LIFE'S FLAVOUR

"Variety's the very spice of life that gives it all its flavour." (William Cowper, 1731-1800)

Maurice Taylor was born in 1926 in Hamilton, Scotland, and after military service, was ordained to the Catholic priesthood in 1950. He became bishop of Galloway in 1981, and retired in 2004. He has served as a priest in the diocese of Motherwell, as a seminary lecturer at St Peter's College, Cardross (photograph, 1959), and as rector of the Royal Scots College in Valladolid, Spain.

Bishop Taylor has made many visits to Central America, especially El Salvador and Guatemala; visits that have taught him so much about those lands and their peoples; friendly, welcoming, beautiful yet, in so many cases, impoverished, oppressed and persecuted. Two of these visits are described in detail.

This book also includes his early memories of the Church's liturgy, a review of the reforms of the Second Vatican Council, a frank portrait of the diocese of Galloway and the author's observations following many visits to the Holy Land.

Published in Great Britain in 2014

Life's Flavour

A VARIETY OF EXPERIENCES

Maurice Taylor

The author would like to thank Chris for his computer skills, Nicola for her rigourous proof reading, and Ranald for his design work.

Contents

Foreword

When my term as bishop of Galloway ended in 2004 I found myself in the unaccustomed state of having time on my hands. Somehow or other I began to start writing, generally on matters with which I was fairly familiar. I also learned how to use a computer rather than a typewriter. This book is the result of these developments in my autumnal days.

So the seven chapters are something of a miscellany and each of them can be read independently of the others. They all have some connection with me and the fact that my life has been intimately bound up with my being a Catholic. But the book is narrative and observations, not argument or polemics.

The title which I chose for the book, *Life's Flavour*, comes from the quotation I selected as a kind of motto for my website. It comes from the works of William Cowper: "*Variety's the very spice of life that gives it all its flavour*".

Writing each chapter and bringing them together has been a pleasure for me. I hope that you will enjoy the result.

A Lifetime of Liturgy is new, and has not been previously published.

Soldier in India was written a few years ago, mainly from notes in a diary which I compiled at the time it describes.

Being a Bishop in Scotland was a book published in 2006. The present text is thoroughly revised and rearranged.

Guatemala was written for the Scottish Catholic International Aid Fund (SCIAF) and published by that organisation in A4 format in 1990. The present text has been revised, extended and updated for this book.

El Salvador was, like *Guatemala*, written for, and published in A4 format, by SCIAF. It describes a period of several months which I spent in a rural parish in El Salvador in 1991. The present text has been revised and updated for this printing.

Portrait of a Diocese is a new essay, written in 2013. The facts and figures are accurate in 2013, but the details are bound to change as time passes.

The Holy Land has been on my website for the past two years, but this is the first occasion on which it has been published in this form.

A Lifetime of Liturgy

INTRODUCTION

To mark the fiftieth anniversary of the Second Vatican Council, the Church celebrated a "Year of Faith". It began on 11th October 2012, exactly fifty years to the day from the start of Vatican II, and continued to the feast of Christ the King on 24th November 2013, just before Advent that year.

During the Year of Faith, we recalled the events of the Council and studied its various documents. My particular interest being liturgy, I spent quite a lot of time on that subject, re-reading the Council's document, the Constitution on the Liturgy, usually called *Sacrosanctum Concilium* (the first two words of its Latin text). I was invited to lead several discussions and give some talks on the Constitution. My knowledge of the Constitution as well as my appreciation of its teaching about the liturgy, and especially on the Eucharist, were both deepened as a result.

Moreover, I began to think more widely about the Church's liturgy and especially on my own experience of the way that we celebrate Mass and the various changes and adaptations that have taken place in it during my life. From those thoughts, the idea of this article emerged. One of its aims is to share with readers some of the memories I have. If you are old enough, they will probably revive your own memories; if you are not, you will, I hope, be interested in learning the varied range of ways, bizarre sometimes and laboured on other occasions, in which we used to celebrate the Church's liturgy and, specifically, the Mass. That is my purpose in the first part of this article.

The second part is a somewhat more serious attempt to review the Liturgy of the Eucharist as reformed by the Council, to explain the changes and to uncover the hidden riches of the Roman rite of Mass, as celebrated in accordance with the Constitution *Sacrosanctum Concilium* of the Second Vatican Council.

SOME PRE-CONCILIAR RECOLLECTIONS

IN THE 1930s AND 1940s

Having been born in 1926, I first became conscious of going to church and being at Mass sometime in the early 1930s. As a family comprising father, mother and children we went to Mass every Sunday morning in St Cuthbert's church, Burnbank, Hamilton, which at that time was in the archdiocese of Glasgow. There were several Masses each Sunday morning: at 8 o'clock, 9.15, 10.30 (principally for schoolchildren) and 12 noon (the only one with singing).

We normally attended the first Mass, at which the church was only half-full although on two Sundays every month the Men's and the Women's Sacred Heart Confraternities occupied the central nave of the church. There were also monthly Masses for the Children of Mary (females, teenage and young adults) and the Boys' Guild (males, similar age range). The 10.30 Mass attracted most of the children who were pupils at the local Catholic primary school. Some of the teachers supervised them while the head teacher led them, phrase by phrase, through Prayers Before and After Holy Communion, with a brief silent break during the Consecration. The last Mass was one that many people, including our family, avoided because (a) it was longer than the others with a choir which sang hymns (with some of the congregation joining in) and even some parts of the Mass: *Gloria, Credo, Sanctus* and/or *Agnus Dei*; and (b) only the priest received Holy Communion since the required Eucharistic fast was total, including even water, and from the previous midnight.

In those days, the attendance at Sunday Mass was much greater than now; at least double the numbers, I should guess. In particular, there were very few primary school children who missed Mass since, on Monday morning, they were brought to the front of the class to be lectured and shamed (and perhaps even given corporal punishment, although I cannot be sure of this). One or other of my siblings frequently was publicly scolded for not having been at the children's Mass, having attended an earlier Mass with the rest of our family.

The general view, in the 1930s and later, was that Mass in the Roman rite was unchangeable and fixed for all time to come; the Council of Trent and Pope Pius V had, in the sixteenth century, made all the changes that we would ever need. Certainly, there were liturgical seasons and there were three prayers said by the priest - Collect, Secret and Post-Communion – which varied from Sunday to Sunday. In addition, the Epistle, Gradual Psalm and Gospel were different each week. The passages chosen were appropriate at special times such as Lent and Easter, Advent and Christmas, but during the rest of the year they seemed to have been completely randomly selected and without any continuity in the passages from week to week. The rest of the Mass was exactly the same each week and, of course, only one Eucharistic Prayer, in those days called the Canon of the Mass, was available.

The entire Mass was in Latin (except for a few words in Hebrew and Greek). On Sundays, however, a break occurred between the Gospel and the Creed, when the priest left the altar, ascended the pulpit, read the announcements for the week, followed by English translations of the Epistle and Gospel already read in Latin, and gave a sermon, which often followed a programme of doctrinal catechesis set for the whole year and therefore unconnected with the Readings used at Mass that week. From time to time, this break in Mass also contained the reading of the names, street by street, of each parishioner or family and the amount each had given at the quarterly collections which the priest had gathered in house to house visits.

The priest celebrated every part of the Mass at the altar with his back to the people. Sometimes the Latin was said audibly; at other times, especially during the Canon, it was entirely silent. Holy Communion for the laity was under the form of bread only, received on the tongue, and kneeling at the altar rails; and mostly from hosts taken from the tabernacle and therefore previously consecrated. The congregation had nothing to say, except the second half of the Hail Mary, recited three times as a postscript at the end of Mass, followed by the Hail, holy Queen and a few other prayers said by the priest in English and ending with an invocation and response to the Sacred Heart of Jesus, all these being "for the conversion of Russia". The requisite responses during Mass, such as *Amen, Et cum spiritu tuo, Deo gratias, Sed libera nos a malo* and others, were said only by the (young male) altar server(s).

We never questioned or doubted the rubrics and rules for the celebration of Mass. No wonder that we spoke of the priest "saying" Mass and the congregation "hearing" Mass. Those verbs were only too true.

Although there is a basic and essential continuity between the Mass in those days and the Mass nowadays, there were also a great number of differences, of which the following are the main ones. The priest and server(s) started Mass by saying Psalm 42 and the *Confiteor* (at the foot of the steps leading up to the altar); the Scripture readings were, on most occasions, set down with little or no attempt at relevance or continuity; there were no General Intercessions; the "Offertory" was longer, more complicated and used language that spoke of the unconsecrated bread and wine in sacrificial terms; the Greeting of Peace did not occur, nor did Communion from the chalice for the laity. The shallowness of our understanding of the Mass and its "Liturgy of the Word" and "Liturgy of the Eucharist" is demonstrated by the rule that, although to miss Mass on Sunday through one's own fault was a mortal sin, it was only a venial sin as long as one managed to be present for the Offertory, the Consecration and the Priest's Communion. Although the priest remained at the altar for all parts of the Mass and was mostly at the centre of the altar, he did move sometimes to one end of the table or the other. Finally, the priest had to learn to perform many different gestures as he "said" Mass; above all there were a great number of little crosses or blessings that had to be performed by the priest's hand over the elements, ten before and fifteen after the Consecration. Some priests performed these crosses so rapidly and vigorously that the effect, seen by the congregation, was of a violent agitation of the back of the chasuble.

An allegorical explanation of the Mass was popular in those days, various elements being thought to represent items or moments connected with Our Lord's Passion and Death. For example, the priest's vestments represented the different garments with which his judges clothed Jesus or cords and ropes which bound him during his trial and journey to Calvary, although the chasuble, with a cross on the back, also stood for his cross; the steps to the altar represented the hill of Calvary. An amice and a cincture, now used only if the priest wishes, and a maniple were always worn. The last, of the same heavy material as the chasuble and stole, had originally (in the early centuries of the Church) been the celebrant's handkerchief, I believe. It was worn on the left forearm; for some odd reason, a bishop had the maniple put on his arm only after the *Confiteor*.

Priest in Amice

Priest in Alb

Priest adjusting the Cincture

Priest putting Maniple on left arm

Priest with the Stole

Priest in Chasuble is now completely vested

What did the congregation do during Mass? In theory, we paid attention to what the priest was doing. Some had missals in English that allowed them to follow what the priest was saying;

there were Sunday Missals and Daily Missals for that purpose. Many people did not have missals but some had other prayer books to read during Mass: *The Key of Heaven* and *The Treasury of the Sacred Heart* were two such books that had some Mass prayers. Some of the congregation said the rosary quietly during Mass. In some parishes, during May and October, the rosary was recited publicly by the congregation while the priest celebrated Mass, although there was a break for silence at the Consecration. Of course, many in the congregation on Sunday gave no visible sign either of book or rosary but may have been trying to watch the priest with care and devotion. In the parish in which I lived as a child, the church pews were covered with carved names of various people, either of the carver himself or of a friend or foe, testifying to the skill in wood of some parishioners of generations past and present as well as to the distractions which had interrupted their attention to the Mass.

It is inaccurate to say that there was no active participation at all by the congregation at Mass in those days. We could leave our seats and go to the altar rails to kneel and receive Holy Communion and, of course, adults could contribute to the collections. My experience was of three collections each Sunday. The first was at the door of the church, as we entered; the second was as the plate was passed from seat to seat at the Offertory; and the last, as we left the church, was for the poor, into a box held by a member of the local branch of the St Vincent de Paul Society. The amount given at each of these collections was, by today's values, very small – a penny, a "threepenny bit", at the most a sixpence. It used to embarrass me that my father, on entering the church, would often place a sixpenny coin or a shilling on the table and wait to receive change from the passkeeper on duty. (References are to pre-decimal coins!)

For some years I was an altar server in our parish, probably from about the age of seven or eight until I was twelve (i.e., from 1933 until 1938). I enjoyed the experience, after I had got over early nervousness and had become familiar with the actions one had to carry out before, during and after Mass, as well as the various responses and other words, nearly all in Latin but a few in Greek, which one had to say. It was all quite complicated and, of course, reliability and punctuality were essential. There were any number of mistakes that could be, and were, made. Perhaps the most common, and one of which I remember being guilty early in my career as an altar boy, was to allow the Missal to slip off its brass stand and fall to the floor, as the server carried it from one side of the altar, down the steps, genuflecting at the foot, then up the steps to the other side of the altar. This manoeuvre was required because the Epistle was read at one end of the altar and the Gospel at the other.

Priests varied in their reaction to altar boys and their mistakes. Some were short-tempered and therefore feared although, of course, most were quite friendly, to varying degrees. Visiting priests were an unknown quantity and therefore caused us to be very nervous. Although the manner of celebrating Mass in those days was so regulated and unvaried, priests did have their idiosyncrasies and we had to be alert to spot our "cues" for action or response.

I had a great uncle who was a Benedictine priest. He came to see us only very, very occasionally; consequently, he was more of a legend than a reality but, on one occasion, when our family was on holiday in Millport, we were told that he was coming to spend a few days with us. He was elderly and ascetic-looking, but to me he looked ancient, grim and frightening. To my dismay, he was told by someone that I would serve his Masses in the local church. I was very nervous, unused to the church in Millport and most anxious to do well despite what seemed to me to be his strange way of celebrating Mass. Later, at breakfast with the family, someone asked him how I had done as his server. "He was all right and will probably be quite good when he has had more practice", he said. His verdict greatly hurt me (proved by my still remembering what he said). Of course, no one asked me how well I thought he had said Mass.

In pre-Vatican II days, the source which was consulted to be sure of the correct rubrics for the celebration of Mass in any of its various forms was Adrian Fortescue's meticulously thorough book, *The Ceremonies of the Roman Rite Described.* I had never heard of the book until I went to the seminary in August 1942. I had completed secondary school and went to Blairs College, near Aberdeen, to begin two years of the philosophy course for the diocesan priesthood. (Blairs, I should mention, was a junior seminary but, because the Scottish major seminaries abroad were closed during the Second World War, students for the first two years of tertiary education for the priesthood were accommodated in Blairs College).

At Blairs, our daily Mass (including Sunday mornings), for the forty or so philosophy students, was a "low Mass", similar to that with which I had been familiar at home. But, later on Sunday mornings, we went with the junior seminarians and a few local parishioners to the large and beautiful neo-gothic college chapel for a "high Mass". There was one celebrant (a priest member of staff), a deacon and subdeacon (both of these being priests and staff members), and full plainchant singing of the parts, both common and proper. Only the priest celebrant received Holy Communion since those were the days when a total fast from midnight was required and we had all been at an earlier low Mass at which we had received Holy Communion, although, of course, only under the form of bread.

For some reason, the sermon at those high Masses was delayed until after the conclusion of the liturgy, when another priest, who had merely attended Mass, appeared and preached. This anomalous practice allowed the further oddity that only two, or at the most three, priests took on the weekly responsibility of the sermon, the others seemingly glad to have one of their few willing colleagues carry out the duty for them. The sermon was often on the feast or season of the time and, on other occasions, at the choice of the preacher; but the idea of the homily, as we now know it, was unknown or ignored. Occasionally, we had the opportunity of serving the high Mass, either as torch-bearer or thurifer or, a special privilege, as master of ceremonies. In my two years at Blairs I had the privilege of being master of ceremonies twice; it was a duty which I performed nervously and carefully but with great personal satisfaction.

From 1944 until 1947 I was in the army, in turn stationed in Britain, Belfast, India and the Suez Canal Zone. On some Sundays I was unable to get to Mass – usually because none was available, rather than due to my duties – while at other times I had the pleasure of being at Mass more frequently than only on Sundays. I often got to know personally the chaplain or the local priest of the place where we were stationed. On such occasions the priest sometimes befriended me and I was delighted to have the chance of serving Mass and also acting as a kind of sacristan. There were no elaborate Masses, of course, and sometimes the Masses were celebrated under cramped conditions. I therefore have no distinct memories of noteworthy celebrations of the Liturgy of Mass during my years as a soldier.

On my release from military service, I was sent to Rome, and to the Pontifical Scots College there, to study the requisite four years of theology. We had low Mass seven days a week, very early in the morning, in the college chapel and then, on Sundays after breakfast, a high Mass if, among the students, there were deacons and/or subdeacons; if not, we had what was called a *Missa Cantata,* celebrated by one of the four priests who formed the resident staff of the college. The *Missa Cantata* was very similar to a high Mass but without deacon and subdeacon; but all parts, both proper and common, that were meant to be sung were sung. Only the priest celebrant received Holy Communion at these Masses and there was a sermon after the gospel, given, if possible, by a student deacon. Priests in those days seemed reluctant, at least in the seminaries where I was a student, to exercise the ministry of preaching.

Quite often, of course, we had the opportunity in Rome of being at Mass in one or other of the basilicas or churches of the city. Occasionally, it was the college community which provided the personnel (ministers and servers). More often, we were in St Peter's basilica for a papal occasion and so witnessed the liturgical ceremonies there. They were long, splendid and very elaborate. However, at least in retrospect, I think that they left a lot to be desired if measured by their prayerfulness. Of course, there was no congregational participation, but the activities around the altar were prolonged and intricate, containing innumerable marks of respect towards the celebrant. A cynic might have described the ceremonies as, largely, liturgical grovelling. The singing by the Sistine choir was no doubt of Mass settings and hymns by highly esteemed composers; for me, however, their rendition (*esecuzione* in Italian - an apt comment) was almost completely unpleasant, being long, tuneless and very noisy. I almost used the word "cacophony", but prefer not to comment further.

IN THE 1950s

My impression is that, in Scotland even in those early post-war years and, no doubt, in many other countries, the Mass of the

Roman rite was accepted without any thought that it needed to be changed or even might be changed in the foreseeable future. Interest in the liturgy, and especially on the possibility of its reform, was regarded by most as rather eccentric.

At the same time, in spite of the very limited active participation permitted to the laity in those days, it would be wrong to imagine that there was a lack of respect or of devotion or that "going to Mass" was less central or less important than nowadays. In fact, people attended Mass in greater numbers than they do now and there was, I think, a greater sense of respect, even of awe, for the sacredness of the Eucharist and of "church things" in general. That does not, of course, imply any desire to revert to those days and to that rather deprived, and placidly accepted, role allotted to the lay people at Mass.

Contrary to the normal apathy and acceptance of things as they were and "always had been", there was slowly increasing interest in the Church's liturgy in some parts of the world. "The liturgical movement", as it came to be called, had begun in the early years of the twentieth century and very gradually had become better known, especially through the books and articles of a number of liturgists and the experience of various Benedictine monasteries. The use of plainchant became more common and there was a desire that it should be as authentic as possible.

The liturgical movement received encouragement during the pontificate of Pius XII (1939 - 1958). Two of his encyclical letters, *Mystici Corporis* (1943) and *Mediator Dei* (1947) were influential. In addition, the same pope, in an Apostolic Constitution of 1953 and, even more, in the *Motu Proprio "Sacram Communionem"* of 1957, decreed that Mass could be celebrated at any pastorally suitable hour of the day (rather than restricted to the morning hours) and reduced the required fast before receiving Holy Communion (until then, from midnight) to three hours for food and alcoholic drink and one hour for other liquids, abolishing the fast entirely for water. These changes were welcome but, of course, they improved only the time of day at which Mass might take place and relaxed the severity of the fast prior to a Mass. The numbers receiving Holy Communion and the frequency thereof were thus much increased. But no alteration was made to the manner of the celebration itself.

It was mainly in France, Germany and the Low Countries (and also in St John's Abbey, Collegeville, Minnesota) that the liturgical movement was most enthusiastically promoted. However, Assisi was the venue for an International Congress of Pastoral Liturgy which took place in 1956. This was a very influential event which became even more widely known because Pope Pius XII sent the congress a very positive letter. In it, he wrote: "The liturgical movement is a sign of the providential dispositions of God for the present time and of the movement of the Holy Spirit in the Church". The papers delivered at Assisi were published and read with great interest in many countries. Awareness of the need for reform of the Roman rite was by now widespread and changes began to be announced by the Holy See. In addition to the *Motu Proprio "Sacram Communionem"* from the pope, the Sacred Congregation of Rites in 1958 issued its "Instruction on Sacred Music and Sacred Liturgy". This document introduced many changes but, in comparison with the changes brought about by Vatican II, these, though welcomed at the time, were relatively minor.

One area of liturgy in the Roman rite – that of Holy Week – had been attracting a great deal of criticism over a number of years. Pope Pius XII had responded to the dissatisfaction by setting up a commission to consider reform of the liturgies of that week. Its deliberations resulted in the Sacred Congregation of Rites issuing the decree or instruction entitled *Ordo Hebdomadae Sanctae* which changed and regulated the ceremonies of Holy Week and especially those of Palm Sunday, Holy Thursday, Good Friday and the Easter Vigil. The decree was issued in 1955 and came into use the following year. The changes it introduced for Holy Week later had their influence in the liturgical reform of Vatican II.

In retrospect, the liturgies of Holy Week that we had prior to 1956 now seem strange and unsuitable; or, as a missal of the time remarked, "they disclose certain anomalies". I give a summary of those liturgies.

The first day of Holy Week was Palm Sunday, the term "Passion Sunday" being then attached to the previous Sunday, the 5th Sunday of Lent. On Palm Sunday, the "Blessing of the Palms" took place at the altar, the priest wearing a purple cope. After an opening prayer, he read a passage from the book of Exodus and the appropriate passage from St Matthew's gospel. Then came the blessing proper: a prayer, a preface followed by the Sanctus, five more prayers ending with the palms being sprinkled with holy water and incensed, followed by another prayer after which the palms were ceremonially distributed. A final prayer was said and then the procession with palms took place outside, ending with the person carrying the processional cross striking the church door with the foot of the cross to call for it to be opened and allow the procession to re-enter. The priest then changed from cope to chasuble and Mass began. The Passion narrative read was always that according to the gospel of St Matthew.

The Passion account according to the gospel of St Mark was read at Mass on the Tuesday of Holy Week and that according to St Luke on the Wednesday.

There was only one Mass in each church on Holy Thursday and it took place in the morning. The readings were accounts of the institution of the Eucharist (1st Corinthians 11) and of Jesus washing the apostles' feet (John 11). However, the washing of feet in each church (or other suitable place), if it took place, was not done during the Mass.

The sacred oils were blessed by the diocesan bishop at his Mass (but there was no renewal of the priests' commitment). There was no specific "Mass of Chrism". The instruction given for the use of the different oils in the sacraments was as follows: "The oils are three in number: the oil for the sacrament of extreme unction; that for anointing those who are to be baptised, and also for anointing the priests' hands at his ordination; and the sacred chrism, a mixture of oil and balsam, used in the sacrament of confirmation and at the ordination of bishops". Now, of course, that instruction is obsolete since chrism is also used at baptism (unless confirmation is to be received immediately) and at the ordination of priests.

The Good Friday liturgy was called Mass of the Presanctified. Black vestments were worn. The ceremony began with two readings from the Old Testament, each followed by a prayer. The account of the Passion from St John's gospel was read. Then came the "Solemn Prayers", similar to the "Solemn Intercessions" of today. However, there were uncomplimentary terms used in the prayers for "heretics and schismatics…deceived by diabolical fraud, that, abandoning all heretical depravity, the hearts of the erring may regain sanity…"; likewise also for "the unfaithful Jews" (*'pro perfidis Judaeis'*), the prayer was made "on behalf of the blindness of that people that, recognising the light of thy truth, which is Christ, they may be delivered from their darkness".

The unveiling and veneration of the cross followed (as today). Then a Sacred Host, consecrated on Holy Thursday, was placed on the altar; so also, a chalice into which was poured wine and a little water. The priest turned to the people and said "*Orate, fratres...*" ("Pray, brethren..."), which on Good Friday received no response from the server(s). The priest (and he alone) received the consecrated host. He then consumed the unconsecrated wine (into which a small particle of the host had been dropped). The priest then "purified" the chalice with wine and water in the usual way and left the sanctuary.

The liturgy of Holy Saturday, until 1955, is best described in the words of a missal of the time, with my explanatory comments here added in italics and within brackets. "The ceremonies of this day begin early in the morning with the blessing (*three prayers*) of a new fire that has been kindled with flint and steel. From this fire, a candle with three stems, and placed on a reed, is lighted and carried up the church by a deacon (*or, if no deacon, the priest*), who three times chants the words *Lumen Christi.* The paschal candle is blessed (*viz., the 'Exsultet' or Easter Proclamation)* by the deacon, who fixes in it five grains of blessed incense in memory of the wounds of Christ and the precious spices with which he was anointed in the tomb, and afterwards lights it from the candle on the reed. The blessing of the candle is followed by the reading of the twelve prophecies (*each followed by a prayer*), and after that the priest goes in procession to bless the font. The water in the font is scattered towards the four quarters of the world, to indicate the catholicity of the Church and the world-wide efficacy of her sacraments; the priest breathes (*three times*) on the water in the form of a cross and plunges the paschal candle (*three times*) into the water (*and then breathes three times on the water in the form of Ψ, the initial letter of 'pneuma'*) for the Spirit of God is to hallow it and the power of Christ is to descend on it; lastly, a few drops of the oil of catechumens and of the chrism are poured into the font, in order to signify the union of Christ, our anointed king, with his people. On the way back from the font, the Litany of Saints is begun, and when it is ended the altar is decked with flowers and the Mass is begun in white vestments. The pictures and statues in the church that have been veiled since

Passion Sunday are uncovered. The organ and bells are heard again and the joyful *Alleluia* is resumed."

The heavy emphasis on symbolism in the various actions of the rite will have been noticed. No provision for baptism on Holy Saturday was made, the Rite of Christian Initiation not being revived until 1972.

The Holy Saturday Mass began, as all Masses then did, with the *Confiteor etc.* The epistle was from Colossians 3 and the gospel from Matthew 28. The *Agnus Dei* was omitted and the communion verse was replaced by a shortened form of Vespers before the Post-Communion prayer, the blessing and *Ite, missa est, alleluia, alleluia.*

It was seldom that more than a very few parishioners attended the Holy Saturday liturgy in those days before the 1955 - 56 reforms, although a number of people would try to estimate when the Mass might start so that they could be there for that. In the 1930s and early 1940s, I recall that that was our family practice. However, our main concern on Holy Saturday morning was to fill a bottle of "Easter water", a large zinc bath of which was left in the priests' garden after the liturgy. Our father sprinkled each room of our house with the blessed water. It probably also was used when one of us was sick, although the Easter water had, in those circumstances, a rival in the small bottle of Lourdes water which someone had given us.

When I was a student in Rome in the late 1940s and early 1950s, we (the Scots College community) used to be invited to celebrate the liturgies of Holy Week in the basilica of Santa Maria degli Angeli, a large church built in the ruins of the Baths of Diocletian. The dramatic climax of the week took place during the Gloria at Holy Saturday Mass. While it was being sung and bells pealed, a large curtain was slowly rolled away from the reredos behind the high altar to reveal, to the eyes of faith as well, the risen Christ. Dramatic, even spine-tingling; theatrical but memorable.

That afternoon, at the request of the parish priest, the students who were already ordained visited all the houses in the parish to bless them with Easter water. Each of us was assigned a section of the parish and given a young altar server who carried the little bucket of water and a burse (which usually contained the corporal, a cloth laid on the altar, but on this occasion was to hold the monetary offerings which we hoped to receive at each house).

Holy Saturday at the cathedral church of Rome, the basilica of St John Lateran, was the scene of one of the longest liturgies of the Roman rite. Not only were the full ceremonies carried out but there were also ordinations. In those days, that involved candidates for tonsure, for each of the four minor orders, for subdiaconate, diaconate and priesthood. The ceremony began, I think, at seven o'clock in the morning and continued, without interruption, until about two in the afternoon. For years, the usual celebrant was Archbishop Luigi Traglia who held the office of vicegerent of the diocese of Rome, a kind of workhorse for the daily tasks to be undertaken on behalf of the bishop of the city. The valiant archbishop was made a cardinal in 1960, a well earned and richly deserved honour.

In 1955, the last year on which the "old rite" was observed, I was assistant priest in a parish in Motherwell. The parish priest there had a novel way of celebrating the Holy Saturday liturgy to overcome its length and thus make it more attractive for parishioners. He told the senior curate to go near the baptismal font and "do" the lighting of the fire, the *Exsultet*, the blessing of water and the litany of the saints. I was directed to the back of the church, there to read the twelve prophecies and associated prayers. "While you two get on with those parts", he informed us, "I shall be celebrating the Mass at the altar". Ingenious and imaginative, but indicative of the need for liturgical reform and renewal!

THE SECOND VATICAN COUNCIL (1962 - 1965)

PREPARATIONS

[In this section, I use the official documents as well as my own experiences and recollections. In addition, I have consulted two published works: Joseph Ratzinger, *Theological Highlights of Vatican II* (the future pope's accounts of the Council sessions, at which he was a *peritus* or expert and acted as a theological adviser to Cardinal Frings of Cologne) and Yves Congar OP, *My Journal of the Council* (the renowned theologian's massive and frank diaries of the events and personalities as well as of his own impressions.]

Pope John XXIII was elected on 28th October 1958. Three months later, on 25th January 1959, he announced that he proposed to call a General Council. The news took everyone by surprise. Yet it was welcomed by many, especially those who were aware that the previous General Council, the Vatican Council of 1870, had left some important areas unfinished and therefore in an unsatisfactory state. I refer to the Church's understanding of itself. The Council had defined the nature and authority of the Supreme Pontiff, the Bishop of Rome, the Pope, but had done little more. There was a great deal more which needed to be considered and taught about the Church taken as a whole, about bishops, priests and laity, about the relationships that exist among them; and even about the pope's correct relationship to the other bishops in the Church. The reason for the abandonment of the Council was mainly political: the outbreak of war between the two great powers, France and Prussia; and the hostilities that ensued in the struggle for the unification of Italy and the consequent conquest of the Papal States, the occupation of Rome and the end of the Pope's temporal power.

It was only when the extent of the agenda which Pope John XXIII envisaged for "the Second Vatican Council" was known that we realised that he planned not only to complete the work on ecclesiology left incomplete nearly a century earlier, but also to deal with a great variety of other matters and, among them, the liturgy of the Church, its worship. Inevitably, therefore, the rite of celebrating Mass would be very prominent in the Council's deliberations.

The Second Vatican Council did not start until the month of October in 1962. But, in the three and a half years between its announcement and its solemn inauguration, much work took place. In particular, a number of preparatory commissions were established to organise the agenda and to draft working papers, called the *schemata* (singular: *schema*). The Central Preparatory Commission was very important. Its members were chosen by Rome and came from all over the Catholic world. From Scotland, the member was Archbishop Donald A. Campbell of Glasgow, also accompanied by Bishop James Ward (and, as adviser to the meetings, Mgr Charles Treanor, who was the rector of the interdiocesan major seminary, St Peter's College at Cardross, near Glasgow). The other preparatory commissions had more limited and defined areas of work; for example the Central Theological Commission and the Commission for the Liturgy.

A considerable amount of the preparatory work done by these commissions turned out to be largely a waste of time and effort. Among them, the commissions produced no less than seventy *schemata* for the Council. It was an impossibly large number, unless the Council Fathers were merely meant to rubber-stamp what had been put before them. In fact, that seems to have been the intention of the Curia in Rome. It was they who chose the subjects of the *schemata* and the people who would be members (all male) of the commissions that produced them. It became evident that the choice of membership had been very selective and had excluded men, even renowned scholars, who were known to have different theological views from those of the very traditional Neo-Scholasticism of the Curia and the Roman universities. The consequence of this crude and less than subtle gerrymandering was probably inevitable.

THE HESITANT START

The Council was solemnly inaugurated with Mass in St Peter's basilica on Thursday morning, 11th October 1962. The impressions of the two theologians, Fathers Ratzinger and Congar, are worthy of mention. The former saw the inaugural Mass as an example of the need for liturgical reform; the liturgy showed the rigidity of a rite encrusted with superfluous duplication and archaism; the language at Mass should be intelligible to those present but Latin was a dead language and not understood; the bishops had been mere spectators. Yves Congar was even less flattering. He thought that the Sistine choir should be abolished, there was no involvement of the congregation, the opulent splendour was grossly excessive and unsuitable. In fact, he could take no more and left after the epistle of the Mass.

The next meeting of the "Fathers" took place two days later, on 13th October. They were designated "Council Fathers" because, although most were bishops, either diocesan or auxiliary, and of the various eastern rites as well as the Roman rite, there were also superiors general of male religious congregations and abbots of major abbeys with a right to be there. Of the 2900 Council Fathers eligible, 2500 were present in the vast nave of St Peter's. These numbers contrasted with those at the 1870 Vatican Council, all of whom were accommodated in one of the basilica's transepts. In addition to the Council Fathers, there were over two hundred *periti*, experts nominated by the Pope and most assigned to advise those Fathers who wished to have advisers; and finally, there were a number of non-Catholic observers, invited to attend the Council sessions.

At the session on 13th October, papers were distributed to the Fathers. These intimated the various *schemata* that were proposed as the Council agenda. In addition, the Fathers were asked to complete a form distributed two days earlier, and thereby nominate those persons whom they wanted to be members of the commissions that would see to any changes or additions or deletions that might be proposed to the texts of the *schemata*. The names of the members of the corresponding preparatory commissions were appended to the forms, the inference being that the Council Fathers could simply re-nominate to the conciliar commissions the same people who had been on the preparatory commissions.

There was some suppressed consternation at these proposals or instructions. Then Cardinal Achille Liénart, archbishop of Lille, asked the presiding cardinal to be allowed to speak. Permission was reluctantly granted. He said that the proposals were unwelcome because (a) the Fathers had come to the Council to discuss and determine what would be decided, and not meekly to agree to texts already substantially written and (b) they needed at least some time to get to know one another before having to nominate members of the commissions. He therefore moved that the proposed procedure be rejected and the session adjourned. Cardinal Josef Frings of Cologne seconded the motion, which was then passed, acclaimed by an ovation. The session was adjourned after only half an hour and the Fathers found themselves leaving St Peter's a great deal earlier than they had expected.

The officials of the Curia were most disconcerted, probably furious, at this turn of events. It upset their plans to steer the Council's deliberations in the direction that they thought best but it was a defeat that was of immense importance for the future of the Council and indeed of the Church as well. Thereafter, it was clear that the bishops would have and would wield authority in the Council's work and would not simply do the Curia's bidding. The

Council was not to be downgraded to a mere executive instrument of the preparatory commissions. Fr Joseph Ratzinger writes very approvingly of the moves by Cardinals Liénart and Frings. He notes that, outside of their own bishops' conferences, there were hardly any proper "horizontal ties" among the bishops. Thus the idea of having on the spot nominations to the conciliar commissions was totally unrealistic. The young Fr Ratzinger (then aged 35) was very much on the progressive wing of opinion, criticising papal centralism, recognising that the Roman Curia needed reform and that the plan for the Council to give more or less unanimous approval to the prepared *schemata* would have meant an end to healthy dynamism and the unwise avoidance of new questions which were being asked and which many bishops, especially those from central Europe, saw as issues that must be considered.

In the Easter Vigil, during the great Proclamation, the *Exsultet*, there occurs a famous phrase: "*O felix culpa!*" ("O happy fault!"). The reference is to Adam's sin because that action was the cause of God the Son becoming man in order to be our Saviour. The same phrase might well be applied to the aborted work done in preparation for the Second Vatican Council since it led to an unexpected but excellent solution being found to validate and justify the Council's very existence.

Pope John had appointed ten cardinals as presidents for the sessions of the Council. Each of them took it in turn to preside. But the unforeseen development placed them and, behind the scenes, officials of the Curia also in a dilemma. "All these bishops brought to Rome and our carefully laid plans for the Council now in ruins. What are we to do?" Something had to be done, and quickly. In the following days, much informal "horizontal" discussion among the Council Fathers took place and, of course, bishops also met in their own linguistic and/or territorial groups. Some tentative lists of commission members began to emerge. In particular, the suggested list of bishops that was compiled by a group of bishops from countries in central Europe had been carefully drawn up to be as international as possible and, in the subsequent formal voting, those whose names figured on it were in large number elected by the Council to the commissions.

Meantime, of course, a decision on another matter was urgent: on which subject should the Council resume, or rather, begin its deliberations? The decision was made, and it was fortuitously a very successful one, to bring forward consideration of the liturgy right away instead of in the later place previously assigned to the subject. This was done because there was a general feeling that the work done on the liturgy during the preparation for the Council made that document stand out as something of an exception, in being capable of immediate serious consideration. It was seen as "carefully balanced and courageous" and not, as much of the rest of the preparatory material, out of touch with the ideas and hopes of many of the Council Fathers.

Why was the document reckoned suitable? There are several reasons. Liturgy is not only an important subject but it is also a prominent one. Every Mass that is celebrated is a public liturgical act of the Church; likewise every time a sacrament is conferred and received. Joseph Ratzinger is eloquent on this matter. The decision to start with the liturgy *schema* was "a profession of faith in what is truly central to the Church…in the true source of the Church's life and the proper point of departure for all renewal… The text implied an entire ecclesiology and anticipated (in a degree that cannot be too highly appreciated) the main theme of the entire Council – its teaching on the Church" (p.31).

Liturgy is something that has to be, by its very nature, in the very forefront of the practice of our faith. So, as already noted, in many countries and particularly in France, Germany and the Low Countries, there had been much discussion at meetings as well as in religious communities and many articles and even books had been written on the subject of liturgical reform. Perhaps 'ferment' is too strong a word for the interest that was increasingly shown in the decades before the Council but the subject was a live one for many people and much research had also been done on the development through the ages of the apparently unchangeable rites that we used.

Although Rome had tended to restrict the membership of the preparatory commissions to local people who were known and trusted by the Curia, there were some exceptions. Among those who had been invited by Rome to help with the preparation of liturgy material for the Council, there were several liturgists who had already become familiar with the ideas for reform that had been circulating in northern and central Europe and elsewhere and who were enthusiastic and confident that these ideas should be on the Council agenda. Thus, the material available to the Council Fathers on the subject of the Church's liturgy was up to date and acceptable to most of them and was deemed suitable for discussion; not to be simply accepted as it was but as matter for debate, amendment and improvement.

There were other very welcome results of this unforeseen change in the Council's schedule. The work done on the liturgy brought out two matters of great importance that were essential to the reform of the liturgy and were then realised to be of vital importance in every other topic which the Council was to discuss. The two were, first, that Scripture had to play an integral part in every aspect of Church life and, second, that the Church was not just the ordained but also all the baptised, male and female, young and old. Furthermore, Pope John XXIII had wanted a Council that would be pastoral, not one that defined and condemned. This aim was realised right from the start of the Council's deliberations and was maintained throughout, following the example set at the very outset by its work on the Constitution on the Liturgy.

Although when he became Pope Benedict XVI years later, Joseph Ratzinger gave the impression of having changed his attitude with regard to liturgical renewal, for example with his use of the phrase "hermeneutic of continuity" and the suggestion that "a reform of the reform" was needed, it is interesting that, when he bade farewell to the priests of the diocese of Rome shortly before his abdication, he told them "it was, let us say, truly an act of providence that at the beginning of the Council was the liturgy… It [the Council] did speak of God! And this was the first thing that it did, that substantial speaking of God and opening up all the people, the whole of God's holy people, to the adoration of God, in the common celebration of the liturgy of the Body and Blood of Christ".

The Council Fathers were convoked again on Tuesday, 16th October. On that day, they were to hand in to the secretariat of the Council the lists of the names of the persons whom they proposed for membership of the nine commissions. On the following Saturday, 20th October, the results of the voting were announced. After some discussion, it was decided that, for each commission, the sixteen Council Fathers who received most votes would be members; to these, the pope added some more names of his own choice. The general impression of the composition of the liturgy commission was that a good range of suitable persons had been elected, although the nine further members chosen by the pope were all from the Curia and were rather conservative in outlook.

CONSTITUTION ON THE LITURGY

At last, on Monday, 22nd October, at the General Congregation, work began on the consideration of the draft liturgy *schema.* It was understood that, although all lawful rites in the Church are of equal dignity and to be preserved and promoted, the practical norms to be discussed would apply only to the Roman rite, unless by their very nature they also affected other rites.

That first day, the subject was the *schema* in general. There were twenty-five addresses, each speaker being limited to ten minutes. Most of the comments were favourable, especially from Fathers who were diocesan bishops; several critical comments were also made, by some Italian prelates and a few others, including Cardinal Spellman of New York.

General Congregations were held daily and, during that week, the subject was the first chapter of the seven chapters of the *schema* on the liturgy. The chapter is entitled "*General Principles for the Restoration and Promotion of the Sacred Liturgy*".

Although there was no shortage of those wishing to speak, the topics debated were relatively few. The one which exercised the Fathers most was the question of the use of "the vernacular". Should local languages be approved for the liturgy or should Latin be retained? If the former, how much was to be permitted? Perhaps the Liturgy of the Word in the vernacular and the Liturgy of the Eucharist kept in Latin? And who should have the right to decide – each local bishop, the conference of bishops, the Holy See?

Yves Congar makes the observation in his *Journal* that the Council Fathers who spoke in favour of the vernacular (and that was the majority) used arguments based only on pragmatic reasons; whereas, as he insists, the fundamental reason was ecclesiological, namely, that the laity were members of the Church and sharers in the priesthood of Christ and therefore had a right to participate as fully as possible in the liturgy of the Church.

Joseph Ratzinger writes on the same subject in his *Highlights* and quotes extensively from the address made, paradoxically, by a bishop not of the Roman rite – the Melchite Patriarch Maximos Saigh, one of the stars of Vatican II: "…The Latin language is dead, but the Church remains alive. So, too, the language that mediates grace and the Holy Spirit must also be a living language since it is intended for men and not for angels. No language can be untouchable…". Ratzinger stresses the importance of the debate on the language of the liturgy since "language is not merely an external, superficial and accidental thing but rather is the incarnation of the human spirit which thinks and lives in its very speech… The sterility to which Catholic theology and philosophy had in many ways been doomed since the end of the Enlightenment was due not least to a language in which the living choices of the human spirit no longer found a place. Theology often bypassed new ideas, was not enriched by them and remained unable to transform them" (pp.36-38).

On the other hand, Cardinal Antonio Bacci, the great Latinist of the Roman Curia, wanted no vernacular in the Mass. He argued that, otherwise, certain texts, for example the Susanna story (Daniel 13), would be understood by the people; and there might be conflicts in multilingual countries such as Canada, Belgium and Switzerland. So, for the laity's benefit, there could be people's missals or sermons or parts of the liturgy read to them by an approved reader.

The question of how much, if any, of the local language should be allowed in the Roman rite and, specifically, in the celebration of the Eucharist, dominated the discussions in those early days. It was by far the topic that proved to be most debated.

The Council Fathers, after considering the first chapter of the liturgy *schema* for a week, moved on to the second chapter, "The Mystery of the Holy Eucharist", at the General Congregation of Monday, 29th October. Various possible innovations in the celebration of Mass attracted some attention: the value of a homily after the Scripture readings; the re-introduction, after many centuries, of the Prayer of the Faithful; the usefulness of allowing concelebration on occasions when it seemed appropriate or convenient…

But, as with the previous week's debates, there was again one subject that captured the attention more than any others – whether the laity at Mass should be permitted to receive Holy Communion under both kinds. There was a considerable degree of hesitation on this matter. Curia officials, led by Cardinal Ottaviani, were opposed; so also were Italian bishops, particularly Cardinal Ruffini of Palermo. Cardinal Spellman of New York was not in favour. And, perhaps surprisingly, from Great Britain and Ireland, Cardinal Godfrey (Westminster) and Archbishop McQuaid (Dublin) were reluctant. The Scottish bishops are not on record as expressing an opinion. In fact, not one of the Scottish bishops spoke on any occasion throughout the four sessions of the Second Vatican Council.

Some of the reasons against allowing lay people to receive Communion under both species were given by Cardinal Godfrey in his speech at the General Congregation. He said that the Church would be seen by some as trying to correct a doctrinal error if it authorised the practice; there was also the question of hygiene and of smears of lipstick; and what about children and alcoholics and teetotallers?

The third chapter, on "The other Sacraments and the Sacramentals" (the latter being various devotions, rites etc. which, although not sacraments, have some similarities to sacraments and are therefore called "sacramentals"), was discussed briefly at the General Congregation of Tuesday, 6th November. On that same day, the announcement was made that the Commission on the Liturgy had had to divide into sub-commissions since, for the Introduction and Chapters One and Two of the Constitution, no fewer than 2000 amendments to the text of the *schema* had been handed in by the Council Fathers and each of them would have to be studied.

The following day, the fourth chapter, "The Divine Office", came under consideration by the Council Fathers. Most of the speakers welcomed the draft *schema* which proposed, for diocesan priests, a shortening of the daily obligation and a simplification of many of the "hours" into which each day's Office is divided. The speech by Cardinal Paul-Emile Léger of Montreal seemed to strike the right note with many; he suggested that reading the Office should be permitted in the vernacular tongue and that the serious obligation for diocesan priests be reduced to the hours of Morning Prayer (Lauds) and Evening Prayer (Vespers), with twenty minutes of *lectio divina* (meditative reading of some spiritual written material) also to be done. (The Constitution on the Liturgy follows the proposals of the *schema* and the general feeling of the Fathers on the subject of the Divine Office. Subsequent regulations issued soon after the Council specified the details that had been decreed by the Constitution. See Paul VI, *Apostolic Constitution*, 1st November 1970, and the accompanying *General Instruction on the Liturgy of the Hours*.)

Around this time, in the second week of November, Yves Congar's *Journal* speaks of a sense of lassitude among the Council Fathers; there is no proper organisation, a lack of direction or method, very inadequate information available, a feeling that the Council's work in the General Congregations is without any apparent order or plan and seems to be going nowhere. Many of the Fathers, their advisers and the non-Catholic observers are complaining and much of the earlier enthusiasm has disappeared.

On Tuesday, 13th November, discussion on the *schema* ended. There had been 328 interventions/speeches and a further 297 were submitted in written form. Congar notes: "This morning, at St Peter's, a not very glorious end to the scheme on the Liturgy. The discussion was brought to a close well before all those wishing to speak had done so. A decision of the Pope was read out stating that, in response to the request of four hundred bishops, St Joseph was to be inserted into the Canon of the Mass… The problem is that, while the Council is in session, and when that Council is discussing the Liturgy, the Pope, on his own authority, decides something… Good John XXIII keeps on combining some lovely gestures with others that are regrettable or retrograde" (p.165).

The next day, Wednesday 14th, the Council voted on two propositions: 1) that the guiding criteria for the *schema De Liturgia* be approved; 2) that the amendments be considered one by one by the Commission. There were 2215 voting, 2162 in favour, 46 against, 7 spoiled votes.

Joseph Ratzinger reports the same voting figures but is clearer on the motion itself: "the liturgical debate that many thought had dragged on too long…ended with a vote for the basic adoption of the *schema,* with the necessary changes left up to the commission". He adds that the vote "was a decision that both looked to the future and showed encouragingly that the forces of renewal were stronger than anyone would have dared hope" (pp.39-40).

The same day, 14th November, the Council began consideration of the next *schema*, that on the Sources of Revelation. That day and subsequently, the new *schema* received a mauling from many of the

Fathers and the subjects with which it dealt were absorbed into other *schemata.* However, that is not our concern here.

To complete the story of the progress through the Council of the Constitution on the Liturgy, some important facts must be noted. The Commission had, during the second session of the Council in autumn 1963, brought to the Council Fathers its proposals on the many amendments that had been submitted. The Council Fathers accepted eighty-six of these amendments. On 18th November 1963, Cardinal Giacomo Lercaro, archbishop of Bologna and chairman of the commission, presented to the Council a full account of the decisions taken on all the many amendments. The final form of the Constitution was then put to a vote on 22nd November and was accepted by 2158 against 19 with one vote void. The Constitution was thus ready for the formal vote and promulgation.

The final day of the second session of the Council was on Wednesday, 4th December 1963. Among the many items on the agenda that day was the formal definitive vote of the Council Fathers on the Constitution *Sacrosanctum Concilium*, on the Sacred Liturgy. The result: *placet* 2147; *non placet* 4; a result that was greeted with applause in the basilica. Then Pope Paul VI made the solemn promulgation of the document, declaring that, since "the Fathers have expressed their agreement with the decrees just read out... We, in virtue of the Apostolic authority passed on to Us from Christ and in union with the reverend Fathers, approve, establish and ordain them in the Holy Spirit..."

The definitive text of the Constitution on the Liturgy has an Introduction and six Chapters, the first four of which have been noted above. The fifth chapter is "The Liturgical Year" and the sixth "Sacred Music". There is also a brief Appendix on "Revision of the Calendar" in which the Council states that it would not oppose the celebration of Easter on a fixed date annually, "provided that others whom it may concern, especially the brethren who are not in communion with the Holy See, are agreed on this matter".

IMPLEMENTING THE CONSTITUTION ON THE LITURGY

It is wise to begin by stating what we mean by the liturgy of the Catholic Church. For that purpose, we cite the teaching of the Second Vatican Council's Constitution on the Liturgy, *Sacrosanctum Concilium* (§7), words repeated in the *Catechism of the Catholic Church* (§1070):-

"The liturgy then is rightly seen as an exercise of the priestly office of Jesus Christ. It involves the presentation of man's sanctification under the guise of signs perceptible by the senses, and its accomplishment in ways appropriate to each of these signs. In it full public worship is performed by the Mystical Body of Jesus Christ, that is, by the Head and his members. From this it follows that every liturgical celebration, because it is an action of Christ the priest and of his Body which is the Church, is a sacred action surpassing all others. No other action of the Church can equal its efficacy by the same title and to the same degree".

More briefly, the liturgy is the public worship of the Church, the Mystical Body of Christ, Head and members.

Among the aims of the Council, the Constitution on the Liturgy states, is the desire "to impart an ever increasing vigour to the Christian life of the faithful…and to strengthen whatever can help to call the whole of mankind into the household of the Church" (*Sacrosanctum Concilium (SC)* 1). "For the liturgy", the document explains, "…is the outstanding means whereby the faithful may express in their lives, and manifest to others, the mystery of Christ and the real nature of the true Church" (*SC* 2). Thus, renewal of the Church is linked closely to renewal of its liturgy.

Fundamental purpose of the Constitution

Since the sacrament of baptism confers membership of the Mystical Body of Christ on its recipients, it follows that all members of the Church have a right to take part in the celebration of the liturgy and especially in the celebration of the Eucharist. It is this truth that is absolutely basic in the Council Fathers' wish to reform the Church's liturgy. The Council's Constitution on the Liturgy not only taught what the various celebrations of the liturgy are, but also decreed changes in the manner of celebration in order to ensure that lay people, in particular, would not be left as mere spectators of liturgy performed by clergy, but would be enabled to participate in it in an appropriate manner and to the full correct extent.

The Constitution, therefore, declares this purpose and intention several times; the laity or, as appropriate, the congregation must be able to participate in the celebration of the Church's liturgy fully, actively, externally, devoutly (e.g., *SC* 11, 14, 19, 21, 30, 48). This is "demanded by the very nature of the liturgy" (*SC* 14). These declarations, moreover, remind us that our involvement should be not only external but also interior. Such participation, if it is achieved, will enable all those who are present to have a better understanding of what they are celebrating and the proper involvement to which they have a right.

At his final meeting with the priests of his diocese, Pope Benedict referred to this primary purpose of the Constitution on the Liturgy, adding his customary word of caution. "Then there were the principles: intelligibility, instead of being locked up in an unknown language that is no longer spoken, and also active participation. Unfortunately, these principles have been misunderstood. Intelligibility does not mean banality, because the great texts of the liturgy – even when, thanks be to God, they are spoken in our mother tongue – are not easily intelligible, they demand ongoing formation on the part of the Christian...[to] arrive at understanding".

[Personally, I agree with Pope Benedict's statement. However, the translation of the Roman Missal, from Latin to English, made by the International Commission on English in the Liturgy (ICEL), of which I was a member at the time, and approved in 1998 by all the English-speaking bishops' conferences which set up ICEL, was then denied the necessary *'recognitio'* by the Holy See. If the Pope is alluding to that translation when he says that "intelligibility does not mean banality", I disagree with the insinuation and believe that he was badly advised.]

This right to understand and to participate in the Church's liturgy is based, of course, on the laity's status as baptised persons and members of the Church and who are therefore entitled to be active in the Church's worship of God, i.e., the liturgy. Perhaps that right was not always recognised in such theological terms in times prior to Vatican II; but there was an acknowledgement that the congregations should be given something to do during Mass or else they would be bored and distracted or even stop attending on Sundays. So various means were employed to keep the minds of the congregation occupied while the celebrant "got on with saying Mass". Such means included the public recitation of the rosary (especially in May and October), hymns, opportunities for confession during Mass, prayers to prepare and give thanks for Holy Communion (especially for children), Holy Communion itself distributed by another priest after the Consecration; and, of course, some of the more thoughtful parishioners brought prayer books which, to differing extents, tried to replicate some of the words that the celebrant was saying in Latin; and some of the more conscientious said the rosary "into themselves". In retrospect, the reforms of the Council were long overdue.

It is important to remember that we are called and enabled to participate not just in the rite of Mass but thereby, through the prayers, readings, actions and even silences, we become present to, and involved in, the one great Liturgy of Christ, his Paschal Mystery of offering himself to the Father (see Peter Cullinane, Bishop Emeritus of Palmerston North, New Zealand, *Openings to Renewal*, p.73).

The full participation of all present at Mass requires, of course, a certain amount of catechesis so that people will understand what occurs and why it does so. Such explanation will have to refer not only to the prayers and Scripture passages that occur but also to the various actions and movements as well as the correct use of music and silence. Perhaps giving the catechesis is a challenge, ensuring not only that the material is suitable and helpful but also that opportunities exist for it to be given. A certain amount can be included in homilies and in explanatory comments (either spoken or written) but a satisfactory outcome will be very gradual and ongoing, and will demand patience and perseverance.

To achieve the desired aim of enabling everyone present at Mass to be active in the celebration, the Council decreed that a number of changes be made and some new elements introduced. Many of the changes are specific and affect only one or other part of the Eucharist. However, before considering these, there are some more general measures which the Council decreed and which should be mentioned first. There are four of them.

Four general directives

First, the recognition that, at Mass, there are, in addition to the priest (and, if present, also a deacon), other ministries and roles which can and should be devolved to lay persons (*SC* 28, 29). These will include readers for the Scripture passages prior to the Gospel, extraordinary ministers of Holy Communion, cantors for the Responsorial Psalm, readers for the General Intercessions, choir, musicians, servers, bringers of the gifts of bread and wine, passkeepers and welcomers (being watchful and helpful, though not intrusive); moreover, everyone present can be participative through the varying bodily postures, joining in the communal prayers, both sung and said, receiving Holy Communion as a member of the worshipping community and, even, showing interest in the others present by affability and approachability both before and after Mass. Those who go to Mass should see themselves as forming a community or, more properly, a communion of the faithful. It is hard to describe the requirements for this to be verified. But one useful criterion is the following: when a regular attender is absent, is it noticed and, if it is, do people care?

It is obvious that all ministers and everyone with a special task to fulfil at Mass should take the responsibility seriously and carry out the work as well as possible. I think that there is a special duty on readers and on leaders of music. They must be competent and prepare sufficiently beforehand. Of course, if a person is unable to achieve the competence needed but is already fulfilling any of these special tasks, it is extremely difficult for anyone, in particular the priest in charge, to rectify matters. The requisite improvement is very unlikely, yet ending the incompetent person's tenure of the post is not at all easy. Perhaps recourse to prayer is the only feasible option.

A second general change is the introduction of the vernacular into the Church's liturgy. This innovation is the one that aroused greatest interest and debate among the Council Fathers and, indeed, among Catholics at large. The issue had been much discussed and enthusiastically urged by some for decades in several countries, especially in France, Germany and the Low Countries as well among liturgists. But it was not seen as a matter of urgency in Scotland. In fact, I recall the possibility of English in the Church's liturgy being a subject at seminary debating societies and the overwhelming verdict being negative; indeed, a positive opinion was regarded as slightly ridiculous, mainly on the grounds that, by retaining Latin, the Mass was in the same language and therefore understandable wherever you went in the world. Very faulty reasoning (perhaps for "understandable", we really meant "equally unintelligible") but easily convincing. However, when it became known that the Council Fathers were seriously debating the issue, many more people began to take the matter as a serious possibility.

We have already seen how the Council Fathers showed so much interest in the suggestion of liturgy in the local language that it became, by far, the most debated issue of the Council's discussion on the liturgy *schema*. Authors and scholars noted and criticised that nearly all of the speeches on the subject at the Council concentrated on practical issues about the benefits or problems that would follow the introduction of vernacular languages; very few of the Fathers spoke of the relationship between liturgical language and the overall purpose of the reform of the liturgy, namely, the full participation of all who are present.

The Constitution is tentative and cautious on the extent to which Latin could be superseded in the Roman rite by a local language. "The use of the Latin language is to be preserved... But since the use of the mother tongue is frequently of great advantage to the people in the Mass, the administration of the sacraments and other parts of the liturgy, the limits of its employment may be extended. This will apply in the first place to the readings and directives and to some of the prayers and chants..." (*SC* 36). And again, "In those Masses which are celebrated with the people, a suitable place may be allotted to their mother-tongue. This is to apply in the first place to the readings and the Prayer of the Faithful but also, as local conditions may warrant, to those items of the liturgy which pertain to the people..." (*SC* 54). The document then reiterates the continuing importance of Latin and indicates the procedure to be followed if an extended use of the mother-tongue appears desirable.

Despite the limited permission for the use of local languages conceded in the Constitution itself, only a few years later, authorisation for the use of the vernacular was extended to the entire liturgy. This concession of the Holy See was widely welcomed but, of course, it made the responsibilities of translators even more onerous.

On 17th October 1963, representatives of ten English-speaking bishops' conferences met in the Venerable English College in Rome and decided that a common English translation would be made and used in all of the countries represented. The ten bishops' conferences were Australia, Canada, England and Wales, India, Ireland, New Zealand, Pakistan, Scotland, Southern Africa and United States of America. Thus was formally constituted the International Commission on English in the Liturgy (ICEL). Soon, the Philippines became an eleventh member and there are a further fifteen bishops' conferences which have associate membership.

ICEL completed its first translation of the Roman Missal in 1972; it was approved by the bishops' conferences, received the "*recognitio*" of the Holy See and was published in 1974. Because it was felt that the first translation could be improved, ICEL produced a second translation in 1998; this also was approved by all the eleven bishops' conferences who are full members of ICEL but the Holy See announced in 2002 that it was refusing "*recognitio*".

The ostensible reason for the denial was the introduction in 2001, by the Congregation for Divine Worship and Discipline of the Sacraments, of a document with new and much stricter rules for the "right implementation" of the Vatican II Constitution "on the use of vernacular languages" in the liturgy. The document, known from the first two words of its Latin text as "*Liturgiam authenticam*", was much criticised for being arbitrary in its criteria and imposing a theory of translation that was much too literal and almost word for word, to such an extent that the vernacular language lost much of its own character and style and became laboured, tedious and even, in some cases, unintelligible. One must also be aware of the fact that the Congregation's attitude to ICEL, previously friendly and cooperative, had become very critical and even hostile.

In his book, *Openings to Renewal*, Bishop Peter Cullinane (now retired bishop of Palmerston North, New Zealand) offers a measured but critical judgment on *Liturgiam authenticam*.. [It] "is more concerned with the individual words of the original text and is ambiguous about the need for the texts to be easy to understand. Consequently, the translations in the new (third) edition of the

Missal tend to be rigorously literal. They better reflect the nuances of the Latin originals and their biblical allusions. This adds a richness beyond what we have been used to. Their main weakness, however, is that their syntax is often still in Latin even though the vocabulary is in English; for example, long sentences with multiple relative clauses. In a culture of sound-bites and shorter attention spans, many will find these prayers difficult to follow. Proclaiming them prayerfully and intelligibly will require serious preparation ahead of every celebration" (pp.78-79).

It may also be claimed that the "*recognitio*" had been wrongly interpreted by the Congregation as equal to "approval", whereas the Council's Constitution enacts that, while decrees of bishops' conferences about which texts will be translated require "to be approved, that is confirmed, by the Holy See", the resulting translations need only the approval of the conferences (*SC* 36 §3, §4). I shall explain this later.

With the deplorable decision of the 2002 refusal, many of ICEL's top officials (including its chairman and its executive secretary) left. A largely reconstituted commission began work on a translation that is conformed to the demands of *Liturgiam authenticam* and which received the approval of the bishops' conferences and the ready "*recognitio*" of the Congregation. Publication of this new translation of the missal took place in 2011. Is that the end of the story of a struggle for an acceptable and permanent translation? Assuredly not. To put it mildly, our latest translation has not been received with unanimous acclamation and, besides, English is a living and a changing language and, sometime in the future, sooner or later, there will be a call for a revision of our English translation of the missal.

Since I was intimately involved in the preparation of the rejected translation and in ICEL's relations with the Congregation during those difficult years, I have written more fully about the entire sorry business in my book, *It's the Eucharist, Thank God* (2009).

Perhaps it is not surprising that the subject which occupied so much time during the debates and discussions on the liturgy at the Second Vatican Council continues to be a matter of great interest and even of dissension. Translations into other languages also have their story which cannot be told here. But it perhaps should be noted that the English translation has special importance, not only because so many Catholics throughout the world use it, but also because it is the translation which, with the Latin original, is most often and most widely employed as a guide by those with the responsibility of translating the missal into many other languages in the developing world and elsewhere, that is, into languages apart from English, French, German, Italian, Spanish and Portuguese.

The third of the general measures decreed by Vatican II for the reform of the liturgy involves the arrangement of various furnishings and the consequent location of participants (cf. *SC* 128). Specifically, for the Eucharist, there should be, in different areas of the sanctuary, the altar, the ambo and the presidential chair. The first should be free standing to allow the ministers to walk around it and the celebrant to face the people during the Liturgy of the Eucharist; the second is for the proclamation of the Word of God and a natural focus for attention at that time; and the third is a symbol of the celebrant's office of presiding and the place where he is during the Liturgy of the Word. In addition, the tabernacle should not be on the altar but should have a place of honour, separate from the altar, and either in the sanctuary or in a side chapel, readily visible and suitable for private adoration and prayer (*General Instruction of the Roman Missal (GIRM)* 299, 309, 310, 315).

"The choir should be so positioned...that its nature may be clearly evident, namely as part of the assembled community of the faithful undertaking a specific function" (*GIRM* 312). The celebration of Mass also calls for certain processions or movements of participants: the entrance procession, the gospel procession, the procession bringing the gifts to the altar, the procession for receiving Holy Communion and the recessional procession, as well as the varying postures of standing, sitting and kneeling corresponding to different parts of the Mass.

The customary arrangement of a church with a sanctuary and a large nave is not ideal in trying to have a sense of everyone actively participating; the impression is too easily conveyed of the congregation spectating as the priest and ministers perform. Perhaps it would be better if the congregation could move around, to be near where the action is at different parts of the Mass. But, given the normal situation, at least on Sundays, with a large number of people and fixed pews, that is hardly possible.

The fourth general measure introduced into the liturgy by the Council is that of inculturation. The Constitution is relatively, even remarkably, profuse on this subject (*SC* 37-40) and encourages "the competent local ecclesiastical authorities" to make adaptations; if such adaptations are "even more radical", the Holy See's permission has to be obtained. Specifically, "provision is to be made, when revising the liturgical books, for the legitimate variations and adaptations to different groups, regions and peoples…provided always that the substantial unity of the Roman rite is preserved" (*SC* 38). In Europe and North America at least, there is little if any evidence of adaptations on grounds of inculturation – and the extremely precise and strict directives of *Liturgiam authenticam* would probably deter anyone courageous or imaginative enough even to envisage proposing such adaptation. The severity of the document just mentioned would seem to make a mockery of the Constitution's assurance that "Even in the liturgy, the Church has no wish to impose a rigid uniformity in matters which do not implicate the faith or the good of the whole community" (*SC* 37).

Before proceeding to consider the specific changes introduced into the celebration of the Eucharist, we should state three criteria which the Constitution declares must govern the choice of such changes.

Three criteria to govern the reform

The first of these criteria is of massive importance since it was on account of this norm that so many changes were made and so many elements which were in the Mass prior to the Council were deleted. The Constitution declares that, to promote intelligibility and participation, the liturgical rites have to be made simpler and clearer. The relevant sections of the Constitution (especially *SC* 34 and 50) are unambiguous: "The rites should be distinguished by a noble simplicity; they should be short, clear and unencumbered by any useless repetitions…" and "The rite of Mass is to be revised…that devout and active participation by the people may be more easily achieved. For this purpose, the rites are to be simplified; elements which, with the passage of time, came to be duplicated, or were added with but little advantage, are now to be discarded; other elements…are now to be restored to the vigour which they had in the days of the holy Fathers (*that is, the early centuries of the Church*), as may seem useful or necessary".

Joseph Ratzinger, writing during and after the Council, welcomes the decision. He speaks of "the pruning of certain accretions often enough concealing the original liturgical nucleus" and that "simple structure had to replace the rampant overgrowth of forms". "Ritual rigidity", he adds, "which almost obliterated the meaning of individual actions, had to be defrosted" (*Theological Highlights of Vatican II*, p.32).

In *It's the Eucharist, Thank God*, I give a detailed description of the rite of Mass before Vatican II. Here, therefore, is a brief account of the changes in Mass that occurred as a result of the Council's instruction that the Roman rite be simplified and made clearer. The Introductory Rites were made shorter and simpler; the Scripture readings were reorganised; the General Intercessions were restored to Mass; the Preparation of the Gifts became much shorter and simpler; the existing Eucharistic Prayer (Roman Canon) was retained, but others were made available to give choices; the Communion Rites became more inclusive of the congregation; and the Concluding Rites were shorn of their "quasi-appendices". Several of these changes will be examined more closely in the following pages.

The second of the three criteria is found in the Constitution on the Liturgy (*SC* 23) and can be summed up in this extract: "Care must be taken that any new forms adopted should in some way grow organically from forms already existing". The document explains that, in order "that sound tradition may be retained and yet the way remain open to legitimate progress, a careful investigation is always to be made into each part of the liturgy which is to be revised". In other words, changes are not to be wanton or made for capricious motives but for reasons that are founded on scholarly grounds and which take account of theological, historical and pastoral considerations.

This is a wise ruling although, if inculturation had been more widespread than it actually is, it is very likely that the correct interpretation of the criterion would have occasioned much debate and even disagreement. Even as things are, this instruction of the Council lacks precision and can, or could, be given rather widely differing interpretations by those who wanted a generous number of changes or as few as possible. The vagueness of the wording and therefore the possibility of disagreement about its exact meaning brings to mind the phrase that Pope Benedict used in order to explain the intention of the Council Fathers; it was necessary, he said, for us to employ "a hermeneutic of continuity", a phrase that itself, I submit, is not without ambiguity.

The third criterion (*SC* 22) exists perhaps for the reason of avoiding such disagreements and even a descent into chaos. The Council decrees that regulation of the liturgy belongs only to the Holy See and, in certain cases, to bishops' conferences and even to the individual bishop. "No other person, even if he be a priest, may remove or change anything in the liturgy on his own authority". I am of the opinion that strict observance of this ruling is better, not only in obedience to authority but also to avoid any confusion to others, especially to concelebrating priests during the Eucharistic Prayer.

In fact, given the Council's teaching, especially that the liturgical rites be made simpler and clearer to foster understanding and participation, I find it difficult to welcome recent legislation that permits, and even seems to encourage, the use of liturgical rites which the Council clearly meant to be superseded. I refer, especially, to what is called the Extraordinary Form of the Roman Rite, using the Missal of Pope John XXIII (in other words, the Tridentine rite of Mass in use from the sixteenth century until the Liturgy Constitution of Vatican II).

The thoughts of the late Cardinal Franz König, Archbishop of Vienna and one of the great figures of the Church, both at the Council and subsequently, are relevant. In *Open to God, Open to the World* (2005), chapter 1, he writes: "To many, however, both inside and outside the Church, the renewal of the liturgy was the Council's most striking reform. Misunderstandings arose because the change was too abrupt and the faithful were not prepared gently enough. Many Catholics were so deeply attached to the liturgical forms they had grown up with and had been familiar with all their lives that the fact that the liturgy was no longer in Latin but in the vernacular and that the priest faced the faithful etc. was almost more than they could cope with. Elderly priests found these changes particularly difficult."

The comments of Joseph Ratzinger on those with authority for "the regulation of the liturgy" are most interesting. He welcomes such authority, within limits, being given to bishops' conferences.

"An especially important development is the decentralization of the liturgical decision-making...and this not by delegation from the Holy See but by virtue of their own independent authority". He declares, "Now that they (*bishops' conferences*) possess in their own right a definite legislative function, they appear as a new element in the Church's structure and form a kind of quasi-synodal agency between individual bishops and the pope... This small paragraph, which for the first time assigns to conferences of bishops their own canonical authority, has more significance for the theology of the episcopacy and for the long desired strengthening of episcopal power than anything in the *Constitution on the Church* itself". By this measure, "the Church had produced a work fundamental in the renewal of ecclesiology" (*Theological Highlights of Vatican II*, pp.34-35). The young Fr Ratzinger's enthusiasm for this element of decentralisation and the exercise of subsidiarity is admirable but was not, it seems, sustained throughout his life. There is little evidence of it when he became prefect of the Congregation for the Doctrine of the Faith nor did he seem, as pope, to foster such measures in the activities of the Roman Curia.

By the way, it might be asked how many bishops' conferences or, indeed, individual bishops have availed themselves of the right, given by the Council, to introduce measures that "regulate the liturgy" "within certain defined limits" and "as laws may determine" in their territory or their diocese (*SC* 22). Are the limits of that right known by conferences or by bishops? Do they even know that they have that right?

Specific reforms of the Eucharistic liturgy

Let us move on to consider the more important of the specific changes that we now have in the celebration of the Eucharist in the Roman rite. Before going through the Mass from its beginning and looking at various different elements during the celebration, we should consider an element that to an extent should pervade the celebration – music.

The Constitution devotes a chapter to this subject (chapter VI, *SC* 112-121) and, since then, there have been other developments. So the following remarks are not merely comments on the Council's teaching but also a consideration of the part music does, or should, play in our celebration of the Eucharist, at least on Sundays and the great feasts.

The first point to make is that, although there is a place for hymns in the celebration of Mass in parishes, the principal purpose of music is that parts of the Mass itself should be sung. In fact, there is nowadays clear encouragement that singing should be welcomed for the three presidential prayers (Collect, Prayer over the Gifts, Post-Communion Prayer), as well as for the Preface and even the entire Eucharistic Prayer.

It is perhaps too much to expect all of this at every Sunday Mass, not only since many priests feel that their vocal talent is limited, but so also are time and the congregation's patience. But at least the acclamations should be sung: Gloria, Gospel Acclamation, Sanctus, Memorial Acclamation, Great Amen, Lamb of God and, if at all possible, the Responsorial Psalm. Congregations should be urged to sing these parts and not listen to a choir. Consequently, settings have to be attractive and should become familiar to the people but not limited to one setting relentlessly and monotonously used Sunday after Sunday. Choirs have a role in the liturgy, to sustain the singing and provide support, with an occasional specially prepared piece of their own if they wish. I suspect that habitual singing, each weekend, of the Creed, the responses to the General Intercessions and, perhaps also, the Lord's Prayer can be tedious for many good people and therefore unnecessarily conscientious.

The Constitution on the Liturgy stresses the special place of plainchant and also polyphony in the Church's music. "The Church acknowledges Gregorian chant as specially suited to the Roman liturgy; therefore, other things being equal, it should be given pride of place in liturgical functions. But other kinds of sacred music, especially polyphony, are by no means excluded from liturgical celebrations..." (*SC* 116).

The same points continue to be urged nowadays, although it has to be admitted that, except in the cathedrals and other churches of large dioceses, it is not easy to make great use of Gregorian chant and even less of polyphony. It is possible and, in some parishes, not uncommon for the Proper of the Mass, or parts of it, to be sung in Latin and using plainchant settings on special occasions; even more at diocesan or national liturgies. Polyphonic motets also feature now and again, properly prepared and practised by choirs. But usage of the classical polyphonic settings of the Mass is a rarity; apart from the inherent difficulty of their performance, the length of the different sections, composed to fill the silences while the celebrant continued with "his" parts, are not at all suitable for today's reformed liturgy.

Hymns? Well, yes. But perhaps we tend to overuse them. It is not decreed that there should be any, but they can and do embellish the celebration. It seems clear that, for many people, the words of a hymn can be very meaningful and provide consolation, inspiration, hope in sadness, appreciation of God's love for us and such like. So let them be well chosen and appropriate for particular seasons and/or themes. There is no rule that there ought to be four at Sunday Masses. Consequently, wise and thoughtful choices should be made, not only what hymns to have but also when they should be sung – at the entrance, during the collection and at the procession of the gifts, during and/or after Holy Communion, recessional: all are possible, but not compulsory, times for a hymn. And all singing is much more attractive when it is not dragged!

That last point is something that is also important for the instrumentalists, whether organists, guitarists or others. Is the excuse that "I need to keep with the congregation because, if I play at the right speed, they simply stop singing" a valid reason?

Musicians are long-suffering and insufficiently appreciated and thanked. On the other hand, perhaps there are cases of parish organists who have been faithful for fifty years or more, not because there is no one to take over but because there is no one brave enough to inform them gently that perhaps they might like to allow another and younger musician to be given at least an occasional opportunity to play at Sunday Mass. Enough on the subject of music. I am not a musician but I know enough to realise that music in the parish is not only important and beautiful but also can be a matter of the utmost delicacy where even immense discretion and tact can fail...

Now to thc important changes in different parts of Mass in the Roman rite; first the Scripture readings. The Constitution (*SC* 51) calls for more readings, more varied and better ordered. Previously, the Scriptures at Mass were an Epistle (from the New Testament) and a Gospel extract, with a short passage called "the gradual" between the two. The readings were in Latin, of course, with the priest with his back to the congregation, although usually on

Sundays he would go to the pulpit after the Gospel to make announcements and then read the day's Epistle and Gospel in English. Except on particular occasions, the two readings would have little relevance to one another, to the Sunday or to the readings of the previous or following Sundays. The result was a limited selection of passages, with no variation from year to year, no continuity from Sunday to Sunday, and many parts of the Bible, including the entire Old Testament, neither read nor heard.

The position on weekdays was even worse. Most days were saints' feasts, usually with the Scripture from the appropriate "Common"; ferial days used the readings of the previous Sunday, while a great many priests preferred to celebrate, as often as they could, daily Masses specifically for the dead and with the same very brief Epistle and Gospel. Nor were the passages read a second time in English on weekdays. They had degenerated into a routine and in danger of losing their essential purpose.

The situation badly needed reform, which was further emphasised by the increased awareness of the importance of the Scriptures among Catholics in general and the Council Fathers in particular. So, in response to the Council's wishes, a totally revised lectionary was drawn up. At weekday Masses, there was be a first reading, varying between extracts from Old and New Testament books. Then follows a psalm, proclaimed by a reader with a response for the congregation after each verse; this so called Responsorial Psalm is to provide a suitable reflection on the first reading. The second weekday reading is a passage from one of the gospels, introduced by an acclamation. Although the two readings are not interrelated, each follows a day-to-day continuous extract from a book of the Bible. In the first reading, the different books are allotted a number of days, few or many, depending on their length and importance. To allow a wider selection, the weekday first reading has a two-year cycle. The weekday gospel passages are read each year and proceed through the three synoptic gospels, Mark in springtime, Matthew in summer and Luke in autumn (approximately). John's gospel is used at various special times of the year, especially Passiontide and Eastertide.

The arrangement of Sunday Scripture readings is somewhat more complicated. In the first place, there are three readings with a responsorial psalm and a gospel acclamation spaced between them. The first reading is usually from the Old Testament, except during the Easter season when it comes from the Acts of the Apostles. When from the Old Testament, it does not follow a semi-continuous path from week to week since the passage is chosen because it has some relation to the Gospel of the day. The second Sunday reading is usually from one of St Paul's letters or the other New Testament letters. Over a number of Sundays, these follow continuous extracts from the one book, but without any explicit relation to the first reading or the gospel. Both the first and the second Sunday readings have a three-year cycle, each year of the three being also devoted to continuous readings from one of the synoptic gospels. There are exceptions to these arrangements, occasionally on a special feast but more commonly at Advent/Christmas and at Lent/Passiontide/Eastertide. At these two seasons, John's gospel is very prominent. For six weeks during the summer of a "Year of Mark", John chapter 6 is inserted, since Mark, being a shorter gospel, "needs help" to cover all the available Sundays.

It is obvious that the new arrangement is a much better one than before Vatican II, and especially the programme for weekdays; but the Sunday arrangement is not perfect. Two related problems may be mentioned. The second reading on Sundays bears no real relation to the other readings and serves to divide them and therefore to distract from the relation that the first and third readings have to one another; and three readings plus a responsorial psalm and a gospel acclamation is fare that is too rich and too rapidly delivered, even if there are short silences. Omission of the second reading is not a solution because then we should have little or nothing of St Paul. Keeping the second reading until the end of Mass (as we used to have a "Last Gospel") would probably find no favour as being liturgically clumsy. Perhaps there is no good solution and we should just be grateful for the amount and variety of Scripture made available and the orderly way it is presented to us.

The readings from Scripture are complemented by the homily, the importance of which is strongly stressed in *Sacrosanctum Concilium* (*SC* 52). In fact, a homily is obligatory on Sundays and days of obligation "and should not be omitted except for a serious reason". The homily is a specific exercise of a priest's and a deacon's ministry of the Word. As the *General Instruction of the Roman Missal* (*GIRM* 65) explains: "It should be an explanation of some aspect of the readings from Sacred Scripture or of another text from the Ordinary or Proper of the Mass of the day and should take into account both the mystery being celebrated and the particular needs of the listeners". Proper fulfilment of this instruction about the homily requires serious effort by the priest or deacon. This involves not only good choice of a subject and adequate preparation, but content and delivery, neither too short nor too long, but able to maintain the interest of the listeners and be of some advantage to them. While sermons are usually about what we should do, homilies tell us what God is doing. "The discovery of God's marvellous, surprising, unmerited love generates our desire to love and to live gratefully in return. It liberates and empowers us for even more than the law asks of us" (Peter Cullinane, *Openings to Renewal*, p.83).

A satisfactory homily is not easy to achieve, especially since the average congregation has such a diverse range of people. Meeting "the particular needs of the listeners", as the General Instruction of the Roman Missal requires, is a real challenge for the priest. "The homily provides an opportunity to flesh out the meaning of God's words in terms of everyday life", writes Kevin T. Kelly, *Fifty years of Receiving Vatican II*, p.56, "yet sadly it is an opportunity we priests rarely make the most of – our words are often up in the air and rarely connect with the 'down-to-earth' lives of people". He continues, "Perhaps this is partly due to the fact that a combination of celibacy and clerical culture leaves us largely out of touch with the nitty-gritty of most people's everyday lives".

Nowadays especially, the homilist will be compared, too easily to his disadvantage, with other modern means of communication. In some parishes or dioceses, there also seem to be too frequent occasions when the homily has a rival and is omitted; for example, a letter to be read, an appeal to be made or some other matter to be announced or explained on "a special occasion". I am tempted to "anecdotalise" at this point, but will resist the temptation and proceed to the next subject.

One part of Mass which dates from the earliest centuries but had disappeared for a long time before its restoration by the Council is the Universal Prayer, also known as the Prayer of the Faithful, or the General Intercessions or, more familiarly, the Bidding Prayers. "By this prayer, in which the people are to take part, intercession will be made for Holy Church, for the civil authorities, for those oppressed by various needs, for all mankind and for the salvation of the entire world" (*SC* 53). The missal notes that, at the Prayer of the Faithful, the people are "exercising the office of their baptismal priesthood" and that "it is desirable that there usually be such a form of prayer" (*GIRM* 69). The missal offers some examples but there is freedom to compose and use words specially prepared and suitable for the occasion; however, it should be borne in mind that the Prayer of the Faithful has to retain a certain character of prayer for the whole Church and for all of humanity. The Intercessions are introduced by an invitation to pray and a concluding prayer by the priest, while a deacon or lay person announces each intention, allows a short silence and then invites the congregation to respond to a phrase such as "Lord, hear us" with, for example, "Lord, graciously hear us". The intercessions should be limited in number (not more than four to six) and in length, because each is the announcement of the intention and not itself a prayer, even less a mini-sermon.

The Prayer of the Faithful had disappeared from the liturgy of Mass many centuries ago but traces of it, so it is said, found their way into the Roman Canon, thus making that Eucharistic Prayer very cluttered, as we shall see.

There are other elements in the first part of the Mass which we have not mentioned, such as the Rites of Introduction (which are still fairly complicated and variable, since a suggested radical simplification was not carried out), the Collect (the first of the three "presidential prayers", said by the priest in the plural and in the name of the assembly, the people responding in each case with the acclamatory assent of "Amen"), the Gloria and the Creed (each said only at Masses of some notable commemoration or feast). The Creed has reverted, in the 2011 translation, from "We believe" of the 1972 translation to "I believe", as a more correct translation of the Latin "*Credo*" but one which was regretted by many as losing the communal sense valuable in a formal Profession of Faith.

After the Prayer of the Faithful, which concludes the Liturgy of the Word, the Liturgy of the Eucharist, its complement, begins with the Preparation of the Gifts of bread and wine. These two elements are brought to the priest, along with the collection of money offerings if such has occurred. It is good that some of the congregation take the bread and wine to the priest with a certain appearance of a formal procession, to indicate that they come as an offering from the people. The priest then says a form of dedication for the bread and the wine, both of which will soon be consecrated and offered to God. But this part of Mass, which ends with the second presidential prayer (the Prayer over the Offerings), has been greatly simplified from the prayers and actions used before the Council. These were not only needlessly fussy but also couched in language that gave the impression that it was the bread and wine, as such, that were being offered to God in sacrifice. In *It's the Eucharist, Thank God*, I have given more details of this part of Mass as it used to be.

The most solemn part of the Mass, the Eucharistic Prayer, then commences. Its first part consists in a short dialogue between priest and people, a paean of praise and thanksgiving to God called the Preface (somewhat confusingly named, because it is an integral part of the Eucharistic Prayer), and ending in an acclamation by all. This first part has been largely unaltered, except that the range of different Prefaces to suit various seasons and feasts has been further increased in the new rite of Mass.

Then comes the principal part of the Eucharistic Prayer, recited by the priest alone. Before Vatican II, the Roman rite used only one unchanging form of this major part of the Eucharistic Prayer. When, after the Council, the official commission, charged with the task of implementing the Council's wish that the liturgical texts should be made simpler and clearer, came to consider the so-called Roman Canon, they found it impossible to effect the necessary reform; the text was too complex and too intricate, with the consequence that any attempt to update it would have destroyed it. Part of the problem is due to the fact that, over the centuries, various additions have been made which have interrupted or damaged the logical flow of the text or have duplicated elements in it and have obscured others. In particular, the prayer makes no mention of the Holy Spirit and includes no explicit epiclesis. So the decision was made to preserve the Roman Canon with only a very few minor changes, to designate it "Eucharistic Prayer I" and to introduce others into the Missal, most entirely new and others adapted from very early and later abandoned forms of the prayer.

The newcomers include Eucharistic Prayers II, III and IV, the Eucharistic Prayers for Reconciliation I and II, the Eucharistic Prayer for use in Masses for various needs (forms I to IV), and the three Eucharistic Prayers for Masses with Children. All of these prayers have the same structure. Following the Preface and its acclamation, there is an address worshipping God, an epiclesis invoking the Holy Spirit to come so that the bread and wine may be consecrated into Christ's body and blood, the institution narrative, elevation and acclamation, an anamnesis relating the Mass to Calvary and offering our sacrifice to the Father, a prayer that those participating may be filled with the Spirit, invocation of the saints, a prayer for the living and the dead, the solemn doxology and final acclamation. The three acclamations in each Eucharistic Prayer, one ("Holy, holy...") after the Preface, another (with three alternative wordings) after the elevation and the third ("the Great Amen"), are the responses made by the entire congregation.

The introduction of a variety of Eucharistic Prayers has been generally welcomed. By the very nature of things, the normal ones used are numbers I, II, III and IV, with numbers II and III said more often than the other two. Not only are they shorter and simpler but, at least as translated in the present English version, numbers I and IV are seen as less pleasing in some respects. The Eucharistic Prayers for Reconciliation and for Various Needs are normally not to be used on Sundays and feast days but at least they should be used occasionally on other appropriate days, even though rather longer than numbers II and III. Personally I have reservations about the use of the Eucharistic Prayers for Children. In addition to the text said by the celebrant, they also have more acclamations at various points, presumably to maintain the children's attention. But the language of these Prayers still seems no more intelligible to children than that of the "adult" Prayers; moreover, a correct and decorous inclusion of the extra acclamations seems seldom achieved.

The Lord's Prayer introduces the Rite of Communion as it did before Vatican II, but now the entire assembly says the prayer. The theme of Christ's gift of peace to his disciples is very evident throughout the Rite of Communion and there is provision for the exchange of a Sign of Peace among those present at Mass. This action used to be seen at Masses at which the priest was assisted by a deacon and subdeacon and the priest offered the Sign of Peace to the other two. Now, however, all participants are invited to exchange the gesture with one or more of those who are nearby. It signifies the wish for peace as well as ecclesial communion and mutual charity (*GIRM* 82).

Sometimes, the gesture embarrasses those unaccustomed to it or, at other times, the exchanges can become too prolonged if attempts are made to reach many or even all present or if the gesture becomes the opportunity for exchanging news. But, if carried out with dignity and warmth, the Sign of Peace expresses something important and useful. The suggestion has been made that the Sign of Peace might find a new location in the liturgy, namely at the start of the Liturgy of the Eucharist. The reason for this is Our Lord's injunction: "…go and be reconciled with your brother first and then come back and present your offering" (Matthew 5:24). However, the proposal has not been taken up, perhaps because the Sign of Peace is by no means limited to seeking to be reconciled.

Holy Communion is Holy Communion, but there have been changes in the way that the congregation receives it. Of course, the regulation of fasting from all food or liquid, even water, from the previous midnight, has now been drastically mitigated and reduced to one hour before reception, with water and medicines unrestricted (Code of Canon Law, *CIC* 919). The procession of people towards the altar indicates that it is the local ecclesial community or communion which takes part in Mass, not just a number of individuals. Reception can be in the hand rather than on the tongue, and while standing instead of kneeling; Holy Communion under both kinds, although not giving us any more of the risen and living Christ, is a more complete sign of what we receive and, by receiving from the chalice, reminds us of the new and eternal covenant sealed by Christ's shedding of his blood.

It is noteworthy that the Constitution *Sacrosanctum Concilium* reiterates the previously official teaching: it is "strongly commended" that the faithful "receive the Lord's body from the same sacrifice", a practice which the Constitution describes as "that more perfect form of participation in the Mass" (*SC* 55). The habit, through carelessness or on purpose, of keeping a large number of consecrated hosts in the tabernacle to be used in future Masses, is clearly wrong and to be deplored.

Finally, in 2008, various versions of the words of dismissal were provided. This follows a request made at a recent Synod of Bishops that the words should indicate not merely that the celebration has come to an end but also that we are being sent forth with a mission to bring God's infinite love and care, mediated through Jesus Christ, to those whom we meet. The laconic "*Ite, missa est*" has been adjudged too abrupt; besides, it defies accurate translation.

Appreciating the Eucharist more fully

That concludes a review of the more important or more drastic changes in the Roman rite of Mass, resulting from the Constitution on the Liturgy of the Second Vatican Council. There are also some aspects of the Eucharist that were not included in the Council's Constitution or are there, but more implicitly than explicitly. These points do have importance, especially for a deeper appreciation of the riches that have been bestowed on us through the gift of the Eucharist. I want, therefore, to describe at least some of them.

The celebration of the Eucharist involves not only looking forward to Christ's second coming "at the end of time" and the eternal life he promised us, but indeed is the pledge and foretaste of that destiny. Two of the three acclamations after the Consecration declare: "We proclaim your death, O Lord…until you come again". And many of the Mass prayers explicitly look forward to eternal life and ask God to grant us that supreme favour. Specifically, Holy Communion is seen as an anticipation of heaven and, when the celebrant shows the consecrated elements to the people as an invitation to receive Communion, he says "Behold the Lamb of God" and refers to "those called to the supper of the Lamb" or "the wedding feast of the Lamb", quoting the phrase used in the Apocalypse as a metaphor for the happiness of eternal life with God: "Happy are those who are called to the wedding feast (*some versions:* "supper") of the Lamb" (Revelation 19:7).

We have already noted that we attend and celebrate the Eucharist not as individuals but as members of the Church, worldwide and local, and therefore as a community or, better, "the communion of saints" here on earth. What does the latter term add to the word "community"? It signifies all that "community" implies, namely a conscious sense of union or relationship with others, a love and care for them, an interest in their welfare, a hope of their reciprocating similar feelings for us; but it also implies that the bond that unites the community is Jesus Christ himself, that together we form his Mystical Body. So, when we are at Mass, we pray for one another and act together with each other. We manifest this at various moments by our bodily postures of standing, kneeling and sitting carried out together as well as by our participating in any procession that occurs, especially in bringing the bread and wine to the altar (a group representing the entire congregation) and in approaching the altar to receive Holy Communion. Perhaps most clearly the "communion" is visible at the Sign of Peace as, in preparing to receive the Body and Blood of Christ, we express our unity in words and in a gesture of peace and fellowship.

Although the "institution narrative" is to be found in the three synoptic gospels (and in the first letter of St Paul to the Corinthians), it is not in the gospel according to John. Instead, that gospel, and it alone, recounts the event at the Last Supper when Jesus washed the feet of the apostles. Clearly this was a very significant action, so why is it repeated only once a year, at the Mass of the Lord's Supper on Holy Thursday evening? The response which I like to offer to that question is as follows.

A precise repetition of Our Lord's action at the Last Supper, if carried out at each Mass, would mean that our love would be expressed to a very limited number of people and to the same people (especially at weekday Mass) and with a gesture that is not clearly significant, at least in our culture. Jesus speaks of himself, and therefore of his disciples, as present "to serve, not to be served". And, in the Apostolic Letter, *Mane nobiscum, Domine*, Pope John Paul II, writing of our duty of concern for all people in need, declares: "This will be the criterion by which the authenticity of our Eucharistic celebrations will be judged" (no. 28). So our constant readiness to serve all and any of our brothers and sisters in need is the appropriate and effective way of continuing Our Lord's gesture of washing the feet of the apostles.

Another important element, and one that is sometimes overlooked, is that, in celebrating the Eucharist, we affirm once more the new and eternal covenant between God and his people, a covenant inaugurated on Calvary and sealed with the blood shed by his Son. The extension of Holy Communion under the form of wine has therefore special added significance for communicants, allowing them to make a personal renewal as members of the community or communion covenanted to God. In Sacred

Scripture, God insists on his having a covenant with his people. It is God's chosen way not only of expressing the bond that exists but also of wishing to have fidelity and permanence as qualities of that relationship. Further, the covenant with God implies not only lasting friendship but also a pledge of help and support from God and of honour and obedience from us. In the Old Testament, the covenant had to be several times re-established due to the infidelity of the chosen people; but the New Covenant is essentially eternal because of the unbreakable fidelity of Jesus Christ and the unending efficacy of his self-sacrifice. In the Eucharist, therefore, we have the privilege of being united to Christ and sharing in his eternal bond with the Father.

The relationship between Christ's Paschal Mystery of his death and resurrection on the one hand and the Last Supper as well as Mass itself on the other is something not considered in the Constitution on the Liturgy. There is an identity among all three (Supper, Calvary and Mass) and clearly Jesus does not offer himself in sacrifice again each time we celebrate Mass. The term "re-presentation" is often used, not "representation" since that might suggest that Mass was only a symbolic depiction of Calvary, much as a passion play is. Is it legitimate to suggest that Jesus, being God as well as human, can abstract himself from the limitations of time and location to which mere humans are subject and so "telescope" Holy Thursday, the Sacred Triduum and every Mass into one and the same action? Would that help to explain the mystery? Because mystery it is and perhaps we have simply to agree that the explanation is beyond us and that we accept the Eucharist as a mystery and a gift for which we can never be grateful enough.

The celebration of Mass is such a rich activity that we are inclined to feel uncomfortable at its length, being aware that people can become impatient and uneasy if anything lasts too long. Perhaps this explains the lack of pauses for silence that ideally should take place at various moments of the Mass. There are several such moments – at the Penitential Rite, after the "Let us pray" before the Collect, after the readings and after the homily, after each intention of the General Intercessions, after Holy Communion. I think we could do better in this respect, but it would take some courage – and some moderation – on the part of the celebrant.

It seems to me an acceptable practice if people can talk to one another, and not only about "holy subjects", both before and after Mass and inside the church, if they wish to. After all, we are human beings, living in the world, with worldly concerns that it helps to share with those whom we may meet only at Mass. However, in some parishes, the custom is to ask the assembly to be silent for two or three minutes before Mass begins and thus give everyone the chance to think about, and prepare for, Mass.

While on the subject of preparing for Mass, it is a kindness to the congregation if those who have a ministry or duties to perform during the celebration do what is needed by way of preparation before Mass starts. This, of course, implies being at the church in good time and not rushing in at the last minute; but it also means that we should not be in the habit of fussily carrying out during Mass what should be done earlier. In particular, the different pages of the missal should have been marked, the lectionary should be open (or at least have been marked), things needed for music and singers and passkeepers already in place and, of course, candles lit and bread, wine and water already prepared. All of this is, or should be, done out of respect to the congregation. Even looking for the correct place in the missal should have been done before Mass and not allowed to be a distraction during it; and (perhaps a minor matter but also out of respect to the congregation) the priest, while in dialogue with the congregation, should look and listen to them rather than occupying himself with some trivial matter that calls for attention. Last but not least (and that cliché is truly appropriate in this case), punctuality is an important and virtuous habit where Mass is concerned; it is a question of showing respect and courtesy to the people attending. The plea that being a few minutes late allows the latecomers to arrive before Mass begins is not a good reason for delay.

Personal observations

There are a few further remarks that I should like to make. They allow me to add some personal observations, the first of which is my opinion and the other two I believe to be factual.

The first concerns statements, often heard or read, to the effect that, since the Vatican Council, abuses are frequent in the Church's liturgy and especially in Masses. The implication is that some priests take advantage of the reform and renewal of the liturgy to include further changes that are of their own making and that are an abuse of the priest's office as presiding celebrant. For example, a former Archbishop Secretary of the Congregation for Divine Worship and the Discipline of the Sacraments claimed, in an interview, that "liturgical free-wheeling has become the order of the day" (cited by Peter Cullinane, *Openings to Renewal*, page 81, footnote). My firm impression is that, although no doubt there have been some unauthorised changes or additions or omissions, the practice is very infrequent indeed and the complaint is much exaggerated. It sometimes appears that the accusation is made gratuitously and as a pretext for criticising the very reforms of the rite of Mass (and of other rites) authorised and promoted by the Council.

Secondly, surprise is sometimes expressed that the changes in the Church's liturgy, and especially at Mass, seem to have exceeded those which are mandated in the text of the Constitution on the Liturgy, *Sacrosanctum Concilium*. The assumption is correct but the changes, though not in the Constitution, are authorised by the subsequent official documents of the Holy See. After the Council ended, the Holy See issued and indeed, from time to time, continues to issue formal instructions on various details concerning the manner of celebrating the liturgy. I suppose the most glaring example of subsequent practice exceeding the Council declarations is with regard to the use of the vernacular. The Council decreed its use but, although not imposing limits on the extent of its use, gives the impression that it did not foresee the subsequent situation which later official documents have authorised (see especially *SC* 40 & 54).

By way of illustration, here are some examples of official documents of the Holy See issued subsequent to the Council and which make specific provisions about the celebration of the liturgy: Instruction on the Proper Implementation of the Constitution of the Liturgy (26th September 1964); Decree on Concelebration and Communion under Both Species (7th March 1965); Instruction on Music in the Liturgy (5th March 1967); Second Instruction on the Proper Implementation of the Constitution on the Liturgy (4th May 1967); Instruction on the Manner of Distributing Holy Communion (29th May 1969). The practice continues of official documents being issued, usually by the Congregation for Divine

Worship and the Discipline of the Sacraments, intimating changes, clarifications etc. in the performance of the Church's liturgy.

The third of these observations is also again on the subject of translations into the local languages. A careful reading of the Constitution (*SC* 36) shows that, while a decree of "the competent ecclesiastical authority" (a local bishops' conference) about the extent of the use of the vernacular requires "to be approved, that is confirmed, by the Holy See (§3)", the actual translation requires only approval "by the competent local authority" (§4).

However, within six weeks of the promulgation of the Constitution on the Liturgy, the Holy See, in an official document, *Sacram Liturgiam* (25th January 1964), declared that, "as provided in article 36 §3", both *which translations* as well as the *translations made* "require due approval, that is, confirmation, by the Holy See". This erroneous statement has, ever since, been enforced by Rome. Whether the extension of the need for Holy See approval was done deliberately or by mistake, the error has usurped the authority of bishops' conferences. In particular, it caused the English translation of the Roman Missal, completed at the behest of English-speaking bishops' conferences and approved by all of them in 1998 but refused '*recognitio*' by the Holy See, to be summarily discarded. Consequently, another translation was made and in 2010 readily received the '*recognitio*'; despite widespread and severe criticism generally and specifically by liturgy scholars and many expert authorities, it is now in (reluctant) use.

Perhaps it is worth mentioning that, after the latest translation was approved by the bishops' conferences and went to Rome, it was subjected to multiple alterations by "Vox Clara", a group set up by the Holy See to help the Congregation for Divine Worship and the Discipline of the Sacraments. The translation was then given the '*recognitio*' of the Holy See! A further infringement of the prescribed and correct procedure?

Some suggestions and reminders

These points, I hope, will be of use in helping us to celebrate Mass as correctly and devoutly as possible, and in accord with the wishes of the Fathers of Vatican II as expressed in the Constitution on the Liturgy. The points are mainly for use on Sundays. They are a revision of the ones which I included in *It's the Eucharist, Thank God* (pp.93-95).

1. Everyone, and especially those who have ministries or other roles to carry out, should be properly prepared and should be present for some time before Mass is due to begin. This applies to priest, readers, servers, extraordinary ministers of the Eucharist, musicians, cantors, choir, passkeepers and welcomers.

2. The entrance procession should be accompanied by suitable music, either instrumental or sung.

3. A Liturgy of the Word for children can take place sometimes, but not on every Sunday. Suitable material and content of sufficient maturity should be prepared and used. Pre-school children may have a separate assembly.

4. The Penitential Rite can be varied. (A rite of sprinkling with holy water can be used occasionally.) The invocations, if the third form is used, can be varied as appropriate; they are a litany to Christ – not to the Trinity and not in a form such as "For the times that we…".

5. Parts of the Mass should be sung. Top priority should be given to the 'Ordinary' and especially to the acclamations (Gloria, Gospel Acclamation, Holy, Holy, Memorial Acclamation, Great Amen, Lamb of God). The sung text of these should be the same as, or close to, the words prescribed. Although there is a role for a choir at Mass, the congregation must be allowed and encouraged to sing.

   It is laudable for the priest to sing parts of the Mass (Presidential prayers, Preface dialogue, Eucharistic Prayer), provided this does not impose a considerable burden upon him or the congregation.

6. At the Collect, there should be a short but definite silence after 'Let us pray'.

7. Readers should be intelligent, prepared, audible, able to make eye contact. There should be sufficient numbers to allow variety. In particular, different readers should be used when there are two readings before the gospel. Some practice is necessary (including practice in moving to and from the lectern). The proper books should be used, not missalettes. The question should be asked: is there a courteous and effective manner of dealing with poor, inadequate or unreliable readers?

8. The psalm should be sung, if possible. Some variation from the prescribed psalm is allowed, as also are metrical versions (but not a non-psalm hymn).

9. General Intercessions: the items are *intentions* for which we are asked to pray, not the prayers themselves. Hence, after each intention and before the invitation for a communal response, there should be a short but definite pause for individual, silent prayer.

   How many intentions should there be? Four or five are enough.

   How long? Quite short; they are intentions, not prayers or disguised sermons.

   They should include topical, important concerns, either local or more general.

10. The Eucharistic Prayer begins with the dialogue before the Preface. The Preface is part of the Eucharistic Prayer.

11. There are other Eucharistic Prayers in addition to nos. II and III.

12. Since the celebrant announces the Memorial Acclamation but does not lead it, a decision about which one to use has to be made beforehand. On weekdays, a convenient method is: Mondays & Thursdays: 1st; Tuesdays & Fridays: 2nd; Wednesday & Saturdays: 3rd.

13. During the doxology at the end of the Eucharistic Prayer, the consecrated bread and wine are raised in a gesture of offering them to the Father, not of showing them to the people.

14. The Sign of Peace should not be prolonged unduly or involve a lot of movement or chatter.

15. "Blessed are those…" before Holy Communion. The Eucharist is a pledge and foretaste of eternal life which, in the Apocalypse, is described as a banquet or supper. The liturgy takes up the eschatalogical theme (e.g., as in the Memorial Acclamations and "Lamb of God…") so 'supper' here refers to heaven, not this Mass.

16. The hosts should be those consecrated at the Mass being celebrated. This is not fully achievable, but the tabernacle should not contain full ciboria "ready for the Sunday Masses".

17. Holy Communion from the chalice should be offered to all the communicants, allowing them to drink "the blood of the new and eternal covenant".

18. A sacred silence should be observed after Holy Communion. If it is, there is no need to pause after 'Let us pray' before the Prayer after Communion.

19. Dismissal: the words indicate the mission with which we leave Mass.

20. Hymns at Mass are often given undue importance. Suitable hymns can be sung at appropriate moments but sometimes silence is preferable. Hymns should have some relation to the liturgy of the day and should not take so much time that they delay unduly the liturgical action.

Concluding thoughts

The Mass is something so familiar and so intimate in the lives of so many people that its fortunes at the Second Vatican Council are of great interest to us; one might even speak of its story during those years holding a fascination for us when we learn the details.

The botched preparations for the Council's deliberations projected the Church's liturgy into the leading place and an unexpected prominence when the Council got under way. In retrospect, the result was favourable not only for the liturgy itself but also for putting down markers for the later debates and discussions on other subjects.

The Liturgy with which we now celebrate the Eucharist in the Roman rite is, to a large extent, taken for granted by most of us and for most of the time. But it is useful to be aware of two things. First, to have some knowledge of the Mass as it was celebrated for centuries before Vatican II; and second, to realise that the Council Fathers only decreed a reform and renewal of the liturgy and set the process in motion, a process to be continued lawfully and authoritatively in the Church.

As we enjoy the privilege of greatly enhanced participation in the Mass, we must know that our Eucharistic celebration is more than a beautiful spectacle or a fulfilling human experience. We remember that, above all, the Mass is a spiritual and religious gift of our Saviour that enables us to be in the closest relationship possible on this earth with Jesus Christ and, through him and by the power of the Holy Spirit, with the Father. That relationship is one which we enjoy because we are members of the Church, united with our brothers and sisters in the communion of saints on earth.

Fr Anscar Chupungco OSB, an erudite and influential liturgist, offers some very basic thoughts on liturgy, declaring it to be "the source of the Church's spirituality because Christ and his saving mystery are present and active in it... The liturgy quickens our spiritual life: in the liturgy we experience spiritual rebirth, communion with the Lord, reconciliation and spiritual comfort". He recalls the teaching of Pope St Leo the Great: "What was visible in Christ (*his person and mission*) passed into the sacraments of the Church" (*Sermon* 72) and then continues: "The liturgy is the summit to which all the other activities of the Church are directed... If the Church engages in the apostolate of education, ministry of healing, political liberation, and the moral and social uplifting of the people, it is in order to lead them to the fount of spirituality, which is the liturgy" (*What, then, is Liturgy?*, p.236).

The 2012 Synod of Bishops makes similar points, also based on the Constitution of the Liturgy, no. 10. "The worthy celebration of the Sacred Liturgy, God's most treasured gift to us, is the source of the highest expression of our life in Christ. It is, therefore, the primary and most powerful expression of the new evangelisation. God desires to manifest the incomparable beauty of his immeasurable and unceasing love for us through the Sacred Liturgy and we, for our part, desire to employ what is most beautiful in our worship of God in response to his gift… Evangelisation in the Church calls for a liturgy that lifts the hearts of men and women to God. The liturgy is not just a human action but an encounter with God which leads to contemplation and deepening friendship with God. In this sense, the liturgy of the Church is the best school of the faith" (*Proposition 35*).

Even after the Year of Faith, we remain People of Faith, called to share in the new evangelisation. So, renewed and strengthened in faith by the Eucharist, let us "go and announce the Gospel of the Lord!"

For all that the Mass means to us, and has meant to countless millions through the centuries, thanks be to God!

Soldier in India

INTRODUCTION

During the Second World War, most young men studying in seminaries were not called up for military service. However, some were – and I was one of them. The distinction was made on the following basis. Those who had begun their studies before the outbreak of war (3rd September 1939) or those on whose behalf their parish priests could vouch that they had manifested their intention to do so were exempt.

I was not included in those categories, so although I had begun my seminary studies in August 1942, I was called up for military service aged eighteen in August 1944.

Hence the account which follows.

MILITARY SERVICE

I was eighteen when, in August 1944, I was called up for military service. The Second World War was already five years old and had another year to run. When I joined the army the Allies were fighting their way through France, having landed in Normandy on D-Day, 6th June 1944. The Allies were also advancing northwards through Italy, the Russian army had withstood the German onslaught on the Soviet Union and was moving inexorably towards Berlin; but the war in Asia and in the Pacific seemed set to last for a considerable time longer.

My first posting in the army, for "initial training", was to Dreghorn barracks in Edinburgh. Life in a barrack room was a culture shock (especially as it immediately followed two years in the seminary, studying philosophy and living a very sheltered existence). The weeks at Dreghorn were physically tiring, intellectually stifling and humanly degrading. But, at eighteen, I seemed to accept things rather stoically, without resentment or even dismay.

During the initial training, decisions were taken about the regiment to which each recruit was to be sent. I was relieved not to be assigned to the infantry or to an armed, fighting regiment. Instead, I was sent to the Royal Army Medical Corps which meant, for me, a few months in each of four places in Britain and Northern Ireland: Crookham in Hampshire for basic first aid and nursing training, Bristol for training as a blood transfusion specialist, Moretonhampstead on Dartmoor for work in a military hospital and Campbell College in Belfast for the same purpose. I was in Bristol when VE Day was celebrated (8th May 1945) and in Belfast on VJ Day (15th August 1945).

In October 1945, along with many others, I was sent to India. Although by then the war was over in the East as well as in Europe, British troops were still being sent to Asia, particularly to Malaya and India. It was very sad saying goodbye to my parents and siblings at the end of my embarkation leave and not knowing then where I was going in Asia or how long it would be before I saw my family again.

I am not an inveterate diarist but I did keep a diary during the time I was in India. Much of it is trivial and tedious, now even for me, but I have picked out some events and some impressions which, as I read them recently, seemed to be not only from a bygone age, but about a different person, a young man whom I did not know or, rather, whose existence I had forgotten.

We embarked at Liverpool on 2nd October 1945 on the troopship *Empress of Scotland* (a Canadian Pacific Steamships liner formerly called *Empress of Japan*). I was among those unfortunate enough to be put on E3 deck, below the water line and with the propeller shafts running through it. E3 deck was a most uncomfortable place, especially as we were given hammocks, not bunks. A year or so later I read in the *Times of India* newspaper that 300 troops had "…walked off the troopship *Empress of Scotland* in Liverpool as a protest against the 'hellish quarters' allotted them". The news did not surprise me.

We called at Taranto in the south of Italy where, from rowing boats, an apple was being bartered for one cigarette and a bottle of wine for fifty. There were further calls (and bartering from rowing boats) at Port Said and Aden. We finally reached Bombay on 19th October and moored very close to the "Gateway of India", a triumphal arch erected for the visit of King George V and Queen

Mary in 1911, and the imposing Taj Mahal Hotel. The voyage was the first time I had ever been abroad and it was all very strange and exotic to me.

It was even stranger on the train from Bombay to Deolali, a huge and rather infamous transit camp about 100 miles north-east of Bombay. Vendors, beggars, smells, sights abounded at every station and yet, aged 19, I seemed to feel unimpressed and impassive. In retrospect, I suppose I may have been as if shell shocked and traumatised!

I was kept only ten days or so in Deolali but got to know some of the words and phrases that soon became familiar to British soldiers in India. We slept on a *charpoy*, (a wooden bed with cords strung from side to side and top to bottom in place of springs). Our bamboo-walled hut was a *basha*; mosquito nets were a must. There were various Indians unofficially attending to our needs: tea and cakes ("*chahwallah, very very hot; double up!*"), barbers, tailors, chiropodists ("*lovely feet wallah*"), launderers (*dhobi wallah*) and bearers. For one rupee – 1/6d – a week, a bearer made your bed, polished your boots, cleaned your equipment and generally ran messages for you. But Deolali was not a particularly enjoyable place. Since it was a transit camp there were constant comings and goings, with frequent parades and kit inspections to impose a measure of discipline. While I was there we were ordered not to go to the nearby bazaar as an outbreak of bubonic plague had occurred or was expected.

I was happy to get away from Deolali. My posting was to Secunderabad, a town on the Deccan, the high plateau of south central India. Secunderabad had many military installations including several army hospitals. I was stationed there for nine months and it was a comparatively happy time. Secunderabad adjoins the city of Hyderabad which was the capital of the state of that name. In those pre-independence days there were many "states" in India, semi-independent territories ruled by Indian hereditary princes. Hyderabad state was the largest and was ruled by the Nizam, a Muslim, although most of the citizens were Hindus. He was a benign, "hands-off" ruler, hardly ever seen in public. I was very content in Secunderabad, particularly as I heard, on arrival, that a three months' course for trainee radiographers was about to start. I immediately violated a military tradition and volunteered for the course.

It was good to get back to something intellectual. With days devoted to classes, practical experience and study, the army discipline became more relaxed and we were treated as intelligent beings. The two men in charge, both excellent teachers and kind persons, were Major Ahmed and RSM MacFarlane. We were a mixed bunch of students, all male, some British, one or two Anglo-Indians (i.e. of mixed race) but most were Indians from different parts of the subcontinent, Hindus, Muslims, Sikhs and Christians. The atmosphere was easy-going and we became colleagues and friends.

There were two Italian missionary priests in the area and, besides being able to go to Mass frequently and becoming a regular server, I got to know them and we became friendly. Mgr Pezzoni was vicar general of Hyderabad archdiocese and, as he was elderly and had a long white beard, was known to the soldiers as Santa Claus. Fr Dal Balcon, a younger priest, was so dedicated to India that he made me wonder whether I also was being called to be a missionary.

We were given Christmas leave during the radiography course and two of us went off to the south for a week's holiday in Bangalore and Mysore. Bangalore had a large British military presence in the area known as the cantonment. Mysore, on the other hand, the capital city of the state of Mysore, was wholly Indian and therefore much stranger and more exciting for us.

Another pleasant memory I have is of the bearer who served a few of us. He was aged about twelve and his face was permanently pock-marked by smallpox from which he had suffered when younger. We called him "Chico" but what his real family name was, or if he had a family, we knew not. He was cheerful, willing and efficient. I often wonder what became of him.

I wrote home frequently and my parents were equally faithful, their letters (to which I always looked forward) normally taking about ten days to arrive. Keeping in touch was very important for me and I never grudged the effort involved. When I could, I bought a daily paper: *The Times of India* preferably but *Madras Mail* and *The Hindu* were also acceptable. These enabled me to take a keen interest in Indian politics at a time of enormous importance for the future of the subcontinent. That interest came from my own choice. We were given no encouragement to learn anything of India's history, art, culture or the issues of the day. As far as language was concerned, again there was no effort to give us tuition in Hindustani or any regional language. We simply picked up useful words, most of them, I fear, being of the peremptory kind of a master-to-servant relationship. "Quickly" in Hindustani was known to, and used frequently by, every British soldier in India.

Occasionally we had worries. Once or twice items of kit went missing, Mass vestments and altar cloths disappeared from the cupboard in which they were kept and sheets were stolen from my bed – by now we had become quite effete/civilised and were using sheets and pillow cases. From time to time there were cases of smallpox and bubonic plague in the vicinity but our camp was not affected. On another occasion there was a rumour (never confirmed) that a tigress and her cubs had been seen in the neighbourhood.

Once we had qualified as radiographers we were anxious to have patients on whom to exercise our newly acquired skills. My very first case was a strange one. A soldier, a Scotsman, was sent to the X-ray unit because he alleged that he had swallowed a nail file, some wire, some razor blades and three prongs of a fork. None of these objects showed on the X-rays and it was concluded that, as he had been sentenced to detention for some misdemeanour, he wanted to spend his sentence in hospital rather than in the detention centre.

I have happy memories of Secunderabad and was delighted when, on a visit to India in 1987, I was able to visit some of the places where I had been stationed so many years before. It was almost like retrospective reincarnation. Thinking of that young man of more than forty years ago, being in the very spot where he had lived and worked and slept, made me feel strangely upset and sad. Perhaps I envied him the years of life that still lay before him.

In August 1946 I was transferred from Secunderabad to the south-east of India, to a military hospital at Avadi, a small town some twelve miles inland from Madras. Conditions there were not as comfortable as at Secunderabad and there wasn't a great deal of radiography work to do. Sometimes when I was free, I took the train to Madras and, on foot or by bus or rickshaw, explored the city, especially the part known as Mylapore which is associated with St Thomas the Apostle. The tradition is that he made his way to India to preach the gospel, and specifically in the area where

Madras now is. There are several churches and shrines in Mylapore linked with St Thomas, a tradition clearly fostered by early Portuguese settlers.

With work slack at Avadi, the radiologist in charge of the X-ray department used to engage me in long discussions. He was Major Fritz Donath, Austrian and Jewish (but why he was in the British army I don't know). He was very unmilitary, wanted to be called "Doctor" and not "Sir" and used to address me as "Mr Taylor". He seemed fascinated to know that I was a believing Catholic and that I wanted to be a priest. He didn't believe in God and, I think, was influenced by the teaching of Sigmund Freud. He used to argue with me about religion and faith and Jesus Christ. Ours was an unusual relationship but he was a kindly man and a thinker. I wish I knew if he ever got back to Vienna.

In October 1946, the X-ray department in Avadi military hospital was closed and the equipment and machines dismantled. Two of us, one Abdul Latif and I, were ordered to accompany the crates to Poona. The journey took four days (4th to 8th) as our freight wagon was attached in turn to several goods trains zigzagging across India. For both of us it was an unusual task, but we were provided with some accommodation on the various trains. The station masters, guards and engine drivers were kind and thoughtful, the last providing us, whenever we asked, with boiling water "on tap" to make tea. The journey back to Madras, just twenty-four hours long and by ordinary passenger train, was short by comparison. I travelled second class and Abdul was in third. We had become friends but class distinction was enforced!

From Avadi I was sent back to Deolali on transit and then north to Bhopal (a city that later became notorious for the tragedy at the Union Carbide factory which killed and maimed many thousands of the inhabitants). The military hospital was a few miles outside Bhopal. On arrival I discovered that it was in process of closing down (as usual!) and so radiography work was scarce. The X-ray department had infra-red and ultra-violet lamps and we had a few welcome clients for those. In addition, I was glad to be given the extra duty of going on foot, twice a day, to collect mail from the post office, a mile distant.

During my time at Bhopal it was evident that there was increasing political unrest in India. Each day seemed to bring news of significant and often alarming developments. There were negotiations between British delegations and Indian leaders, many Muslims were demanding partition of the subcontinent, there were demonstrations in several cities, the government decreed that any acts of sabotage against the railways would be punished with the death penalty, politicians held rallies which attracted huge crowds and some were even demanding revolution.

For Sunday Mass we were taken by lorry to a church in Bhopal where the priest was a Fr Beck, a German who had been interned during the war. The server looked to be very old and could hardly negotiate the sanctuary steps. I noticed that the Indian women and children at Mass were behind a curtain and that several pairs of shoes had been left outside the curtain. Bhopal state in those days had a Muslim ruler and I wondered whether some Islamic practices had been adopted by Catholics. In front of the altar were three tombs of Isabella, Bonaventure and Balthasar Bourbon, the first of these persons being described on the stone as "*hujus ecclesiae fundatrix*". About the Bourbons of Bhopal I know nothing, except (if there is any connection) a vague tale about a Moghul emperor and some Portuguese girls captured while en route from Lisbon to Goa.

Christmas Midnight Mass at Bhopal was crowded. The Common of the Mass was sung (in Latin, of course) as well as the familiar hymns *Silent night, Angels we have heard on high, Adeste fideles* and (yes) *O come all ye faithful.* The singing was enthusiastic but of indifferent quality, being in a kind of minor key, dragged, flat and each person choosing to sing at his or her own speed. But it was unfair to criticise Indians trying to cope with western music.

By that Christmas 1946 the Bhopal hospital staff numbers were very low so the normal segregation between officers and "other ranks", Indians and British, men and women was fairly relaxed. It made for some informal meals and parties at the festive season. Somehow we had acquired a large tin of mincemeat from Britain which the Indian cooks, misunderstanding the label, served to us with potatoes. On those communal occasions we enjoyed a friendly atmosphere and got to know one another, where previously we had just been faces and names. One person I remember with affection is Parvathi, a girl of sixteen who had been an Indian Army nurse for a year. She was from the south, was well educated and belonged to a Brahmin family. Her father, though a civil servant, had been jailed by the British authorities during the

1942 civil disobedience campaign. When the nurses were served glasses of milk, Parvathi put hers aside to offer it later in *puja* to the god (statue) she had in her room, and then she would drink it.

However we had little real contact with Indians (except in army matters) and such meetings as I have mentioned were a pleasant rarity. An Indian colleague on the radiography course in Secunderabad did invite me to stay with him and his family for a few days but I made some excuse which I regret now.

Shortly after Christmas I was transferred from Bhopal. Half-a-dozen of the Indian nurses accompanied me to the station – that was friendship, often in short supply in the army. I got the train coming from Delhi (running more than three hours late) which, two nights and a day later, arrived in Madras.

In those days the long distance trains in India stopped at breakfast, lunch and dinner time for about forty-five minutes or an hour at stations which boasted a good restaurant – Spencer's or Brandon's. Wealthy travellers alighted and made their way across the tracks or along the platform to eat in the restaurant while the rest of the people bought food or drinks from platform vendors carrying tin trunks with eatables and, strapped on their backs, large tea urns. On one sweltering occasion we were glad, in the restaurant, to have a large blanket fan swinging back and forth over us and providing us with a pleasant breeze as we ate. After the meal and before re-boarding the train, I went round to the back of the restaurant building and discovered the source of the ventilation we had enjoyed. A "*punkah wallah*" in the full heat of the midday sun was rhythmically hauling on the ropes which operated the fan inside. God reward him and the rickshaw pullers and all the other poor people who, to keep themselves and their families alive, have to work with every ounce of their strength and energy to serve the affluent.

From Madras I had to go on to Bangalore where, for the next three and a half months, I served as radiographer in two military hospitals near the city. There was little work to be done since, with British troops being gradually withdrawn from India, both hospitals were being run down.

There were Good Shepherd sisters in two convents in Bangalore and one in Madras. These communities had up to a dozen Scots sisters in them, most of whom were from Lanarkshire. It was the famous Canon (later Mgr) Thomas N. Taylor of Carfin who, if not responsible for the Scots sisters' vocations, had nonetheless encouraged them to join the Congregation of the Good Shepherd and become missionaries in India. I visited the convents on several occasions and was received with genuine hospitality. It was good also to have the chance of talking to Scottish people who were not in the army! In those days, the sisters had no expectation of ever being allowed to see their parents or families again – heroic women!

The sisters told me of the marriage agency which they operated for Catholics in Bangalore. For example, a priest would write to the convent and then send a young man of his parish whom he would like to see settled. The sisters would present to him five or six of their "rescued" girls living in the convent. If one attracted him (and a fair skin was most important), he selected that girl and, if she agreed, the marriage was arranged there and then.

Bangalore has perhaps the highest percentage of Catholics of any large city in the subcontinent. There are many Catholic churches and, not being very busy, I was often able to visit them and to attend Mass. At the Mass on Palm Sunday 1947, while the celebrant was reading the Passion (in Latin), another priest went to the pulpit, read the announcements and gave us a sermon.

During my time in Bangalore, serious communal riots between Hindus and Muslims occurred in the city. During a particularly bad riot, we were "confined to barracks" for five days, a curfew was in operation in the city and five people were killed and seventy injured, many of them by stab wounds. It was thought that the trouble began because a Hindu band, part of a procession, was playing objectionable sectarian music as it passed a mosque. Sounded somewhat familiar for someone from the west of Scotland!

In the last week of April 1947 I was sent once more to the transit depot at Deolali, to await being shipped to another "theatre", either Malaya or Egypt. I hoped that it would be the former as the latter involved the probability of my going to Palestine where British troops were being targeted by Jewish militant organisations, Irgun and the Stern Gang terrorists/freedom fighters. We were in Deolali for three long weeks, being set odd jobs to keep us from being idle: gardening, cleaning huts, packing equipment and stores and (my preference) running errands for the commanding officer. Eventually our orders came through – we were to embark on the Cunard White Star liner/troopship *Georgic* for the Middle East. In 1941 *Georgic* had been sunk by German bombers in shallow waters at the entrance to the Suez Canal; after being salvaged and extensively repaired, the liner was able to resume service.

We embarked on *Georgic* in Bombay on 18th May and eventually sailed two days later. We cast off at 10.40 am and ninety minutes later India was only a low line of hills on the eastern horizon. The ship's tannoy announced, "If you look astern you will see the finest sight in the world – Bombay from the deck of a troopship."

I wasn't at all sure of that. I felt sad to be leaving India. I had been fortunate to be there at a fascinating time as the British Raj was ending and India was preparing for independence. But there was more to it than that. I had grown to love India which had and still does have a powerful hold on my affection. It is that mysterious spell which India casts on all who have known her.

A week after leaving Bombay we disembarked at Suez at the south end of the canal. Two days later, on 29th May, we were put on a train north, via Ismailia, to the RAMC Base Depot at El Ballah, a mile or so west of the canal. We were assigned to tents and there I remained for the next two weeks, worried, like most other transients there, about the prospect of being sent to Palestine and the unpleasant conditions there.

While being held at El Ballah we were given various duties such as cleaning latrines and washplaces and peeling potatoes. We also had to take our turn at guarding the perimeter of the camp at night, two hours on and four hours off. We were given rifles and fifteen bullets each. It was a rather scary and lonely duty, despite the presence nearby of a couple of friendly Sudanese soldiers. My specific personal anxieties were twofold: first, we had been severely warned that to lose one's rifle or have it stolen was a very serious offence tried by court martial; second, I was not at all sure how to load and fire the rifle. Fortunately neither eventuality occurred. Daytime sentry duty at the camp gate was less fraught. You had merely to check the passes of pedestrians and lorry drivers and then wave then through. I did that successfully although most of the passes handed to me for inspection meant nothing to me.

The depot had more army-style discipline than I had been used to in India There were parades, inspections, marching about and a number of officers and NCOs who seemed to enjoy being unpleasant and fault-finding. I sought relief on my off-duty evenings by walking across the desert and sitting on the bank of the Suez Canal, cooling my feet in the water and gazing wistfully at any ships passing northwards.

During my short time in the Canal Zone word arrived that I was to be given home leave. It was good news because it meant that Palestine was at least delayed. But before I left the depot we had a practice for a big parade (for the King's Birthday, I think). The parade itself I missed, but not the rehearsal. During the march round the parade ground my glasses (which for weeks had shown signs of wear and tear) disintegrated and parts fell to the ground. Somehow and by sheer good luck I was able to scoop up the fallen bits without causing too much confusion in the marching ranks. My unmilitary and disruptive activity fortunately went unnoticed by the officer in charge. Before the rehearsal finished we were informed that, at the parade itself, an order would be given just before the end: "You will now give three cheers for His Majesty. On the command, 'Remove headgear', the cap will be lifted off the head…" That was to be followed by "Three cheers for His Majesty – hip, hip" to which everyone was to respond by shouting "Hurrah!", at the same time smartly raising his cap to the required height as a sign of shared joy and unconditional allegiance. I can only imagine the embarrassment of the soldiers and the bemused incomprehension of any Egyptian bystanders at this performance because, luckily, the parade was held a few hours after those of us going on leave had left the camp for Port Said.

Our troopship was the Cunard liner *Franconia* (which, in 1945, had been the headquarters ship at the Yalta Conference). A few of us were assigned to look after any who took ill on the voyage. This duty carried with it the advantage of having our quarters in the ship's hospital – and very comfortable quarters they were. We boarded the *Franconia* (which we had passed three weeks previously as she made her way across the Indian Ocean to Bombay) and were due to sail on Friday 13th June, but the captain said that ships did not sail on Friday 13th. So departure time was set for 00.01 hrs. on Saturday 14th.

After an uneventful voyage we berthed at Liverpool on Sunday 22nd June. We were disembarked almost at once. I remember having a dreadful struggle carrying all my luggage – big pack, small pack, kitbag and, worst of all, a large metal case which I had bought in India – as I staggered my way down the gangway, along the ship's side, through customs and then on to a bus which took us to a transit camp. There I was quickly "processed" and then rushed to the station for an overnight train to Glasgow. My father met me there and later that morning, Monday 23rd June 1947, I got the bus to Hamilton and was reunited with the rest of the family at home.

I think I had been given something like twenty-eight days leave but during that time a telegram reached me, offering "Class B Release" (i.e. release earlier than normal, given to university students and their equivalents). Having accepted an offer which I could hardly refuse, I had to go for the necessary demobilisation procedures to Cowglen, Glasgow, on 5th August and to York the following day. One of the procedures at York was to be given a civilian suit. They didn't supply black suits (hadn't they heard of seminarians and undertakers?) so I chose something that I hoped would fit my father. Thus ended my army career.

Looking back, I have no regrets that I was conscripted. I was eighteen in 1944 and so "did my bit". I realise that that avoids the question of how Britain and its allies conducted the war and the related question – which did not occur to me at the time – of a possible duty of conscientious objection; besides, I was in the non-armed RAMC. On the whole, I think that my army service was beneficial for me. There were unpleasant times but also some wonderful experiences. Even with the three years' interruption, I was only twenty-four when ordained. And despite having gone straight from school to seminary, I did see a bit of life before becoming a priest.

Being a Bishop in Scotland

INTRODUCTION

Demobilised from the army in the summer of 1947, I resumed my studies to be a priest that autumn. To do so, I was sent to the Pontifical Scots College in Rome. I was ordained to the priesthood on 2nd July 1950 and finally returned to Scotland in the summer of 1954.

From 1955 to 1965 I was on the teaching staff of St Peter's College in Cardross, a major interdiocesan seminary, and then was appointed rector of the Royal Scots College in Valladolid, Spain. I was there for nine years and, for seven years, I was parish priest of Our Lady of Lourdes' parish, East Kilbride. In 1981, I received the phone call which changed my life, as I recount below and at some length.

BECOMING A BISHOP

Since relatively few people become bishops, some details of my experience may be of interest.

On the afternoon of Wednesday 1st April 1981 I was running off some work on the duplicator in Our Lady of Lourdes presbytery, East Kilbride, where I was parish priest. When the phone rang I answered it and was surprised when the voice asked for me and then said "The Apostolic Delegate wants to speak to you." Archbishop Bruno Heim came on and asked me to go to the Delegation in London as he wanted to see me. I said I was fairly busy the following week, would the week after that be suitable? "No, come this week". No details of the reason for the summons were given, but I did think it might be either to be bishop of Galloway (I knew Bishop McGee had retired) or to be reprimanded for something wrong I had said or done.

The following morning I told the other priests in the parish that I'd be away all day. I drove to Glasgow airport and got a plane to Heathrow. It was the days of the shuttle service – no booking needed, just turn up and go. At London I was met by a priest and driven to the Apostolic Delegation where I was put into a large empty room. In a few minutes Archbishop Heim came in, eyed me up and down (he did not know me) and then told me that the Holy Father wanted me to be the bishop of Galloway.

Having realised this might well be asked of me, I had decided, if asked, to say Yes. The Delegate told me a story of Cardinal Gasparri – therefore probably early in the twentieth century – having to ask a "candidate" (the official term) the same question; when the priest said that, before responding, he would like time to consider, pray and listen to the prompting of the Holy Spirit. Gasparri grew impatient. "Nothing to do with the Holy Spirit. Yes or no?"

Almost immediately after I said Yes, Archbishop Heim, an expert on heraldry, brought up the question of a coat-of-arms and produced a large book to help him give me advice. At that moment I wasn't a bit interested in a coat-of-arms; but I accepted his offer of guidance and it was he who supplied me with the design.

The Delegate invited me to wait for lunch but, as there was still some time before that, I was put in the back garden to walk up and down on my own and think my thoughts.

After lunch (it was roast lamb and I could not help thinking of its sacrificial connotation), I had a further solitary spell in the garden before being taken to the airport. On arrival at East Kilbride, I celebrated the usual Thursday evening Mass which, on that day, was a special one – the silver wedding of two parishioners. I hope I did the occasion justice but my mind was elsewhere and of course "my lips were sealed".

At that time I was minutes secretary of the Scottish bishops' conference so the following Sunday, 5th April, I had to go to Blairs College for the Lent meeting of the bishops' conference. Archbishop Heim arrived the following day and my appointment was made public at 11am. I do not know whether the bishops already knew of it, or not. But as we were walking along the corridor from the conference room to go to lunch Bishop McGee took me by the elbow and said "I'm glad it's you because it might have been someone much worse". At lunch, my health was drunk and, in my reply, I suggested that my appointment might be seen as a great encouragement for the no longer young since, aged almost 55, I was older than any of the bishops present had been at appointment.

Cardinal Gray and Bishop McGee discussed details of my ordination and decided it would be on Tuesday 9th June, the feast of St Columba, at 4pm in the grounds of Fatima House, Coodham. The outdoor venue was chosen because large crowds were to be expected, especially from East Kilbride. Cardinal Gray made a special plea to Archbishop Heim that he wear his *cappa magna* at my ordination – the last occasion, I think, that the garment, with its hugely long train requiring pages to keep it off the ground, was seen in Scotland.

My episcopal ordination took place as scheduled with Cardinal Gray principal "consecrator", assisted by Bishops McGee and Thomson; Archbishop Winning preached the homily and my two assistant priests were Mgr Frank Duffy (whom I had asked to continue as vicar general) and Fr John Walls (who had succeeded me as rector of the Royal Scots College in Valladolid). It was a cold day but, although it had been raining earlier, it was dry with some sunshine during the ordination.

I don't remember a great deal about the ordination except for the large crowds, the solemnity of the occasion, the welcome of the people – and the sense of awe which I experienced. I was glad to have been made a bishop but nervous because very aware of my weaknesses and my need for God's grace and the support of my new brothers and sisters of "Scotland's oldest diocese".

Very proud to be a successor of the apostles and of St Ninian, I had chosen as my motto the one chosen by another Scottish bishop of two hundred years before, a man whom I greatly admired, John Geddes, rector and second founder of the Royal Scots College in Spain. "*Ambula coram Deo*" means "Walk in God's presence". The phrase comes from the Book of Genesis where Abraham is told to leave his country and to walk in God's presence as he goes to the land to which God has chosen to send him.

I like the motto not only for its link with John Geddes but also because it indicates pilgrimage which is the image of the Church which appeals most to me.

Needless to say, there have been several attempts at flippant translations. The best, I think, is "You'll never walk alone". I have the Latin motto engraved on a ram's horn crozier which was presented to me. The horn has also a little white house carved into it (Candida Casa, another name for Galloway Diocese). I once asked some altar servers if they knew what "*Ambula coram Deo*" meant. None did, though one imaginative boy had a look at the crozier and its carving and suggested "Home, sweet home".

YES OR NO? DECISIONS, DECISIONS!

On several occasions as bishop of Galloway, I found myself making important pastoral choices that might have seemed unwise at worst, risky at best. Let me list them, reflecting on my motivation at the time and the success, or lack of it, in each case.

RENEW

After the Second Vatican Council there was a widespread and sincere desire for spiritual and pastoral renewal. We knew that the Council had taught that all of us are called to holiness – but how were we to move towards that? It would be the work of the Holy Spirit, but we would have to cooperate, to be available. But how?

Similarly there was an awareness that dioceses and parishes needed to be communities of faith and committed to building God's kingdom on earth – not just administrative units for governance and convenience or a select group representing and serving the rest.

A full account of how we attempted to respond to these challenges in the diocese of Galloway is given in *Portrait of a Diocese*, chapter 6 of this book.

HOLY COMMUNION UNDER BOTH KINDS

Having previously been content with the Liturgy of the Mass prior to Vatican II and suspicious of any radical changes, I underwent a "conversion" in the light of the Council's Constitution on the Liturgy (*Sacrosanctum Concilium)* and its subsequent reception by the Church in general and theologians in particular. Above all, I was enthusiastic about the Council's wish that participation should be full, active and understood. This has a number of obvious applications (still not always and fully used) but the one that somehow most caught my attention was the possibility of frequent reception of Holy Communion under both kinds by the laity.

There were arguments against (no real need, danger of spilling, undue expense) and some people felt intinction (dipping the host in the chalice) was sufficient. But I was convinced that such views were unacceptable. The normal method of human consumption is not by dipping the solid food in the liquid; Jesus told us to *eat* and to *drink* – which is a much more complete sign of the sacrament – and, besides, our taking of the Lord's blood expresses our belief that, in Holy Communion, we are renewing the new and eternal covenant, which was and is sealed in Christ's blood.

So, with my encouragement, Holy Communion under both kinds became more and more common in most parishes. We discovered that a) "danger of spilling" was an unnecessary fear, b) the expense was minimal, and c) the anticipated long queues and undue delays were easily avoided.

The Holy See was granting the required permissions to bishops' conferences' requests. In our case in Scotland, the authorisation was generous indeed: "Sundays and weekdays, as long as there was no danger of irreverence or spillage". That gave greater impetus to the developing usage and I am glad to say that Holy Communion under both kinds is now practically taken for granted in Galloway, even at St Ninian's Cave where, despite the uneven terrain, the practice is perfectly possible and without any serious danger.

The directive to give Holy Communion to the faithful with hosts consecrated at that Mass (if at all possible) is still, I am sorry to say, not observed as well as it should be. Yet it was Pope Pius XII back in 1947 who urged this practice; he was not the first pope to do so and, indeed, the request has been repeated and explained many times since. The only consolation is that the request seems to be even more widely neglected elsewhere than in Scotland.

PRIESTS' CHANGES

This subject, which is one of great difficulty, is fully treated in *Portrait of a Diocese.* Trying to deal with it satisfactorily was never easy and, on one occasion, led to a very serious situation in the diocese and a dispute in which Rome became involved.

After that experience, I confess that I asked priests to change only when it was necessary and not in caes when I thought such changes would be merely beneficial.

As I said, priests' changes are never easy. For me, they were a source of real distress.

MINISTRY TO PRIESTS

A bishop must have special care of his priests. That has become ever more clearly a most important duty of the bishop. Perhaps like other bishops, I have to confess that I wish I had done more and done it more effectively. May the Lord – and my brother priests – forgive my shortcomings in this respect.

There may have been a time when the personal needs and welfare of priests were not considered or were overlooked or assumed to be each priest's own responsibility.

However, I had not long been in Galloway when I heard of the programme called "Ministry to Priests", designed in the United States by Fr Vince Dwyer. How matters developed from then on is told in *Portrait of a Diocese.*

Nevertheless, years later, we decided that, since not all the priests had become involved in the Ministry to Priests programme, we should try to widen things so that those priests would not feel that they were in any way excluded from "ongoing formation" (as urged by the Pope in his 1992 document *Pastores Dabo Vobis*). So, although the elements of the Ministry to Priests programme remain, the priests elected an ongoing formation team to arrange retreats, study days etc. and to keep a watchful eye on the needs of priests, both individually and as the presbyterate.

I feel that we did as much as we could in this respect and that, if some priests felt overlooked or neglected, the remedy was at hand if they wished to avail themselves of it.

PERMANENT DEACONS

Partly to respond to the decreasing number of priests and partly to restore the practice of the early Church, the permanent diaconate was authorised by the Holy See in 1967 and can be introduced by any bishop in his diocese, provided the local bishops' conference has agreed.

Permanent deacons are used especially in the English-speaking world, above all in the United States. In Scotland, Aberdeen was the first diocese to train and ordain permanent deacons and, in more recent years, Aberdeen's lead has been followed by all the other dioceses.

Without denying the appropriateness and the usefulness of permanent deacons, I did not adopt this innovation or, rather, restoration, during my time as bishop of Galloway. An explanation of this decision and the reasons for it will be found in *Portrait of a Diocese*.

Of course, my attitude was not inflexible and unalterable, especially if conditions or the priests' advice were to change. Indeed, my successor takes the positive view – which, of course, he has every right to do and which may well be a wiser one than mine. After all, the permanent diaconate is an ordained ministry with its own specific character.

Galloway now has a growing number of permanent deacons and I am very content that that is the case.

CHRISTIAN INITIATION OF CHILDREN

The wonderful and beautiful rite which we nowadays use for Christian initiation of adults (RCIA, itself the restoration of a process used in the early Church) led to a review of our method of carrying out the Christian initiation of children.

Above all, we re-discovered that the three sacraments which children receive (baptism, confirmation and first communion) are not just three distinct events in a child's life but do form a real and necessary process, namely a child's initiation as a full and active member of Christ's Church, the people of God.

Hence, there would seem to be a correct sequence for the reception of these sacraments. Clearly baptism must be first, but then, in the previous experience of most of us, it did not seem to matter if we were confirmed before or after first communion; rather, that depended, somewhat fortuitously, on the bishop's practice and availability regarding his visits to parishes to confirm the children.

It is evident, however, and for theological and liturgical reasons, that confirmation is the completion of baptism and should precede first communion, which is the culmination of our children's initiation. This reasoning is confirmed by the correct usage to be followed in the Rite of Christian Initiation of Adults.

Undeniably, this fact poses problems. There are several practical problems; moreover, we lose the pastoral benefit of seeking a confirmation commitment which young children cannot make; and we abandon an accustomed and familiar way for a possibly unwise restoration.

Over several years the bishops' conference discussed, argued, hesitated. Finally I suggested, and the bishops agreed, that Galloway diocese be allowed to go ahead, by way of experiment and trial, with a new or, rather, re-discovered, process of children's initiation into full membership of the Church. Essentially this meant keeping to the order: baptism, confirmation, first communion; and, of course, retaining infant baptism and delaying the other two sacraments until at least "the use of reason".

In fact we decided in Galloway that, where previously the normal had been first communion after Easter in primary 3 (therefore age 7 and 8) and confirmation in primary 6 or 7 (age 10 to 12), we would now have both confirmation and first communion in primary 4 (age 8 and 9). Moreover we recommended that, since the children were becoming full members of the Church (including the local Church), it was right that the sacraments be conferred at a Sunday Mass, when far more members of the local Church would be present.

A consequence of this was that I no longer was able to confirm personally many of the candidates. I went to as many Sunday confirmations as I could and, to maintain as far as possible the connection between the bishop and the sacrament of confirmation, I issued each year an official letter delegating the local parish priest to confirm in my name and asked that the letter be read out at the start of the ceremony. In addition I suggested, but without great success, that I be invited to a class or parish Mass after the children had been initiated in order that I might acknowledge them as newly full members of the Church.

Perhaps surprisingly, the whole new arrangement was generally accepted by the priests, the teachers, the parents and the parishes. The RE syllabus in the primary school needed some adaptation but this was carried out effectively by Sister Dorothy McCaffrey SND (our RE adviser for primary schools) and well implemented by the teachers.

Further details on this subject are considered in *Portrait of a Diocese.*

To conclude: our re-discovered process of initiation of children as full and active members of the Church is theologically, liturgically and historically correct, the method contains all the potential to achieve great benefits for each person, each family, each parish and the diocese.

As bishop, it was my earnest hope that the people of the diocese would seize the opportunity offered to them in the Christian initiation of their children. However, the loss of much of the bishop's involvement and the comparative smothering of confirmation by first holy communion, with all the latter's accessories and trappings, cause me concern. These are pastoral issues which make the ideal solution very difficult to decide.

EMBRACING THE FUTURE

The obvious decline in the number of priests – and what to do about it – has been a long term concern. During my absence from work because of cancer, July - December 2002, the Council of Priests commissioned and produced a paper called *Embracing the Future.* This listed what, with fewer priests, the laity had a right to expect of their pastors and also what limitations the latter had a right to put on such demands. More positively, it also suggested the provision that should be available to priests for their own welfare. Furthermore, the document asked the priests of each deanery to indicate what the deployment of priests in the deanery would be if a) there were one fewer priest than at present; b) two fewer; c) only half the present number.

When I returned to health and to work early in 2003, I was grateful for the priests' initiative and approved of it.

Moreover, I felt that we should build upon that foundation in two ways. First, by encouraging a greater number of lay people to become actively involved in pastoral ministries. Parishes were asked to ascertain their own needs of lay ministries, not only liturgical but also in evangelisation, catechesis, justice and peace, those in need, sacramental preparation; then, keeping their specific local needs in mind, to ensure adequate and proper training as required. For this, our Pastoral Ministry Course, provided a two-year part-time non-residential course of teaching, reading, essays and practical work for those who wanted to minister in their parishes or deepen their knowledge and appreciation of Scripture, liturgy, Church teaching and social care.

The success of these plans to provide extended and trained lay ministry is perhaps for others to judge. Let me say we have tried our best, we have had some success but probably "there is still room for improvement".

The second initiative, built on the foundation of *Embracing the Future* ("How are we to manage with fewer priests?"), was to take up John Paul II's call, in *Tertio Millennio Ineunte,* for spiritual and pastoral renewal in the local Church. The pope speaks of the opportunity we have after the 2000 Jubilee Year and the beginning of a new millennium, but he leaves the details of such a plan of renewal to each local Church. I feel that, in Galloway for the years ahead, we can use the five areas highlighted by the pope and the three activities he recommends in which the diocese can seek pastoral and spiritual renewal for itself, its parishes and its families. The five areas are holiness, prayer, Sunday Eucharist, sacrament of reconciliation and Scripture; and the three activities: the development of communion, evangelisation and care for those in need.

These five-plus-three headings are sufficiently wide to allow all manner of practical initiatives in the diocese and in the parishes (or deaneries). The pope's idea is that the parish should be a community of small communities. The work was only in its initial stages when I was made "bishop emeritus" but I had great hope that it would be continued prayerfully, conscientiously and faithfully.

The phrase or slogan "Embracing the Future" was chosen carefully, especially the first word. It indicates not a negative attitude ("We had better do something although we are not sure what") but a truly hopeful outlook to circumstances and conditions which will be very different but full of challenge and opportunity.

ACCOUNTABILITY

In his "Apostolic Exhortation on the Formation of Priests" (*Pastores Dabo Vobis*, 1992) Pope John Paul II, in the final chapter, speaks of the necessity of ongoing formation for all priests. Apart from theological reasons (St Paul instructs Timothy, "I remind you to rekindle the gift of God that is within you"), there are also compelling human reasons. Ongoing formation, says the Pope, "is demanded by the priestly ministry seen in a general way and taken in common with other professions, that is as a service directed to others. There is no profession, job or work that does not require constant updating if it is to remain current and effective".

On the same subject the Norms for Priestly Formation issued by the Scottish bishops' conference (2005) point out that a priest's continuing formation is an obligation. "In the first place he is answerable to God should he neglect the gift he received at ordination. At the same time he also has a responsibility before his bishop and the rest of the presbyterate, as well as to the people to whom he is sent, to make sure he is as well prepared as possible to do what is expected of him" (Norms 11.1).

So the need for, and the obligation of, ongoing formation are clearly stated. The exact manner in which that obligation is to be fulfilled will vary from priest to priest and from diocese to diocese.

It is not for me to guess how well the responsibility is being carried out. Perhaps it is enough to say that, for many of us – or most of us – we are aware of the need and the duty, we are doing something to respond, but we probably could be doing more.

A related subject that has often exercised my thoughts is the accountability of priests and bishops – and to whom are we accountable? To God, certainly; we shall all be called to "give an account of our stewardship". To whom else? To the Church, surely; that is, to those whom the priest or bishop is sent to serve.

Accountability is concerned not only with the duty of seeking ongoing formation or attending in-service courses. It includes these but is wider. It is about competence, commitment, fulfilment of one's responsibilities, doing a good job, giving "value for money".

At present this is largely left to a priest's (or bishop's) own conscience. Parishioners may feel dissatisfied, a few may even write to the bishop to complain. But, except in cases of serious dereliction of duty, the bishop (or, indeed, the Holy See) will do little more than exhort and hope that things will improve. Apart from the canonical protection that priests and bishops have against sanctions, priests are very scarce nowadays...

Sometimes I have felt unhappy about this apparent freedom that we have from any real accountability (in this life). More seems to be demanded in Reformed Churches.

In the Church of Scotland, for example, a parish does not have to "take what it gets" but, at least, ministers have to apply for positions and a parish decides whether it wants the applicant. I am afraid that this would not work in the Catholic Church with our diocesan structures and with priests constrained to working in the diocese for which they have been ordained. The diocese has an obligation to look after all its priests (unless they have chosen to leave the active ministry) and the idea of having to support priests whom no parish community wants is practically unthinkable for the poor (in more senses than one) bishop.

I remember an occasion, before I became a bishop, asking a bishop (now dead) what he did if and when there was an incompetent or lazy priest – did he move him to another parish? No, he replied, better to have one (possibly) unhappy parish than two. That, incidentally, is merely by way of being anecdotal.

Many professional people and/or institutions are now subject to published league tables. I don't know if that would work for priests (or bishops) and parishes (or dioceses). At the very least it would be good if there were some recognisable and objective standards against which we could be measured. But are there? And would we consent to be judged? And who would do the judging?

Perhaps there has been too much negativity in what I have said – an apparent desire to go after those who seem to be failing. So, to be positive also, I think it would be good for priests and bishops to have "supervision" in the sense of someone, properly qualified, to listen to a man (in private), to ask wise questions, to explore with him sensitive areas about his work, to advise, to encourage and so on.

This would require qualified people to be available as well as priests and bishops willing to have supervision. We are a long way from that at present, but could we not try to make a start? It would help those who would welcome such an opportunity – and it would assuage the unease, or guilt, of bishops like me!

SCHOOLS

Children in school are something of a captive audience for the priest (or bishop) who wants to visit. Despite that, it was my pleasure to pay an annual visit to all the primary schools in the diocese. There were thirty-seven of them in 1981 but five or six had been closed by 2004. On each occasion I tried to visit each class in the school, a task which in the bigger schools occupied practically the whole day.

Depending on the age of the children I attempted to say something religious but not to the exclusion of showing an interest in the children's lives or projects and to share nursery rhymes (with infants) or to give friendly "tests" (to the older children). In the early days I also tried to tell a joke or pose a riddle but I stopped that when the children would ask if I wanted to hear their jokes; one girl regaled us with a joke which embarrassed the class teacher and me, though it was greatly enjoyed by the other children. In the classes in which the children were preparing for first holy communion or confirmation I tried to say something appropriate and, from time to time, I invited the children in the confirmation class to write to me telling me about their preparation and asking me to confer the sacrament on them. Here are some of the letters I received.

"I am now 11. Over the past ten years my faith has been going up and down. If you confirm me, it will go up and stay there. Please confirm me and stop this yo-yo of love and hate." (John, Kilbirnie)

"I especially want to be confirmed by you because, to me, you're the next best thing to God or the Pope." (Martin, Troon)

"I am hoping to get better from the confirmation by helping others and not to be so mean and cruel to my little brother. Also around the home I don't usually help but this great occasion will bring me back to my senses, I hope." (Debbie, Cumnock)

"I wish to be confirmed. I feel I am ready to become a member of the Christian community. I have been going to church now for eleven years. Ten of these years meant nothing to me. I hope my wish is granted." (Margaret, Irvine)

And a post- Confirmation verdict :-

"I enjoyed my confirmation more than I thought I would. I am very glad you have a gentle hand. When we practised for confirmation I found that Father…hasn't got a gentle hand." (Alice, Kilmarnock)

In general children in primary schools were open, friendly and talkative. On one occasion when I arrived at a school, it was the morning interval and the children were in the playground. As they gathered round, I asked one child "Who's your teacher?" "Fine" was the prompt reply.

I am afraid that I was not so conscientious in visiting the Catholic secondary schools, seven of them in 1981 but only five in 2004 and now four. It wasn't only because in secondary schools the children move constantly from room to room while primary children are more static. I just found that I got very little response from the older children and I suppose I wasn't brave enough to persevere, except if I was asked by the head teacher to visit a fifth or six year class. Such "by appointment" visits were pleasant for me and, I hope, for the pupils.

There are no Catholic special schools (schools for pupils with special needs) in the Galloway diocese but I did try to visit all the non-denominational special schools every year or two. When I first began this custom, I think some of the head teachers were a little suspicious of my motives but, as I got to know them, I believe I became a welcome visitor. I used to receive invitations to their Christmas plays and carol concerts and, on one occasion, I was invited to have lunch with the older pupils, eating what they themselves had cooked.

Teachers, in fact, I always found unfailingly welcoming and, over the years, I think we got to know one another and in many cases have become friends. I hope I am also friends of the pupils although, since they grow and change rapidly, I confess that, after a while, I find it difficult to recognise them again. May they forgive me for the apparent and unintended discourtesy.

(The above provides only some anecdotes from my visits to schools. A more general and objective account of the schools in the diocese will be found in *Portrait of a Diocese.*)

BISHOPS' CONFERENCE

It seems natural for all the bishops of a country to meet from time to time. Nowadays such meetings and indeed the institution of bishops' conferences are enshrined in the law of the Church.

"The Bishops' Conference is the assembly of the bishops of a country…exercising together certain pastoral offices for Christ's faithful of that territory" (*Code of Canon Law* no. 447). "The Bishops' Conference can make general decrees only in cases where the universal law has so prescribed or by special mandate of the Apostolic See…(otherwise) the competence of each diocesan bishop remains intact" (*Code of Canon Law* no. 455).

So except on rare occasions a bishops' conference does not make laws; it exists principally for pastoral and administrative purposes.

There are eight dioceses in Scotland and so normally there are eight members of the Bishops' Conference of Scotland. That number is increased if and when there are also some auxiliary and/or retired bishops, although attendance of the latter is not obligatory. The Scottish conference has two three-day statutory meetings, one in Lent and the other in November and, in addition, five or six overnight meetings. In my latter years as bishop of Galloway, the meetings were held in Scotus College, the national seminary situated in Bearsden, Glasgow, but now closed.

Meetings of our bishops' conference I normally enjoyed. The principal reason for this was the companionship. We were, indeed are, a band of brothers who got on well together. With only eight members, we knew one another well, were on first name terms, and were relaxed in each other's company. The meetings had become more informal than when I first joined the conference.

There is, moreover, a sense of satisfaction in the conference that we can share each other's concerns and try our best to do a useful job. The amount of work to be done keeps increasing, and so, worryingly, do costs. Since these costs are raised by levies on each diocese, we are constantly in a dilemma. We ought, for example, to set up another commission, employ a new professional, take on extra commitments: yet is it right, or even possible, for the dioceses to meet the increased expense? Also, there is the need to avoid unnecessary expense and to be as sure as we can be that we are getting value for money.

Our agenda seemed constantly and ineluctably to get longer and longer. That put us under pressure and it was the president's responsibility, as chairperson, to keep things moving, to try to limit digressions and unnecessary discussion and to ensure that we reached, where required, a clear and agreed decision. Some chairmen were better than others at these tasks so it would be wrong to imply that the conference never suffered frustration or that there were never moments of irritation and tension.

To give you an idea of the agenda, here are some of the items discussed: our seminaries, the various national commissions and other agencies of the conference (about twelve or fifteen of them), items received from the Vatican, matters concerning schools, ecumenical relations, various issues of the day (usually of an ethical or moral nature), pastoral planning, the needs of priests, and correspondence (sometimes weird and wonderful).

The conference has the valuable help of its General Secretary, its Minutes Secretary and its Media Officer and most meetings involve receiving personal reports from various persons or groups, including seminary rectors, commission presidents, lawyers etc.

I don't think that either the role or the work of our Scottish bishops' conference is well recognised and I sometimes wished that (a) our published bulletins were more widely distributed and read by priests and people and (b) the conference would speak out more often on national and international issues so that the voice of the Catholic Church in Scotland would be heard more clearly. We could not expect that all our statements would escape criticism but, as has often been said, "There is no such thing as bad publicity".

As a postscript to what I have said about the Bishops' Conference of Scotland, let me mention something called "The Mount Carmel Group" meetings. These were held twice yearly, each bishop being accompanied by three of his close pastoral advisors, clerical or lay. The Mount Carmel Group's purpose was to share pastoral ideas and initiatives, to plan common pastoral activities, to discuss and decide pastoral priorities. Such topics as marriage and the family, preparing for and celebrating the millennium, being the Church in today's world, have occupied our attention. The agenda was always pastoral and, on the whole, I think most of us considered the meetings to have proved worthwhile.

Why "Mount Carmel"? Because the first meetings were held in Mount Carmel Monastery in Glasgow. For lack of a better alternative the name was kept, though meetings were soon transferred to other venues. It all added to the slightly arcane and obfuscated reputation that unfortunately attached to the group. That is of little importance now, since the meetings were discontinued some years ago, and the Mount Carmel Group is just a footnote in the story of the Bishops' Conference of Scotland.

AUTOBIOGRAPHICAL

EARLY YEARS

I was born early in the morning of Wednesday 5th May 1926 in my maternal grandmother's house in Hamilton and baptised in St Mary's church there on 9th May. My parents were Maurice and Lucy (McLaughlin) and I was the first born in a family of four.

A few months after I was born the family moved to the Burnbank district of Hamilton where I lived until I was sixteen. First Communion in St Cuthbert's church on 25th May 1933 and confirmation on 22nd September 1936 (by Archbishop Mackintosh or Bishop Graham) and education at St Cuthbert's primary school (1931 - 1936), St Aloysius College, Glasgow (1936 - 1939), and then Our Lady's High School, Motherwell (1939 -1942), sum up my early years.

Our family life was extremely happy, our home was truly Catholic and our parents loving and caring. I was a very reluctant schoolboy at the age of five but cannot remember whether I enjoyed primary school; I was not particularly happy at St Aloysius, happier at Our Lady's High School but I have never subscribed to the suspect assertion by my elders that schooldays are or were the happiest of my life. On the whole I was glad when they were over.

Sometimes I have wondered how the idea of priesthood developed in me. My parents made our home a place of faith and religious practice; going to Mass on Sundays and "devotions" on Sunday evenings and some weekdays was routine. From perhaps the age of nine or ten, I went to Mass on weekdays when I could. Sometimes this involved a rush to be in time for school and I remember one occasion when I left my place immediately the priest disappeared into the sacristy; a devout old gentleman told me to kneel down again and finish my thanksgiving after Communion!

I was also an altar server for a few years. On my first debut, the "head altar boy" told me to go and "tim the thurible". I guessed that the contraption he handed me must be the thurible but I hadn't the faintest idea what "tim" meant and to my shame and embarrassment had to ask. Another memorably embarrassing experience was "dropping the Missal", the very heavy book sliding off its stand to the floor as I struggled to carry it from the "epistle side" to the "gospel side".

Much more embarrassing in retrospect (though it seemed to me a generous gesture at the time) occurred one Hallowe'en when I invited my fellow altar servers to come home with me because we had peanuts for them. On arrival, I indicated that they should stand in the street while I threw handfuls of nuts to them! May the Lord – and they – forgive the little prig that I was.

I was in my second to last year at secondary school and getting worried about "what I wanted to be" when, one evening at confession, a priest whom I greatly admired in Burnbank (Fr Daniel B White) asked me that very question. To my surprise but without hesitation, I said I thought I'd like to be a priest, so in the spring of 1942 the parish priest made formal application for me to the archdiocese of Glasgow (the establishment of the dioceses of Motherwell and Paisley did not take place until 1947). I was interviewed by a panel of formidable and venerable old priests who asked me to read a passage of the gospel in Latin; a few days later I was informed that I had been accepted as a student for the priesthood and that I would start my philosophy course at Blairs College, Aberdeen, that summer (August 1942).

SEMINARY

Having been told that I would be studying philosophy when I began my seminary training at the age of sixteen, I felt slightly embarrassed since I imagined that philosophers were not usually teenagers. Would we be sitting in deep leather armchairs, smoking pipes and solemnly discussing the problems of mankind and such like arcane matters? Teenage philosopher? Surely an oxymoron!

The reality was different. We were housed in part of Blairs College. In normal times, Blairs was a "junior seminary" housing boys of secondary school age but, because of the wartime unavailability of Rome, Valladolid and Paris, it had to make room for students in the first two years of their senior seminary course – the "philosophers". Our accommodation was worse than basic – tiny cubicles, the entrances being screened by an inadequate curtain, many without a window and all part of a large dormitory which doubled as our common room. We went to bed breathing air thick with cigarette smoke. And the food was equally sub-basic, predictable and monotonous. But it was wartime, we wanted to be priests, we accepted the conditions without complaint (this was the 1940s!) and I was very happy there, once recovered from initial homesickness.

By today's standards the regime was austere and exacting, with a strict discipline, a full daily programme of religious activities (Mass, morning, midday and night prayers, meditation, visit to the Blessed Sacrament, rosary, spiritual reading plus occasional extras). Academically there were classes and exams in various branches of Scholastic philosophy such as logic, metaphysics, psychology, cosmology and the history of philosophy: quite demanding because so different from the subjects we had studied for our Highers.

Conditions for those in seminary training nowadays are necessarily very different and far less spartan and rigorous but in those days we were told if we felt hard done by, that we were lucky not to be students of sixty years previously.

And despite everything, they were an enjoyable two years at Blairs College with many happy memories, two of which I recall with special pleasure – my first opportunity to be "master of ceremonies" at the weekly solemn High Mass (on Passion Sunday 1944), an honour I performed successfully and with great pride; and a completely unexpected victory in the final of the Blairs billiards tournament.

The Blairs song contained the brainwashing declaration that "Joys of home how sweet so ever can't compare with those of Blairs". A wicked exaggeration but I have happy memories of my two years there.

MILITARY SERVICE

(A much fuller account of my time in the army, and especially the years in India, is given in chapter 2, *Soldier in India.*)

I was eighteen in May 1944 and had to register for military service. In August that year my calling-up papers required me to report at Dreghorn Barracks, Edinburgh, for initial training.

If joining the seminary had been a culture shock, joining the army was a cultural cataclysm. And yet, at eighteen, I did not feel as traumatised as I would have done if I had been older. To contemplate the prospect now would terrify me and it is a consolation of old age to know that, even in dire necessity, it is unlikely that the country will ever need me again.

People have often said "I thought students for the priesthood were exempt from call-up". Well, it depended. Exemption was granted to those who had begun their studies before the outbreak of war in 1939 (thus if I had been at Blairs College for my secondary education) or if one's parish priest could declare that, before 1939, he knew of one's intention to apply to go to a seminary (mine couldn't and didn't).

Army life was a strange experience for me. I certainly didn't revel in it nor was I totally miserable. The first six weeks (at Dreghorn Barracks in Edinburgh) were pretty awful – a strict regime (as at Blairs) but with hardly any intellectual or spiritual content. Drill, route marches, rifle firing, grenade lobbing, bayonet practice (on hanging bags full of sand), kit inspections, lectures on various aspects of warfare and fighting, and barrack room conversation on topics and with vocabulary new and startling to my tender ears.

Having successfully avoided assignment to an infantry regiment by achieving a low score at rifle and Bren gun target practice (and thereby failing to win the sweepstake that was organised for us at sixpence each), I was enrolled in the Royal Army Medical Corps and posted to its central barracks at Crookham in Hampshire. Life there was somewhat more civilised than at Dreghorn and it became even more so when, two months later, I was sent to Bristol to be trained in blood transfusion work. Much of our time there was taken up with cleaning used blood transfusion kits but, instead of barrack rooms, we were billeted in local civilian homes. Then to Moretonhampstead in Devon where a huge hotel on the edge of

Dartmoor had been made into a military hospital; and later to Belfast where Campbell College had been similarly commandeered. In Belfast I watched the huge parade on the twelfth of July (1945) and was a frequent attender at the weekly novena to Our Lady of Perpetual Succour at Clonard Redemptorist Monastery in the Falls Road district. It was only many years later, on a visit to Northern Ireland and with an audience of committed Catholics, that I realised the anomaly. My mention of having gone to the weekly novena – wearing a British Army uniform – caused some astonishment. Those people (understandably after all their experiences) did not normally associate a young British soldier with someone who attended novenas in the nationalist district and who wanted to be a priest.

In October 1945 – by this time it was two months after Japan's surrender – I was sent to India. From Liverpool the Canadian Pacific Steamship Company liner serving as a wartime troopship, *Empress of Scotland* (formerly *Empress of Japan* but renamed for obvious reasons) took us, with calls at Taranto, Port Said and Aden, to Bombay. The voyage lasted three weeks with many of us assigned hammocks on E deck. This location was well below the waterline and in normal times was the place for steerage baggage, I think. It was so hot, airless and uncomfortable that, when we got to warm nights, we slept on the open decks.

India was totally fascinating and on the whole I was happy. The ethos was generally relaxed and friendly. I got the chance of training and working as a radiographer and I became extremely interested in India – its history, its people, its culture, its politics as it moved uneasily towards independence and partition.

After an initial few weeks in Deolali, north of Bombay (where we were warned about bubonic plague in the district and inevitably I felt very ill for a few days and practically certain that I had succumbed to the dreaded disease), I was sent to Secunderabad (near Hyderabad) where I qualified as a radiographer and worked in a military hospital there for several months. While there I got to know and admire two local priests, both Italians – one was a parish priest as well as vicar general, elderly with a long white beard (inevitably called Santa Claus by the soldiers) and the other a much younger priest with whom I became very friendly. He was a zealous man who wanted to identify so much with his parishioners that he tried various methods, unsuccessfully, to dye his skin. Later I had postings to Avadi (outside Madras), Bangalore and Bhopal.

I got to love India and its people – although my 21st birthday (5th May 1947) passed unnoticed and unremarked by anyone and I felt very lonely that day and greatly missing my family.

British troops were being withdrawn from India in preparation for the country's independence in August 1947. As the liner *Georgic* sailed westward from Bombay I stood on deck looking back wistfully and indeed sadly at the receding coastline of a beautiful and wonderful land.

At the Suez Canal we were disembarked and taken to a camp at a place called El Ballah, near the Canal, awaiting transfer to Palestine – not a pleasant prospect at that time with Jewish "terrorists" (or "freedom fighters") targeting British soldiers who garrisoned the country. Demobilisation was in progress and, although normally I would not have got out of the army for many months, I applied for exceptional "Class B release" to enable me to resume my seminary studies.

While awaiting authority's decision (release or Palestine), I used in the evening to go, if I could, to the Canal, sit on the stony bank and dangle my feet in the cooling water. Occasionally a ship would pass and, if it were going northwards, I would watch it longingly.

After six or eight weeks in Egypt, I was given "leave" to go to Scotland for a few weeks, and I sailed from Port Said to Liverpool, accommodated in the comfort and luxury of the *Franconia's* sick quarters, not because I was ill but because I and a few others were entrusted with caring for any who might be. No one was, so the voyage became a pleasant ending to my army career, made even happier as when I was on leave I was granted "Class B release".

I have tried to give some idea of my feelings during my three years in the army rather than details of all that happened. In retrospect, I now think that the experience was beneficial. I don't know if it "made a man of me" but it was a wonderful opportunity to get to know new places, new people – and myself. Moreover, even with my three years away from the seminary, I was still only 24 at ordination.

Did I reflect on the morality of World War II? Did my conscience bother me while in the army? Did I ever think of being a conscientious objector? The answer to all three questions is No. If I had been older, the questions might have occurred to me, even bothered me. The Allies were opposed to powerful and unjust aggressors whose leaders were guilty of horrible crimes – but we were allies of the evil Soviet regime, we got involved with immoral and indiscriminate bombing of Germany, we collaborated in dropping atom bombs on Japanese cities.

I now doubt very much whether any war can be just – yet is there always and in every case an alternative? May God grant us the blessing of peace, guide the powerful to forswear all violence and protect the innocent, the weak and those without power.

ROME: STUDENT FOR THE PRIESTHOOD

"Demobbed" in the summer of 1947, I applied to return to my seminary training but I was in an uncertain frame of mind. Did I really want to be a priest? And if so, did I want to be a diocesan priest in Scotland or a missionary in India? However, I made my presence known to the diocesan authorities (still uncertain if I was doing the right thing), was assigned to St Peter's College, Cardross – but my destination was changed at the last minute to the Scots College, Rome. That change pleased me. I was excited at the prospect of living in Rome and I suppose that helped to resolve my indecision about my future.

Anyway, I found the College, both during the academic year in Rome and during three hot summer months in Marino (to the south of Rome and near Castel Gandolfo) a very happy place.

In the city we were living in those days in the Via Quattro Fontane, right in the centre of things, and I took full advantage of getting to know the city, and especially its churches, very well. Things were still somewhat spartan only two years after the war but it was a marvellous and unexpected privilege to have been sent to Rome.

Papal occasions were awesome to this newcomer to the Eternal City. To be present in St Peter's when Pius XII was there – carried in on a throne borne on men's shoulders, surrounded by cardinals, monsignori, and I don't know what other great people, with trumpets filling the basilica with Grieg's *Homage March* and other solemn music, thousands of people reaching out to try to touch the

Holy Father as he was carried past and screaming "*Viva il Papa*" – for me it was breathtaking and unforgettable.

Of course, there had to be a fly in the ointment in those happy years. It was study, classes at the Gregorian University and exams. I found it all quite difficult, perhaps because I had been away from books for three years, perhaps because I found classes in Latin, and as spoken by "foreigners" and so rapidly, not at all easy to follow, and maybe – no, I must admit, certainly – because I was lazy.

Anyway, somehow or other I got through the courses and the exams. I had four years of "undergraduate" theology and, after an interval of a year back in Scotland, a further two years as a "post-graduate" student for a doctorate in theology. One memorable academic triumph is worth recalling. Among the courses we had to do was Hebrew, admittedly at a very elementary level. As usual, I had left my study for the exam until the last minute. The night before the exam I realised I hadn't the faintest idea of the subject. In a panic I asked the resident student genius to explain a few things. He gave me an hour's tuition. The next morning I not only passed the Hebrew exam but got ten out of ten – "*summa cum laude*". If that proves anything, it is not something that should be spoken about – especially to those studying for exams. You may not be able to fool all the people all the time but you do seem to be able to fool some of the people some of the time.

The custom in those days was that the senior student due to begin his fourth year of theology was ordained at the end of his third year. The reason for this was that most of the students moved to the college's summer villa in Marino and there were some days when no member of the staff was there. Hence the arrangement meant that there would always be a student who could celebrate Mass for the other students. I was the senior student in my year by reason of being alone in the year, so I was ordained to the priesthood at the end of my third year in Rome: to be precise on Sunday 2nd July 1950 in the chapel of the International Carmelite College in Rome, with about twenty other ordinands from various countries and by Bishop Eliseu Van de Weijar, a Dutch Carmelite, bishop of the Territorial Prelature (later the diocese) of Paracatú in the remote west of the Minas Gerais region of Brazil.

My parents, sisters, brother and a few relatives travelled by train from Scotland to be present at my ordination. They boarded at *Pensione Maravilla* on the top floor of a building in Via Napoleone III and it was there we had a celebratory meal after the ordination. The following day I "said my first Mass", with my father and brother serving, in the chapel of the Scots College villa in Marino.

Making the trip to Rome was a severe financial burden on my family but I was honoured by their presence and I believe they gladly made the sacrifice to be there – and to make their first visit to the Eternal City.

As seminarians, we didn't have much contact with Italians, at least "ordinary" Italians. Some of us made friends with people from other colleges who were fellow students at the University. My special friend was Marcial Ramirez from Venezuela; we spoke in Latin because he knew no English and I had no Spanish. We lost contact for many years until I discovered, in the late 1980s, that he too had been made a bishop. The result was renewed contact by letter and phone, leading to exchange visits to each other's countries and homes.

Our social life in Rome was therefore fairly restricted and, to a large extent, was lived in our own Scots community in the college. But it was a happy place and the city was a wonderful experience. I was really sad when it came time to leave.

PALE YOUNG CURATE

The archdiocese of Glasgow was divided in 1947 with the formation of the new dioceses of Motherwell and Paisley and (a change that would much later be of great personal interest to me) the northern part of Ayrshire, from Largs to Stevenston and from Beith to Kilwinning, territory which had belonged to the archdiocese since 1878, was given to the diocese of Galloway. Priests who were in the affected parishes at the time of the split became priests of the new dioceses. Some priests who knew or guessed that change was coming made frantic efforts to be moved to the city of Glasgow "before the music stopped" – a clerical amalgam of pass the parcel and musical chairs. Those of us who were still seminarians in 1948 were allocated to the diocese in which our home parish was situated. Hence I was assigned to the diocese of Motherwell as my home parish was Burnbank, Hamilton.

On each side of my two years' post-graduate course in Rome, I was given a year's parish work, first in St Bartholomew's, Coatbridge (1951 - 1952) and then in St Bernadette's, Motherwell (1954 - 1955).

St Bartholomew's was a new parish. Fr Tom McGhie, the parish priest, lived in a council house and had Sunday Mass in the local school. I was very green but Fr McGhie was a kind mentor. Apart from the obvious duties of a priest, he taught me many useful activities – how to play pontoon (I was apathetic and therefore pathetic), how to visit parishioners (keep your hat on for hygienic reasons and, if you felt that that was rude, lay your hat upside down on wood, not upholstery), how to eat a large meal in ten minutes so as to get to Celtic Park in time.

I tried my hand at a boys' club and was an abject failure – see elsewhere for a full account; and at "instructing a convert", as we called it in those days. The poor lady must have been totally bored with my inadequate efforts to "instruct" her which ended, to her astonishment and alarm, with her baptism over the bath in our council house toilet. The recollection still gives me frissons of embarrassment.

St Bernadette's in Motherwell was also a new parish, but we had a church and an adequate house for us three priests as well as for a housekeeper and maid, both resident. The problem was that there was over a mile between the house and church. That was an incentive for me to learn to drive. By the way, I think that the driving test(s) can well stand comparison with any other of life's ordeals and emerge near the top.

Fr Peter Sexton was what I suppose would be described as an old-fashioned Irish parish priest. He was a character, eccentric, respected, a mixture of homespun philosophy and Shakespearean erudition. He had his own solution to the Easter Vigil liturgy, in those days celebrated in an empty church on Holy Saturday morning. That ingenious solution is described in *A Lifetime of Liturgy*, chapter 1. It certainly shortened the Easter Vigil. I wonder if similar ingenuity is in use anywhere today!

CARDROSS: SEMINARY LECTURER

Not unexpectedly, because of my postgraduate spell in Rome, I was appointed in 1955 to the teaching staff at St Peter's College, Cardross. This was the major seminary which, in those days, took students from Glasgow, Motherwell and Paisley.

Also not unexpectedly, having specialised in theology, I was sent to teach philosophy, or more accurately, certain subjects in the philosophy course. Formal logic, metaphysics and the history of ancient and medieval philosophy were my assigned subjects. Pedagogical methods were left more or less entirely to oneself while as far as subject matter was concerned I had, it is true, done a philosophy course, as a student in Blairs College, in 1942 - 1944 but had not looked at the matter since then. So it was a case of buying the books, keeping a few pages ahead of the students and hoping nervously for the best.

I started my lecturing career inauspiciously. Seeking to be thorough, I decided, before embarking on the history of early Greek philosophy, to devote twenty minutes or so each to the history of the even earlier philosophies of China and Egypt. As examples of the former, my book mentioned Confucianism and Tao-ism so I remarked that Tao-ism still had its followers as there was a Tao institute in Glasgow. One of the students raised his hand to tell me, publicly, that the Tao Centre was "for the removal of surplus hair".

It was a humbling start to my lecturing career – like being ordered off after scoring an own goal on your home debut – but it taught me a lesson difficult to forget. Pride certainly went before a fall on that occasion. And a little knowledge is a dangerous thing.

After five generally happy years in the philosophy section (Darleith) of St Peter's College – during which I bought my first car for £30 (second hand, no heater, no radio, little orange lateral indicators which sometimes worked), I was transferred to the senior of the two houses (Kilmahew) to teach theology. This was more familiar ground and I was asked to teach the second, third and fourth years of dogmatic theology as a cycle course. Perhaps the general atmosphere in Kilmahew was not as relaxed and "homely" as Darleith but I was happier with the subjects I had to teach.

After all these years since then, it is too easy to be critical of St Peter's College and especially Kilmahew in the years from 1960 to 1965. But I think the leadership was weak, discipline was lax and a proper sense of community was missing. Moreover the roles of the three bishops, Archbishop Campbell, Bishop Scanlan and Bishop Black, were unclear, their relationship among themselves apparently not close and their attitude towards the seminary ambiguous.

The sixties were generally a time of change, of turmoil, of student revolt, of crisis of authority – and it would have been naïve to imagine that a seminary would be uninfluenced and exempt. Besides, the construction of the new building had begun alongside the Kilmahew nineteenth-century house and, among us from the start, the whole project was a source of concern and dismay. The design and architecture of the new building may have impressed architects and others who were not going to live and work in it but to us it was clearly impractical and unsuitable. For example, it was evident that, as a result of the Second Vatican Council, the style of liturgical celebration was about to change but the arrangements of the new building did not cater for that. I remember that, at one stage, the teaching staff at Cardross became so worried at the design and proposed arrangements of the building that, although we had never been consulted about the project, the senior priest among us sought to bring our views to the Glasgow archdiocesan authorities. I don't remember whether he was granted a hearing or not, but no heed was paid to our concerns or suggestions.

So they weren't altogether easy, happy days in my later years in Cardross. One bitter incident remains vivid in my memory. It was the time of student riots and the struggle for desegregation in the United States. One morning, our students had been refused a day off which they wanted and, as I waited to go into the lecture hall to give a class, they began to sing loudly "We shall overcome". In retrospect, the incident was trivial and somewhat ludicrous, but it was serious for us then and menacing. I was very shaken. It was not a pleasant experience.

One element of life at Kilmahew gave me satisfaction as well as a continuing challenge. I was asked to take on the editorship of the college magazine. It was set up at the beginning of the century, I think, and had two names: one, the obvious and unimaginative *St Peter's College Magazine;* and the other, the more adventurous *Claves*

Regni. It appeared twice a year and had a few fairly scholarly articles, plus a number of regular features including a diary of college events, letters from other Scottish seminaries and, since my years as editor coincided with the sessions of the Second Vatican Council, I introduced a section in which we summarised an update of the activities and decisions of the Council. I do not now have access to what we said about the council and perhaps that is good since I suspect that, reading our efforts today, we would be embarrassed at our attempts to be accurate and usefully informative. Not only was our knowledge of what was going on very limited but I suspect that we did not properly appreciate the import and relevance even of what we did know.

It was part of the editor's job to liaise with the Glasgow firm which printed the magazine, a more complicated and tedious task than nowadays since it involved visits to the printers at various stages of the publishing process, reading galley proofs, discussing editing technicalities etc. In addition, I tried hard to increase circulation through contacting likely or possible people: priests, parishes, schools. And, of course, I had to try to ensure that one-off articles and material for the regular items were commissioned and were being written, and punctually, for each forthcoming issue. Those who have had similar responsibilities will know the anxieties and the occasional subterfuge of having to write an article oneself and publish it under a pseudonym. It was all hard work, but I found it enjoyable enough and fulfilling.

One day in 1965, before the summer holidays, I received a letter from the newly-ordained bishop of Motherwell, Bishop Frank Thomson. I expected it to be a reply to my request for a photograph and message from him for our college magazine but, to my utter astonishment, it told me that the bishops' conference had appointed me to be rector of the Royal Scots College in Spain. Total surprise and shock – I had hardly adverted to the fact of the vacancy in Valladolid and certainly had not ever dreamed of being asked to fill it. The letter bluntly added "Your ignorance of Spanish will not be accepted as grounds for refusal. You will just have to learn the language."

VALLADOLID: SEMINARY RECTOR

The thought of going to Spain and of being rector of the Royal Scots College seemed very, very strange to me and exciting also. I wasn't a reluctant appointee, but intrigued at the prospect of a new job in a country new to me – and I felt very honoured to have been chosen.

When you start a new job, you are not aware of all the duties that await you – and that was true for me in July 1965. But obviously there was the language and my ignorance of it. True, among the community of priests and students we spoke English – but we had constant contact with Spaniards. I felt like Zechariah, John the Baptist's father, but his speech was fully restored after nine months. I was gradually learning some Spanish right from the start (for example, when meeting someone for the first time, you can say "*mucho gusto*" or "*encantado*") but it was a struggle, first to understand what people were saying, then to answer them intelligently. Gradually my vocabulary increased, my grammar improved and I gained confidence. If I were now asked for advice for someone in my plight it would be twofold: don't be afraid to make mistakes and never decide you are good enough!

It wasn't long before I discovered that being rector of the Royal Scots College was more than being in charge of the students (usually about twenty, all training to be priests in Scottish dioceses). That was difficult enough, especially in the worldwide turmoil of the late '60s, with student riots, crisis in authority etc. But I also had to deal with the college domestic staff, with tradesmen and workmen and local officialdom. The college owned a large estate called Canterac in another part of Valladolid, a summer house, a pine wood and extensive vineyards in Boecillo (ten miles south of Valladolid, on the River Duero), and property in Madrid. It had to be a very steep learning curve but I was helped, supported and consoled by the two other staff members, already there when I arrived and indeed former students, Fr (now Bishop) Ian Murray and Fr (now Mgr) Jack Sheridan.

Shortly after I arrived in Spain, the college got involved in court action against a man who had done a lot of paid work for the college and had become friendly with my predecessor. The problem was to dislodge him from a portion of our Canterac estate which he had occupied (illegally, we maintained). It was a very disagreeable business, employing lawyers and taking our dispute through the courts. We lost the criminal case so were advised to take civil action – which we also lost. I felt disheartened and cynical. We were sure that justice had been denied us but we lost the land and had to meet the cost of our lawyers' fees.

My main duty as rector was, of course, to look after the students. They received most of their classes in the local diocesan seminary and, later, in an Augustinian Institute affiliated to the University of Comillas. But we gave additional classes in the college and were responsible for the students' human, spiritual and pastoral development as well as generally being responsible for their safety, welfare, health and happiness. End of term assessments had to be made, progress reports on each student sent to his bishop in Scotland and, a task I greatly disliked, having occasionally from time to time to dismiss a student or recommend to his bishop that he be withdrawn. In such cases, I was only too well aware of the responsibility I had – and indeed the power – to make a decision of such great importance for the student himself and for his diocese. In the majority of occasions when a student left, of course, it was of his own volition. That was a preferable and better way.

Attending the bishops' conference once a year and giving a report was another task, thankfully worse in anticipation than in reality. I used to remind bishops that we needed students and would be grateful for new recruits to the community; one year I appealed especially for a goalkeeper who could play the organ. One bishop obliged. The new man could do both (just) but unfortunately was not called to be a priest.

The college summer house at Boecillo was a great favourite of mine. In my day some of the students went home for the summer but most went to Boecillo. So did I (since I went to Scotland each spring and autumn). They were happy times – an old 1795 large solid building (used by Wellington during the Peninsular War), away from the city, in a commanding situation with extensive views, the river Duero nearby for swimming, priests visiting from Scotland, a real sense of community (in Spanish "*convivencia*" which I once saw unfortunately translated as "cohabitation"). Our summer house was for relaxation and tranquillity. There were, however, occasional exceptions to our bucolic quiescence; for example, when we erected scaffolding round the whole building and all of us worked together to restore the walls to perfect whiteness, painting them with quicklime; or on another occasion when I was foolhardy enough to drive a tractor with trailer attached, lost control and was very lucky not to capsize or collide as we careered down a short but steep hill. There were students on the trailer, some of whom received cuts and scrapes as they leapt off in panic.

In the years until 1971, much of my spare time was occupied by preparing and writing "*The Scots College in Spain*", a history of the college from its foundation in Madrid in 1627. The college had been transferred to Valladolid in 1771 and, to celebrate the bicentenary of that event, the book was published. Moreover, for a period of three days at the end of May and the beginning of June 1971, the college hosted a number of events (Masses, meals, receptions) for the Scottish bishops, many former students now priests in Scotland and a great collection of Spanish people, some of them dignitaries, some with an official connection to the college and others simply friends. They were successful and memorable days despite the fact that we were being picketed by people who lived near our Canterac estate and who thought we were selling it for housing development. Groups of them were standing in the street outside the college, holding placards. Cardinal Gray gave them his blessing and a cheery wave, thinking that they had come to express their delight and congratulations on the occasion of the bicentenary.

My being sent to Valladolid, such an unexpected appointment, turned out to be very much to my liking. There were difficult moments but I was extremely happy in Spain. However, after nine years I felt it was time for me to ask the bishops to let me return to Scotland. The college needed a change and I didn't want to be in Spain so long that I would not be glad to resume parish work in Scotland. So, nine years to the day from my arrival, on 2nd July 1974, I bade the college, the community and Spain a sad, indeed tearful, *Adiós*.

The question has often been asked: why have a college or seminary in Spain? Only through having experienced life there can one answer the question adequately but let me list some reasons: the college (and its assets) cannot easily be sold or funds removed from Spain; the college is well endowed so that the cost to a diocese of having a student there is a small fraction of the cost in the other seminaries; the Spanish pontifical universities offer an excellent academic formation; it is a very broadening and enriching experience to live abroad for a time; to learn at first hand the history, culture and language of Spain is an invaluable advantage in today's world; Scots seminarians in Spain can and do have lots of contacts outside the college; the students really enjoy being in Spain and remember it with great affection; finally the priests educated in Spain are second to none, are they not?

At present and due to the dearth of seminarians, the Royal Scots College, now located in Salamanca since 1988, has no students doing their full undergraduate course before priesthood. The college is still very much in use for the ongoing formation of bishops, priests and deacons as well as providing a valuable resource, in a variety of ways, for the Catholics of Scotland. Nevertheless, my fervent hope is that once again, and soon, the college may resume its work as a fully active seminary, training priests for Scotland. Then, we shall all be the beneficiaries.

EAST KILBRIDE

Our Lady of Lourdes, East Kilbride, to which Bishop Thomson appointed me as parish priest in August 1974 is large, completely post-World War II and welcoming. I took to it very easily and readily, despite my parish experience being limited and twenty years out of date. I got great support and understanding from the other two priests and from the people. And of course, settling into East Kilbride was not as challenging as it had been in Valladolid.

I was very happy as a parish priest, perhaps because it was a good time: long enough after the Second Vatican Council to be introducing "new" insights from its teaching on the nature of the Church, on liturgy, on ecumenism etc. But it would have been quite wrong to abandon all previous religious practices and ideas.

This sat very comfortably with me and while we were introducing a parish pastoral council, a more participative liturgy and more frequent contact with Christians from other churches and traditions, we still had Rosary and Benediction, Holy Hours, visits to parishioners in their homes and regular visiting of the hospital and the schools.

As I look back on those seven years in East Kilbride (1974 – 1981), there are certain aspects of life there that I remember with particular appreciation. One was the happiness of "collaborative ministry", sharing the work with parishioners through discussion, planning and carrying out various activities. It was good not to be solely responsible, to help people become aware that, through baptism, they were as much the Church as the priests were and that they were called to be active, to use the gifts the Holy Spirit had given them. Not everyone responded but it was heart warming that so many did.

Another source of happiness for me was the parish charismatic prayer group that met each Thursday evening. We had our struggles to keep it going in its early days but then it did truly flourish and, for many of us, was a real grace as we learned to pray communally, spontaneously and without embarrassment. The Scriptures became more familiar and meaningful, hymns became prayers, and we became, in grace, closer to God and to each other. The Holy Spirit was present and active in our midst.

Nor do I forget the feeling I gradually experienced in the parish of being understood, accepted and appreciated. In a seminary I think that the students tend to take one for granted or, at least, are not good at showing appreciation or expressing gratitude. So it was really affirming to be thanked and appreciated. In return, I became able, indeed sought, to be seen as a human being, imperfect and vulnerable, with feelings and emotions, making mistakes, grateful for being allowed to grow in friendship. It can be difficult for parishioners to achieve the right attitude towards their priest. He must be seen as having a ministry different from lay people and being respected for that, but also allowed and enabled to be a human being who needs relationships, who needs to love and be loved. Our Lady of Lourdes parish meant that for me.

TRAVEL

Being a bishop increased my opportunities for travel to far off lands. It gave some justification to the riddle: "What is the difference between God and a bishop?" "God is everywhere but a bishop is everywhere except in his own diocese". I always enjoyed the overseas trips and found them most interesting. So I am happy to recall some memories of them. An added bonus was that, on many occasions, the air fare was not my responsibility.

Before I became a bishop in 1981 and for a few years thereafter, I was secretary to the Bishops' Conference of Scotland and during my term of office the custom of an annual meeting of the secretaries of European bishops' conferences was begun. That provided trips to Bruges, Malta and Budapest. In Hungary we were accommodated in a Redemptorist house on the Danube, a few miles west of the capital. Hungary was still in the Soviet bloc and, when we had Mass during the meeting, the man in the house next door put on his radio as loud as he could, presumably to annoy us. On the Sunday, however, we had a splendid celebration of Mass in Budapest cathedral, with the archbishop as principal celebrant, organ, choir, candles, incense and the first "altar girls" I had ever seen. Two other Hungarian memories – the reckless speed of the taxis especially when overtaking on bends; and the genial Redemptorist superior who insisted on our having a glass of plum brandy each morning before breakfast.

At one of the European secretaries' meetings, there was an announcement that the Federation of Asian Bishops would like a European representative to attend their forthcoming meeting. As I, by then, fulfilled the two conditions (a bishop who spoke English) I found myself in Tokyo for the meeting. My memory of that city is its size, its bewildering bustle and the archbishop's house where I was given warm hospitality despite having committed an initial solecism of not having changed my outdoor shoes to one of the pairs of slippers at the entrance.

I also managed to spend a few days in Kyoto, the old capital of Japan with many religious shrines and temples and where the local bishop took me to have a private and traditional meal of about ten (small) courses with a spoon courteously provided for me in addition to chopsticks. A further bonus was a day in Hiroshima where the devastation caused by the 1945 atom bomb is still poignantly "preserved" as an affront, a reproach and a plea to humankind. Although when I was in Japan, I was constantly aware of the part which the country had played in the Second World War and of the atom bombs which had been dropped there, it was also heartening to see the progress made since those days and the frequent evidence of modern life. This last is best illustrated by the *shinkansen* ("bullet trains") network, travel on which is a truly astonishing experience. I enjoyed that experience on journeys from Tokyo to Kyoto and to Hiroshima.

Invitations to speak at charismatic meetings took me to Australia, Ireland, Malta, the Czech Republic as well as to Canada. In the last-named, it was Winnipeg in Manitoba and Kamloops in British Columbia – it should have been Vancouver but the archbishop of that city refused permission.

Appointment as the Scottish representative on the Episcopal Board of the International Commission for English in the Liturgy took me quite frequently to Washington DC. For that journey my preferred route was via Reykjavik, not only because it was more pleasant than via London but also because the airline seemed very appropriate for my purposes: ICELandair I remember one occasion when we left Iceland for Washington after dusk and, as we flew across the ocean, I saw the sun rise in the west.

Perhaps most interesting of all was travel in connection with and deriving from my membership of the Catholic Institute for International Relations, which has brought me many visits to Central America, especially El Salvador and Guatemala. I hope that I can continue to visit Central America because I now have some good friends there but I found, on my trip there in October 2004, that some of the hardships and discomforts of life there were becoming more difficult to accept than they used to be. There is more about my visits in the following sections.

Various contacts, and my knowledge of Spanish, have afforded opportunities to visit South America on several occasions. Venezuela (where I went to meet a bishop who had been a fellow-student in Rome in the late 1940s), Chile (I had been invited to be a member of a delegation when the people there voted against General Augusto Pinochet in a national plebiscite), Ecuador (to visit Scottish priests working there), Peru (to visit the Columban missionary priests in Lima) and Colombia (as a member of a Pax Christi delegation from the Netherlands – fascinating, memorable but not for the faint-hearted).

After retiring as bishop of the diocese and chairman of ICEL, I went to visit two bishops who had been colleagues on the Episcopal Board of the latter. From Bishop Peter Cullinane of Palmerston North in New Zealand and Bishop James Foley of Cairns in Australia I received a very genuine welcome and fine hospitality. In both places, I had the pleasure of meeting priests and people of the dioceses, as well as being taken by my tireless hosts to visit a number of very interesting places.

I remember with pleasure two trips I made and without any official purpose. One was to Zimbabwe, with a priest colleague, to visit Mgr Peter Magee, the first priest that I ordained (on 2nd July 1981) and, at the time of our visit, the secretary in the Nunciature in Harare. We managed to travel extensively in various parts of the country, meeting many people including, in Bulawayo, Fr Pius Neube, now the courageous archbishop of that city, and seeing some wonderful sights, above all Victoria Falls.

The other trip was to India, nearly fifty years after my time there as a soldier. I managed to visit two cities, Delhi and Agra, that I had not visited before; but perhaps the highlight was to visit places where I had been stationed while I was in the army. I particularly remember going to the very barrack room near Secunderabad where I had spent some months in 1946. It was a very strange feeling to stand on the spot where my bed and belongings (and I) had been so many years before and so many miles from home and to realise that that young man had been me, unaware of all that was to befall me. An uncanny experience.

CHAPLAIN TO THE CANARIES

One raw December afternoon in the early 1960s I walked down Fish Street Hill in London past Billingsgate Market and then, for the first time in my life, stepped on to Spanish territory. The particular piece of Spain on which I trod was the Bilbao-registered ship, *Monte Urquiola,* which maintains, or maintained, a fortnightly service between London and the Canary Islands, carrying bananas, tomatoes and people. The ministrations of a Catholic chaplain were deemed necessary, not for any of these three categories – apparently only the occasional English Catholic had the necessary leisure or inclination to winter in Tenerife – but for the crew who, being Spanish, were, of course, all Catholics.

Those were happy days as we sped sunwards at twelve knots – and memorable too, since we enjoyed the roughest weather anyone could remember. Lunch on New Year's Day was taken in, or at least on, bed – a cup of weak tea and a water biscuit. But not every day was as bad and I recall having had *some* meals in the dining room. There was the occasion, for example, when, during afternoon tea, one lady was a little late in clutching the edge of the table and with a cry of "My God!" was tipped off her chair and slid ungracefully across the room and into the far corner, followed closely by her chair and a large amount of the ship's crockery.

However, I restrict myself to recalling some incidents of a more strictly religious character. On the Sunday, I was informed that I would be saying two Masses, one at an early hour for the ordinary seamen and another at ten for the officers. The weekday Mass had not been exactly a sell-out, but it was reasonable enough to have two Masses on Sunday since a ship sailing the high *(sic)* seas with every member of the crew attending Mass at the same time is somewhat unusual and even perilous. It was disappointing to have, as the total congregation at the first Mass, the altar server (of whom more later) and about six seamen, lurking sheepishly in the further corners of the room.

For the second Mass, I was ready and vested at ten, but the turnout was equally sparse. I thought I'd wait a few minutes just in case any more came, but by five past the situation was unchanged. So I began Mass. During the first reading, the door opened and in trooped the captain, followed, to a man, by all the other officers. Perhaps there is some unwritten law of the Spanish main that ordinary seamen don't attend Mass but that officers do. My feeling, afterwards, that at least the latter did come to Mass even if they had not quite been on time – this smug reflection – was devastatingly dispelled when it was communicated to me that the 10am Mass began only when the officers had arrived and that the captain was very displeased at my non-compliance with the rule.

The ship's barman was called Jesús and, perhaps for that reason, had been the Mass server for a long time. But recently he had acquired a young assistant, Ramón, who had once been a seminarian for three weeks and to him had naturally been delegated the liturgical duties. Ramón took me under his wing at once and felt it incumbent upon himself to undertake an apostolate of liturgical pedagogy. In other words, he dedicated himself to teaching me, during Mass each morning, how to celebrate it properly. Those were pre-Vatican II days, by the way.

Apparently he felt that I needed speeding up with the prayers at the foot of the altar, since he would give the answer to the verse that I had been hoping to say next; this is good training in patience and concentration – try it sometime. He would disappear discreetly for considerable periods during Mass to see, I think, if I could manage on my own for a while. Each morning he presented me with the water cruet first so that he could then correct my attempt to say "wine" in Spanish and teach me to pronounce the word properly; when he considered that I had at least made a praiseworthy effort, he would hand over the wine cruet with a word of congratulation. He was a most helpful youth who gave me all the assistance in his power. In those days at the end of Mass, the priest had to say, "*Benedicat vos omnipotens Deus*" facing the altar and then turn round to finish the blessing. Ramón used to allow me to say the first four words, but, by the time I had turned round, he had already piously intoned "*Pater et Filius et Spiritus Sanctus*" to which I responded a dutiful if sheepish "*Amen*". An estimable youth. I wonder where he is now. A leading figure in Catholic action, perhaps. Or a bishop.

The passengers treated me with respect under the impression that I was a permanent member of the crew. "How long do you reckon this storm will last, padre?" "Does this ship always roll as much as this?" There was also a certain reserve, increased perhaps by the fact that the passengers were English as well as non-Catholic. I recall with affection, however, one very pleasant, elderly Englishman who, from time to time in the intervals between dreadful bouts of seasickness, would emerge from his cabin. He was a Church of England clergyman, a gentle soul, who was going to Tenerife for a few months for the sake of his health. On the Saturday afternoon he asked me whether I thought it would be a good idea if he were to hold a Holy Communion service the following morning for the benefit of those passengers who were interested. I said it was an excellent idea and then he disclosed that he had none of the wherewithal and wondered would I be willing to co-operate. I felt that I could hardly lend him the chalice and paten for which he asked, nor allow him to use the altar. I explained that these objects were consecrated and set apart so that even Catholics were forbidden to use them for anything except Mass. He was so understanding that I thought no harm would be done by giving him some hosts and wine and, putting our heads together, we decided that a coffee table, a wineglass and a small plate, while not ideal, would be fairly acceptable to the Lord in the special circumstances. Finally, he asked if nine o'clock the following day would be suitable, so as not to be in the way at the time of my Masses.

So all was arranged and off he went to let the captain know, so that the matter might be announced to the passengers. He returned a few minutes later, utterly crestfallen. He had explained all the arrangements to the captain, who then informed him that we were on a Spanish ship and that therefore he would not permit any non-Catholic religious rites. And that was that.

My friend, by this time thoroughly demoralised, asked if I thought there would be any objection to his coming to Mass, as otherwise he would not be present at any act of worship. I assured him that, as far as I was concerned, there was no objection. And so next morning, he was a member of the congregation at the ten o'clock Mass, taking his place at ten minutes to ten.

THE DELIGHTS OF TURKISH TRAVEL

[I wrote this essay in 1963. Travel in Turkey nowadays must be different and so the article has acquired a "*period-piece*" *quality*.]

"Fly!" urged the travel agent, "It's the only way to get around this country". A priest friend and I were in Istanbul, planning a tour of Asia Minor, Turkey-in-Asia. Had we taken the travel agent's advice, we should have deprived ourselves of not the least of the delights which Turkey offers the visitor. Turkish surface transport may not be the last word in luxury but is certainly an experience that the conscientious tourist should not try to avoid.

Most popular for long distance travel are the buses. You go along to the local bus depot a day or two beforehand to book a seat. Scores of bus lines operate out of the larger cities with perhaps two or three specialising in each route. The buses may, in many cases, be ancient lurching juggernauts but the companies all have the word "Jet" incorporated in their name. "Express" would presumably denote a company still using horse-buses. Before departure time, you present yourself at the bus stance to have your cases securely but crudely roped on the roof and to claim your seat – and the journey begins. One's fellow travellers are a cross-section of the Turkish people, young and old, comfortable and poor, modern and old-fashioned. Nor is it long before a foreigner has attracted the interest of at least one or two of them. Halting conversation is begun and you are offered a share in the food-hampers that nearly everyone seems to have – cherries, some figs or tomatoes. It is at such moments that you are faced with the dilemma of remaining true to the rule of never eating unwashed, unpeeled fruit and so seeming ungrateful or just going ahead and immediately experiencing all sorts of aches and pains that can only presage cholera or typhoid, if not both. Much better if your new-found acquaintances produce oranges, peaches or even a water-melon. Anything, as long as it's peelable.

The bus driver is much more important than in our own country. Apart from his obvious duties and responsibilities, it is he who decides when and where the next stops will be made, for how long they will last, whether the passengers will be allowed off or whether they will remain on the bus, to be ministered to by an invasion of vendors of *ayran*, the cool refreshing drink of diluted yoghurt that is almost a national beverage. He also decides whether the bus radio will be turned on and just how deafening the music will be; and whether every other road-user that passes or is passed will be treated to several blasts of the ear-shattering horn. These are important decisions when you are condemned to spending all day in a bus, in a temperature approaching 100 degrees and when your nerves tend, after a little, to become ever so slightly frayed at the edges.

However, I must be fair. No matter its length, the driver has to do the full journey on his own, without benefit of a relief driver. I recall a magnificent specimen of Turkish manhood – bullet-headed, moustachioed with whiskers more like buffalo horns than handlebars, who drove his bus from Izmir to Adana, 600 - 700 miles, from 1pm until 10am the following morning.

After some hours on the bus, of course, a sticky lethargy tends to take over and you hardly bother to notice the string of camels by the roadside or to register that the village with the unpronounceable name through which the bus is passing was once Nicomedia or Thyatira or Laodicea or some other place mentioned in the New Testament. Stretches of ruts and potholes are much more effective for jolting you back to full consciousness, but such are not very frequent, most of the roads, even if only with a gravel surface, being fairly smooth.

One drawback in bus travel is the difficulty you have in discovering the estimated time of arrival. Timetables seem unavailable, the booking agent who hopes to sell you a ticket is very optimistic and reassuring but as the journey gets under way the rumours that circulate become gloomier and gloomier. The best plan is to be mentally detached from such worries and anxieties. The information is largely irrelevant in such an easy-going country as Turkey and, besides, the fare is less than £1 for 400 miles.

The railways issue timetables of course, but their value is rather curtailed when you realise that, due to bus competition and cheapness, many trains do not run daily and that the train at the time most suitable for your needs runs on "Pazartesi and Cuma only" (or is it "excepted"?). The safest plan in this case would seem to be to present yourself at the station at the correct time each day and eventually, one day, the train is bound to appear. There are some fast diesel services but the steam trains have much more character. They go slowly enough to allow peasants in the fields to give a friendly wave to the travellers, if not actually to jog along beside them. I recall an all-day journey from Konya (Iconium in the New Testament) to Tarsus. The scenery was remarkable, often breathtaking, as we crossed the barren central plateau of Anatolia, passed through the towering mountains of the Taurus range and dropped down through the narrow defiles of the Cilician Gates to the semi-tropical maritime plain of southern Turkey.

Despite the magnificence, the journey was just as memorable on account of our compartment co-passengers – the little old man, for example, sitting quietly in a corner who suddenly slid his feet out of his shoes, drew his legs up under him, put a prayer cap on his head, turned towards Mecca and unconcernedly went through his evening prayer ritual. Then there were the three boys who had been on the train since the previous day but had sought us out in the milling crowds to let us know that they had a spare seat and would crush up to make a second seat available. They were friendly and full of fun. They soon produced a pack of cards and were delighted to be taught some games that we knew. By the end of the journey, with the aid of a little good-natured cheating, they could beat us every time. And let any anthropologist beware of oversimplification if he decides to write a thesis on the card games indigenous to the remote areas of south-east Asia Minor. I am afraid we have contaminated the evidence and complicated his task.

Shorter journeys can be made by private taxi, if you are an American or a former pasha. Everyone else uses a dolmus, an admirable institution for cheap and convenient movement between two points. A dolmus is a shared-taxi and in the bigger cities this form of conveyance does a constant trade. You simply go to a square or other central point and help to fill up the dolmus whose destination is where you want to go. In a few moments, the car is full and off you go – only a little dearer than the city bus, yet much quicker and more comfortable. Dolmuses also make longer trips out of town. In these cases the dolmus is often a minibus with room for about eight passengers and you may have to wait for a little longer before the vehicle is full. For example, dolmuses regularly ply between Izmir and the ruins of Ephesus, 50 miles to the south, take their passengers round the various places of interest there and bring them back to Izmir in the evening. And they are frequently used as land ferries to the beaches, from Istanbul to the Black Sea, for instance, or from Mersin to the ruins-cum-beach at Soli where the inhabitants once spoke such execrable Greek that they gave the world a new word – solecism.

Perhaps the most attractive of all Turkish transport, however, is the horse-cab. Some of the holiday islands in the Sea of Marmara have banned all internal combustion engines from their streets and a gentle ride along them by horse-cab, past pine woods and summer villas, is a balm to the nerves after the clamour and crowds of Istanbul. But when you get to some of the towns of Asia Minor, it is to discover that the horse-cab is there not as a tourist attraction but as the only form of transport in the place. No doubt there are compensations for being so far behind the times but please do not suggest freedom from breakdowns as one such compensation. At Mersin, on the south coast, the railway station is a mile from town and so a cab is a necessity. We had just passed one of the only two possible hotels in the town, having rejected the entreaties of its owner to put up there, when a wheel rib came off our cab; in full view of the disappointed hotel owner we had to dismount and, carrying our cases, walk to the other hotel. Our "humiliation" was not yet complete: no accommodation available there and so nothing for it but a sheepish return to the hotel we had previously spurned and a servile request to be forgiven.

Although our journeying in Turkey had been accomplished without leaving the ground, fate, in the form of a Syrian refusal to grant us visas, decreed that we should have to take to the air to leave the country and continue our journey southwards. And so it was that we alighted from a dolmus at the end of the side road in which the entrance to Adana airport is located. Not a taxi or cab was in sight and there was nothing for it but to cover the half mile on foot and carrying our own luggage – hardly the way in which the best people arrive at airports. Our self-esteem was restored, however, by a glance at our plane tickets for we were travelling by the national airline Turk Hava Yollari and there, on the cover of our tickets, were the very charming and flattering words "THY Airline".

CENTRAL AMERICA: FIRST IMPRESSIONS

One of the most enriching and interesting aspects of my life has been my association with Central America. It all began in 1984 when I attended a meeting in Glasgow, organised by the Scottish Catholic International Aid Fund (SCIAF) and at which the Catholic Institute for International Relations (CIIR) had been invited to speak of its work in Central America. CIIR had been founded as "Sword of the Spirit" during World War II and has recently been renamed "Progressio". Its work is described as "tackling the causes of poverty and injustice internationally through advocacy and skill sharing". It is active in countries in Asia, Africa, and Latin America and, in addition, seeks to raise awareness at home concerning issues of poverty and injustice in the developing world.

At that meeting in Glasgow, the principal speaker was Fr Ricardo Falla, a Jesuit anthropologist who was living and working with Guatemalan "internal refugees", indigenous Mayan people in hiding from the Guatemalan army which was pursuing a policy of near genocide against them. Fr Falla was accompanied that day by the then head of the Latin American desk of CIIR, Mrs Kathy Piper. She told me that CIIR, which is based in London, wanted to have more visibility in Scotland. To that end, would I, as bishop and able to speak Spanish, consider being made a vice-president of the Institute? I readily agreed – and thus began a series of visits to Central America that taught me so much about those lands and their peoples – friendly, welcoming, beautiful yet, in so many cases, impoverished, oppressed and persecuted.

My first visit to Central America took place in October/November 1984. We were a party of four: Kathy Piper, Bishop James O'Brien (auxiliary in Westminster), Duncan MacLaren (executive director, Scottish Catholic International Aid Fund) and myself. That first visit I found fascinating, disturbing and very bewildering.

We spent a day in Mexico City where we met a number of exiled Guatemalan church people. Kathy Piper knew the issues being discussed – but I had little idea of what was being spoken about; moreover, I found it difficult to understand what people were saying. But Bishop O'Brien and I did manage a quick visit to the Basilica of Nuestra Señora de Guadalupe! The following day, our party travelled to Guatemala City.

Guatemala City seemed unattractive to me – narrow, crowded, dirty streets, a somewhat menacing atmosphere; we knew that the regime was cruel and tyrannical and used death squads as well as informers. However, the Hotel del Centro was clean and comfortable, with a bar, restaurant, a pianist and a singer. During our days in the capital we had many meetings with priests, religious, human rights groups, women whose husbands had been murdered or abducted; but, on that first visit, I am afraid that I didn't really get fully in touch – due partly to my ignorance of the specific matters under discussion, partly to my (then) poor comprehension skills.

On the Sunday morning we went to the outskirts of the city for an open-air Mass. The priest was a Belgian missionary who told us that, in the congregation, there were "*orejas*" (ears), i.e. informers ready to carry tales to the authorities about what he said.

The number of small evangelical churches was also evident. Many of them are financed by US evangelicals, they are hostile to the Catholic Church – but many Catholics have joined them and they are much more acceptable to the authorities than is the Catholic Church.

During my stay in Guatemala, the group made one excursion outside the capital – to the province of Quiché in the northwest highlands. Quiché has a majority of indigenous inhabitants and it is probably the area that has suffered most from the activities of the Guatemalan army. Many thousands of people, including many catechists and other active Catholics, have been brutally killed or "disappeared", the people there have endured a reign of terror, the inhumanity and savagery of which can scarcely be exaggerated. On that first occasion, in Quiché, we visited only two centres, both in the south of the province: Santa Cruz, the provincial capital where we met the apostolic administrator, Mons. Urízar (there being no bishop at the time), and Chichicastenango, where we lodged in the beautiful, but almost empty, Hotel Santo Tomás (a former monastery) and marvelled at the exotic open-air market which sold anything and everything but especially the wonderful woven cloth in a dazzling variety of bright colours and so typical of Guatemala. The huge church of Santo Tomás was packed for the feast of All Saints. It was a brilliant liturgy with clouds of incense and enthusiastic singing accompanied by "*conjuntos*" of accordions and marimbas. Duncan MacLaren had written out for me, and coached me how to say, a phrase of greeting in Quiché language. I delivered it nervously and it was received in total silence, possibly out of respect for a visiting bishop but much more probably because my pronunciation was awful and totally unintelligible.

From Guatemala we continued to Nicaragua. The differences were immediately obvious. The country had had its revolution, the tyrannical and murderous Somoza regime was gone, the left-wing Sandinistas were in power, the people, though living in great poverty, were not living in fear and terror. There were no distinctive indigenous people – all were of European descent or mixed race, although with people of African descent on the Atlantic coast.

In Managua, we were given lodgings in the house of the Jesuit Fathers who taught in the University of Central America. The university rector, Fr César Jerez SJ, was kind enough to give me his room. I soon learned that the university, its faculty and many other priests were viewed with hostility and suspicion by the archbishop of Managua, Cardinal Obando y Bravo SDB, and most of the bishops because of their support of the revolution and the new Sandinista government.

During that first visit, we had meetings with several of the Jesuits, with religious and with a number of government people, all of whom seemed intelligent, very aware of the problems which the country faced, yet determined to do all they could to bring health, education and a better future to the people of Nicaragua. Once again, however, as in Guatemala, I felt frustrated that, because I was unfamiliar with the issues discussed and slow to pick up what people were saying, I did not contribute to the discussions as I should have liked.

One obvious element in the situation both in Guatemala and Nicaragua was the role of the United States. Menacing, bullying, interfering and with a very right-wing agenda that tended to equate anything else as Marxist and therefore unacceptable, the United States was implicated in the Guatemalan army's strategy of terror against the indigenous population; while it was promoting and equipping the armed resistance of the so-called "Contras" against the government and the great majority of the people of Nicaragua.

Although it was my first experience of Central America and I was not nearly as aware of the situation as I later became, I was interviewed, on my return to Scotland, by Brian Wilson (later MP for North Ayrshire) and his report appeared in *New Statesman* for 23rd November 1984.

"Bishop Maurice Taylor of Galloway says…the Guatemalan bishops – on the basis of what they understand Lord Colville's report to be – are 'distraught that a man of such experience and influence could put in such a report'.

"Lord Colville of Culross…was until last year British representative on the United Nations Human Rights Commission… He was appointed to carry out a special report on Guatemala and completed his researches in September.

"Bishop Taylor asserts 'Wherever we went, people were complaining about this very unsatisfactory report put in by Lord Colville, a U.N. appointed observer who couldn't speak Spanish and who went around with representatives of the Guatemalan government'.

"Bishop Taylor was deeply impressed to meet a group of representatives from the wives, mothers and sisters of 225 men who have disappeared in recent months. 'We hope that by speaking out we'll be doing something for the people of Guatemala. We were so convinced of the evils of the regime and the violations of human rights as well as the restrictions on the practice of religion'.

"Of the current regime, (Bishop Taylor says) 'There's no sign that the army of Guatemala intends to relinquish its total control of power or to implement serious reforms – such as the desperately needed agrarian reform. Without such fundamental structural changes, there appears no hope that the situation of gross injustice and fear will come to an end in the near future'.

"In response to Bishop Taylor, Lord Colville emphasises that his report hasn't yet been published and says he assumes that any conjecture about what it will say must be based on a press conference he gave in Guatemala.

"'It's a document intended to be read as a whole,' he says. 'Some things I am critical of, some things I give them a pat on the back for. The bishop will have to wait and see what's in the report.' Lord Colville isn't prepared to go into it in more detail pre-publication.

"Lord Colville responds to the criticism of his appropriateness on linguistic grounds by saying that he can speak Spanish, but not speak it very well. 'There isn't time for me to fumble around with a language at which I am not very good.'"

After my first visit to Central America in 1984, I returned there frequently. This book contains separate chapters on Guatemala and El Salvador. In the sections following, I merely mention a few details, along with a somewhat larger piece on Nicaragua.

EL SALVADOR

El Salvador is by far the smallest of the Central American republics (the books all say it is approximately the size of Wales) and it is the only one lacking two ocean coastlines – it has only a Pacific coast. Its people are possibly the most energetic and combative in Central America and their history is at least as violent as any in the region.

The recent civil war began in 1980 in a country where military dictatorship and right wing tyranny were the rule. There was an oligarchy of fourteen powerful families who owned most of the land and most of the wealth. Death squads, murderers hired by the army and their associates, were very active; tens of thousands of people were killed in the violence of the 1970s and 1980s. It was perhaps inevitable that a popular uprising should take place, which it did in 1980 with the creation of a guerilla army, the FMLN (*Farabundo Martí National Liberation Front*). The civil war continued into the 1990s, there were thousands of casualties, the death squads were active, people lived in terror – the whole country was in a state of confusion. Following the 1992 cease fire, the FMLN,

Liberation Theology?

or its political successor, gained many successes in local elections but had to wait until 2009 before gaining tenuous power at national level. It defeated ARENA, the conservative right-wing party favoured by El Salvador's rich and powerful. *Alianza Republicana Nacionalista* was founded in 1981 by Roberto D'Aubuisson, who, in all probability, was guilty of many crimes, especially murders carried out by death squads.

Although the country is officially at peace, the post-war years have brought a wave of violence – kidnapping, armed robbery, revenge killing – due, probably, to the number of guns and ex-combatants available, as well as to drug trafficking and to widespread poverty.

Of course most of the events which made news all over the world took place in the capital, San Salvador. One such event was the murder of the city's archbishop, Oscar Romero. When made archbishop in February 1977 he was not expected to "rock the boat" but, in fact, the almost daily violence changed him and he became increasingly courageous in his condemnation of the assassinations and the atrocities either carried out or tolerated by the army and the government. His weekly homilies, broadcast throughout the nation, were particularly outspoken and he began to receive ominous threats. Finally on Monday 24th March 1980 he was shot by a hired marksman (who may himself then have been shot by his hirers as a "precaution") as he celebrated Mass in the convent chapel of the Hospitalito de la Divina Providencia, a little hospital run by religious sisters and where the archbishop lived very simply in a cottage in the grounds.

Archbishop Romero's body is in a tomb in San Salvador cathedral and, despite Rome's reluctance, or at least slowness, in proceeding towards canonisation, he is popularly venerated as a saint by most Salvadoreans. One can visit the chapel where he was killed and the cottage where he lived. I have done so more than once.

I have also been fortunate enough to have met the next two archbishops: Archbishop Arturo Rivera y Damas, Romero's successor and also a heroic figure who unfortunately died very suddenly and unexpectedly, and Archbishop Fernando Sáenz Lacalle, who is Spanish and a member of Opus Dei. The auxiliary bishop, Gregorio Rosa Chávez, was one of Archbishop Romero's closest collaborators and, although after the arrival of Archbishop

Sáenz Lacalle he has been much less involved in diocesan affairs, his accounts of Archbishop Romero's activities and of his assassination are still heard with awe by those who meet him.

Nowadays there is not the same degree of tension between the archdiocese and the civil authorities, in large measure due to the great decrease in government and army violence against citizens, especially articulate and socially concerned Catholics.

It is astonishing that, at the funeral Mass for Archbishop Romero, only Mons. Arturo Rivera y Damas, soon to be Romero's successor, of all the bishops from other dioceses in El Salvador, was present. Most of the others disagreed with Romero's outspoken criticisms of the regime; but about thirty foreign bishops were there. At the end of the Mass, which had taken place in the square outside the cathedral with the altar and the coffin on the cathedral steps, shots were fired from the windows of the National Palace into the massive crowd. Several (estimates varying between thirty and fifty) were killed, some by the bullets and others crushed in the resultant panic.

Another event in San Salvador which made the country's reputation even grimmer took place on 16th November 1989 – the assassination of six Jesuit priests, faculty members of the University of Central America, along with their housekeeper and her teenage daughter. UCA had been for some years critical of the human rights record of the Salvadorean government and army. One night, during a period of great tension and fear in the city, a death squad, commissioned and protected by the authorities, entered the Jesuits' residence, ordered the six priests to go to the little garden outside and shot them there in cold blood. Because of the tension, the two women had been advised not to walk home after work that day but, for safety's sake, to spend the night in the residence. To prevent their being able to give their account of the priests' murders, they also were taken out and shot.

A few months before the crime, our CIIR delegation had visited the university and had been welcomed and shown round by Fr Segundo Montes SJ, soon to be one of the victims. On later visits to the country, I have tried to make a little pilgrimage to the university and the place where the Jesuits and the two women were murdered. Their residence has been refurbished and is again in use, there is a small museum which tells the story of the murder and has various documents, photographs and personal articles on view and, perhaps most moving, the little garden has now six red rose bushes and two white, planted and blooming on the spot where the bodies were found after the crime. The tombs of the six priests are on one side of the sanctuary in the modern university chapel – now very much a shrine to their memory – only a few steps from their residence. May they rest in peace.

I met some remarkable people in El Salvador – people who have suffered greatly, people with dreadful memories, heroic people. Among these last, I must mention María Julia Hernández, director of *Tutela Legal* ("Legal Protection"), the human rights office of the archdiocese of San Salvador. *Tutela Legal* was formed in 1982 and María Julia has been its director from the start. She is a small, affable, friendly person who sits behind a desk totally covered with documents, reports, letters and other papers to a height of at least a foot – but she is a remarkably active lady always ready to travel to anywhere in the country where she is needed.

The work that she and her staff do is to monitor the human rights situation, to investigate reports of murders and disappearances, to follow up people's complaints of torture or ill-treatment in prisons, especially pre-trial treatment etc. When I visited her in 2004, she told me that she has to work as hard as ever, investigating war crimes, clandestine cemeteries which have been discovered, and complaints by victims of injustices. El Salvador, she said, had more violent deaths in 2003 than had occurred in the final years of the civil war.

The following morning she was leaving at 3 am to drive to a distant town to investigate certain allegations about human rights violations. She is indefatigable, fearless. She could have been murdered or "disappeared" on many occasions when her reports were unwelcome to the authorities. This truly heroic woman survived all such dangers but died, aged 68, after a short illness, on 30 March 2007. May she rest in peace. The present archbishop, José Luis Escobar Alas, disbanded *Tutela Legal* in 2013.

It is through knowing people like María Julia Hernández that one is humbled and yet enriched, aware that Central America, though it has suffered so much from poverty, violence and injustice, can also be so uplifting to one's spirit and make one praise God for such goodness and beauty.

Chapter 5 describes my experiences as an acting parish priest in Dulce Nombre de María (a parish in the north of El Salvador) in 1991.

NICARAGUA

Nicaragua is, in many ways, a bizarre country, certainly different from its Central American neighbours and even, it seems to me, surreal. It endured the cruel tyranny of the Somoza dynasty from 1937 until the revolution in 1979 led by the Sandinistas – FSLN (*Frente Sandinista Liberación Nacional*), founded in 1962 and named after Augusto César Sandino who led an unsuccessful revolt in 1920 and was later executed.

Elections held in 1980 and again in 1984 returned the Sandinistas under the presidency of their leader, Daniel Ortega. While in power, they distributed the vast lands of Anastasio Somoza and his family and began successful national health and literacy campaigns.

Since 1981, guerilla warfare led by the "Contras" against the Sandinistas had been a serious problem, especially since the Contras were supported financially, politically and militarily by the United States which did everything it could to destabilise the country.

A peace agreement was reached in 1988 and, in the subsequent general elections, the Sandinistas were unexpectedly defeated. A coalition government, led by Violeta Chamorro and composed mainly of right-wing parties, held power from 1990 until 2006. Some of the leaders were jailed for fraud and corruption, while the Sandinistas were weakened by internal splits. However, the latter regained power in 2006, under the leadership of Daniel Ortega, who declared himself to be no longer a Marxist but a Christian.

I visited Nicaragua several times during the 1980s from 1984 onwards. Let me quote from the report made by our CIIR/SCIAF delegation of 1987:

"Managua must be one of the strangest of all capital cities. The centre was almost totally flattened in the 1972 earthquake and, because of the continuing danger and the need to use available funds for other purposes, it has not been rebuilt. To stand and look around gives one the eerie impression of being somewhere that is a cross between Pompeii and Hiroshima. The cathedral is roofless and overgrown with weeds, the National Palace (the former parliament building) has been patched up and is in use as government offices, the Intercontinental Hotel stands in splendid isolation and the rebuilt National Stadium was solemnly inaugurated during our visit. Ironically the occasion was marked by an international baseball series – the Nicaraguans may be at odds with the US, but they love the US national game – with teams from Nicaragua, Cuba, Mexico and the Dominican Republic. But there is little else except the streets, neatly and regularly intersecting a vast area of grassland.

As a result, 'sprawling' is a word that might have been coined with Managua in mind, since a large number of widely separated suburbs have been constructed. Even if you have transport, it is extremely difficult to locate an address and, of course, for the great majority of people who are without cars and who must rely on the skeletal bus service, the daily journey from home to work and back is an ordeal." (CIIR/SCIAF, *A Thousand Times Heroic*, 1988, p.64)

It was obvious that, in the 1980s, the Catholic Church in Nicaragua was divided in its attitude to the Sandinistas. The bishops, some priests and some lay people were against them and regarded the government as Marxist and dangerous. On the other hand, most religious (male and female), many diocesan priests and most lay people supported the Sandinistas. It was an unhappy division and produced a lot of bitterness.

During our visits to Nicaragua, we had many meetings with government ministers and officials and with religious leaders. Perhaps the two most interesting occasions were our meetings with Cardinal Miguel Obando y Bravo SDB and with Violeta Chamorro.

Despite many requests, the archbishop of Managua was unable to see us until at last he agreed to a short meeting early one morning. He was courteous but very firm in his dislike of the Sandinista government. This attitude made him very unpopular with many Nicaraguans ("the Church once again siding with the rich") but he did not seem upset by this. He had, of course, the support of the Vatican for his stance, exemplified by his being made a cardinal in 1985 and, for many years, the only Central American member of the Sacred College.

The Chamorro family is famous in Nicaragua. Violeta's husband was murdered by the Somocistas and her children were to be found in the ranks of both the Sandinistas and the Contras. At the time we met her she was owner and editor of a daily newspaper but she later became the country's president. She was violently against the Sandinistas, fanatically so and to such an extent that I thought she was unbalanced. The meeting was a strange experience. She talked incessantly and her views were totally black and white. It must have been one of her bad days. I believe that, when she became president, her manner, if not her politics, was more controlled.

I did not meet Daniel Ortega in Nicaragua but did so later, when he was given a civic reception in Glasgow and attended Sunday Mass in St Aloysius' church in the city. I remember that, at the reception, he pointed to Cardinal Winning and asked me if he was a Catholic.

Several times during CIIR delegations to Nicaragua, we left the capital to visit other parts of the country. One such visit, in 1987, is especially memorable and I quote the account of it which we included in our subsequent published report.

"The most memorable experience we had in Nicaragua was the weekend we spent with Fr John Medcalf of Arundel and Brighton diocese, the only English priest working in Nicaragua. Fr Medcalf is parish priest in an area of the Atlantic Coast region, deep in the war zone.

Two weeks before we arrived the parish had been the target of a Contra attack, along with four other towns along the Rama road, the only road that connects the Atlantic Coast region with Managua.

In his regular newsletter Fr Medcalf described what happened.

> On October 15 this village of Muelle was attacked by over 500 well-equipped Contras. The battle began at 3 am and continued uninterrupted until 6 am. The din of mortars, machine-guns and ricocheting shrapnel was horrendous. The attackers penetrated simultaneously at three different points – the high road, the bridge over Monkey River and Death Canyon. Their chief objective was probably to blow up the bridge.

> The Contras surged into several of the village streets. We heard them shouting slogans. The Sandinistas made a temporary retreat, only to return with reinforcements for the street fighting. The bridge was saved and the Contras dispersed when their supply of ammunition came to an end.
>
> We opened up the parish hall to the wounded and dead. They were brought in from all parts of the village. Our canvas stretcher-beds were quickly drenched in blood since we used them for those worst wounded. Others were laid on the tiled floor. I have so many indelible impressions of that day... There were more than 30 gravely injured and 20 dead. The morning seemed endless as we waited for an ambulance to transport the injured to hospital.
>
> Rumours began to reach us that four other villages had been attacked that night. At 2 pm a Sandinista driver made a bad mistake. Having found the dead bodies of three Contras near the bridge, he strung them up on the back of his open lorry, heads down, like sides of beef bound for an unhygienic market. The driver's fury was understandable, but many villagers protested as he drove through the streets with the almost naked bodies waving grotesquely. I spoke with the mayor and we agreed to give them a Christian burial in a common grave in the village cemetery, as soon as possible. There were no more coffins available by this hour of the day, but by 4 pm the three soldiers had been buried in plastic sheeting and a rustic cross marks their grave.

When we arrived in Muelle de los Bueyes, where the parish house and centre are located, the people were still stunned by the attack. There was a constant, pervasive fear that there could be a repeat attack and for that weekend we experienced what it is like to live with that kind of insecurity and tension, never knowing when the Contras will strike again and listening all night to the exchange of fire as the fighting raged a few miles away.

There was also the moment, about 11 pm, of sheer and sudden terror when a machine-gun opened up right outside the presbytery and convent where we were staying. We immediately jumped – literally! – to the conclusion that the Contras had invaded the village again and that we were caught in the middle of a battle. In fact, the cause of the disturbance was one of the villagers who regularly got drunk and liked to mark the occasion by firing off a few bursts. Some of the party were given this explanation immediately, others not until the next morning. For the latter it was a long and anxious night.

Our journey from Managua to Muelle had not been without incident… Until we reached Juigalpa we had seen very few people on the road and little sign of any special security measures. On the second stage of the journey, however, it was very different – we were now in 'Contra territory'. Bridges over every stream and gully – and there are many in this rolling hill country – are guarded by the military and a good many carry signs indicating that the area around the bridge has been mined. At one point we had to make a slight detour when we reached one bridge which had been badly damaged in the Contra attack on the night described by Fr Medcalf.

From time to time we came across open trucks packed with people jammed shoulder to shoulder in the back – Nicaragua's inter-city express coach service. The journey to Muelle de los Bueyes taught us many things about the daily hardships and difficulties faced by many ordinary people in Nicaragua.

There are approximately 40,000 people in Fr John's parish, which is made up of several small towns or villages and 66 outlying hamlets. The parish centre is located in Muelle de los Bueyes, where we stayed. The parish has a team of two priests, three Franciscan sisters from the United States and six deacons. There are also 120 delegates of the Word and 500 catechists. The sisters' home had been caught in the crossfire during the recent battle and was now, as they commented, 'air-conditioned' by bullet holes. As in other parts of Central America, the area covered by the parish is huge and the priests can get to the various hamlets only once every few months when they go out on one of their regular 'safaris'. The journeys are very arduous and involve long distances which have to be covered on foot, on horseback or by mule through difficult jungle terrain.

There is also always a danger of running into groups of armed Contras, as indeed both priests have done in the past. Sunday Mass is a rarity in the remote areas and the weekly religious celebration is usually led by a delegate who conducts a Liturgy of the Word and presides at the distribution of Communion. The delegates of the Word, here as elsewhere in the region, are of any age and either sex, but are chosen not only for leadership qualities but also because of their exemplary lives. Another quality required in delegates is courage. In other parts of Central America they are often seen as a threat to privilege and wealth, and become victims of the army's suspicion and repressive measures; some have been killed, others tortured, kidnapped or imprisoned. In this part of Nicaragua the delegates face similar dangers, but in this case it is from the Contras, who have often targeted delegates of the Word, as well as health workers and teachers, as being supporters of the Sandinistas.

On Sunday morning we went with Fr Medcalf along the Rama road and across the bridge which had been the Contras' target in the recent attack, to the nearby village of Cara de Mono, literally 'Monkey Face' but, in deference to the feelings of its inhabitants, also called Santa Ana, which is the name of the parish church. There we joined the local community for Mass. It was a most moving experience, especially when some mothers in the congregation, who had lost sons in the war, began to speak of their pain and sadness. It was the day before All Souls' Day, the Day of the Dead, a very important day in Latin America. The delegate of the Word in this village is also the local midwife and a very fit and active grandmother. She told us that she has to carry a gun when she is fulfilling her duties because health workers are a particular target of the Contras. It is a sad irony that this woman, whose job it is to assist in bringing new life into the world, is forced to carry an instrument of death.

The following day we returned to Managua but, before leaving Muelle, we celebrated Mass. It was All Souls' Day and Mass with the people of Muelle, several of whom had sons killed, was a poignant and memorable occasion. We were privileged to share in their grief and in their faith. Our last act, as we drove out of the village, was to stop at the cemetery, thronged that day, and to pray at the graves of the young men, both Sandinistas and Contras, who had lost their lives in such a tragic and needless way." (CIIR/SCIAF, *A Thousand Times Heroic*,1988, pp.64-68)

Through all their woes, the Nicaraguans have not lost their mordant wit. "Poor Nicaragua", they would say, "God seems to send us one disaster after another – the Somoza dictatorship, the 1972 earthquake, hurricanes, the papal visit..." This referred to Pope John Paul II's pastoral visit in 1983 when, at the open-air

Mass in Managua, some mothers pleaded aloud with the pope to pray for their sons killed by the Contras. The Holy Father became very angry and ordered them to be silent – a most embarrassing incident which, along with the pope's public rebuke to those priests who were ministers in the Sandinista government, left Nicaraguans with unpleasant memories of the papal visit to their country. Since then, Nicaragua's troubles have continued – a rolling back of the literacy and health campaigns which had been set up by the Sandinista government, a devastating hurricane in 1998. a severe drought in 2001 – and most of the population still living at subsistence level or worse.

HONDURAS AND COSTA RICA

Having been in Honduras only twice, and once in Costa Rica – each time as a member of CIIR delegations – my experience of the countries is very limited and my impressions superficial.

Honduras is a country in which the civilian population is tightly controlled by the military, where most of the people live in poverty and which, compared with other Central American republics, has shown little organised resistance to a repressive regime. To an extent this may be due to some limited land reform in the 1970s but traditionally the Hondurans see themselves as lacking the energy, initiative or drive that would produce violent and armed resistance. "We are not belligerent like the Salvadoreans", I was told.

For decades there was hostility between El Salvador and Honduras which, in June 1969, erupted in the "soccer war" between the two nations, El Salvador being furious at being defeated by Honduras in a World Cup eliminator. There were other reasons for the short war, but the match result seems to have been the last straw.

Honduras, in return for considerable financial aid, has allowed itself to become the principal US military base in Central America. Large numbers of United States army and air force personnel are stationed in Honduras for training purposes and as supply headquarters for the region and also, presumably, to "defend" Central America from communism and Marxist revolutionaries.

During my two visits we spent some time in the capital, Tegucigalpa, a busy, congested city with an airport perilously near dense and high-rise housing close to the city centre. We also managed to visit some towns, villages and parishes to the north and to the south of the country and listened, sadly, to the usual stories of poverty, oppression and fear.

Costa Rica is the most southerly of the Central American republics. Its southern border is the frontier with Panama which, formerly part of Colombia, is therefore not considered to be a Central American country.

Costa Rica is different from the other four Central American nations. It has no armed forces, is peaceful, relatively prosperous and with better social, educational and cultural resources than the others. Hence it does not attract human rights organisations such as CIIR.

On my one brief visit to Costa Rica – for a conference about the situation elsewhere in Central America – my impression was it seemed to live up to its reputation: orderly, clean, modern and quiet, at least compared with its neighbours.

GUATEMALA

Guatemala is a land of enchantment with a tragic history. It has natural beauty in abundance: Lake Atitlán surrounded by volcanoes is breathtakingly lovely; the Cuchumatanes mountains are like a huge wall or barrier behind which lies the mysterious district of Ixil; the historic city of Antigua was the Conquistadores' capital of all Central America; and most of the Guatemalan people are Mayans with the women in their traditional and dazzlingly colourful costumes – what a wonderful country but what a tragic history.

My first visit to Guatemala took place in October 1984 but I have been back many times, early on as a member of CIIR delegations but, more recently, on my own to visit friends, especially Bishop Julio Cabrera Ovalle, a dedicated and fearless pastor and a dear friend.

Monseñor Cabrera was bishop of the diocese of Quiché for fifteen years (1987 – 2002). He had been rector of the national major seminary and then a parish priest in Guatemala City. I first met him in his diocese in 1987. From then on, he would introduce me as the first bishop to visit him in the "afflicted" diocese of martyrs of which he was pastor.

Let me explain a little. Quiché is in the high plains and mountains of northwest Guatemala, with a largely indigenous population. For some years it was under martial law of the most vicious and cruel kind. The government and the army saw the people as rebellious and were determined to subdue them. This they tried to do by terror, with massacres, kidnappings, disappearances, all finally and fully catalogued in 1998 in the volumes of "*Guatemala: Nunca Más*". Specifically, the Church was the principal target of the oppression, above all the catechists, sacristans and others active in the parishes.

The diocese of Quiché had been staffed, since its creation in 1967, by Spanish priests, Missionaries of the Sacred Heart. In June and July 1980, two of them were assassinated at the behest of the military and, with other assassinations threatened, including his own, the bishop of the time, Mons. Juan Gerardi and most of the priests fled temporarily from Quiché. A few priests remained and one of them was murdered in February 1981.

Since the Guatemalan government refused to allow Mons. Gerardi to re-enter Guatemala on his return from a meeting with Pope John Paul II, the Vatican then appointed, as an interim measure, an apostolic administrator, Mons. Pablo Urízar, whom I met when I first went to Quiché in 1984.

To achieve a solution to the problem, Mons. Gerardi, when permitted to return to Guatemala, did not resume as bishop of Quiché, but was made an auxiliary bishop of Guatemala City. Later he led the editorial team which published "*Guatemala: Nunca Más*" and was himself assassinated in April 1998 a few days after the work was published! Bishop Gerardi told me once that his decision to leave the diocese of Quiché temporarily with most of the priests in 1980 was the most difficult decision of his life; he didn't know if he had done the right thing but at least it produced worldwide publicity for the atrocities being carried out in Quiché.

With the transfer of Mons. Gerardi to Guatemala City, the way was open for the appointment of a new bishop – and Mons. Julio Cabrera was chosen by Rome for the post.

During my visits to Quiché, I accompanied Mons. Cabrera to nearly all of the parishes in the vast diocese. On one occasion he took me to the parish of Playa Grande in the area known as Ixcán in the north of the diocese, near the Mexican border. There is no road directly through the diocese to Playa Grande, so our journey, in a 4-wheel drive vehicle, took us two days and was by road and track round, as it were, three sides of a square. Although the military presence was still very evident, new villages and settlements were slowly springing up, many of them peopled by those who had been refugees from the terror, some having fled to Mexico and others, amazingly, having survived hidden in the mountains, forests and jungles of Guatemala.

The story that these internal refugees had to tell was astonishing. The army never succeeded in capturing them, they lived in desperate poverty but somehow managed to grow food, to educate their children, to care for those who became ill. They survived thus for years, their existence known to only a very few. Bishop Cabrera heard about them and made a memorable visit where he received an emotional welcome. Gradually, as conditions got a little less dangerous, the CPRs as they were known ("*Comunidades de Población en Resistencia*") emerged from hiding; it was some of them, as well as those who had fled to Mexico, who were repopulating Ixcán. Conditions were very primitive in the new settlements and I was privileged to hear many tales of heroism amid murders, disappearances and cruelty as well as of escapes and survival against all the odds. The strong, simple faith of so many of these people was truly edifying and their unfailing kindness was heart-warming.

I have already spoken of the area known as Ixil, to the north of the diocese, but south of Playa Grande and Ixcán. It is hidden behind the enormous barrier of the Cuchumatanes range and is reached by a track (now with an asphalt surface) that consists of hairpin bends, steep inclines and many stretches with cliffs on one side and precipices on the other. The views are stupendous if you are not too frightened to look.

Ixil has three huge parishes – Nebaj, Chajul and Cotzal, each with many outstations. It is a beautiful area among the mountains but the people, who have their own language, different from those further south and further north, are poor peasants with very few educational possibilities and a history of violent and bloody repression by the Guatemalan army. I visited Ixil many times and became very friendly with the German parish priest of Cotzal and the Italian parish priest of Chajul. All three of the parishes had had many martyrs and there had been several instances of "massacres", where whole communities had been murdered.

Yet, somehow or other, normal life continues despite the fear which had been added to the people's poverty-stricken daily existence. A guerilla army of sorts operated in Ixil, as in other war-torn parts of Guatemala, but without the organisation that characterised the FMLN in El Salvador or the FSLN in Nicaragua.

On one occasion, however, when the parish priest of Chajul was driving me back from Nebaj to his parish, we were stopped by a group of guerrilla fighters who suddenly emerged from the maize plants growing at the road side. They were very courteous, especially when they discovered we were priests, but explained their reasons for having taken up arms, and "asked", probably expecting, some help from us. On other occasions the men might have taken clothes or watches or radios or money but on that occasion they seemed satisfied with a share of the bread we had bought in Nebaj.

In Chajul the parish priest has been very active in establishing and promoting the "Asociación Chajulense Va'l Vaq Quyol" in the parish. It is basically a cooperative of which all local small farmers and producers, whether parishioners or not, can become members. The cooperative then markets their produce, especially coffee, much more widely than the individuals could, not only in Guatemala but in the United States, Canada and Europe. Moreover, the cooperative has now gone over to organic products exclusively. This initiative has brought some prosperity to an area in which, previously, only the owners of the large estates lived above subsistence level.

After forty years of violence with, it is reckoned, 160,000 killed, the civil war in Guatemala came to an end in 1996 but unfortunately the nation has now entered another era of violence and personal danger as the result of a great wave of murders, kidnappings (particularly of children) and armed robbery. Unemployment, especially after demobilisation, drug trafficking and revenge feuds have all contributed to the wave of crime.

So Guatemala remains an uneasy country and, in my opinion, the basic reason for generations of unrest, violence and oppression is the inequality of land ownership. Relatively few families own huge amounts of the best land, millions of peasants have either a few hectares of poor land – or none at all, seeking work on the big estates in dreadful conditions and with miserable levels of pay. Moreover, through their power, their influence and widespread corruption, the rich become richer, proper land redistribution never takes place, and nothing changes.

Another powerful influence for decades has been the Latin American policy of the United States. Not only has the USA. defended the interests of the estate owners, some of whom are United States multinational companies, but it has tended to condemn peasant unrest and denounce those who took up arms, accusing them of being agents of Communist subversion. Hence the United States has aided the Guatemalan government policy of repression by awarding huge financial grants, by sending expert military advisors and by training Guatemalan officers in counter-terrorist warfare. United States policy in Guatemala, and in Central America generally, has been interfering, shameful and immoral. The massive violation of human rights by the United States in Central America is one of the great scandals of our age, yet its perpetrators seem either unaware or, even worse, unconcerned.

On one memorable occasion in Guatemala, I spent a week in the parish of Chajul in Ixil, visiting a number of villages in the mountains, experiencing the people's living conditions, listening to their stories, ministering to their spiritual needs. That experience I have narrated in Chapter 4, which describes in full my visit to Guatemala in 1989.

Throughout his fifteen years as bishop of the diocese of Quiché, Julio Cabrera had shown himself to be a caring, energetic, courageous and dedicated pastor. He knew the people, became aware of their culture, their problems and their sufferings, became a father to the priests and religious, fostered vocations to the priesthood, encouraged lay people to be active and involved, and was always available to everyone. Quiché was a very dangerous place but the bishop did not flinch from criticising the authorities and especially the military – his Sunday homilies were broadcast each week – and in every possible way encouraging the people in their lives of suffering and fear. On several occasions he was "warned about his conduct" by the military and I often thought that, fearless as he was and determined to be faithful to his mission, he would be murdered.

But in fact, early in 2002, he was transferred by the pope to the diocese of Jalapa, in south-east Guatemala, an area where there had been, over the years, a great deal less unrest and violence. He accepted the decision obediently and moved to his new diocese, accompanied by his personal staff of five remarkable indigenous ladies, two to assist in his office and three to look after the domestic arrangements. When I spent some time with him in October 2004 he had already made a great impression, inaugurating a new pastoral centre for the diocese and inspiring priests, religious and laity to share his untiring zeal.

PRESENT THOUGHTS AND PAST EXPERIENCES

FAITH

Life is God's first gift to us and then consequently God gives us those gifts which are needed for life's preservation and development, especially the gift of loving parents.

As Catholics we also thank God for the special and additional gifts that are sometimes called supernatural – and basic among these is faith.

To the question "What is faith?" the *Catechism of Christian Doctrine* which we used when I was at school answered that "Faith is a supernatural gift of God that enables us to believe without doubting whatever God has revealed".

"*The Catechism of the Catholic Church*" (1992) is similar but longer: "Faith is the theological virtue by which we believe in God and believe all that he has said and revealed to us and that Holy Church proposes for our belief, because he is truth itself" (§1814).

These descriptions are fine as far as they go, but they do not go very far. They intend to tell us what faith is, they analyse its essence, but questions remain. Are the two definitions not in danger of begging the question by using the word "believe"? What does that word mean? And I am sure that most of us seek not to have a definition of faith, but to have faith. And by that I do not mean the body of teaching that is sometimes called "the faith" (as in "We have the true faith") but a total conviction of the truth of what God reveals to us (through Jesus and the Church). Am I totally convinced – and on the grounds of God's truthfulness and trustworthiness, and not only on human motives, either my own or others'?

These are vitally important matters obviously. Am I convinced that God exists? Am I convinced that there is a life after death? Eternal life with God?

In the seminary during our philosophy course we were taught the "Five Ways" as laid out by St Thomas Aquinas – five ways of proving by reason that there is (or rather must be) a God. They are metaphysical proofs and convince me; in summary, that you cannot have even an infinite number of caused causes – there has also to be a first cause, a being that is not dependent on another for its existence. There are also the powerful arguments for God's existence based on the order, complexity, beauty of the universe and its components – all of which cannot have happened by chance but demand a supreme intelligence.

But never forget that faith is a gift of God to us and, though we can use our reasoning to develop it and discover its implications, its source is not ourselves or our powers of reasoning. As Pope Benedict XVI has pointed out: "The first act by which one comes to faith is God's gift" (*Porta Fidei,* no. 10). The Second Vatican Council declares: "Before faith can be exercised, we must have the grace of God to move and assist us; we must have the interior helps of the Holy Spirit" (Constitution on Divine Revelation, *Dei Verbum*, no. 5).

One could continue to ask questions and some of them still challenge us as well as theologians. For example, does God offer the gift of faith to every human being (because if not, that would seem unjust)? If Catholic Christianity possesses the truth about God etc., where does that leave others? Do Jews and Muslims not have the same utter conviction of faith that we should have, but whose tenets contradict some Christian beliefs? But I digress and prefer to leave such questions to better theologians than me.

God gives us faith – and God will strengthen that gift if I pray. I often think of the incident in the gospel and identify with the man who said to Jesus "Lord, I believe. Help my unbelief" (Mark 9:24).

And God does just that. Personally, I find my faith strengthened when I am with others and worshipping in particularly moving circumstances – on a pilgrimage, at an ordination or funeral, when celebrating the sacrament of reconciliation, at a charismatic event. We need Tabor occasions to restore and strengthen our faith on the journey through life to death, to reassure us that there is a beyond and that God awaits us there.

One personal memory, a powerful Tabor occasion, will always be vivid with me. It was in September 1967 and I had been called home from Spain because my father was dying. Although he was very weak I was able to spend a lot of time with him. He liked when I said Night Prayer aloud from the Breviary. One psalm spoke of death and the grave – and I broke down and wept. He called me over to his bed, to embrace me and console me and to tell me that he had no fear of death since he was, and would be, in God's hands. At that moment, I experienced a renewal of faith, an awareness that, no matter what doubts might tempt me in the future, I had been totally convinced of God's loving providence. The memory of that experience sustains me as a very personal support to the faith I received at baptism.

PRAYING

Praying is not easy. At least, for me, it isn't. Perhaps that statement needs to be qualified. It is easy enough to *say* prayers and perhaps also it should be added that the near inevitability of distractions while saying prayers does not destroy their value. But when I say that praying is difficult I mean the quality and amount of time I am willing to give, the priority that praying has in my life, the faith which I bring to prayer, the daily commitment, the perseverance…

It is humbling when people presume that a priest, indeed a bishop, is good at praying, that he knows the secret that they don't know, that he is an expert because he is ordained. I feel like saying "it's not so" but such a disclaimer is taken for humility and only increases the fiction.

Anyway, having got that off my chest, let me offer some thoughts, experiences and preferences on prayer. (For the present, I prescind from writing about praying the Eucharist – the best of all prayers – and the sacraments, as they are in a class apart from other prayer).

The Divine Office (the Breviary and/or the Prayer of the Church) is not the burden that it was until Vatican II. That Council decreed that in order that the Office be better and more perfectly prayed it was to be "restored" in accordance with certain principles. The two obvious results of this decree were a) a considerable shortening of the Breviary and b) permission to have it in translation. So nowadays the psalms, prayers and readings of the Divine Office are more accessible. (A Canadian priest once told me how glad he was to have the Breviary in English "because the only Latin word I know is 'Alleluia!'")

There is less excuse nowadays for "fulfilling the obligation" by merely verbal recitation. It is not too difficult to pay attention to the meaning of at least some of what we are saying. A further advantage is the fact that we should distribute the different parts of the Office throughout the day, Morning Prayer in the morning, etc. (where, pre-Vatican II, it was permissible to say the whole Office, including Night Prayer, first thing in the morning or, perhaps more commonly, the entire Office, including Morning Prayer, last thing at night).

However, there are suggestions that further reform of the Breviary would help. The "Office of Readings" (formerly called Matins) could do with a better and wider selection of readings; the Divine Office which diocesan priests are obliged to pray daily is probably still too monastic (i.e. more suited to the needs of a community of monks); and the Breviary should be able to attract wider use by lay people, whether individually or in groups or as the parish community.

The Divine Office is a wonderful treasury (of psalms as Christian prayer, of specifically Christian prayers, and of Scripture and other sacred readings) awaiting further discovery and use in the Church.

The Rosary is still a favourite prayer for many Catholics, sometimes said in common but more often, I think, by individuals. It used to be said daily by priests and religious, but less so nowadays. Yet Pope John Paul II prayed the Rosary and constantly recommended it to us.

I have found the new "Mysteries of Light" which Pope John Paul introduced in 2002 - 2003 to be extremely usable and helpful. Not only do they fill a huge gulf between the Fifth Joyful Mystery and the First Sorrowful Mystery, but they cover the period of Our Lord's public ministry and highlight five events of outstanding importance, each of which challenges us to repeated reflection on its significance.

On a personal note, I am especially glad to have the Transfiguration included as one of the Mysteries of Light. For a number of reasons I have a particular affection for that event and am delighted at its increased prominence in our devotion. The Transfiguration is relevant for all of us –we need to have our own Tabors in our journey of faith!

Contemplative prayer is a beautiful experience and, for many, a new discovery. When I was in the seminary, we had a daily period of "mental prayer" or "meditation". We were given some instruction on how to do it and books that provided thoughts for each day's meditation. But I have to admit defeat – probably failure is more accurate. Were the instructions and materials too structured? Or not one's own? Or therefore boring? Or was six o'clock in the morning an unsuitable time?

However, in recent times, there has been the discovery that contemplative prayer is not forbidden territory for ordinary mortals or reserved only for very holy people living in monasteries. The methods are various, the structure much freer, help and advice readily available and, provided we are willing to give the time, the "technique" is simple and the result a beautiful intimacy with the God who loves us.

Charismatic prayer has, in the comparatively short time since its re-discovery, proved to be a powerful grace for many and a cause of bewilderment, even hostility, for others. Hundreds of books have been written about it but I restrict myself here to some personal reflections.

It is unfortunate, I think, that charismatic renewal became so distinct in the Catholic Church and so differentiated from other ways of praying. Perhaps that was inevitable since charismatic renewal and charismatic prayer take place in groups which meet regularly and therefore are seen as "different". Further, these groups were perceived, especially by some who did not join them, as being places of bizarre and even suspect practices (especially "speaking in tongues") and whose members had an elitist view of themselves.

In reality, charismatic renewal arose from an ardent wish to seek closer union with God, to be more open to the Holy Spirit, to receive the grace of conversion, to be holy (as Vatican II taught). Some gifts of the Holy Spirit which had not been conferred (requested) for centuries were received but so were more usual gifts, maybe with greater intensity (because sought more earnestly).

In a charismatic group there is much use of Scripture for prayer and also for learning about God and his plans for us and the world. There should also be authentic teaching by competent persons, prayer of praise, thanksgiving and intercession, and hymns. There can be opportunities for some to witness to God's action in their lives and for people to use God's gifts (which in New Testament Greek are called *charismata* – hence "charismatic").

One of these gifts is called "speaking in tongues" or, more frequently and simply, "speaking or singing without words". If this strikes one as silly or pointless, read what St Augustine said about it early in the fifth century:

"This is the way of singing that God gives you: do not search for words. You cannot express in words the sentiments that please God; so praise him with your jubilant singing. This is fine praise of God when you sing with jubilation. You ask, what is singing in jubilation? It means to realise that words are not enough to express what we are singing in our hearts. At the harvest, in the vineyard, whenever men must labour hard, they begin with songs whose words express their joy. But when their joy brims over and words are not enough, they abandon this coherence and give themselves up to the sheer sound of singing.

What is this jubilation, this exultant song? It is the melody that means our hearts are bursting with feelings that words cannot express. And to whom does this jubilation most belong? Surely to God... What else can you do when the rejoicing heart has no words and the immensity of your joy will not be imprisoned in speech? What else but 'sing out with jubilation'?" (*Sermon on Psalm 32*)

In Scotland Catholic charismatic prayer groups are fewer, smaller and probably less enthusiastic than they were in the 1970s and 1980s. This is at least partly explained, I believe, by the fact that much of what comprises charismatic renewal has already made its way into mainstream Catholic life in our parishes – a desire for conversion and holiness, a sense of community, sharing of faith and prayer, a greater use of Scripture and, not least, the widespread popularity of the contemporary Scripture-based hymns which charismatic prayer groups had known and used for years.

I first met Catholic charismatic renewal in the summer of 1974 when I was working for a couple of months in St Saviour's parish in Brooklyn. When subsequently, I was parish priest in Our Lady of Lourdes, East Kilbride, we had a prayer group which, having had a somewhat embarrassed birth and an extremely fragile infancy, developed into a thriving weekly meeting that brought powerful graces and much happiness to many.

I want to mention one grace of a charismatic prayer group that sometimes goes unnoticed or unmentioned – the group itself, which gives the participants so much support, friendship and joy in praying. That was one of the things which I most missed on leaving the parish – and yet, at the start, I confess that I had often been glad of an excuse to miss the weekly meetings.

Some final thoughts on prayer. Isn't it good that so many people want to learn to pray well? And that people see prayer as important and a means to holiness? One indication of this in Galloway diocese has been the growth of weeks of guided prayer. Lay people, familiar with Ignatian spirituality and trained as prayer guides, spend a week in any parish community that invites them. They share their knowledge and experience of prayer with individual parishioners seeking guidance and support. Prayer is indeed more and more on our agenda.

YOUTH MINISTRY

When we have meetings to discuss how things are in the parish or in the diocese, you can be fairly sure that someone will ask "Why is the Church not doing more for our youth?"

This always struck me not so much as a question but rather an accusation. The implication (to my guilty mind) seemed to be "You are the Church and you should be doing more for our young people"; perhaps also meaning "our young people have stopped going to Mass because they say it's boring".

I count myself fortunate in having had little direct responsibility for parish youth clubs. An early experience, it would be in 1951 or 1952 in Coatbridge, perhaps was sufficiently unnerving that it destroyed any confidence I might have had.

I was told by my parish priest that he thought I should set up a Boys' Guild in the parish. A meeting was called, a reasonable number of teenage boys turned up, and by common consent, indeed acclaim, we decided to form a football team. In those days Boys' Guild teams were frequent in Lanarkshire and there existed both a league and a cup competition.

Our first venture was to enter the cup tournament and St Bartholomew's, Coatbridge, was drawn against formidable opponents, St Joseph's, Blantyre. We had no kit and very limited funds so I accepted a "special offer" and bought the necessary jerseys and shorts. The jerseys were light blue in colour and this may have had a psychologically negative effect on our team because we did not do very well.

The referee had no watch so he asked the two touchline "managers" to let him know when it was time to blow for full-time. I recall, when the score was 16 – 0 in favour of St Joseph's, saying to my opposite number "I think it's time-up", whereupon he looked at his watch and replied "No, still two minutes to go". I am glad to report that, despite their manager's machinations, his team did not add to their score.

I forget what happened to our Boys' Guild but I suspect that our cup experience shattered their morale – and probably has obliterated my recollection of any subsequent activities.

As a teenager myself I had been enrolled in our local parish Boys' Guild. My only memory is of Sunday afternoon meetings in the parochial hall. About twenty of us would turn up and the main item on the agenda was calling the register. This consisted of a member of the Catholic Young Men's Society intoning several hundred names (or so it seemed), the effect being of an interminable succession of names, the great majority being followed either by a stony silence or a mumbled suggestion ("not here", "sick", maybe even "dead"). An occasional "present" did little to relieve the total boredom of this weekly performance. Other parishes must have done it better but, at that age, my reactions were limited to an anticipatory dread and a post-meeting sense of relief.

No wonder I feel guilty when someone asks why the Church is not doing more for the youth. My heart goes out to fellow inadequates and my total respect to the few, priests or laity, who are blessed with success.

After I became a bishop, people sometimes wrote to me with helpful suggestions. Here is one letter I received, from a young person, with his proposals for a youth-friendly parish.

"I am writing a letter to tell you how I am getting on. I am fine. How are you? The other day at school our teacher told us to write about our ideal parish. My story was like this. My ideal parish is to have a football team and a club where we could all meet just like a youth club. We could have a disco. We could have one night when all the children could meet and talk about the football games they have played lately and what the telly has been like." (Ryan, Kilmarnock)

Undoubtedly young people nowadays are generous and thoughtful. They have a highly developed sense of social justice. They will repeatedly help those in need and will protest against instances of institutionalised and social injustice. Issues of justice, peace and the environment are important for them. But older Catholics lament their absence from Mass and their apparent indifference to parish activities and "churchy" things.

Why, above all, do we see so few teenagers at Mass on Sundays? After all, we say, Mass is not offered as entertainment; it is not what we get out of it but what we put into it.

All of this is true but I do often sympathise with those who say that Mass is boring. Could we not make use of the opportunities and variations available and, without flouting liturgical rules and good taste, be more imaginative?

In addition, there is the menace called peer pressure. Why, to cite the most extreme case, do hundreds of thousands of young people take part so enthusiastically when the pope holds a World Youth Day? Why do they enjoy Lourdes or Taizé? Such places and events can make us feel very guilty about our own lack of success. One explanation, which I think has much to commend it, is that young people feel comfortable and will be involved provided they know that their peers are present and are also enthusiastic. If others of their generation are not there or are not obvious participants or, worst of all, if they feel that they will be ridiculed for even being there – is it any wonder that they "vote with their feet"?

I suspect that demanding to know "What can be done for our youth?" will not solve the problem. I really don't know the answer but I admire the priests and others who try – and the young people who still witness courageously to the faith they have received.

PILGRIMAGES

Not everyone enjoys pilgrimages. I suspect they are something of an acquired taste. You know the sequence: "No thanks, I don't like being organised", then "Well, I'll go if you think I ought to"; next, "it wasn't as bad as I expected" and finally "Yes, sure, I'll be there again."

Of course, we have to admit that pilgrimages nowadays are not nearly as arduous as they once were. With the notable exception of the *Camino de Santiago de Compostela* and its growing popularity, very few people these days can or do spend months in walking great distances to far-off shrines: apart from the danger of being killed or injured by traffic, we are no longer sufficiently fit! But a pilgrimage can still be difficult physically and/or financially.

The essential pilgrimage is the process of getting there rather than having reached one's goal. Even if that be the case, I have to confess that I have visited many shrines but with little effort in getting there – Guadalupe, Esquipulas, Beaupré, Fatima, Santiago de Compostela, Walsingham, Carfin…

I was a late convert to pilgrimages, both their value and their enjoyment. Perhaps in earlier years I resisted what I imagined would be the organised religiosity of pilgrimages, the enforced communal piety that I thought would be present – or perhaps I was just resistant to community. Whatever it was, I am now pro-pilgrimages and know their importance and the pleasure they can give.

On the last Sunday of August each year the Whithorn pilgrimage takes place, to the town on the south coast of Scotland where St Ninian established the first Christian community in Scotland and to the Cave at the edge of the sea where, two or three miles from the town, the saint would spend periods in solitude and prayer.

Hills enfold the bay, the sea is wide, the outline of the Isle of Man is visible away to the south. The setting is beautiful with the altar placed on a natural platform at the mouth of the Cave and the pilgrims on the beach and on the rocks around, below and even precipitously above. Moreover, despite the difficulty of the terrain, we have contrived a fine liturgy with sound system, keyboard or small organ, cantors and full ceremony and involvement, including (perhaps a little boldly but without mishap) communion under both kinds for all. The swampy path and the stony beach are made as easy as possible by hard-working Kilmarnock scouts and guides and the painful walk across the beach seems shorter by the presence of a faithful pilgrim piper.

The pilgrimage is memorable not only for the natural beauty, but also for the sense of history, tradition and sacred heritage we feel as today's pilgrims, worshipping God like so many generations of Christians have done for centuries. It is on such occasions and at such places that one has a sense of the faith having been handed down to us and of the presence of God still with his people and making the place sacred.

Of course there are also cheerful aspects to the Whithorn pilgrimage and people do enjoy themselves. I remember the only occasion I was at St Ninian's Cave before I became bishop of the diocese. Bishop McGee invited me to preach at the Mass at the Cave, the day was hot and sunny and, somewhat to my dismay, I noticed, as I began the homily, that a number of the pilgrims had left the Cave to go in for a bathe before returning when the homily was over.

There are more details about the Whithorn Pilgrimage in *Portrait of a Diocese*, at the start of the section, *Deanery by deanery*.

The Galloway custom for many years has been to have our diocesan pilgrimage to Lourdes take place every second year. The routine is too well known to require description but, for me, the great element of a Lourdes pilgrimage is the presence and involvement of the sick. It is they who are central to the pilgrimage. Their spirit, courage and cheerfulness are an inspiration to us all. They are a source of spiritual healing for everyone. For those privileged to be with them – doctors, nurses, helpers (male and female, young and old), priests, everyone – they bring out the best in us. They are the soul of the pilgrimage and the main reason for its success.

Let me make a couple of observations. First, there always seems to be a shortage of nurses and, even more, of helpers, male and female. The work can be long and tiring and does demand sacrifice but it is rewarding in several ways. Indeed I would go so far as to say that, as a helper, a pilgrim will experience a satisfaction and happiness from the pilgrimage at a greater intensity than otherwise. Nor can I overstate the value of the presence of young adults of secondary school age and older. They are asked to work hard and at unsocial hours but unfailingly it is a good experience for them, and a reassuring witness to the older pilgrims.

Regrettably it is not cheap to take part in the diocesan pilgrimage to Lourdes. For a week's "holiday", the price seems extortionate. Various ways of reducing the cost have been suggested but without any great success. Perhaps it is a sacrifice that has to be borne in order to have the graces that a Lourdes pilgrimage always gives. Miracles in the strict sense of the word are few at Lourdes, but all of us, sick and healthy, receive true healing from God, mediated through the Blessed Virgin.

We began Galloway pilgrimages to the Holy Land in the early 1980s and soon they began to alternate with our Galloway Lourdes pilgrimages, taking place every second year. Sadly, due to the disturbed state and violence of the Holy Land, we had fewer pilgrimages during the first decade of this century. Our pilgrimages have now resumed, even though conditions are by no means settled in that sacred but unsettled land. Unfortunately, there is no assurance that further interruptions will not occur.

For me the Holy Land pilgrimage – I have been there about twelve times – is always a wonderful experience. The reasons are obvious – the opportunity to be in the land where Jesus lived, to see the hills and valleys, the plains and the mountains which he knew, to sail on the Sea of Galilee on which he sailed (and walked), to visit the churches and shrines which mark the great events of his life in Bethlehem, Nazareth, Capernaum and Jerusalem. And to be on pilgrimage with other people of faith, to share their happiness, to witness the awed delight of first-timers – all of these greatly enhance the experience of being a pilgrim in the Holy Land.

Of course one cannot be a pilgrim in the Holy Land without being aware of the people who live there and of the sadness of their lives. There is still violence and conflict, innocent people are being killed or maimed and, generally, people live in fear and with little hope of peace. It is a dreadful situation and so pitifully ironic that all this should be happening in the land called holy. The violence is to be condemned but that is not sufficient. One has to ask why there is such violence, what causes it? The reason is injustice and I believe that the world must not only condemn the violence but also be courageous enough to name the injustices and do all it can to put an end to them. Much easier said than done, but I think that the violence will not be ended by "defeating the terrorists" until we have also ended the injustices that produce them. May God help the Holy Land, its Christians (who, sadly, are emigrating in large numbers to seek a peaceful life) and all its inhabitants, Jewish and Muslim as well as Christian.

An extended essay on the Holy Land is to be found as chapter 7 of this book.

I have said that I really enjoy pilgrimages, not only because of the locations and their associations but also because the company of so many "brothers and sisters in Christ" is always, for me, an enriching experience.

There is another reason also. The image of the Church that I find the most helpful is that of the Pilgrim Church. A pilgrimage is the Church in miniature, a living illustration of what the Church should be and is – a band of people with a common purpose and goal, travelling thither together, but inevitably with stragglers and strugglers, even some getting lost now and again; not too regimented as if on a route march but keeping our own individuality, ready to support, help, forgive and enjoy one another, and animated by a faith that allows us to be aware of the presence of Christ in our midst, encouraging us to continue in faith and hope and without fear.

Yes, there is nothing like a pilgrimage to enable us to know who and what we are in God's sight.

POLITICS

"The Church should keep out of politics". Yes, I agree that those who "speak for the Church" should not use that privilege in order to support or promote one side of a political issue or dispute – provided the issue is not one that involves morality as well as politics. In other words, many political issues are also ethical issues and, in such cases, the Church has the right, indeed the duty, of making its teaching known. This duty is not to be restricted to matters of individual and merely personal morality.

There are obvious examples of political issues which are also moral issues, such as a country's legislation on abortion and euthanasia but, in today's climate, the moral or ethical dimension of many problems is ignored or not understood and, as a result, there is a resentment at what is seen as Church "interference". But to keep quiet to avoid offence or resentment would be a dereliction of duty. As well as the right to life, I am thinking also of issues of social justice and human rights, of relations between the affluent nations and the "developing" world.

There is one issue current in this country that may, or may not, have its ethical dimension, so when I give my own opinion, I am speaking only personally and as a citizen and not in any way presuming to "speak for the Church".

I refer to the controversy regarding Britain and Europe. Should we approve the European Constitution? Should we change our currency to the euro? Should we leave, or stay in, the European Union?

I am a European and pro-European. I want to share in the culture of our continent as fully as possible, to be a citizen of a country with full membership in the community of Europe. Moreover I believe that the EU (in its earlier and developing stages, as it is now and as it will grow in the future) is our best safeguard for peace in a continent riven by conflict and violence since history began; as well as a means of bringing friendship, acceptance, toleration and cooperation to the nations and peoples whom it comprises.

The arguments against seem to me to be weak. At their worst, I suspect there is at times an element of xenophobia (and maybe even of religious antipathy) which is non-Christian and perhaps, to some extent at least, based on ignorance and fear.

Also weak, in my opinion, are the arguments (both pro and con, actually) that put all their emphasis on whether "it will be good *for us*". "Will it be to Britain's advantage?" seems to me to be a very selfish criterion if it does not also take into account the benefits to others of our being in (or not in). "National interest" may seem an obvious yardstick – but is it not also a selfish one? Indeed, if our country possesses so many advantages, should we not be sharing them rather than keeping them to ourselves?

Words can be demonised so that sometimes it is necessary only to mention them in order to dismiss what they signify as unacceptable; such words as constitution, integration, community, federation. Moreover, arguments against Europe often presume, erroneously, that Britain has been one nation for a thousand years or more – "our parliament", "our legal system", "our currency". Have they never heard what happened in 1707 or that, even today, not all of Britain has the same legal and education systems as England? There is an arrogance, I hope unconscious, in such specious assumptions.

My pro-European views are, I suspect, in part the result of my having lived "on the continent" for fifteen years, six in Italy and nine in Spain. I feel at home in Europe, I like the people, the music, the art, the scenery and the food. Even if Britain were to leave the EU, I could still go abroad and enjoy those things – but I do hope that we shall never turn away from being genuinely citizens of Europe as well as of our own nation.

Let us not stand aside, an island race that wants little part in European civilisation and culture, content to see "the continent" as not much more than a trading partner or a holiday destination.

It is encouraging to know that the Holy See and the Council of European Bishops' Conferences (CCEE) are strong and constant supporters of European integration. But perhaps that very support which they give is part of the problem for Britain.

MUSIC

When I was ten years old, all the children in our class were graded for singing – A, B or C. I was put among the Cs.

Then when I was in my first year in the seminary (I was 16 or 17), we each got a turn of singing, solo, the short prayer which opened Compline in Latin: "*Iube Domine, benedicere... Noctem quietam et finem perfectum...*". The prospect of making a fool of myself made me almost sick with fear, but the reality was even worse than I dreaded. It was one of those occasions when I should have been happy for the ground to open and swallow me.

Despite those incidents, which I remember vividly and with embarrassment, I love music and enjoy singing, as long as I am one among several.

I trace my awakening to the delights of music to a quartet of musicians who, again when I was 16 or 17, were brought to Blairs College one evening to entertain us young seminarians. Their programme was a series of popular classics which were totally new to me. Until then I had imagined classical music to be highbrow and boring. The quartet played Delibes' *Pizzicato Polka*, some of Saint Saens' *Carnival of the Animals,* Sibelius' *Valse Triste,* and a few other pieces. I thoroughly enjoyed that concert when "good music" was revealed to me.

When I was in the army, I saw my first opera – Puccini's *La Bohème* – and enjoyed it even if my sixpence (or shilling) got me only a standing place in the gods of a Belfast theatre. As students in Rome we frequently went to the Sunday evening concerts in the Teatro Argentina. The orchestra was usually the Accademia di Santa Cecilia and there were famous guest conductors and soloists – and on one occasion, a concert with Beniamino Gigli. He was the second world famous tenor I had heard. When I was much younger, my father took me to a church hall to hear Sir Harry Lauder, then semi-retired. "You will be able to say that you once saw and heard the great Harry Lauder", my father impressed on me.

Over the years my tastes have become wider – not just symphonies and operas, but chamber music of many kinds – and especially of course the great Spanish composers: Falla, Granados, Albéniz, Rodrigo… But I have to confess a difficulty in appreciating and enjoying what I suppose may be called contemporary music. Enough of this, however, because what I really meant to write about is church music and music in the liturgy.

Before I went to Blairs College in 1942, my experience of church music was limited to a small number of hymns that comprised the choir's repertoire in my home parish: *I rise from dreams of time, Sweet Sacrament divine, I'll sing a hymn to Mary, Hail Queen of heaven* and a few others.

The seminary introduced me to singing plainchant at Sunday High Mass. We had to learn and sing the various settings of the Common of the Mass (*Missa de Angelis*, *Credo III* etc). In addition, each week we practised the Proper of the Mass for the following Sunday: introit, gradual, offertory and communion antiphons. For this, each of us had acquired a thick volume called the *Liber Usualis.* For some months I was bewildered – I would vaguely follow the notes which accompanied the text of the introit but was totally mystified how we got through in such a short time the much greater number of notes which accompanied the text of the gradual. The mystery was eventually solved for me. Apparently we were simply using a psalm tone for the gradual (and not the full version) but that had not been explained (or if it was, I missed it).

I never cared much for the plainchant of the Mass, especially the Propers. Had we had a monastic choir properly trained, it would probably have been more attractive to me – but I particularly disliked choir practice and must have been a trial for successive choir masters.

Since English began to be used in the liturgy, church music has, of course, changed greatly. Much of it I find inspiring, moving and enjoyable – not only hymns but also settings of the liturgical texts and especially of the Mass. When the diocese of Galloway was preparing to celebrate 1997, the sixteenth centenary of its foundation by St Ninian, I asked James MacMillan, an Ayrshire man brought up in Cumnock, to compose a Mass setting. The result was *The Galloway Mass,* for which he refused to accept any fee and with which he honoured me by dedicating it to me.

As bishop I tried to encourage singing at Mass – not only suitable and good hymns but also, and more importantly, the parts of the Mass themselves. Some parts make little sense if not sung (the Acclamations) but it is also better if the psalm is sung. Many parishes responded very courageously and successfully – but I sometimes feel a) that, when the psalm is sung and there are four or five verses, it can be disproportionately long, especially if the first reading is a short one; and b) that, when a parish does not have a cantor to sing the psalm verses, a psalm-based hymn could be sung by the congregation, instead of merely "saying" the psalm.

I do not like paraphrases of, for example, the *Gloria* or the *Sanctus*, especially if the same melody is used for all the sung Mass parts, in spite of the very different themes and moods of the parts, from joyful praise to a prayer for forgiveness. And to return to the psalm, it should bear some relation to the foregoing reading.

People sometimes say that they would prefer "a quiet Mass with no singing " but I feel that such a request is a little unreasonable since some Mass texts *should* be sung. Not to sing them diminishes that liturgy.

The subject of music in church is, of course, a difficult one and can produce very mixed reactions and bad feelings. But most of us, I believe, are grateful for the fact that our worship, and especially at Mass, allows us to participate more fully by the fact that it contains music – and not just for a choir but for everyone to sing. Though well-known, the saying (mistakenly attributed to St Augustine?) is worth recalling: "They who sing pray twice".

THE ECCLESIOLOGY OF VATICAN II

The Second Vatican Council (1962 - 1965) was a total surprise, a cause of bewilderment and confusion, and an event whose effect has been to produce a revolution in our Church, a source of deep division but also a Spirit-led pastoral renewal.

I was a member of the teaching staff at St Peter's College, Cardross (the interdiocesan seminary for Glasgow, Motherwell and Paisley dioceses) when the Council was announced and during the first three of its four sessions. The world's bishops met for two or three months in St Peter's, Rome, each autumn from 1962 to 1965. My early reactions, which probably many priests and others shared, were not enthusiastic. Did we need a Council? Were things not all right in the Church? John XXIII seemed to have called the Council more or less on a sudden impulse while on a visit to St Paul's Basilica on the outskirts of Rome. And was he not simply imposing on the whole Church what he had already done in Venice and then, when he became pope, in the diocese of Rome? And the decrees of those two diocesan synods, as we had heard, had been very restrictive and authoritarian.

Despite prior doubts and uncertainty, the Council got down to business and over the four years of activity produced some very fine pastoral decrees to guide the Church's varied activities plus four "Constitutions" which are even more important – teaching documents on the Sacred Liturgy (*Sacrosanctum Concilium*), on the Church (*Lumen Gentium*), on Divine Revelation (*Dei Verbum*) and on the Church in the Modern World (*Gaudium et Spes*). These four Constitutions were truly innovative and, each in its own way, has changed not only the Church's teaching but the Church itself. The Holy Spirit spoke through the Popes (Paul VI having succeeded John XXIII in 1963) and the bishops of the Church.

Have we, the Church, listened?

It would be foolish to attempt to put the various teaching documents of the Second Vatican Council in order of importance, but surely the most basic is the Constitution *Lumen Gentium* on the Church.

Over the years since the Council I have gone through a learning curve about that Constitution and its implications as they have been developed, especially in the teaching of Pope John Paul II. The learning process has brought me joy, affirmation and a real sense of freedom.

As seminarians in Rome in the late 1940s, one of our major subjects was *De Ecclesia*, taught in Latin by a Jesuit, Fr Timoteo Zapalena. His Latin, spoken the Spanish way, was nearly incomprehensible to me but fortunately his lectures were all in his book.

It started by proving that the Church was monarchical (the Roman Pontiff) and hierarchical (the bishops). The vision was pyramidal and legalistic – but I wouldn't blame our professor because that was the accepted theology of those days and I had no problems with it. It was the theology that sustained and justified the ministry of bishops and priests at that time and, as far as I am aware, was questioned by few, if any, "ordinary Catholics".

The "*schema*" on the Church which was prepared for and presented to the bishops at the Second Vatican Council followed these lines. To the surprise and annoyance of some bishops, especially members of the Roman Curia, it was rejected by the majority of bishops and a new draft document was demanded.

That new document was *Lumen Gentium.* It still speaks of the hierarchical nature of the Church and the teaching authority of pope and bishops – but that is in chapter 3. The opening of the Constitution is on "the mystery of the Church", viz. it is God's kingdom on earth, inaugurated but not yet fully achieved, poor, persecuted, imperfect yet possessing the Holy Spirit; and the second chapter treats of "the People of God", i.e. all of us who are baptised members of the Church. There are later chapters on the laity, dealt with positively and not contrasted with clergy in a negative way, and on the universal call to holiness in the Church.

The Council's teaching on the Church was new for most of us in Scotland, it was refreshing and, at the same time, seemed daring, indeed revolutionary. Yet it is the teaching of an ecumenical council of pope and the world's bishops and so is certain and reliable. Since 1964, when *Lumen Gentium* was published, much authoritative teaching has been based on it, especially many documents from John Paul II. These include *Christifideles Laici* of 1988, his letters announcing and concluding the Millennium Jubilee Year, and his letter for the start of the third Christian millennium.

How much influence has all this had on our thinking and on our behaviour as members of the Church? A considerable amount, I think, but not yet enough. For example, what do we mean when we ask "What is the Church doing about it?"; again do we still assume that, somehow, priests and nuns should be, and are, holier than "ordinary" people? Do we still tend to see priests, and I suppose bishops, as if they were on pedestals? Is baptism properly recognised as the moment of God's greatest gift to us?

It cannot be denied that increasingly in recent post-conciliar years the Holy See itself has attracted criticism on such grounds as excessive centralisation, unwillingness to allow decisions to be made locally, an apparent lack of trust in regard to bishops and bishops' conferences, a Roman Curia which seems to take more and more power to itself and so on. Furthermore, such criticisms are being voiced by responsible people, experienced bishops some of them, and should not be ignored. Let me develop this.

I describe, when writing about ICEL (International Commission on English in the Liturgy), the unseemly way in which, in recent years, the Congregation for Divine Worship and Discipline of the Sacraments has treated not only the agency of English-speaking bishops' conferences (ICEL) but also and directly the conferences themselves.

The appointment of bishops is another area of discontent, both in the manner in which this is carried out – secretly and by Rome itself without any genuine discussion with the local church or the local conference of bishops – and in some appointments that have been made, especially in North and Latin America, as well as for some of the larger dioceses elsewhere. Rome's regulation that it alone will choose who are to be bishops is not traditional or historic. Moreover, there appears to be an agenda that often favours appointments of men who are conservative and not in tune with Vatican II and its ecclesiology.

There has also been quite an amount of disappointment over the way in which synods of bishops have developed. These synods were begun in order to continue the ethos of collegiality generated by the Second Vatican Council. The idea was that a certain number of bishops, representing their conferences from all over the world, should be convened in Rome every two or three years in order to deliberate, for a month, on one or more topics of importance to the Church e.g. penance and reconciliation, priesthood, consecrated life, laity.

However, after a few synods it became clear that they were only consultative and not deliberative – they would not be allowed to make decisions or offer teaching. Further and even within these narrow parameters, it seemed that the Roman Curia was manipulating the process in the sense that, at certain stages of the synod process when choices had to be made, those choices were made not by the synod bishops nor by the conferences but by the synod officials (members of the Curia) and in secret. They were thus able to "censor" those topics which were "inconvenient".

For example, bishops' conferences are asked to make suggestions for the synod's "*Instrumentum Laboris*" (working document) but the document is compiled by the Roman officials; it is they also who decide the agenda for the small groups into which the synod divides for its second fortnight; it is they who, from the reports of the small groups, decide the final report presented to the Holy Father; and it is he, not the synod, who writes the "Apostolic Exhortation", the only document which is made public from the synod. The effectiveness of the synod is further limited because, during the plenary sessions which take up the first fortnight, each bishop can make only one short speech – but these speeches are not in any logical order and there is no public discussion allowed of any proposals or suggestions made in the speeches.

Many bishops now feel that the synods are so controlled that their effectiveness has been severely diminished and they serve little purpose.

Perhaps it is a less important matter, but I have always felt that the daily newspaper of the Holy See, "*L'Osservatore Romano*", is more of an official bulletin than a true newspaper. The news that it contains is always favourable to the Church and so are the articles. Real controversy, criticism of the Church and adult discussion of its problems are absent from its columns and the impression is given of manipulated content by a fortress mentality out of touch with the real world.

There is, nevertheless, one very important aspect of this whole matter to be kept in mind – the need to preserve unity of teaching in the Church. Certainly, present practice of centralisation is an effective way of achieving this, but is it the right way? The difficulties which the worldwide Anglican Communion is experiencing in trying to have unity in such matters as the appointment of practising homosexuals and the ordination of women shows the danger of a lack of a firm central authority. If Rome relaxed its stance and devolved more authority and decisions to local churches would that inevitably lead to disunity in teaching?

That is a question perhaps impossible to answer with any assurance. One hopes that the Holy Spirit guides not only the bishop of Rome but all bishops and indeed all the baptised. And this touches on a disputed ecclesiological question: which has priority, the worldwide Catholic Church from which the local churches derive their validity or the local churches which are in communion with each other and with the bishop of Rome to form the worldwide Church?

The extent of decentralisation, using the principle of subsidiarity, that would be best is a matter for discussion. But that there should be more than at present, I think is right and necessary and widely hoped for.

Vatican II teaching on ecclesiology challenges us and we should be aware of it and embrace it, not only in theory but in practice too. That applies to everyone in the Church. Please God we may increasingly understand and try to implement the Council's inspired ecclesiology.

THE LOCAL CHURCH AFTER VATICAN II

The most disturbing document of the Second Vatican Council is the Constitution *Lumen Gentium* on the Church. Disturbing in the sense that it was meant to change us, to change the Church. Has it? Is the local Church changed? Are we, individual Catholics, changed?

Well, it depends. In theory, the Church is changed. Some local churches are changed or slowly changing, and it is the same with individual members. Some are changed, some not; some think they have changed; some think they have not changed...

Even though the essentials of Mass remain unchanged, the way in which we celebrate Mass is very different from what it was in pre-Vatican II days. That is so evident as to make further explanation unnecessary and tedious. But that everyone in the Church is called to be holy, to be active (using the gifts received through baptism and confirmation), to seek to make the local church a true community, indeed a communion of sharers in the one and only priesthood of Christ – is this Vatican II teaching a reality in parishes yet? The Council also radically advanced the Catholic Church's views on ecumenism, on our relations with non-Christians, on the role we should have in today's world. Have these ideas been accepted and put into practice yet?

Through the sacraments of Christian initiation we are full members of the Church, gifted, empowered, with rights and responsibilities. Yet there are many Catholics who are unaware of this and therefore not actively involved. There are many, also, who show such deference to priests that the relationship, if not one of fear, can be something approaching infantilism and servility. Of course I am not recommending an absence of law and order, for collaborative ministry does not mean chaos.

Besides, infantile servility or fear in lay people doesn't help a priest. Most priests feel frustrated in such circumstances and a few of us may, God forgive us, relapse into clericalism ("only the priest has the right to decide"), paternalism ("I know best") or, worse still, hypocrisy or pomposity. Yes, we can be tempted if we are spoiled by misplaced respect.

Most Catholics nowadays worry about falling numbers – fewer people at Mass, fewer vocations to priesthood and religious life, fewer marriages, fewer children and, incidentally, less income for parishes and dioceses at a time of increasing expenses. These concerns produce explanations galore but far fewer solutions – materialism, individualism, relativism, selfishness, hedonism, influence of the media, peer pressure, we should pray more, have less boring Masses, do more for youth and for families, provide better marriage preparation.

I do not want to discuss these explanations or remedies. There are other occasions to do so, occasions, I am afraid, to make ourselves feel depressed or guilty. Let us be content with saying that we are aware of these negative developments, that we regret them and are not complacent, but that we shall simply try to give witness to what we believe, to the faith we have received – and leave the situation in the hands of the God who is in charge and in whom we trust.

"Jesus said 'Do you also want to go away?' Simon Peter answered 'Lord, to whom shall we go? You have the message of eternal life and we believe'" (John 6:67-68).

ICEL

An important task that came my way as bishop was to be the Scottish representative on the Episcopal Board of ICEL. The International Commission on English in the Liturgy was established by English-speaking bishops' conferences during the Second Vatican Council when it became obvious that the vernacular languages would be permitted in the liturgy. Since the recommendation was that there should be one translation for countries using the same language, an organisation like ICEL was needed, a mixed commission with representatives from the various bishops' conferences requiring English translations.

The basic work in ICEL was done by teams of experts in various disciplines, charged with the responsibility of producing translations that would be faithful to the Latin original – but not so literal as to be stilted; and suitable for proclamation and for public prayer. The translators' work was examined and, if necessary, revised by an Advisory Committee which then passed their texts to the Episcopal Board, a team of eleven bishops each representing his own bishops' conference: Australia, Canada, England and Wales, India, Ireland, New Zealand, Pakistan, Philippines, Scotland, Southern Africa and the United States of America. Once the Episcopal Board had approved the texts, they were sent to the bishops' conferences. Each conference could then give formal approval, with any changes if it felt they were required; formal rejection was also possible. Finally the conference, when satisfied, would send the document to the Roman Congregation for Divine Worship and Discipline of the Sacraments seeking *recognitio;* once this last was given, the text could be published for use in that particular country.

That summarises the process but it was a process that demanded and received meticulous attention by many experts and authorities, debate and discussion and possible admission of amendments or alternative translations – a long, careful and demanding process.

The documents which ICEL translated comprised the rites of all the sacraments, the various liturgical books (RCIA, reconciliation, care of the sick, funerals…) but, of course, the principal texts were those of the Roman Missal which includes the unchanging "Order of Mass", prefaces, Eucharistic Prayers, presidential prayers for Sundays, feasts, commons, votive Masses – an enormous production of more than 2000 texts. The Scripture readings are in the Lectionary, not in the Missal; nor does ICEL translate them as various versions in English already exist and, from these, each conference makes its choice.

During the years that I was involved with ICEL, most of our work was on the revised translation of the Missal. The first English translation, issued in 1973, had stood the test of time and was recognised as, in general, a very adequate version. However, it had had to be done quickly and there was a widespread feeling that improvement was possible and appropriate. The language of the 1973 translation was spare, its style sometimes "bitty" and it was clear that, in some parts of it, more accurate translations could be made. In addition to its translating work, ICEL had also been charged by the conferences with providing "original texts" i.e. not translations of Latin texts, but directly composed in English, especially to provide alternative Opening Prayers on Sundays and some new votive Masses.

As an Episcopal Board member and, later, as one of the three-man Executive Committee of the Board, I was frequently throughout each year sent bundles of texts for study and report. So our work was by no means limited to our annual meetings in Washington.

ICEL had its headquarters in that city where the ICEL Secretariat (six or seven persons headed by the Executive Secretary) did wonderful things not only in managing the work of all the experts and bishops but also in providing us with background information and advice, the result of their intimate knowledge of the history of the Latin liturgy, of the situation regarding translations in other languages (French, German, Italian, Spanish, Portuguese) and of the particular problems and possibilities associated with the various texts.

I found the work extremely interesting, even fascinating; very time-consuming but time given gladly because we were serving English-speaking Catholics all over the world.

There was another aspect that made me very happy – the comradeship that grew up among us, bishops, priests, religious, lay people, men and women. We came from a variety of countries, we had a wide range of skills and expertise and we respected each other's work and enjoyed each other's company, especially when we met. I miss the work and the meetings but, thanks be to God, the friendships and the occasional contacts continue.

By the time our work on the revised translation of the Missal was completed in 1997, I had succeeded Archbishop Daniel Pilarczyk of Cincinnati as chairman of the Episcopal Board of ICEL. The various English-speaking bishops' conferences were sent the finished product and all but one approved it with overwhelming majorities; the one exception was the United States. A minority of the bishops of that conference did vote against the revised translation but, even so, the majority there was sufficiently large to secure its approval for the whole nation.

However, the entire scene was to change and our revised translation, on which we had worked so hard and of which we were proud, was to be rejected, not by the bishops' conferences but by Rome.

The problem became apparent in 1996 with the arrival of the Chilean Cardinal Jorge Arturo Medina Estévez to be Prefect (i.e. head) of the Roman Congregation for Divine Worship and Discipline of the Sacraments. Although with some previous prefects, relations between the Congregation and ICEL had been strained, the difficulties were to do with specific matters. For some years before Cardinal Medina, relations were cordial and ICEL had some useful and very friendly meetings in Rome with officials of the Congregation.

Whether due to Cardinal Medina or whether only concomitant with his appointment, things changed and at ICEL we began to feel very threatened. The change, as I say, may have been of the cardinal's making or he may have been advised, either by higher authority or by some Congregation officials, to "bring ICEL to heel".

At any rate, I, as ICEL chairman, began to receive letters from Cardinal Medina, couched in formal, seemingly courteous language, either deploring some of ICEL's activities or "requesting" changes or announcing new regulations. Letters were exchanged between us, the tone was always superficially polite in an old-fashioned way, but there was no real dialogue or attempt to hear our views and consider them. Decisions had been made, consultation was not on the agenda.

I remember one occasion in particular when I wrote to the cardinal to say that I would be happy to go to Rome if he would be willing to meet me. The reply was that, as a bishop I was welcome to go to Rome and he would receive me – as he would any bishop – but I would not be received as chairman of ICEL to discuss its concerns.

Some years earlier I did have a private meeting with the cardinal but discussion was difficult as he does not speak English and conversation in Spanish about translation from Latin to English is not very satisfactory. So perhaps the snub to which I have referred merely avoided another frustrating encounter.

What is good translation? A simple question but not an easy one to answer. Fidelity and accuracy to what is being translated, yes; but also the result must be acceptable for those who have to use it. The two extremes, both unacceptable, are, first, a translation that is so "word for word" that it is stilted and artificial; and, second, a translation that is so "free" that it is paraphrase rather than translation. The good translation, and this is true for the liturgy as well as everything else, lies somewhere between the two extremes.

To enable the translators to know just where the right "middle way" lies, some authoritative guidance is necessary. This guidance was provided until 2001 by a document issued in 1969 by the "Consilium" established by the Holy See after Vatican II for this – and other – reasons. The document is called "*Instruction on Translation of Liturgical Texts*" and was used by ICEL in its work.

Although there were rumours that another document was under preparation in Rome, ICEL was told by Congregation officials that work done before its publication, including the revised translation of the Missal, would be judged not by its norms but by those of the 1969 instruction.

After a long delay, the new document, called "*Liturgiam Authenticam*" (from the first two words of its Latin text), was finally published in May 2001 – after ICEL's revised Missal had been completed and approved by the English-speaking bishops' conferences. Despite previous assurances, ICEL was told that the revised Missal was subject to its norms! This seemed not only like changing the goalposts but changing them after the game was over. Or again, if a new 30 mph speed limit is introduced on a road, should motorists who, before the new law is enacted or known, exceeded that limit, be found guilty of its infringement?

"*Liturgiam Authenticam*" is a long and prolix document produced without any consultation either with mixed commissions such as ICEL or even with bishops' conferences. It is a document that has been widely and severely criticised. It certainly requires translation from Latin to be closer to "word for word" rather than a somewhat freer style that is faithful to the meaning and sense of the Latin but nearer an English that is both intelligible and usable, prayerful and proclaimable.

In addition to its stricter norms for translation, "*Liturgiam Authenticam*" also lays down rules for mixed commissions such as ICEL; for example, all those who work for ICEL must, unless they are bishops, have prior authorisation from the Roman Congregation; only translation work may be undertaken and not, as hitherto, the composition of original extra prayers even if requested by bishops' conferences; ecumenical contacts have to be discontinued.

These developments took place against a background of expressions of dismay from many liturgical and theological scholars and, on the other side, of attacks on ICEL, especially from a number of very conservative publications and letters, and which condemned the mixed commission as anything from arrogant and disobedient to heretical.

I realise that, as a leading member of ICEL, I tend to see the dispute from one point of view. Was the Congregation justified in its denial of its *recognitio* to the revised translation of the Missal and in its generally hostile and very critical attitude to ICEL? Opinions do, and will, vary on this. In order to be as fair as I think possible, let me say that ICEL may sometimes have appeared intolerant or arrogant; but ICEL did use the very best people it could find – liturgists, theologians, Scripture scholars, Latinists, English writers – and in this sense its scholarly resources were second to none and inevitably superior to those which the Congregation for Divine Worship could employ. Again, one could admit that, apart from their one bishop representative on ICEL's Episcopal Board, some bishops' conferences did not normally take an active part in ICEL's work; but neither did the Congregation, despite our frequent invitations to do so. In fact, various "Progress Reports" were issued by ICEL – we were not secretive about our work – and these reports were sent to bishops' conferences and also to Rome. If our work was so unacceptable to Rome, why did the Congregation not stop it sooner? Why, at least, were we not contacted?

Wherever the blame lies, the whole business was extremely sad and, to those who are aware of its details, unedifying and even scandalous. Many years' serious work was wasted and the people had more long years to wait, bewildered by the delay, for the promised revised Missal in English.

Radical changes took place in ICEL's statutes, leadership and procedures at the Episcopal Board meeting in July 2002. Both the Chairman (myself) and the Executive Secretary (Dr John Page) left ICEL. The latter resigned because he felt he could not continue under the new ways of working and I did not stand for re-election because I was 76 years old and due to retire as bishop of the diocese; I felt that it was not appropriate for ICEL to be led by a retired bishop, especially one with cancer. Unfortunately, it so happened that, at the same meeting, several of the Episcopal Board were newcomers. Nevertheless, the Board elected a new chairman, a new executive secretary and a new executive committee of the Episcopal Board, abolished the Consultants' (formerly, Advisory) Committee (as required by the Congregation) and accepted all the directives in "*Liturgiam Authenticam*". I left ICEL with regret but with truly happy memories and with good wishes for those who were to assume the task of producing a translation of the Missal that would be acceptable to Rome.

I have already spoken about the activities of the Roman Congregation for Divine Worship and about its criticisms of ICEL. I have also said that there are those who consider those criticisms to be justified. However, there is another player in the drama – the

English-speaking bishops' conferences. I believe that they ought to have played a much stronger part in the whole affair and not only because they had all approved the ICEL revised translation of the Missal, yet, without any complaint or question, they allowed the Congregation, in denying its *recognitio*, to overturn their approval. The *recognitio* is not the same as a further "approval"; it is rather "ratification" and is supposed to be only a way in which the Congregation recognises a conference's decision and accepts it (or not – but this last merely and only for very serious reasons such as heresy or similar grave error). Indeed, the Second Vatican Council decreed that translated liturgical texts from Latin require the approval of bishops' conferences, without mentioning any need of involvement by the Holy See (*Sacrosanctum Concilium*, 36 §4).

Moreover, *Liturgiam Authenticam* arrogates to the Congregation certain powers which properly belong to the conferences, especially the right to set up mixed commissions such as ICEL, to approve their statutes, their personnel, their programmes and their way of working. All of these duties are declared by *Liturgiam Authenticam* to belong to the Congregation – and the bishops' conferences have meekly accepted this.

Not only is all this against the original statutes of ICEL but it goes against the ecclesiology that was taught by Vatican II: collegiality, the authority of bishops (who are not merely Rome's branch managers), subsidiarity. Much has been written in recent years of the increasing power which the Roman Curia is giving itself – and all this is a further example of the centralisation of authority or simply, if you like, a further example of the use of power.

In my opinion, things need to be rectified to recapture the spirit and the teaching of the Second Vatican Council. Ecclesiology is the main problem, and the liturgical situation is a sad illustration of the problem. And specifically, the Roman Curia needs that reform which recent popes have acknowledged but not achieved.

RETIREMENT

A retired bishop used to be an unusual thing. Bishops just kept on as diocesan leaders until death. But since the introduction of the new Code of Canon Law in 1983, "a diocesan bishop who has completed his seventy-fifth year of age is requested to offer his resignation from office to the Supreme Pontiff who, taking all the circumstances into account, will make provision accordingly" (canon 401 §1).

Having "completed my seventy-fifth year of age" on 5th May 2001, I offered my resignation to the Holy Father in a letter dated 6th May 2001. My resignation was soon accepted with the phrase "*nunc pro tunc*", i.e. accepted, but to be effective later. In fact, I ceased to be bishop of Galloway only when my successor's appointment was published on 7th April 2004.

The following month, in *The Galloway Newsletter* for May 2004, I gave my retiring reflections.

GOING, GOING, (ALMOST) GONE!

Since the announcement, on 7th April, that Pope John Paul II had appointed Mgr John Cunningham as my successor, many people have congratulated me on my retirement (after a delay lasting almost three years, since I became seventy-five on 5th May 2001). Usually, people added "You must be delighted" but a few have asked whether I am sad to be retiring. That question challenges me.

I want to say that I truly welcome my retirement, partly for my sake and certainly for the sake of the diocese. Not only will the diocese benefit from new and fresh leadership but the uncertainty that has lasted three years has been unsettling (especially for the priests) and the appointment of a new bishop is long overdue.

For these reasons (and because Mgr Cunningham is such an excellent choice), I am very happy that my retirement has come at last.

It would be wrong, however, not to admit to some feelings of sadness that my years as bishop of this wonderful diocese are over. But instead of sadness I prefer to thank God for all the happiness and fulfilment I have had and for the prospect of having so many memories to enjoy in the days ahead.

Memories of ordaining priests, which I always found an awesome privilege. Memories of the annual Mass of Chrism when the cathedral church of the Good Shepherd is filled to overflowing and the liturgy is celebrated with such deep emotion (especially when the priests solemnly and publicly renew their commitment to serve the people). Memories of the Whithorn pilgrimage in sunshine and rain, in calm and storm, always a physical effort but richly symbolic as we of today recognise the antiquity and tradition of the diocese to which we belong.

Visits to parishes brought me great pleasure, whether for confirmation (and also, latterly, first communion) or jubilees and anniversaries or simply pastoral visits which I tried to carry out each weekend since 1981. Annual visits to schools were happy occasions ("Who's your teacher?" "Fine!") but quite demanding. Diocesan pilgrimages to the Holy Land and to Lourdes were unfailingly rewarding, not only because we were in holy places but also because of the bonds of friendship and support that so rapidly developed.

I have been fortunate enough to get to know several countries in Latin America and to experience their poverty, their faith and their friendship. Nor must I forget the privilege of my association with the International Commission on English in the Liturgy (ICEL) which involved a great deal of fascinating work, becoming friends with many fine people from all over the English-speaking world and, ultimately, the disappointment of having our work approved by all the bishops' conferences which ICEL serves but then rejected by the Congregation for Divine Worship in Rome.

Perhaps most of all my memory will be of people – you, the priests, religious and lay people, young and old, of this diocese who have been so supportive, so cooperative, so forgiving, so good to me. I am truly happy to have been your bishop and I am happy that, for the time that remains to me, I shall continue to live in this diocese whose people I have grown to love so much.

Retired bishops in the past were "transferred" to "titular sees *in partibus infidelium*", i.e. dioceses that no longer existed. Now that somewhat coy fiction has been abandoned and "a bishop whose resignation from office has been accepted acquires the title 'emeritus' of his diocese" (canon 402 §1). The word sounds fitting and worthy, perhaps something like "meritorious". So I looked up my Latin dictionary:– "*emeritus – one who has served his time, a veteran, unfit for service, worn out*".

So that's what I am! It just goes to confirm the old adage that no one is indispensable. Ah, well! So be it. Amen.

Episcopal ordination

Troopship *Empress of Scotland*: 26,000 tons

Rome: Pontifical Scots College
(former building on Via Quattro Fontane)

Rome: River Tiber with Castel Sant' Angelo and
St Peter's Basilica, 1953

Marino (south of Rome): Scots College Villa (for the summer vacation from study) with surrounding vineyards; property now sold

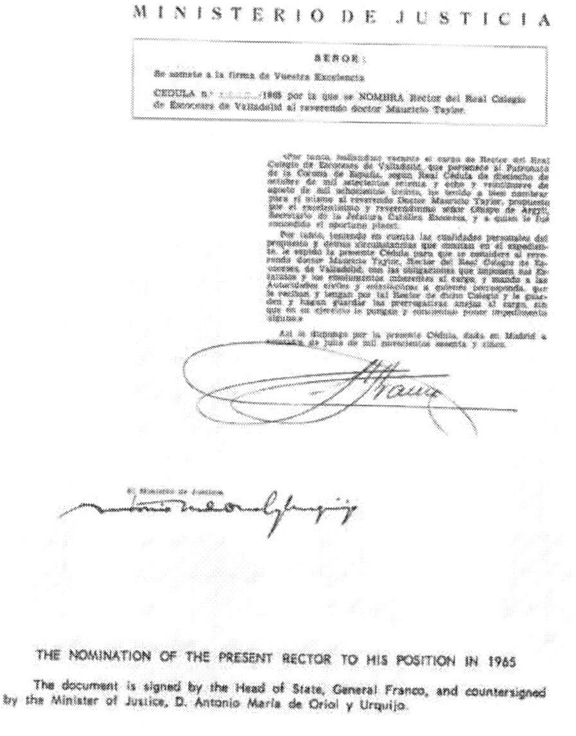

MINISTERIO DE JUSTICIA

SEÑOR:

Se somete a la firma de Vuestra Excelencia

CEDULA n.º ..../1965 por la que se NOMBRA Rector del Real Colegio de Escoceses de Valladolid al reverendo doctor Mauricio Taylor.

[illegible]

[illegible]

[illegible]

THE NOMINATION OF THE PRESENT RECTOR TO HIS POSITION IN 1965

The document is signed by the Head of State, General Franco, and countersigned by the Minister of Justice, D. Antonio Maria de Oriol y Urquijo.

"Il Reverendo Doctor Mauricio Taylor" appointed "Rector del Real Colegio de Escoceses de Valladolid"; official document signed by Head of State, General Franco, 1965

Valladolid: Community of the Royal Scots College, 1970

Lourdes 2013: Galloway Diocesan Pilgrimage; large banner was made for Pope John Paul II visit, 1982

Guatemala:
A tale of brutality, survival and faith

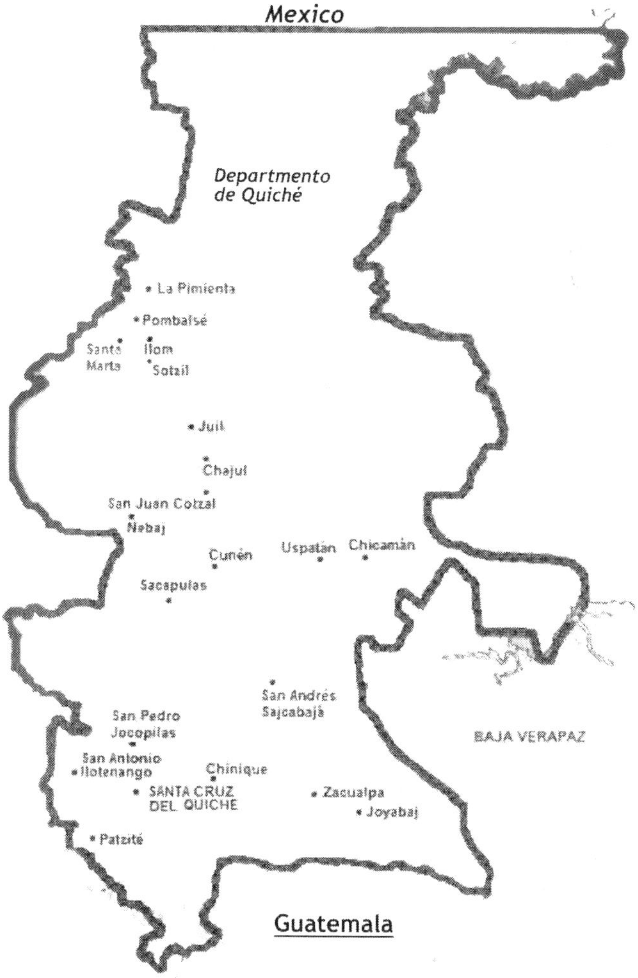

INTRODUCTION

This is the story of a journey I made to Guatemala in 1989 during July and August – our summer, but winter there, not because it is cold but because it is the rainy season.

My time was spent in the Department of El Quiché, in the north-west of the country. During previous visits as a member of delegations from the Scottish Catholic International Aid Fund (SCIAF) and the Catholic Institute for International Relations (CIIR, now Progressio), I had made the acquaintance of Monseñor Julio Cabrera, bishop of Quiché.

The diocese of Quiché is an extremely difficult one – roads are non-existent in many parts of it, there are five main languages spoken and the Department, coterminous with the diocese, has been very "conflictive" with countless people murdered and kidnapped.

When it was suggested to Bishop Cabrera that it might be possible for me to spend a few weeks with him to give a clear sign of our solidarity with him and with his diocese, he was very enthusiastic. If the Church is worldwide, it is good to show one's concern and support for those parts of it which are suffering most by actually going there, being with the people and sharing their lives.

The bishop invited me as a fellow-bishop and a friend to go to Quiché, to experience something of the reality of the diocese, to accompany him on his travels and his visits to the parishes. What follows is a day-by-day account of my impressions and experiences over a period of three weeks.

TUESDAY 18TH JULY

Bishop Julio Cabrera welcomed me to Guatemala. Our meeting in Guatemala City was a little illustration of communication difficulties that can occur. The bishop had asked Roberto Paz, one of the students in the national seminary, to go to the airport to meet me. Roberto was there at 3.00 pm, to meet, as he thought, "a Venezuelan arriving from Costa Rica". I had spent the previous week in Venezuela and had changed planes in Panama, so the confusion was understandable. Eventually, at 8.30 pm, as Roberto was about to abandon his long vigil, I turned up and was taken to Bishop Cabrera. He himself had just arrived in the capital since he had been making a pastoral visit to a parish in his diocese – a parish which is accessible only by many hours on foot or by light aircraft from Cobán in another diocese. He had opted for the latter and had left his car in Cobán. The weather closed in, however, and he was marooned for three days before a plane could make the journey to pick him up and fly him back to Cobán, his car and the road. So he told me that he had been getting desperate and more and more worried, knowing that he had told me that he would be in Guatemala City to meet me.

WEDNESDAY 19TH JULY

The bishop has brought me to Santa Cruz del Quiché, the town in the south of the diocese where he has his cathedral and his house. It is a drive of more than two hours from Guatemala City and we are to spend the night here before going northwards tomorrow.

At supper the local priest of Santa Cruz came to greet us. Padre Teodoro Chitic is one of the few indigenous priests in Guatemala – despite the fact that most Guatemalans are indigenous; in Quiché, the overwhelming majority. I asked Teodoro if his house was near the cathedral and he said, "It's just beside it, but it's more a cave than a house!" The bishop explained that the house, so called, is really just part of a wide corridor converted into rooms.

The indigenous people of Guatemala (Mayan Indians) have preserved their own separate identity. Elsewhere in Central America intermarriage between the indigenous people and those of European descent has blurred the distinction.

It is also true that the Guatemalan Indians have been oppressed ever since the Spanish conquest early in the sixteenth century. Partly for racial reasons, partly for economic, the indigenous people have endured poverty, marginalisation and often violence from the ruling class who are, partially at least, of European ("*ladino*") descent. In the early 1980s the repression reached new heights of cruelty. On the pretext of destroying the guerrillas, rooting out their sympathisers and pacifying the country, the army carried out a campaign that was little short of genocide. Hundreds of individuals, sometimes entire villages, were massacred, people disappeared in their thousands and whole communities fled to the mountains in terror.

THURSDAY 20TH JULY

The day has been quite a long one although, in terms of miles or kilometres, we haven't travelled all that far. We took the road north from Santa Cruz. It's really just a wide track, very precipitous in parts, with hairpin bends and very little level. Not a very comfortable ride, although the bishop is a competent driver and the Toyota Landcruiser is adequate for the task. An ordinary car would have had its springs and suspension wrecked within a very few miles.

We made a brief stop in Sacapulas and visited the parochial house. Four priests who are Oblates of Mary Immaculate came to the diocese a year ago and one of them is parish priest here. There are also in the town a religious sister and a young lay woman, a biologist from Guatemala City, giving a year's work to the diocese.

Extensive repair work is taking place in the parochial house and adjoining parish offices because, during the time of the worst violence some years ago, the premises were occupied by the military. Appalling things had occurred in the buildings and just outside – interrogation, torture and killings. Many bodies are buried in a kind of backyard of the premises, now concreted, but the people who live there say that from time to time they are conscious of terrible smells and of a sense of evil around the place. It brought home to me something of the reality of what has been happening in Quiché.

We resumed our journey northwards over the great barrier of the Cuchumatanes mountains and into Ixil, an area with a population of around 70,000. Here more atrocities perhaps than anywhere else in Guatemala have been perpetrated and the people have lived through years of indescribable violence and terror.

Ixil is a vast mountainous area with three towns ("*pueblos*") or parishes: Nebaj, Chajul and Cotzal, each with many villages ("*aldeas*" or "*cantones*").

By lunchtime we had reached Nebaj and a convent of Sisters of Charity. The sisters look after a home for orphan children – those whose parents have been killed or "disappeared". The children – there were thirty or forty – were brought to the convent to meet the bishops. They were extremely friendly to us and, after a polite handshake, would give us a hug. They are obviously in need of a great deal of love. After we had eaten, we had musical entertainment from the children, dressed in traditional style: the girls in the long red skirt called *corte*, the richly embroidered blouse called *guipil* and the turban called *cinta*; the boys in red jackets, white trousers and panama hats. They danced, sang and played the marimba, a local form of the xylophone.

It was outside the church in Nebaj that a particularly frightful atrocity occurred in May 1980. A crowd of women were protesting about the kidnappings and disappearances when the army opened fire on them and thirteen were killed.

Thousands of people from Nebaj and district fled to the mountains. Many of these refugees have now come back. Some of them are to be found in "model villages" such as Acul, where they are under surveillance by the army; others are in resettlements run by the diocese such as Las Violetas, where 325 children as well as many adults are cared for.

Finally this evening we got to Chajul. We are staying overnight in the parish premises and are being looked after by a group of Carmelite sisters. The parish priest has gone ahead to await us in the village where we are due to arrive tomorrow night. It was about five o'clock when we reached Chajul, through some quite heavy rain and watery roads, still very precipitous and rough. It took us more than an hour between each of the places that we visited today.

The countryside here is very dramatic and very mountainous. There is hardly any flat level ground. The mountains, covered with trees, grass and crops right to their summits, are very beautiful, with occasional vistas of valleys.

Three times on the road we were stopped by "civil defence patrols" or by the army itself. We were asked who we were and where we were going. After the bishop had simply replied "to work" to the second question, the wooden barrier across the road was lifted and we were allowed to proceed.

After our arrival in Chajul we had a meeting with some men of the parish about whether we were to continue our journey tomorrow in a small plane or on horseback or a bit of each. There does not seem to be any decision yet – it all depends on the plane being induced to come here tomorrow to pick us up.

The church in Chajul is enormous. It is under the patronage of Saint Gaspar, one of the names traditionally given to the Wise Men from the East. There are some very bizarre statues in the church, including a group consisting of Jesus nailed to the Cross, flanked by Gaspar and Baltasar. Popular devotion clearly outweighed considerations of historical accuracy.

We were told of a horrible event that took place in Chajul less than two weeks ago, on Saturday 8th July. There was a commotion in the streets, thought at first to be people coming down from the mountains to surrender to the army. In fact, however, it was a crowd surrounding two or three men; these were carrying a pole, from which there hung the body of a dead man. The body was left lying in the street from one o'clock until six. It was almost naked and the soldiers invited the people to come and kick it and spit on it. They said that this was a guerrilla, "the kind of person who destroys your crops, brings violence to the area and makes life terrible for everyone – so show what you think of him". Some of the people accepted the invitation and behaved in a frightful way, but others were disgusted at the spectacle. It was just one of the many violent incidents that occur in this country; and no one talks about them in public.

Perhaps the way that some people responded to the army's invitation is a warning against over-simplifying the issues here. Basically, it is the army versus the peasants and the pretext for the repression is the presence in the area of the guerrillas. But does no one in the army feel any compassion for the victims? And, among the peasants, are there not some who, as informers or sympathisers, do side with the military? Protestant fundamentalist sects have made great inroads in these districts and the peasants who have joined them are not likely to be subversive or pro-guerrilla because their theology is about saving one's soul for the next life and does not include a commitment to God's kingdom of peace, justice and love on this earth.

[Throughout this chapter, when I mention sects I am referring to some Protestant groupings, never mainstream, or denominations which present a 'distorted' gospel. The common characteristic is that these sects are very 'pushy' in attempting to convert to their particular message and belief system.]

Even among practising Catholics, there is a certain division between those who belong to "Catholic Action" and those who belong to charismatic renewal. The former, much more than the latter, tend to be involved in issues of human rights and social justice and therefore are much more likely to be seen by the army as subversives.

So to some extent it is understandable that observers may over-simplify the situation. One has to realise that, among the local population, there are different attitudes to the army and to resistance. The people are largely illiterate, minimally educated and very unsophisticated. Their response to the oppression and the violence is, in many cases, pragmatic, not ideological.

FRIDAY 21ST JULY

Today has been some day! As it turned out, there was no plane. So we left Chajul for La Perla at about 9.00 am, driving over an extremely bumpy track, up and down hill, with lots of holes and rivulets. We made our way for probably about fifteen kilometres, past a village named Juil and past the spot where, on 4th June 1980, Fr José María Gran, parish priest of Chajul, and his companion, Domingo Batz, were ambushed and murdered. Fr Gran was the first of three parish priests of the diocese – all Spanish Missionaries of the Sacred Heart – to be killed in the space of nine months.

At one point we encountered a tree which had fallen across the road, practically blocking it. It would have been very dangerous for the car to have tried to edge past it because there was a precipice at the side of the road. So the men produced their *machetes* and before very long had hacked right through the trunk of the tree; then, with a lot of levering and heaving, they got the branches out of the mud and toppled the tree over the cliff, so allowing the car to continue. Soon, however, the "road" came to a halt and we had to transfer to horses which had preceded us up the hill from Chajul. The two young men, Domingo and Baltasar, who had been with us in the car became our guides, while the three who had brought the horses went back in the car with one of the sisters. Our cases and bags were loaded on one of the horses and Bishop Julio and I mounted on the other two.

I found horse riding not merely uncomfortable but really painful. I constantly felt, especially at first, that I was going to fall off, above all when the horse was trying to climb up rock. Climbing on mud or gravel was not too bad, but rock was quite frightening and I held on to the pommel with both hands and as firmly as I could. Descending also had its problems – the inside of my thighs got extremely sore with the position that you have to keep your legs in. I wished that the horse had been much thinner!

So we rode, and sometimes – to get relief from the pain and fear – I walked, for many kilometres, up and down hills, along narrow paths, across a river, through mud and rain until at last we reached La Perla at dusk, some time after 5.00 pm. I thought that it would never come. My companions' thoughtfulness induced them to try to help me with encouraging words like "It's mainly level from now on" or "In twenty-five minutes we shall be in La Perla". God bless their wildly optimistic forecasts!

When we arrived at the church at La Perla – inevitably at the top end of the village – we were all soaked and I was really exhausted. But a great crowd of people awaited us, some outside the church and others crammed inside, singing and applauding and welcoming us. It was very moving. Fr Rosolino, who had come up from Chajul ahead of us, led us to the sacristy – just a shed – where, in the midst of much confusion and many people, we managed to change some of our wet clothes, have a couple of bottles of Pepsi-Cola and get ready for Mass. The Mass was by candlelight and, during it, there were weddings, performed by Bishop Julio, and about twenty or thirty confirmations, by me. All very makeshift, I admit, but very satisfying, with a great deal of enthusiastic singing.

La Perla is not called an "*aldea*" (village) but a "*finca*" because it is owned by a local family as part of their estate. Most of the people, who are employees of the family, are *ladinos*. After the Mass we were taken by Doña Amparo, mother of the present owner, to the big house and introduced to her son, Don Enrique Arenas, and his wife, Doña Beatriz. The house is large and comfortable and the bishop and I were assigned a room with two beds, sheets and blankets.

The family were hospitable and have a high standard of living. There was good food, Scotch whisky and Heineken beer. Don Enrique explained that the village has about five hundred families, practically all the men being his employees. His main crops are coffee and cardamom. All his supplies, including water for drinking, are brought from Guatemala City by plane – that is the only way that you can reach La Perla, apart from walking or on horseback. He told us that he was probably unique in Guatemala in trying to make his business into a genuine cooperative, with the workers having an opportunity to share in the ownership and the profits.

This, he informed us, has had excellent results in terms of increased production and of his workers' contentment. In Washington he had met President Reagan who had praised him for his far-sighted policy and had wished that the other landowners of Guatemala were similarly enlightened. We did hear that his father, the husband of Doña Amparo, was called "The Tiger" and was much disliked in the village. It was apparently no real surprise to anyone when he was murdered.

Don Enrique and Doña Beatriz have five children but only two were at home – a girl of about ten and a boy of three; the other three were at a junior golf championship in Los Angeles. The family were very hospitable and anxious to give us the impression that they had a very reasonable attitude to the troubles in Guatemala and especially in Ixil. Our discussion continued until midnight. Sometimes it became an argument but the tone remained friendly. Don Enrique's general thesis was that, if the peasants were treated as he treats his workers, they would be reasonable and contented, knowing that people like him had their best interests at heart. The guerrillas and their supporters were starry-eyed idealists who needed a bit of realism in their outlook – or else they were Marxist agitators aiming to subvert Christian values in Guatemala. His manner was very civilised and he appealed to Bishop Julio and myself as men of intelligence…!

Near La Perla there is a village called La Estrella. In the church there, in the early 1980s, the army lined up ninety-seven men of the village round the walls and killed them all with machine guns. The building was like a charnel house, with blood everywhere and bodies lying scattered on the floor. When the army departed and the women and children ventured to come back and saw what had taken place, the scenes of grief and anguish were indescribable. La Estrella was not an isolated event or untypical of the kind of treatment that the people of Ixil – and so many other places in Guatemala – have suffered.

SATURDAY 22ND JULY

Don Enrique Arenas' jeep, with about twelve of us crowded into it, took us a couple of kilometres along the track to where the horses awaited us. Fr Rosolino, our guide Baltasar and I got out, said farewell to Bishop Cabrera who was going to other villages, and began to climb to our next stop, the village of Saxiván. The journey was not nearly as difficult as yesterday's and I thought that I would try and walk. Soon I had to admit defeat and mount the horse for the ascent. My legs were very sore because of the length of the stirrups. Shorter makeshift stirrups of rope allowed my legs to be less stretched and we eventually arrived at Saxiván fairly easily a little before noon.

Saxiván is a village that was reconstructed only two years ago. Before that, the people, who are originally from the Nebaj area and overwhelmingly indigenous, lived dispersed in this district. Then, during the worst of the violence, many of them fled to the mountains. When they came down, the army grouped them into a compact village which, although not a so-called "model village", is still very much under military surveillance.

Our trio of Rosolino, Baltasar and I was expected in Saxiván and received a warm welcome. We have been given part of the house of Jacinto, the sacristan and catechist. He, his wife and family are on the other side of a partition. Our "beds" are planks raised a few inches above the earthen floor, on which has been spread a carpet of grass cuttings. The walls are of planks of wood – very open, with gaps everywhere – and the roof is of corrugated zinc. We are well over 2000 metres high in the village and it can become very chilly at night.

Mass was to begin at 4.00 pm prompt which, in reality, was just before 6.00 pm. A big crowd assembled under a zinc canopy, hastily erected because of the threat of rain. Marimba and bass fiddle were the accompaniment to our singing. I gave a short homily in Spanish, pausing after each sentence or two to allow Jacinto to translate into Ixil. Most of the men understand Spanish and speak it haltingly, but many of the women know only Ixil.

We finished the Mass at about 7.30 pm, met the people informally and then went to Jacinto's house for supper. This was a chicken broth (*caldo*) into which you put spoonfuls of boiled rice. You take the pieces of chicken in your fingers to eat because spoons are the only cutlery here. Then we went to bed with the aid of a candle or two and a torch. There are six of us in the small room since a man and his two boys have arrived in Saxiván to be our guides tomorrow.

It's a very strange experience, this journey, and obviously very hard for someone like myself, unaccustomed to the conditions. So much uphill and downhill, there is hardly a square metre of level ground. And living conditions are primitive – no running water, no electricity, no furniture, monotonous food. But no complaints either, because the people are so kind, so good, so faithful. They have endured so much and are so glad to see us that all discomfort disappears in the smiles and welcomes and thanks that we receive from everyone. I feel very privileged.

SUNDAY 23RD JULY

The hard boards and the barking dogs wakened me several times during the night but I must have slept reasonably well. The cocks began to crow at about four in the morning and we were up before six. Someone brought a basin of water and I managed to wash and shave at the door of the hut, watched by a number of onlookers. It was a beautiful morning and there was quite a lot of activity in the village – people of course, but also pigs snorting and looking around for food; dogs, hens, ducks, a few small turkeys, cockerels and even a cat or two. During the night I could sometimes hear the far-off sounds of a marimba because there was a dance in another part of the village. It did not finish until about 6.30 am and then, shortly afterwards, four or five young men passed me, climbing the hill. One of them was being propelled by his companions because he was obviously inebriated. Alcoholism is a severe social problem among these people who have been subjected to so much suffering and terror.

We continued our journey, riding sometimes and walking at other times, always supported caringly by those accompanying us, especially the admirable Baltasar, tireless and cheerful though loaded like a pack animal.

Our first stop was at Santa Marta, a very new village since the people have only recently come out of hiding in the mountains. Before they fled, all had suffered terribly, many people having been butchered, and there had been some awful atrocities perpetrated by the military. We were welcomed in the traditional way – the whole village out to greet us, fire crackers going off like a machine gun right beside us. You get used to the noise, although babies, wrapped very tightly in shawls on their mothers' backs, usually begin to cry. We were escorted into a very new and rather makeshift chapel where we had a hymn and a few prayers before a big cauldron of coffee and plates of bread were brought in.

It wasn't far to our next village – Las Pilas – and a number of people from Santa Marta accompanied us along the uneven, muddy path. The church there was packed as we began Mass at noon. There were about twenty people to be confirmed, most of them grown-ups. Getting a correct list of their names caused quite a delay before Mass and I could see Fr Rosolino becoming rather agitated as very often the surnames they claimed to have did not correspond to those which they gave as their parents' surname.

I have been puzzled by the small number of those who go to Holy Communion on these occasions. Only those who were confirmed, and maybe even not all of them – plus a few others – come to Communion; in other words, a very small proportion of those attending. This, despite the fact that, before Mass began, Rosolino and I had sat outside the church, hearing confessions.

After Mass we were taken to a house and served our midday meal. It was soup (*caldo*) with a bit of chicken in the middle of it, and we added rice to the soup as desired. The usual menu, of course, and quite pleasant, but this time we didn't even have spoons. In such circumstances, you dip a *tortilla* in the soup – but a *tortilla* (a pancake made of maize flour, about ten or twelve centimetres in diameter) isn't very absorbent. So another option is to use the *tortilla* to scoop up the rice; then you just tilt the plate or bowl to your mouth, before taking the chicken in your fingers.

In the afternoon we went to our third village for the day – Las Amelias. Again we had Mass with confirmations, preceded by confessions and the same confusion about the correct names of the confirmation candidates. During Mass we also celebrated the marriage of a couple who, they told me happily, had lived together for ten years and had five children. They were a joyful pair. As a liturgical postscript at the end of Mass, Rosolino baptised four babies. Life is vibrant here, even in the midst of such deprivation and oppression.

My homily in Las Amelias did not need a catechist-interpreter to translate my Spanish words into Ixil. Most of the people here are *ladinos* and use Spanish; but every now and again the liturgy was punctuated by a kind of instruction or short homily by Rosolino. He does this in an extrovert and enthusiastic manner and often you can see that what he is trying to do is to insist that to be a Catholic is to belong to a worldwide Church. He is well aware of the inroads that the fundamentalist sects have made in these parts. A number of villages seem to have a fifty-fifty situation, as in Las Amelias where the larger of the two churches belongs to a group that the people call *La Iglesia Centro-Americana*. As we entered the village, it was broadcasting tapes of Scriptural homilies from its loudspeaker for all – and especially us – to hear. That so many have joined the sects is a sad situation, partly due to the fact that the diocese was "closed" for a time in the early 1980s.

Quiché became a diocese on its own only in 1967, but already it has had five bishops. The first died fairly soon – he had a heart condition; the second left the active ministry (having already had problems, it is said, before being made a bishop). The third bishop was Monseñor Juan Gerardi who, after two of his priests had been murdered and he himself had narrowly escaped assassination, decided in the second half of 1980 to withdraw all the clergy and religious from the diocese. Bishop Gerardi has told me that the decision was an exceptionally difficult one to take and he will never know if it was correct. Opinions are very divided among the priests and religious who are now back in Quiché but, in addition to the avoidance of further murders, Bishop Gerardi felt that the dramatic decision would draw the attention of people throughout the world to what was happening in Quiché. He is now an auxiliary bishop in Guatemala City and heads the new human rights agency of the archdiocese.

[Later, Bishop Gerardi edited '*Guatemala: Nunca Más*', the official and detailed Church account of the atrocities in Guatemala in recent times and which shows that the Guatemalan army was responsible for the overwhelming majority of the murders and disappearances; a few days after the three volumes were published, Bishop Gerardi himself was murdered.]

Not long after the "closure" of the diocese in 1980, a few priests and religious began making their way back and in 1983 the diocese of Quiché was officially "re-opened". Mons. Pablo Urízar was appointed administrator, but not actually ordained a bishop. His nomination was something of a stopgap measure until Mons. Julio Cabrera (rector of the national seminary) was fit. He had had a long illness but was finally nominated and ordained bishop of Quiché in 1987.

To return to the account of my journey, Mass in Las Amelias came to an end and we all gradually dispersed. Quite a number of people, as usual, came to me and said how much they appreciated my visit and that it was heartening for them to know that I cared about them and that I had taken the trouble to come. I don't think that Bishop Julio has yet managed to get to the villages that I have been visiting. It has probably been something like eighteen years since a bishop has been in Las Amelias but I know that Mons. Julio will come here – and to the other places – as soon as he can.

This evening there was unexpected luxury: supper at a table laid with a proper cloth, turkey instead of chicken, and a bed to sleep on.

MONDAY 24TH JULY

At 3.30 am Fr Rosolino and Baltasar crept stealthily out of the hut and began the journey back to Chajul to prepare for tomorrow's festivities there. For a few moments I felt lonely and a little frightened – "there's nobody here if anything happens to me" – but that soon passed. I thought of today's journey and how I would cope with the walking and the riding. I'm afraid I'm no horseman and don't use the reins much because I have both hands clasped tightly on the pommel for fear of falling off.

As usual I was assured that today's journey would take only two and a half hours and that the path was wide and good – but I have learned from experience that estimates are over-optimistic and made mainly to encourage me! The whole area of Ixil is extremely mountainous and very, very beautiful.

Some of the people in Ixil are *ladinos* (i.e. with European blood in their veins) but the great majority are indigenous. I asked Fr Rosolino yesterday if the two racial groups ever mixed. He said that marriages between the two are extremely rare but they have been known to take place where there is a kind of fifty-fifty division. If there is a dance, then both races will attend but they don't dance with one another. Although the poor *ladinos* do not look down on the *indígenas*, the richer *ladinos*, for example, shopkeepers or storekeepers, do, as also, of course, do the landowners.

The other night, when we had dinner with the Arenas family in La Perla, Rosolino brought one of our guides with him to the house. He told me that he did this for two reasons: first, so that he (the guide) would be able to lead him back in the dark to the church where the two of them were going to sleep; second, because he wanted to make the point that an indigenous person was good enough to be a guest in the house, sit at the log fire in the sitting room before the meal and at table with the rest of us during it.

The people here are friendly and welcoming, but there is obviously a big problem of the fundamentalist sects and of the people who don't practise any religion. I have been a little disappointed that, in the absence of a priest except for an occasional visit, the lay-led liturgical ministry is not more developed. But I believe that much of this is due to the recent history of these people who have suffered such violence and who have only lately come down from the mountains and are only now bonding into new village communities.

Many of the people we have spoken to, including the catechists, are members of the civil defence patrols. All able-bodied men have to go on duty once or twice a week in some cases or once a month, depending on the number of men available. Being in a patrol is not the same as being in favour of the regime – there is no choice –

and there does not appear to be any politicisation. Nevertheless, there remain the terrible economic and social evils that these people have suffered, with human rights and social justice so frequently and blatantly flouted. Even if the danger of violence is not so immediate these days, the people do live with a constant sense of foreboding.

Any priest coming here would have to be very special. The work is most demanding and living conditions, while visiting the far-flung parish, are uncomfortable and primitive. There is also the question of language and of culture. Rosolino considered it extremely important to be able to speak not just Spanish but also the local indigenous language. Pity the poor bishop who is trying to learn four new languages spoken in various parts of the diocese of Quiché! To understand the rich Mayan culture means that you must be constantly with the people and not merely come to celebrate Mass or hear their confessions.

So, all in all, I think that priests and any other pastoral workers who come here would have to be exceptional people – fairly young, fit and dedicated. I just don't know if they are available but, please God, they are because, at least in the meantime, there is still a great scarcity of vocations to priesthood and religious life among the indigenous people of Guatemala. Have the centuries during which they have been treated as second-rate and sometimes even as sub-human affected their self-esteem and deafened them to God's call in those directions?

Having completed all these reflections I got up before 6.00 am – the cockerels make sure you don't oversleep – found running water outside the hut (a length of hosepipe coming down the hill from a stream) and had the luxury of a good, if partial, wash with only a handful of curious onlookers.

After breakfast our group set off, with me again, painfully, on horseback. It rained heavily all the way to Santa Delfina where we stopped briefly for greetings, a prayer, a hymn or two and coffee. Then back to the "road" and the saddle. By now the rain had stopped and our group was augmented by a number of people, mostly girls, who had come from Ilom to Santa Delfina to accompany us to their village. We made a merry party, the girls just splashing through puddles and across streams, even though some had shoes on and others hadn't. They were all dressed in the red skirts and white blouses of the district. We must have been a colourful sight – quite medieval and princely, in fact – with me on horseback and accompanied by dozens of admiring maidens as a retinue! On the way we met up with Bishop Julio and his small group, soaked and bedraggled after a walk of four and a half hours through constant rain.

He told me later that, when we appeared, we seemed to his tired eyes to be like a truly magnificent vision of pomp and circumstance. Thus we made our solemn entry into Ilom, the biggest village in the area with about 1500 inhabitants. After a brief stop in the church, I left Bishop Julio there and continued, no longer with my charming escorts, for another couple of hours to Sotzil.

The church there was home for the next eighteen hours or so – meals, Mass and sleep. The Mass was packed and joyful, with confirmations. When the Mass was over, no one left and in fact the hymns continued for another couple of hours, making up in enthusiasm and noise what was lacking in finesse. The musical accompaniment during Mass was with guitars and a bass fiddle but these were augmented for the hymns after Mass by a marimba, a drum and two saxophones. Following his Mass in Ilom, Bishop Julio joined me during the evening. We supped and slept in the church after the departure of the last exuberant member of the congregation.

TUESDAY 25TH JULY

Since I was assured that the journey we had to make, from Sotzil to La Perla, was short and easy, I decided to try and walk. The first mile was downhill, steep, rough and muddy. Supported on each side by two sturdy men, I scrambled and stumbled my way down to the bottom of the valley or ravine but then, for the uphill stretch, I lacked the strength needed and had to go on horseback. On reaching La Perla, whence we had set out on Saturday morning, I was helped to dismount or, rather, I was more or less tilted off the horse into waiting arms, while others lifted my right leg across the horse's tail – inelegant and embarrassing, but effective!

La Perla airfield is just a gravel track about 500 metres long, down a distinct slope, the idea being to give a plane a good chance to pick up speed before the runway ends at a ravine. We had a long and frustrating wait before the little plane eventually arrived to take us to Nebaj. Only the pilot had a chair; the other five people on board sat on the floor or on bags of coffee beans. We threaded our way between the mountains and along the valleys and in fifteen minutes landed at Nebaj, on a military airfield, with guns and soldiers and a large notice proclaiming:

Welcome to the home of the men with gruff voices and long arms who, with their 105 mm guns, crush, neutralise and destroy the terrorist criminals, and thus contribute to the peace, security and development of Guatemala

We hitched a lift into Nebaj on a pick-up truck which happened to be at the airfield. I was given the comfortable place beside the driver. He told me that he was a teacher but that he wasn't working at present. There is a national teachers' strike on, as well as a postal strike that has lasted three months so far. Once a month he brings a photographer from Nebaj to the barracks at the airfield to take photographs of the soldiers for them to send home to their families, when there is not a postal strike. My informant also mentioned some interesting things about guerrillas. He spoke about two recent occasions. On one of them he himself had been stopped on the road between the airfield and Nebaj by about fifteen men, accompanied by a woman and a child. They told him that they would buy any clothes, particularly sweaters, that he had to give them and they assured him that they were not going to harm him or rob him. On another occasion some of the guerrillas appeared in one of the villages on market day and bought provisions for themselves. So they are certainly around this area and they seem to have the ability to keep going and to have the basic necessities of life. However, there can be times of great difficulty when they are reduced to eating roots and are very ill-clad.

[Some years later I was again in Ixil and with Fr Rosolino on the road between Nebaj and Chajul when a group of guerrillas suddenly emerged from the cornfield at the side of the road and stopped our car. Their leader was courteous. He told us of their reasons for having taken up arms, we gave him some of the bread that we had bought in Nebaj, and we bade one another farewell.]

After lunch in the Nebaj convent we reached Chajul about 4.30 pm, just in time for the Mass and the inauguration of the "*Asociación Chajulense Va'l Vaq Quyol*". This is a kind of cooperative set up by Fr Rosolino for the people of Chajul. Members will be able to buy necessities at a fairly cheap rate or have their coffee ground or their maize (corn) made into flour for *tortillas*. Moreover, they can bring their produce – principally coffee and maize – to sell to the *Asociación* and receive better prices for it.

The hall where we had the Mass was packed and among the guests were the mayor, who is Protestant, and the local military commander. The idea is that the *Asociación* should not be merely a parish venture but something for all the people of Chajul and its villages.

[The Asociación has subsequently thrived, both locally and also internationally. It has outlets in Europe and North America for the sale of its coffee and also, interestingly, for marketing the multicoloured woven cloth so characteristic of this part of Guatemala.]

WEDNESDAY 26TH JULY

This morning we left Chajul and drove to Cotzal, the town and parish in Ixil which will soon have a resident priest from Germany and a community of religious sisters. Cotzal has been a very difficult place with a recent history of violence and massacres. Those in authority there have tried to frustrate efforts by the diocese to re-establish a presence in the town.

Bishop Julio and I passed through the town of Cotzal and continued for perhaps some twelve kilometres to a village (actually a *finca*) called Santa Abelina to celebrate the third anniversary of the opening of its rebuilt church. It is fairly large, built of *adobe* and wood, with a roof of corrugated zinc.

About two hundred metres short of the church our car was stopped because the road ahead was blocked by people who had assembled to greet us. Someone made a short speech of welcome to which the bishop replied and then girls scattered flower petals over the two of us as we walked down the road between two rows of people, shaking hands with them all, under a blazing sun. We were taken first to a building alongside the church where we were given something to drink and the bishop was measured by the local tailor for a traditional Cotzal suit (red jacket with facings, white trousers). The measurements included places which other tailors do not reach and the bishop was promised that, in due course, he would receive a suit, a gift of the local community.

The Mass was due to start at 9.00 am but, due to the welcoming ceremonies and because we were hearing confessions for an hour beforehand, it was about 11.00 am when the Mass began, with a packed congregation. The liturgy was very joyful, with two *conjuntos* or bands: no marimbas, but plenty of guitars and accordions.

There was segregation of the sexes, men on the right as we looked towards them and women on the left. At the bringing of the gifts there were not only the bread and wine but a lot of presents for the bishop and me. People handed over flowers and fruit and maize as well as a towel for each of us. Most weird of all, the bishop was given a live hen and I received a duck which we had to take in our hands and clasp tightly so that they didn't escape, before handing them over to someone who was standing nearby. We took the presents away with us but later left the fowl with the nuns at Nebaj.

After Mass there were ten baptisms, but done by the Nebaj priest, Fr Tomás Ventura, who is filling in at Cotzal until the new parish priest arrives. Meanwhile, Bishop Cabrera and I went to the same room as we had been in prior to Mass and there was something to eat before we moved off in the midst of the most effusive of farewells. We were treated with great friendship and kindness by the people of Santa Abelina. Our welcome there, though not any more sincere than in the other places we had been to, was probably on a bigger scale and more carefully prepared.

By way of Nebaj and Sacapulas and about half a dozen checkpoints with either the army or the civil defence patrols, we reached Santa Cruz and the bishop's house at about seven o'clock. A good hot shower, a change of clothes and an enjoyable supper ended a full day and an unforgettable trip.

THURSDAY 27TH JULY

Not much activity today, but a chance to rest, to recuperate and to reflect.

Most of the people who live in the *aldeas* or villages which we visited are *indigenas*. The villages do not have any streets in them. Most of them are built on hillsides or on hilly ground and in among trees also, with the result that one tends to see roofs rather than buildings if looking from any distance. The walls of most houses are made from planks of wood, but others are just sticks of bamboo or even maize stalks stuck into the ground close together. The insides of the walls sometimes have plastic sheets attached to them, sometimes not. A few times you see buildings of *adobe*. The roofs of some houses are of corrugated zinc sheets but more often are thatched.

Inside the houses the floors are of earth and there is very little furniture. In some cases the family has a wood stove but in other houses the people simply put the firewood on the ground and light a fire there, maybe arranging stones around it on which the pots can be placed. It is a very common sight in the evenings to see men returning home and bent almost double under huge loads of firewood. Deforestation continues apace because wood is the only fuel that the people have and they cannot afford alternatives or to replant.

When, often, we were invited to eat in their houses, the people pulled the stops out. There was usually some kind of rickety table, with maybe a bench along one side (no chairs) and a piece of plastic sometimes placed on the table. People have soup plates or bowls, perhaps also a cup or a mug, but none of them matching one another and normally showing their age. For us, special guests, a chicken was killed to add to the staples of soup, *tortillas,* rice and, sometimes, beans.

The usual drink is coffee with sugar, occasionally also with cinnamon, but no milk. On the bishop's advice I avoided drinking water but there is often, even in remote villages, Pepsi-Cola. The bottle is opened by inserting the neck in your mouth and wrenching or levering off the cap between your back teeth – not a practice I engaged in!

The men dress in "western" clothes and nearly always with a straw hat. The indigenous women wear the traditional – and expensive – clothes: blouse (*guipil*), long skirt (*corte*) and turban-like headdress (*cinta*), each group of villages having its distinctive colours and styles.

In the houses there is no electricity; candles or torches are used when it gets dark. No running water, no telephone or television, of course. Sometimes one will hear a transistor radio and there are often a few pictures stuck on the walls, and maybe an out-of-date calendar. Occasionally I saw beds; some people sleep on raised planks, some just sleep on the ground. Little hammocks are slung from the roof beams for the babies. The love of the people for children is evident. It is very noticeable that most women of child-bearing age, whether walking or working, seem to have a baby slung on their back and tied tightly in a shawl.

Despite the conditions in which they live, most people keep themselves and their clothes remarkably clean. Some families share what they call "*un baño*"or "*un excusado*" which is a little cabin about a metre square and a short distance from the house. It is made of maize stalks on three sides and a piece of plastic as the door. These stalks rise to about shoulder height and then there is a gap and some kind of a roof over the whole thing, held up by four corner posts. Inside there is just the earth floor but, in addition, there is a plank of wood which has been smoothed and sandpapered and which takes up about half of the floor area. It is raised about forty centimetres from the ground and, in the middle of the plank, there is a hole very much like a toilet seat – because of course that is what it is – and this hole goes down about three metres. The alternative is a nearby bush.

Each family seems to have quite a collection of hens and chickens, ducks and ducklings, sometimes also turkeys, pigs and piglets and often dogs and even cats. I didn't see any mice or rats but was told that they are around. The dogs and cats are pets but the other animals are kept for food.

The people were astonishingly kind to me, not just with presents – that was particularly true in Santa Abelina – but good and thoughtful, wanting to make sure that I was comfortable, helping me on the road and giving me of the very best food that they have. Even though it is simple, monotonous and sometimes difficult to eat, it is in abundance and that is very touching.

Concerning the amount of food that I had been offered, I said to the bishop when we were on our way back to Santa Cruz yesterday that I was sometimes asked in Scotland whether there is any starvation in Guatemala. He replied that in some cases there may be hunger and malnutrition, but not generally. It is not one of the major problems in Guatemala, especially since the land is so fertile and the weather so propitious, with a good amount of rain. Anything grows anywhere, or at least in most places there is some ground for cultivating something. In addition, he said, the people have a tremendous sense of community. If they see one of their number going hungry, they will certainly take measures to ensure it does not continue. So on the whole the people here look well nourished.

Yesterday, just as we were leaving Chajul on our way to Cotzal and Santa Abelina, Bishop Julio noticed a house on the left side of the road and exclaimed, "Oh, there's Mek's house". Mek (Miguel) was our chief guide on our trip, so we stopped and he invited us into his house where we met his wife and his two infant children, plus a third infant (Francisco) who is an orphan. I asked the bishop afterwards and he said that the Catholic Church has tried to have orphans adopted by families and has asked families to do this. Mek's was one family which had agreed to do so. Were they paid or given an allowance? Bishop Julio replied, "Well, if there is absolute need; but in many cases they just take the orphan and don't ask for any allowance and the orphan simply becomes a member of the family." It struck me as poignant and yet very noble.

FRIDAY 28TH JULY

Much of the time these past twenty-four hours I have spent reading the book called (in English) *Guatemala – Eternal Spring, Eternal Tyranny* by Jean-Marie Simon. Published in 1987, it gives a good outline, both in text and in pictures, of the recent history and present state of Guatemala.

Some points from the book have struck me as particularly significant. For example, it is reckoned that, over the last ten years, between fifty and sixty thousand people have been killed in

Guatemala; second, that the killings have mainly been of two kinds, the first being of what might be called selective disappearances and murders, kidnappings and assassinations. The other has been wholesale massacres which have usually occurred in towns and villages, especially in this department of Quiché. Tens of thousands of peasants have fled in fear of the army, sometimes going into exile in Mexico or, I suppose, further afield; but the great majority have just fled into the mountains. Many have been recaptured or have surrendered to the military authorities but, strictly speaking, these are not guerrillas – merely people who fled in terror, many of them women and children.

To a large extent these people, after surrender or discovery and recapture, have been re-housed in the "*aldeas modelo*" or model villages, so-called, which have often been set up on or near the site of villages razed to the ground under the army's scorched earth policy of some years ago. The situation is simply appalling. God help them. God alone knows what is going to become of the people of this country. And I know, from what I have seen and heard myself, that conditions, especially in Ixil, are just sheer brutal slavery, with indescribable atrocities and a complete lack, on the part of the authorities, of any sense of humanity.

[Some years later, details became known of the CPRs (Comunidades de Población en Resistencia) – men, women and children who had fled into the mountains and had survived there for years. They organised themselves as communities, providing basic health care for themselves and some education for the children. They were in constant danger of being discovered by the army and sometimes had to flee hurriedly from where they had established themselves to another site. Some people, including Bishop Julio, knew of the CPRs' existence and even visited them on rare occasions; but there was always fear of discovery or betrayal.]

SATURDAY 29TH JULY

Bishop Cabrera and I spent most of today in Chichicastenango, in the south of the diocese. It is or, rather, was a great tourist centre since it is the nearest Quiché town to Guatemala City and has a very colourful market on Sundays and Thursdays. Our destination was a pastoral retreat centre run by Marist Brothers on the outskirts of the town and we were taking part in a day for young people who were interested in the possibility of a vocation to priesthood or religious life. Eleven boys and sixteen girls were present, most of them indigenous. Also attending were three or four religious sisters, two Marist Brothers, Padre Teodoro from the cathedral in Santa Cruz, a German missionary called Andrea, Bishop Cabrera and myself. It was a very interesting day and the young ones seemed quite open and uncomplicated and keen to know.

The programme consisted of talks and small groups and games, and we ended with Mass. A couple of people were invited to give testimonies of how God was active in their lives. One was Fulvia, a young lady in her twenties who comes from the Guatemalan town of Escuintla and who is working for the diocese in Patzité, a parish west of here. The other witness was Fr Teodoro who told us that he had had a hard struggle to become a priest. Part of the trouble was that his father, although a good Christian, was very much against his son's wish. He is the eldest son and the father wanted him to marry. In fact, at one stage, Teodoro's father said, "I'll sell my house and smallholding and spend the money I get to allow you to qualify for any profession you like, whether it be doctor or teacher or anything at all, if you will just give up the idea of priesthood". But the young man would not and, after several problems which included his moving from seminary to seminary, he was ordained a priest last year. I asked him privately after his testimony whether his father now accepted the fact that he was a priest. He answered, "My father was killed in the violence".

The Marists told me that they had taken possession of the house after several years of occupation there by the army. The army left around 1983 and one of the brothers said to me that, in the grounds, there were several deep wells or pits ("*pozos*") and, when I asked if there were bodies in them, he shrugged his shoulders and said, "Presumably".

When he was speaking to the young people before the Mass and also during the homily, the bishop dwelt very movingly on the fact that Quiché was a land of martyrs where blood had been shed by countless people for the faith and the ground was therefore sacred; but he also said that Quiché's need was for indigenous priests and religious. There must be a serious effort to overcome the reluctance and the feeling of unworthiness that affects indigenous people with regard to priestly and religious ministry. He strongly urged the young ones there to reflect seriously on whether God was calling them to that kind of service in the Church.

On the way back into Santa Cruz we stopped at the town hospital to visit two people whom the bishop knows. Conditions inside the hospital are practically indescribable for dirt and antiquity. We were shown into the men's surgical ward. The beds are about a metre apart. The mattresses were filthy. There was sometimes a kind of sheet which hardly covered the mattress and the pillow had no pillowslip. There was a blanket and a cover on each bed but God knows if the cover was washed each time between patients. It didn't look like it.

There was a rickety table at the side of each bed on which the remains of the supper lay. The supper had been served, without plates, on a circular metal dish with three compartments. I could see, from the remains, that each man had been given a corn (maize) on the cob and some beans (*frijoles*).

One single light hung in the centre of the room – no bedside lamps (which would have looked incongruous in the midst of the squalor). The men themselves were dressed in any old dirty clothes. The whole place was truly awful.

The patients had various surgical complaints – sometimes an operation for things that were wrong with them, sometimes it was the result of an accident. In one case a man had been gored by a bull, in another a man had been badly burned. One of the men whom we had gone to see had been hit on the foot by a small rock and it was only two or three weeks later that things had begun to trouble him; but now several of his toes looked black and, although I could not see the rest for bandages, it seemed that gangrene had set in.

We spoke to about a dozen men in the ward, if you could call it a ward. It was divided into sections by shoulder–high partitions, each section containing four, five or six beds, not all of which were occupied. Two of the men could not speak any Spanish at all. This surprised me because I thought that all the men – but far fewer women – knew the language, at least to some extent. Two of the patients were on drips and quite ill, but the whole place seemed depressed and depressing and, I have to say, filthy by our standards.

We usually get the newspapers here in Santa Cruz some time during the day. The two dailies (*Prensa Libre* and *El Gráfico*) are both full of reports about the teachers'strike in the state schools throughout the country. It has been going on for weeks now and I suppose that most of the incidents take place in Guatemala City. There have been attempts to have a meeting with the President, the archbishop has been brought into the situation by people invading the cathedral and also his residence; and four of the main access roads to the capital city were blocked by strikers for two or three hours one morning.

The other day there was an open letter published in one of the newspapers by the *Procurador de Derechos Humanos*. He is an official appointed by the government, I suppose as a kind of ombudsman for human rights. Not that much has been achieved so far, but the letter itself was extremely strong and highly critical, especially of Vinicio Cerezo. "You, Mr President, were elected by the people of this country to run the country and you are doing nothing; you are simply allowing it to drift into chaos". The letter instanced the stalemate in the teachers' strike and the many bombings that have occurred recently in Guatemala – not necessarily by guerrillas or death squads but perhaps simply criminal bombings, though God knows who is responsible for all this violence. All this, the *Procurador* added, illustrated how the President was allowing the country to drift and not taking any responsibility for the situation.

The people have said that it was an extremely brave letter. However, when I asked whether he had put his life in jeopardy by writing and publishing it, I was told that was unlikely because he was doing the job that he had been given and he is a highly respected eighty-one year old lawyer.

But the situation is almost "cloud cuckoo land" because, in addition to all the bombings and the strikes and the Procurator's letter, the papers carry reports of coming-out parties and society weddings. Yesterday there was a full page dedicated to photographs of a party celebrating a girl's fifteenth birthday. This is an important milestone in a girl's life and demands a big celebration in Central America, especially among the wealthy classes. A great deal of money is spent on it, with lavish entertainment and so on, just like a big wedding. I saw another similar fawning report a few days ago and in each case the girl's father was a high-ranking officer. One just wonders what the stories of those colonels are and how all the make-believe of joy and celebration can take place in a country in which so much evil has been perpetrated over the years – and in which those who have power have every intention of keeping things as they are. Are such people aware of the evils? Or of the poverty, injustice and terror? Do any of them care?

SUNDAY 30TH JULY

Each Sunday, if he is in Santa Cruz, Bishop Cabrera celebrates the 7.00 am Mass in the cathedral and it is broadcast on Radio Quiché, the diocesan radio station which provides a contact with people in the remote areas of the diocese such as Ixil. Before beginning the homily today, the bishop spoke about the journey which he and I had made recently in Chajul. Here are some of the things he said.

"…I send my greetings to my brothers and sisters who live in the parish of Chajul and to those who accompanied us on our journey – Miguel, Domingo and Baltasar – as well as to all the communities we visited with Mgr Maurice Taylor, a Scottish bishop who is visiting this diocese and who wanted to accompany me on this long and difficult journey. I greet all the communities I visited and thank them for all the signs of affection which I received – La Perla, Ilom, Sotzil, Pombolsé, Santa Eulalia, Santa Cecilia, La Pimienta. I also greet the communities visited by Bishop Maurice and thank them for the welcome they gave him – La Perla, Saxiván, Santa Marta, Las Pilas, Las Amelias, Santa Delfina, Ilom and Sotzil. I thank my brothers and sisters in Santa Abelina for the celebration we had there, a truly fraternal celebration of the third anniversary of the blessing of their church… These journeys, many of them on foot and for many days, or on horseback as well as by car and by plane, are very hard. In many of the villages visited, it is the first time the bishop has been there. It was more than twenty years since a bishop had been in Ilom… The only thing that I seek is to encourage my brothers and sisters, to nourish their faith, to assure them that they form a part of a community much bigger than the small one where they live…"

The streets in the centre of Santa Cruz were the scene of the weekly market today. The goods on sale were laid out on stalls or on mats on the road – fruits, vegetables, lumps of soda for use when making *tortillas,* bleached palm fronds for making the hats that the men wear, lengths of cloth, ready-made clothes for men and *ladino* women, household goods, cheap plastic items, unvarnished pine furniture…

The people here are even more colourful than the goods, both the vendors and their customers, most of whom are women with baskets on their heads and babies on their backs. The Santa Cruz market seems a genuine one for local people and not in any way an attraction for the benefit of tourists, who do not come here anyway.

One section of the market runs along the back of the military establishment which, with the cathedral, is the most prominent building in the town. As I passed, a crowd of people were looking in or watching the few soldiers who were standing there. The people were very passive and there wasn't any great excitement but, when I returned to the bishop's house, I discovered that in fact several youths had been grabbed by the soldiers and pulled inside the building. When I asked why the people did not protest, the answer was that, if they had protested, they might have been shot. Apparently this is the way in which the army gets its recruits. On a market day or a feast day, the military just seize any young men who are about, if they want them, and take them away to be drafted into the army. The same thing can happen on buses: the bus is stopped by the army and the young men on the bus are removed. No permission is given by their parents, or anything like that. The young men are just grabbed. "Come on! We're going to make men of you!" and they reappear some time later in some barracks in another part of the country. The period of military service is three years but, of course, there is no proper registration or organised call-up. It seems a frightfully inhuman way of doing things, like a press gang. Apparently this method is not used in the capital city but only in the interior of the country, as it is called. I asked if the system was something new but it seems to have been the way of recruiting for the military since time immemorial. The practice is called "*agarrando*" (grabbing) or "*pescando*" (fishing).

This afternoon I met three of the leaders of "*Conavigua*" which is an association of widows whose husbands have been killed or have disappeared. They had come in to ask Bishop Julio if they could have a Mass next month to mark the first anniversary of their foundation. The members of the association accept that, in all probability, their menfolk have perished and they seek official protection and assistance, financial and other, for themselves and their children.

Conavigua stands for *Co-ordinadora Nacional de Viudas de Guatemala* (National Coordinating Committee of Widows of Guatemala). It came into being in September 1988 because of the desperate plight of so many thousands of widows whose husbands had been murdered or had disappeared. One of its aims is to get the government to take responsibility for the education of their children. The authorities have allocated certain funds for this but no one has yet received anything. There have been some food handouts, but these have been selective, minimal in quantity and with strings attached. Conavigua demands that any funds should be given directly to the widows because, if they are channelled through officials, they may never reach the intended beneficiaries. It also asks that women in Guatemala be treated with proper respect and not with the traditional disdain because they are often illiterate or poorly educated or unable to speak Spanish.

Although Conavigua is not a clandestine organisation but operates openly and legally, the authorities' attitude has been suspicious and unhelpful and some members have received threats from local military commandants. But, as the leaders told me, "We are *for* the widows and orphans; we are not *against* anyone, not even the army".

I went to the cathedral in order to celebrate Mass there at 5.00 pm. The church was fairly full and there was a choir there from charismatic renewal. The singing wasn't very great nor did the congregation join in to any extent. Incongruously, the *Gloria* was sung to the tune of "*John Brown's Body*", the chorus being "*Gloria, Gloria, Alleluia*", ending with "*En el nombre del Señor*".

The gospel was about God's goodness in giving us what we need, what we ask for, but in the homily I made the point that that does not absolve the rest of us who have plenty from giving to those who are in want. I spoke about the way in which I hoped to encourage my fellow countrymen and women not only to be more generous towards a nation like Guatemala but to be more aware of the situation here. I hope that I did not go too far. I certainly did not attempt to assert who had been responsible, but I did mention the suffering, the massacres, the disappearances, the widows, the orphans, the deaths, the poverty and the fear, so I think that I went as far as I probably should have. At the end of Mass a number of people, about ten perhaps, came to the sacristy to thank me for coming and for what I had said. It was good of them to bother.

MONDAY 31ST JULY

Fr Juan Vásquez, the parish priest of Joyabaj, came to see the bishop this afternoon and I had the chance of a long talk with him. He is interesting, not only because he is in Joyabaj but also because he was the first priest to arrive in Ixil after the worst of the violence in the early 1980s and when the diocese was being "re-opened". For three years, until 1987, he had to look after what are now the three parishes of Ixil – Nebaj, Chajul and Cotzal – with all the villages and settlements around them. He said that, on arrival, he did not receive a rapturous welcome from the people because everything was so tense. Many of the people had just come back from months or years hiding in the mountains. The military and the civil defence patrols carry out what are called "*rastreos*" – "raking" or "combing" through the mountains – and those who are found are brought down and now live in settlements under the control of the army. He himself had found life very difficult because of the demands made upon him by the army. On one occasion he was told that he was needed to bless a new "*aldea modelo*" ("model village") but since he had a previous appointment he declined to go. The fact that the administrator of the diocese, Mons. Pablo Urízar, was taken there to do the blessing in his stead did not make things any easier for Juan Vásquez. There were other times, too, when the army more or less tried to dictate to him where he should go and what he should do.

I asked him about the villages I had visited and whether the people there had been among those who had suffered. His answer was a laconic "Everyone suffered".

Two incidents which someone described to me illustrate the conditions under which people lived. The first happened in Cotzal. The people there, it is said, are more openly emotional than those in Nebaj and Chajul and the guerrillas had been particularly active in the district. On one occasion they attacked the barracks and, as a reprisal, the army went into the town and picked at random a large number of men, women and children, took them to the cemetery and shot them.

The other incident occurred in Sacapulas, on the other side of the mountains from Ixil. A boy of about sixteen had had the notion of going to the seminary and he asked permission of the military to leave Sacapulas. Since his family were under surveillance because of suspicion that some of his relations were involved with the guerrillas, the army was very reluctant to allow him to go to Guatemala City. However, they did give him permission and he was to leave the following day. That night, the civil defence patrols were ordered by the army to keep away from the area where the boy lived and, during the night, the boy and his father were taken out of their house and were not seen again.

I asked Fr Vásquez about his work in Joyabaj. He told me that it was difficult because he has something like sixty *cantones* (villages) to look after and he has to go out every week, from Monday to Friday, to visit some of them; and then he goes back to Joyabaj for the Masses at the weekend. The community leaders of the *cantones* go to Joyabaj on Saturdays to meet, study and reflect. They take part in the Saturday evening Mass and spend the night in Joyabaj, sleeping on the floor of the parish hall, and go back to their villages on Sunday morning. These leaders then have a catechesis class every Monday in their villages which the great majority of people attend.

He said that, in the villages, there is no Sunday liturgy, neither a Liturgy of Holy Communion nor even a Liturgy of the Word, but that they were gradually moving in that direction. Some parishes in the diocese had begun to have lay-led Sunday liturgies but he felt that it was important to build good foundations, otherwise things might just get out of control. He added that, although there are no women yet in lay leadership in his parish, he would like to work towards that.

He himself is from Guatemala City but it had always been his wish to work among the people who were least privileged. That is why he had wanted to be in the diocese of Quiché and why he was pleased to go to Ixil when asked. That appointment, however, had been very much against his mother's wishes because she had been a cook for the military and she knew the kind of life and dangers that he would experience.

Fr Vásquez confirmed something that I had already heard. He tended to distinguish between two ways of being an active Catholic in Guatemala. One was to be in "Catholic Action" and the other was to be in charismatic renewal. He said that the latter, when it became popular about ten years ago, was much favoured by the army because the style of spirituality that it fostered was more individualistic and somewhat cocooned, with enthusiastic singing, an atmosphere of noisy joy and a concentration on preparing for the next life; whereas "Catholic Action" was seen as a threat because there was stress on the need for justice in the here and now. What he seemed to suggest was that most Catholics, or at least most of those who are active, were in one or the other group. In some parishes, as I had already heard, one group is much stronger than the other.

The preference that the army has for a charismatic type of Catholicism and one that is less likely to ask awkward questions or to seek to change structures is clearly in accordance with the encouragement shown to the fundamentalist sects by those in power. These are obviously much less of a threat to the status quo than a Christianity which has embraced a preferential option for the poor and all that that implies.

TUESDAY 1ST AUGUST

There were quite a number of people at supper in the bishop's house this evening, including Fr Rosolino from Chajul and Fr Federico. Both priests are originally from the same diocese of Crema, near Milan. Fr Federico works in Lancetillo, in the east of Quiché diocese, and is parish priest of the area known as La Reina.

The situation there during the awful years from 1981 to 1984 beggared description; the persecution, killings and destruction carried out by the army were appalling. Gradually and under conditions of great hardship, people have been returning to the area. The land there is not as mountainous as in Ixil but getting there and moving around are even more difficult because of the lack of roads. Incidentally, it was La Reina that the bishop had been visiting just before I arrived in Guatemala and in which he had experienced such delay before being able to get out.

WEDNESDAY 2ND AUGUST

One of the sisters of St Joseph of the Apparition, a Congregation working in Santa Cruz, took me today to see the parishes in the south-east of the diocese. The road is good by Quiché standards.

We stopped first in Zacualpa, at the church of the Holy Spirit, served by two Franciscan fathers. In the garden behind the church there is a little stone building where people were taken to be tortured in the repression of the early 1980s. There are still bloodstains on the walls and, screwed to the ceiling beams, there are hooks to which were attached the ropes that bound prisoners' wrists so that their arms were kept raised above their heads. The room is now a little chapel and beside the altar there are photographs of Archbishop Romero of San Salvador (assassinated in 1980) and of the three priests who were murdered in this diocese.

We continued east to Joyabaj. The parish priest, Fr Juan Vásquez, had not yet returned from some villages he was visiting, but his housekeeper showed us around the town. In an old cemetery a man was, we were told, "*haciendo costumbre*" – i.e. performing traditional Mayan rites – at the foot of a stone cross. He had a small fire burning and three candles on the step at the bottom of the cross. He put something like incense on the fire and then sprinkled liquor on it. Our guide whispered that he was a "*brujo*" and that he was carrying out "*brujerías*" (witchcraft). A woman approached and spoke to the man. We were informed that she was asking the man to cast an evil spell on one of her enemies. When we met Juan Vásquez later, he ridiculed this explanation and

I learned that, although witchcraft is sometimes practised, it happens in secret.

The Catholic Church is showing a growing interest in Mayan rites as practised by "*los de la Costumbre*", as they are called. There was a time when these pre-Christian rites were regarded by the Church as quite unacceptable and therefore to be totally rejected. But now there is an increasing opinion that many of them are acceptable and even praiseworthy. One clear exception to this seems to be the use of alcohol in the rites, which sometimes degenerates into drunkenness. As serious study is done on Mayan beliefs and practices, there are those who see the possibility of their being integrated into Catholic ritual. Some of those who follow Mayan rites consider themselves to be Catholics; others do not.

In another part of Joyabaj I saw a curious sight – a child of about three or four holding a piece of thread a metre or more long, the other end of the thread being tied to a butterfly which was flying around like a miniature kite. Very incongruous. It reminded me of something I had seen in Saxiván: one of the ducks in the house next to ours was walking around with a feather threaded through its nostrils and sticking out at each side. Its owner said that this was a punishment for the duck's wrongdoing.

In the parish house in Joyabaj we visited the room where Fr Faustino Villanueva was murdered on 10th July 1980. Two men knocked at the door of the house and asked him if he would celebrate Mass for a special intention. He took them to the room which he used as an office in order to make a note of their request. As he was about to do so, they produced a gun and killed him at point blank range. A stone tablet to his memory is placed in front of the high altar in the church nearby.

On the way back to Santa Cruz we stopped at Chinique and met Sister Colette, from St-Etienne in France. She lives a solitary life in a small house beside the church. The inhabitants here are mostly *ladinos*, rather indifferent to religion and quite hostile to the *indigenas*, so much so that they have asked the priest to give them a Mass for themselves on Saturday evenings in order to avoid the *indigenas*, who come into Mass on Sundays from the outlying villages.

There has been a lot of killing in Chinique but much of it was due to vendettas between families, some of whom took advantage of the conditions in order to kill their enemies. We were told that the atmosphere in the town is still very tense because of the murders that had taken place; even the children knew what had happened and were conscious of the bad feeling. There was much bitterness in particular that some people, through their dubious activities and the friendships they had cultivated with the military, had become quite wealthy and at the expense of their fellow townspeople. I had the clear impression that things are not pleasant in Chinique and that not all the problems are directly the fault of the army.

Finally we made a brief stop at Chiché where we visited a community of young indigenous women. Their mentor is Sister Andrea, the German lady we met at Chichicastenango on Saturday. Their main work is with the widows, of whom there are many in this area, teaching them the skills of cooking and dressmaking. They seemed a happy community despite, or because of, living a very ordered and disciplined life with a demanding routine of prayer.

THURSDAY 3RD AUGUST

Bishop Cabrera's housekeepers are two sisters, María and Ignacia. Their parents have a smallholding in Río Blanco, very near Sacapulas. Since the patron saint of that town is St Dominic and his feast is still kept on 4th August there (for the rest of the Church it was changed to 8th August some years ago), the four of us went to Sacapulas today for the annual celebrations.

The church was packed for the vigil Mass, before which we had confessions. I was assigned a place in the sanctuary and a long line of men and women, nearly all indigenous, came and confessed. I was working under some difficulty because most of the women confessed in Quiché and I could tell that they had finished only because they said the Spanish word "*solamente*" at the end of their confession (and I listened carefully for that word). In addition, there were frequent deafening bursts of firecrackers ("*bombas*" and "*cohetes*") which made it impossible to hear myself speak, let alone my clients. I am sure that the Lord understood.

The Mass was joyful and enthusiastic. To distribute Holy Communion, we were all dispatched to various parts of the church. I ended up near the main entrance at the back of the church. As it was extremely dark there, I had great difficulty in avoiding treading on the young children lying asleep wherever there was a tiny space on the floor.

After Mass the Blessed Sacrament was exposed and the timetable for "watches" throughout the night was announced, each village of the parish being assigned its half-hour. The streets of the town would be filled with noisy revellers most of the night and so the bishop and I were given hospitality, at some distance away from the town, in his housekeepers' parents' home.

The family were extremely thoughtful and kind. On a little table at my bedside there was a rose in a vase and a note which read, "*Bienvenido a su casa, Mons, Mauricio*".

FRIDAY 4TH AUGUST

I was up and about in the early morning sun and had a stroll round the smallholding. There are two cows and a calf, a mare and her colt, a donkey, some chickens and hens plus about two hectares of land around the house, planted with various things, principally maize and beans. The land is irrigated from the river nearby and gives two crops each year.

This is the traditional style for the indigenous people of Quiché. Because of the close bond that Mayans have with the earth, they want to live on the land they cultivate. So each dwelling house is surrounded by its owner's land and the houses in a village are not all clustered together, as is now the case in the villages which I visited last week in Ixil. There the army has forced the people, when rebuilding their villages, to keep the houses close to each other so that it is easier to have the people under surveillance.

In addition to Don Pedro and Doña Isabel, parents of the bishop's housekeepers, a widow and her two young children also live on the smallholding. They are not relations but, in fact, the woman arrived about 1985 seeking shelter when her husband either disappeared or was killed and the older couple took her in and befriended her.

Doña Isabel told us that, when her children were younger and the family were poor, they used to have to go to the Pacific coast each year to work in the coffee and cotton plantations and that the wage was 50 *centavos* (10p) a day. The work was very hard, they got very little to eat – just six *tortillas* per family three times a day – water was scarce and they slept in one large room, all the families together, lying on the floor. But they had to do it because otherwise they would have starved. The conditions were dreadful and the wages poor but, before they set out, the man who hired them would give them an advance of perhaps five *quetzales* (about £1.00).

We returned to the church in Sacapulas for another Mass (more or less a repeat of last night). During it about twenty children made their first Holy Communion and the bishop commissioned a number of lay ministers for the outlying villages of Sacapulas parish. Some were to be ministers of the Eucharist, others were to be "*animadores*" or "*formadores*" (lay leaders and catechists). The bishop, in addressing them, made the point that people like them had suffered greatly from the persecutions of recent years, accused of being subversives or even Marxists, and that the Church in Quiché was rising and growing from soil consecrated by the blood of martyrs.

I have been struck by the friendliness of the people in all the places I have been to. They are very natural. As you are walking around, many will approach – total strangers – clap you on the shoulder or shake hands and say "Good morning" or "Good evening" or offer a word of welcome.

The custom is for children up to the age of about ten to stand before a priest with their heads bowed so that he can place his hand on their heads as a kind of blessing. It's done very naturally and spontaneously. Even babies, strapped to their mothers' backs, have been taught to lean forward with their heads bowed.

SATURDAY 5TH AUGUST

The bishop and I have been in San Antonio Ilotenango today. It is a town about fifteen or twenty kilometres west of Santa Cruz, reached quite easily over a gravel road. When we got to the outskirts our car had to stop because hundreds of people were there to welcome us – and me in particular, as was obvious from the banners they carried. The parish priest is a young man from the Pacific coast, Fr Rudi, and San Antonio has its "Sunday Mass" on Saturdays because he has to go elsewhere on Sundays.

We were introduced to the leaders of charismatic renewal, "Catholic Action" and "*La Costumbre*". The last are those who, at least nominally Catholic, continue to practise traditional Mayan rites, including the veneration of their ancestors. They all seemed to be elderly and were dressed, men as well as women, in indigenous costume with a white veil around their shoulders. Most of the men carried some kind of "pious object" like a small monstrance or a reliquary or a wooden statue, as a symbol of office. I was told that these people of *La Costumbre* have been baptised in the Catholic Church but do not usually receive other sacraments.

After the introductions, everyone formed up in a kind of procession and, with music and song and firecrackers, we made our way up the main street under a blazing sun to the church for Mass with a packed congregation. There was the usual joyful and noisy liturgy which included the presentation of quite a variety of gifts, both to Bishop Julio and to me. Among the items I was given were a *cinta* (the turban worn by indigenous women), a painting of the town and a vase of plastic flowers. I was glad to observe that, as in Sacapulas, the numbers receiving Holy Communion were large. Perhaps the small numbers of communicants that I noticed in Ixil were due to the circumstances there – communities newly formed and the recent history of violence and terror.

After Mass, the lay leaders of the parish – about twenty and all men – led us proudly on a tour of inspection of the priest's house and the various parochial offices, classrooms etc. alongside the church. Then we had lunch in one of the biggest rooms – Bishop Cabrera and I at the top table with the twenty leaders, and over a hundred parishioners at two long tables at right angles to the top table. All the women who were there sat at one side of one of the long tables. In most churches also I noticed that the women tend to be together on one side and the men on the other. Our visit to San Antonio Ilotenango ended with a dramatic and musical presentation by the teenagers – scenes from the weekly market and a stately traditional dance.

I had the chance of some informal conversation with about a dozen of the men of the parish and they were full of questions about the country I came from. "Where was Scotland?" "Near England" meant nothing to them but "Near Spain" seemed to satisfy them. "How much did people earn?" "What was the climate like?"… Until then they had never heard of Scotland and, frankly, after our conversation I don't think they felt much wiser.

However the whole day was hugely enjoyable, if a bit embarrassing for me as the centre of attraction, and yet another sign of the warmth of the friendship and hospitality that one receives in this part of the world.

On the way back to Santa Cruz, the bishop pointed out to me the road on which men were waiting, one Saturday afternoon in 1980, to ambush and kill Bishop Juan Gerardi. He often went to a village called La Estancia to celebrate Saturday evening Mass. Actually on that occasion the Superior General of the Sacred Heart Fathers, who was on a visit to the diocese, was to accompany Bishop Gerardi. Most of the priests in the diocese at that time were members of the Congregation of the Sacred Heart and two had been murdered in the recent past – the parish priests of Chajul and Joyabaj. Fortunately a man spotted the group waiting to carry out the ambush and succeeded in getting word to the bishop just before he left his house.

I asked Bishop Cabrera if any of the young widows in Quiché ever remarried. He said that remarriage was very unusual, not only because there was a shortage of men due to the murders and disappearances, but also because many of the women were not absolutely sure whether they were widows or not. It is not unknown for a man who has been missing to reappear, perhaps because, instead of having been kidnapped, he had been in hiding. Also, most of the widows have children and that is an added complication – the mothers are afraid that a stepfather might not take to the children or might even ill-treat them, while men are not particularly keen to marry women who already have children by a previous husband.

Fr Bernard Gosse, a French priest, arrived at the bishop's house today. He is engaged in making the first Catholic translation of the New Testament into Quiché and has just completed the initial stage – St Luke's gospel. The sects do have a translation of sorts but it seems that it is more of a version or interpretation to fit in with their doctrines, rather than a faithful rendering.

The lights failed tonight all over town, so we had supper by candlelight and went to bed in the dark.

SUNDAY 6TH AUGUST

Bishop Cabrera and I concelebrated 7.00 am Mass in the cathedral in Santa Cruz. There was still no electricity and so the Mass could not be broadcast, as it usually is, on Radio Quiché. At the start of Mass the bishop introduced me to the packed congregation, indigenous women on the left as we looked down the church, men and other women on the right. As on several occasions during my visit to the diocese, he told them that I had been the first bishop to visit him in Quiché (that was in October 1987) and that I am now the first to spend some time with him and that he has felt very affirmed as a result. The bishop's homily was lengthy. The translation into Quiché also took time and Holy Communions were very numerous so that it was after 8.30 am when Mass finished.

On the way back to the bishop's house I met Raimundo, aged eight, very bright and precocious. He told me that he was interested in space exploration and technology. When I enquired of him why the moon was sometimes round and sometimes a crescent – "like a banana", suggested Raimundo – he said he believed that it was because the United States astronauts who had landed there were in the habit of taking some home with them for examination.

I asked him if he would like to put a message on my tape recorder for the children of Scotland and he was delighted to do so. Here it is, spoken quite extempore (in Spanish):

"To the children of Scotland, to those who are poor: pray a lot to the Lord because the Lord is going to bless you with his glory because he is very pleasant and very holy. It is because of this that we have life, because Jesus sacrificed himself on the cross. And so, to the children I say that they should take good care of themselves and say their prayers".

After breakfast Bishop Julio and I set out for Patzité, fifteen or twenty kilometres south-west of Santa Cruz. Fr Rudi of San Antonio Ilotenango is also parish priest of Patzité so, after yesterday, I had a good idea of what to expect. In Petzité he is fortunate enough to have Srta Fulvia resident there. She is the full-time "*animadora*" (or lay leader of the parish community) whom I met in Chichicastenango a week ago. Both Fr Rudi and the bishop were full of praise for her and for the work she is doing.

A few hundred metres outside Patzité there was an arch of welcome and a crowd around it so we got out of the car and went forward to be greeted by the *Junta Directiva* (Parish Pastoral Council) and then by the *Alcalde* and the *Concejales* (Mayor and Town Councillors), holding their batons of office. Firecrackers were exploding all over the place. We then formed up into a procession of many hundreds of men and women and walked into Patzité and to the church. In the procession we also had a band and in the middle of the band was a small elderly man, staggering rather than walking and bent nearly double because he was carrying on his back a huge battery or accumulator so that the music – and announcements by a man with a megaphone – could be amplified through loudspeakers.

Again the church was crammed to the doors. I was invited to be principal celebrant at Mass on the feast of the Transfiguration. During my homily I chose to speak about the history of Scotland with particular reference to what the peasants there had suffered in the eighteenth century at the hands of the English armed forces. I hope that the parallel was clear and the message understood.

At the General Intercessions of the Mass, Bishop Cabrera invited anyone who so wished to come to the microphone and mention an intention spontaneously. About ten or twelve took up the offer, including some women. Most spoke in Quiché but I was told that many of the prayers had been about me and my work and the hope that I would have a safe journey back to Scotland.

A whole procession of people came forward, bringing gifts for Bishop Julio and me; probably about twenty presents, most of them food and fruit. There were also a large red tablecloth and a live hen in a cardboard box. Several old women approached and gave me money, usually a *quetzal* (about 20p.) but one gave me 25 *centavos* (5p.) Each of them said something like "We are happy to have you here, so please accept this as a sign of our gratitude". I was very moved.

At the end of Mass, the bishop and I, still in our vestments, made our way to the door of the church to greet the people as they came out. This lasted a long time and there were moments when I thought that I was going to be pushed over, such was the crush and the enthusiasm. Then we were taken to the parish hall where, with some of the local dignitaries, we were served a meal while the youth entertained us with drama, music and dancing.

MONDAY 7TH AUGUST

Fr Rosolino was in Santa Cruz today. It was a pleasure to see him again and to have a long discussion with him. He had left Chajul very early after a fairly sleepless night because the army had been firing shells from the town at supposed concentrations of guerrillas in the hills around.

Rosolino reminded me that all the villages which I had visited in his parish, with the exception of La Perla and Sotzil, had been destroyed by the army and only recently reconstructed. Most of their inhabitants have spent years in the mountains as refugees and only in the last few months have come down and surrendered to the army. Even so, many of the former inhabitants, up to half in some cases, are still in hiding in the mountains. In addition, a certain number of newcomers now live in the reconstructed villages.

The villages of Chajul parish, as elsewhere in Ixil, witnessed frightful violence and brutality in the early 1980s. There are authenticated stories of hundreds of people being shot or hacked to death with *machetes*. Rosolino thought that, in some cases, the fact that people were massacred in their villages was because they hadn't fled in time. When they heard rumours of other villages in the vicinity being attacked and burned, many people took to the hills. Others decided to sit it out and these were the ones who were often killed a few days later.

When one hears accounts of the killings in Quiché and especially in Ixil – at first, selected victims and later indiscriminately, with entire villages being massacred – it is hard to avoid the conclusion that this is genocide. Merely to be an indigenous person was to be a subversive, therefore an enemy of the state, therefore deserving of death. And this appalling reasoning was carried in thousands of cases to a cruel conclusion.

In the evening I called to visit the Sisters of the Holy Family, who have a community of four in Santa Cruz. Their convent building was formerly the headquarters of the Sacred Heart Fathers in the diocese. There used to be thirty of these, all Spaniards, and there were hardly any other priests in the diocese. Three of the Spanish priests were murdered, two in June and July 1980 (after which the diocese was "closed" by Bishop Gerardi) and the third, who had returned independently, in February 1981. Since the official "re-opening" of the diocese in 1983, the Sacred Heart Fathers have not returned. They are not allowed back because, in the authorities' view, they are associated with subversion.

The sisters have part of the building for their living quarters and the rest of the building is used for various activities to help the widows and orphans of Santa Cruz and district: teaching the women how to weave and to use sewing machines, giving them literacy lessons, helping to educate the orphans. There are reckoned to be about two hundred young widows in Santa Cruz itself and considerable numbers in the neighbouring villages. Some of the widows manage to obtain employment as servants, washerwomen, house cleaners. The wages they receive for this kind of work are paltry by our standards, perhaps twenty *quetzales* (£4.00) per month or thirty at the most. One woman gets her food and nothing else for her work as a servant in a house.

One of the sisters is a native of the diocese and she had been among the first to return to Quiché when it re-opened. The official re-opening took place in January 1983 when Mons. Pablo Urizar was appointed Administrator. Nevertheless, a few priests and sisters began to infiltrate back to the diocese before that, in fact within several months of its closure in 1980. Padre Axel, the present vicar general, was one of these. He returned to Santa Cruz but did not dare go to any of the other towns or villages for quite some time. Another who went back soon was Fr Juan Alonso, who returned to look after the parishes of Uspantán, Cunén and Chicamán, all to the east of Sacapulas. He was assassinated on 15th February 1981, very soon after his return, on the road between

Uspantán and Cunén, the third Spanish Sacred Heart Father to give his life in Quiché diocese.

The same sister who told me of her experiences during the years of violence had had a brother and several other relatives assassinated in those years. She spoke of having to go to the mortuary to identify victims. Sometimes she did not find the body of the person she was seeking but would recognise other people whom she knew, their faces and bodies bearing the marks of torture and mutilation as well as death. It had been an extremely harrowing and painful time for her and for thousands like her.

TUESDAY 8TH AUGUST

Bishop Cabrera drove me to Guatemala City. I found it very hard to leave his house where I have received so much kindness and affection and very hard to leave Quiché whose beautiful and heroic people I have grown to love and admire.

The diocese has three young men preparing for the priesthood in the seminary in Guatemala City and we met them in the evening. Bishop Julio has succeeded in bringing a good number of priests and religious to Quiché since he became bishop but there is still need for many more. It was heartening to meet the three students who are all Guatemalans and who should be able to serve the diocese well for many years.

WEDNESDAY 9TH AUGUST

Today in Guatemala City I met a number of people whom I had met on previous visits to the country – priests, religious and others concerned with human rights and involved in various ways with justice and peace issues. In a way it was strange to hear them talking of the problems and obstacles and possible solutions; to me there seemed an air of unreality about the discussions. It was like medical staff talking about unconscious patients or like parents discussing their infant children. Those people whom I had been with for the previous three weeks – it was their past, present and future that was under consideration – but they were not part of the discussion.

Some of the people to whom I was listening knew that it was not enough to try to secure basic human rights for the peasants. Much better to help *them* to recognise the injustices in their situation and so enable *them* to seek redress and change for themselves. But that seems still a long way off. The lack of communications, the language barriers, illiteracy, cultural differences are all obstacles to allowing the peasants to "take ownership" of their problems and to assume responsibility for their solution.

I felt sad that the victims of injustice and violence in Guatemala are also still the objects of pity. Even those who work for human rights and social justice tend to see the victims as "them". In that sense, their condition seems even more poignant.

Yet, despite the apparent absence of serious and mature discussion on human rights in the towns and villages of Quiché, despite the fact that the people have been ill-treated and kicked around and are truly poor in worldly terms, they possess a joy and serenity and dignity that can come only from being close to God. Our faith tells us of God's special nearness to the poor, of his preferential option for them – and my experience in Quiché provided ample confirmation of that fact.

THURSDAY 10TH AUGUST

As my plane took off for Europe I knew how privileged I had been for the last three weeks, and how happy too. It was an unforgettable experience. In many ways it was very hard, especially the days spent trekking in the mountains of Chajul parish. I don't think I could have gone on doing that for much longer. But I received so much in friendship, acceptance and affirmation. In return I hope that I gave a little bit of myself to build up the bishop, the priests and the people of Quiché.

Perhaps also the story of my journey will help to make a heroic people better known and admired and will arouse interest in, and practical concern for, their plight.

POSTSCRIPT

In the years since I wrote the journal some changes have taken place in Quiché and in Guatemala. Mons. Julio Cabrera has been transferred to another diocese, that of Jalapa, to the east of Guatemala City. The war between the Guatemalan army and the guerrillas officially ended in 1996 and a number of reforms, meant to improve the living conditions of the poor and especially of the indigenous people of the country, have been enacted or are planned.

But matters have not changed radically. Rich people are still as rich as before and still retain the real power. Corruption is endemic, even in "the corridors of power". The poor, especially peasants, are still marginalised and do not look forward to any improvement in that respect. They still live in poverty; many have migrated, in near hopelessness, to the cities. To be poor in Guatemala is to be denied good education and proper health care; it means to be without power and without the means of gaining power or being able to change things.

Perhaps worse than that is the very great increase in violence that has occurred in Guatemala. Armed robberies, kidnappings (of childen and others) for ransom, vendetta killings have become common; armed gangs of youths (called "*maras*") cause much of the violence, as well as the activities of individual criminals and death squads. Around five thousand people are murdered every year. And the reasons for all this? Because many ex-combatants have nothing better to do with their time, because guns are easily available, because crime is seen by many to pay, and because of the trafficking in drugs, in particular cocaine from Colombia and elsewhere in South America, for sale and use in Guatemala and especially for onward export.

It is a sad situation that, although Guatemala now has no official armed conflict, the country is as violent as ever. Peace and justice seem far off in Guatemala.

Ciudad de Guatemala: Metropolitan Cathedral

Departamento de Quiché: Santa Cruz de Quiché (capital of the department), Santa Cruz Cathedral

On the way north to Ixil, ascending the Cuchumatanes mountain range: below, Rio Blanco valley and Sacapulas town

Nebaj (in Ixil): orphans of the violence

Chajul: Mek (our guide) and family, outside their house; Mek has *un azadón*, the big boy *un machete*, the smallest *una mochila*

Sotzil: a village on our trek through Ixil; eleven young males curiously watch the strange photographer

Cotzal (in Ixil): Church of San Juan; shrine to the 'martyrs' of Cotzal in the war and repression; each little cross bears the name of a victim and date of death ('I am the resurrection and the life. They who believe in me, even though they may die, will live' – John 11:25)

Cotzal: Church of San Juan; an indigenous lady distributing Holy Communion at Mass

Cotzal: some friendly Mayan peasants; the females wear beautiful traditional clothes, the males do not, except on very special occasions

Member of Civil Defence Patrol: with rifle and embroidery

Sacapulas: preparing tortillas (1), the maize is ground to flour, made into a dough, then rolled

Sacapulas: preparing tortillas (2), the rolled pancakes are further flattened and shaped by hands and then cooked on large pans over a wood fire

Santa Cruz: market day; the knack of balancing a full basket on your head!

Santa Cruz: going back to their village after market day; ice cream cones to lick on the journey; the conveyance is a second-hand US school bus

San Antonio Ilotenango (a village in Quiché): the village and countryside; painting by Vicente Simaj (local indigenous artist)

San Antonio Ilotenango: a view from the balcony beside the church; faces ranging from the curious and surprised to outright astonishment

A day at lake Atitlán (among the Guatemalan volcanoes): Bishop Cabrera (the photographer), his housekeepers Maria and Ignacia (the taller sisters, indigenous from Rio Blanco, near Sacapulas) and his secretaries Eugenia and Norma (sisters, indigenous from Santa Cruz)

Bishop Julio Cabrera: formerly bishop of Quiché, now bishop of Jalapa

El Salvador: Portrait of a Parish

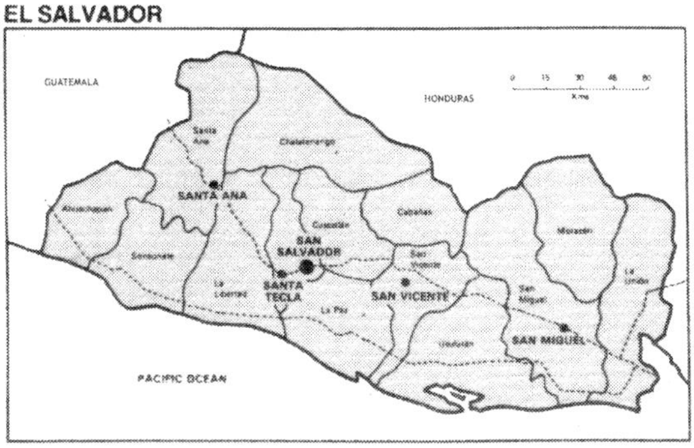

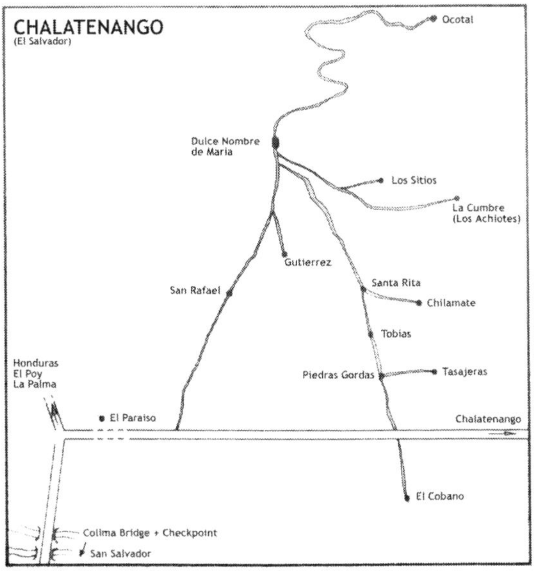

INTRODUCTION

From 1984 onwards I visited El Salvador frequently. While there in 1990, I was told by one of the priests of the archdiocese of St Andrews and Edinburgh working in the diocese of Chalatenango (in the north of El Salvador, near the border with Honduras) that he would take a few months' leave the following year if a priest from Scotland could take his place while he was away.

That is how I managed to spend two and a half months as acting parish priest in the parish of Dulce Nombre de María in El Salvador from late June until early September 1991; and how this "Portrait of a Parish" came to be written.

Before taking up the temporary appointment, I discovered that I had a problem to solve. The Code of Canon Law states (canon 395 §2): "Apart from the visit *ad limina*, attendance at councils or at the synod of Bishops or at the Bishops' Conference...he [the diocesan Bishop] may be absent from the diocese, for a just reason, for not longer than one month, continuously or otherwise, provided he ensures that the diocese is not harmed by this absence". In view of these rather threatening words, I wrote to Rome, to the Congregation for Bishops, for permission to be away from the diocese of Galloway for three months, explaining the reasons for my request. I added that, as I had been bishop for ten years, the object of the request might also be considered as a kind of sabbatical. The reply stated that my request was an unusual one but, for this particular occasion and for the reasons given, it had been granted. The permission seemed to have been grudgingly agreed; at least the tone and the expressions employed gave me that impression. Perhaps Rome does not like to appear over-generous. However, the main thing was that I was free to go to El Salvador.

ARRIVAL

If place names meant anything, El Salvador would be the holiest nation on earth. "El Salvador" means "The Saviour". Its capital is San Salvador and the next two largest cities are Santa Ana and San

Miguel. But the country has a grim reputation and El Salvador is synonymous with violence. Even by Central American standards it is notorious for institutionalised injustice, for corruption and for death squads. [Despite the signing of the Peace Accord in 1992 the country remained deeply troubled.]

El Salvador is a small country with a Pacific Ocean coastline which runs roughly east-west (not north-south). The country measures 250 kms (160 miles) from east to west and only 100 kms (60 miles) from north to south, that is, from the mountains to the coast. With a population of over five million people it is the smallest and the most densely populated country of Central America. The inhabitants have the reputation of being intelligent, energetic, resourceful – and combative! The last is certainly true. El Salvador is the home of the very effective *Frente Farabundo Martí para la Liberación Nacional* (FMLN) guerrilla army and of the notorious death squads. Archbishop Oscar Romero, shot on 24th March 1980, and the six Jesuits of the University of Central America, murdered in the early hours of 16th November 1989, are only the most famous of the seventy thousand people killed in the violence since 1980.

The priest I was replacing, Fr Basil Postlethwaite, met me at the airport and, after one night in San Salvador, we set out for Dulce Nombre de María. About thirty miles north of the capital we came to the heavily guarded Colima bridge over the river Lempa. This is also a very strict military checkpoint so we had to get out of the car – in a downpour – and prove our identities. It was easy for Fr Basil as he is well enough known and has an identity card issued by the diocese. The bishop had fortunately remembered to inform the local military headquarters that I was arriving and the soldier in charge of the checkpoint had a note to that effect. After a laborious and somewhat inaccurate copying of my passport details and a radio telephone call to headquarters for further confirmation, we were allowed to proceed.

"Welcome to Chaletenango!" said Fr Basil as we crossed the bridge. It was exciting – and a little frightening – to enter the diocese where there has been so much violence and suffering in recent years. After a courtesy call on Bishop Eduardo Alas in Chalatenango town, we left the tarmacadamed road and travelled north along a broad but rough track for about seven miles to reach the town of Dulce Nombre de María at 6.00 pm, just as darkness fell.

Dulce Nombre de María – those religious names again! – is a town of about six thousand people. It lies at the foot of the mountain range known as the Cordillera Matapán Alotepeque and which forms the northern boundary of El Salvador. The town is divided into four districts or zones: San José, Carmen, Concepción and Calvario.

The church and the priest's house are in the centre of the town, where the four districts meet. The house is quite large, comfortable and well furnished. It has a patio or garden, round which the rooms are built. Because of the heat, much of one's living and reading and eating etc. are done in the open corridor or verandah along one side of the patio. There is even a refrigerator which works when there is electricity, and a black and white television set, so that the standard of living in the house is good – better than I, in my pessimism, had anticipated!

WELCOME

The morning after my arrival, Fr Basil explained to me that the people did not know that I was already in Dulce Nombre and he did not want to spoil the welcome ceremony they had prepared. So I was taken by car, through back streets and as unobtrusively as possible, to the outskirts of the town. At a prearranged exact time (8.30 am) I was then driven a few hundred yards to the beginning of the houses where hundreds of people had assembled, awaiting my arrival. I got out of the car and was formally welcomed by Fr Basil and the president of the parish council as well as other leaders. Looking as happy as I could in the somewhat embarrassing situation, I tried to show my pleasure at arriving in Dulce Nombre de María.

The people were certainly kind and courteous and many of them came forward to shake hands. I was given bunches of flowers and then we formed up to walk in procession, up the main street to the church, about half a mile away. As we went, rockets were let off with a "whoosh" and then a tremendous bang as they exploded about a hundred feet in the air. I always find it ironic that, in a country which has suffered so badly from gunfire, the noise of exploding rockets should be so much a part of popular rejoicing. A brass band, whose members had been hired from near and far, accompanied us. Their selection included a lively rendition of the march "*Old Comrades*". During intervals in the music, there were cries of "Long live Bishop Maurice Taylor", "Long live Father Basil", "Long live the parish of Dulce Nombre de María" and "Long live all the communities who are here today". The street was decorated with bunting and many people carried little yellow and white paper flags.

On arrival at the church we had Mass with a packed congregation. After the gospel, most of the communities present, from the various *cantones* or villages which, with Dulce Nombre de María, make up the parish, brought gifts to me at the altar – fruit, vegetables, eggs, money, a travel bag and a hammock. I felt really welcome among such kind and courteous people.

SUNDAY MASSES

The following day Fr Basil taught me the Sunday routine. The first Mass was in Santa Rita, a few miles south of Dulce Nombre, along a wide track that presents no problems for the parish four-wheel-drive Toyota Landcruiser. There are a couple of streams to cross where there are no bridges. Fifteen minutes driving got us to Santa Rita, which is the only other official "*pueblo*" i.e. town, in the parish, the other places being "*cantones*" i.e. villages, or "*caseríos*" i.e. hamlets.

Confessions in Santa Rita are at 7.15 am and, with apologies for those still in the queue for the sacrament, Mass begins fairly promptly at 7.30 am – punctuality being one of Fr Basil's innovations – and lasts about an hour. The singing, which includes some parts of the Mass as well as hymns, is led, as in all the Mass stations, by a choir of girls accompanied usually by some instruments. Santa Rita is particularly well off for musicians since it has three guitars, a bass guitar and an electronic keyboard. Each church in the parish has a group of women wearing white dresses and with yellow veils on their heads. These are the *Guardia del*

Santísimo (Blessed Sacrament Guild) who look after the church – cleaning, flowers, altar linen etc.

Back to Dulce Nombre for Mass at 10.00 am, preceded by confessions. The Mass is similar to the one in Santa Rita but on a much bigger scale because the town and church are both considerably larger; and the church is packed.

In Dulce Nombre, Fr Basil has moved the altar away from the apse (where the tabernacle still is) so that it is now halfway down the church, along the side wall. The seats are therefore in a semicircle or shell-shaped arrangement. It is a better plan, not only because it separates altar and tabernacle but because, given the size of the church, it allows the congregation to be nearer the altar and the ministers to be more visible and audible.

On the side wall, behind the altar, there is a new and very large painting on wood in the typical Salvadorean "primitive" style. It is colourful and bright, with Christ in the centre and around him, without perspective or correct scale, a broad landscape with scenes of everyday life and activity. It is a very striking piece of work, painted in 1990 by Roberto Burgos and his pupils in his workshop in La Palma, north-west of Dulce Nombre. Quite a number of people were upset when the altar was taken away from its "right" place. Although I was told that complaints are now fewer, one still hears the nostalgic sigh for things as they used to be.

The third and final Mass of the day is at 4.00 pm in the church at Piedras Gordas. The way there is back through Santa Rita and southwards along a track, which in fact is the first part of the road from Dulce Nombre to Chalatenango and San Salvador. Again, the church was full and the people there, though lacking any musical instrument to accompany their singing, are enthusiastic and lively. One advantage of Piedras Gordas is that the ladies of its *Guardia del Santísimo* provide a glass of fresh orange juice for the priest – very acceptable in the afternoon heat.

Three Masses on a Sunday is not an inordinately exhausting task but when they were over I did feel quite tired and drained. The heat was responsible for this; moreover, the vestments did make me perspire profusely so that often I had to be helped out of the alb because of its being "stuck" to my arms and back. There is the strain of confessions and preaching in a foreign language; and, to cap it all, people have a habit of arriving just as one is about to begin Mass or as soon as one has finished, to ask for Mass intentions to be announced or other notices or reminders to be given or to seek advice or information or merely to tell you their troubles.

After three Masses I needed "space" to relax and unwind, but the priest's special helpers in Dulce Nombre were most anxious to ensure that I was not lonely or felt neglected. Still, I didn't complain because it's good to feel wanted!

PARISH COUNCIL

Dulce Nombre has a parish council. It was set up at Easter 1991 and so is still finding its feet. There are between forty and fifty members, three from each village or Mass station (there are twelve of these) and three from each of the districts or zones into which Dulce Nombre is divided (Calvary, Immaculate Conception, Our Lady of Mount Carmel and St Joseph). It meets on the last Saturday of each month, from nine o'clock until noon, and many of the members have to walk several hours to be present. The representatives are elected; perhaps "chosen" by the people might be more accurate because often they "emerge" from the communities since they already have some sort of leadership role there, e.g. as catechists. The majority of the parish council are men, but ten are women.

Most of the business, after an opening prayer and a gospel reflection from the priest, consists of reports from the various communities and then announcements about plans and projects followed by discussion and questions thereon. The reports, for example, were about doctrine classes for children (all schools are secular and so specific religious education is not given in them) or about repairs to the churches in the villages or about efforts to get nightly rosary groups started.

The announcements were usually about my programme of visits to the various villages for the month ahead or about arrangements for the sacrament of confirmation which the bishop authorised me to confer while I was in the parish. What age? How to apply to be a candidate? Who was to give the *charlas* (i.e. pre-confirmation talks to candidates, parents and sponsors) in each village? What text was to be used for these? Could you receive confirmation even though you hadn't made your first communion? Must a boy's sponsor be male and a girl's female?

One recurring item at the parish council, somewhat embarrassing for me, concerned the cost of my official welcome, 1250 *colones*, about £100. One-fifth of that sum was still owed to other funds from which the money had been borrowed. The expense and the debt aroused some concern, even complaint.

The parish council members have been told that they have to serve the people they represent and to show leadership and to help the community to work together, as well as keeping the people informed about what is happening in the parish. It is all still at a fairly simple level and the quality of leadership given varies quite a lot. Some members were still very timid and seemed to see their role as little more than bearers of announcements from the priest. But I was impressed that a parish council had been started in such a widespread and impoverished parish and that each community had designated its representatives and that they had consented even though not all of them were literate. The seriousness with which the agenda was carried out and the desire of the council to become a valued instrument of pastoral growth and service were also most impressive and very hopeful signs for the future.

OTHER LAY INVOLVEMENT

In Dulce Nombre itself, where the priest lives and is to be found for much of the time, there was considerable lay involvement in the liturgy, viz., readers, musicians, choir, servers; but not yet extraordinary ministers of the Eucharist. In fact, the number of communicants in proportion to the attendance at Sunday or weekday Mass was surprisingly low – perhaps about 15-20% of the congregation on Sundays and 30% during the week. Hardly anyone received in the hand and Holy Communion was not given under both kinds – perhaps because wine is expensive.

In the villages (where there is no Mass on Sundays), there was usually a liturgy of the word, but in only one village was Communion also distributed. Yet many of the villages have the Blessed Sacrament reserved in the tabernacle, and people do visit the churches.

Each village (and each zone of Dulce Nombre) has its catechists, both those who give doctrine lessons to the children and those whose work is to give pre-sacramental preparation for baptism, confirmation, first communion and marriage. Attendance at such talks is obligatory and more or less taken for granted.

There are quite a number of groups that gather in the evenings, either in each other's homes or in the local church, to say the rosary, with lots of trimmings. I tried to encourage such groups not to limit themselves to saying prayers but to use Scripture, to discuss its relevance for their own lives and so experience faith sharing. Charismatic renewal groups and marriage encounter groups are also found in a number of the villages. Relations between charismatics and others are often strained. The reason for this state of affairs is, partly, that the former are not seen as being much involved in that area of religion that is concerned with social justice and partly, I think, that non-charismatics feel themselves threatened by novel forms of prayer and gifts like speaking in tongues and healing. Such suspicion is understandable in a country in which Pentecostal and fundamentalist sects, to which Catholic charismatic renewal bears some superficial resemblance, are making considerable inroads among the people.

I would say that lay involvement still has some way to go before everyone sees it as his or her vocation to be actively involved in building the Kingdom. But is this not true of Scotland as well? It is the delicate matter of getting priestly leadership into correct focus so that people see themselves as called to share responsibility with the priest in the local church, without diminishing in any way the importance of his ministry.

Two further points may be mentioned. Apart from rosary groups and charismatic prayer groups, I saw little evidence of people coming together to form basic Christian communities; in order to reflect on the reality of their lives in the light of gospel values. Something of this was certainly taking place in the monthly meetings of the parish council so perhaps that will be a model for future developments. In various places in El Salvador basic Christian communities have been regarded as subversive by the civil and military authorities and members have been targeted by death squads. So caution and discretion are very necessary.

Second, although the churches are normally full and even packed when Mass is celebrated, the reality is that in the town of

Dulce Nombre perhaps one thousand people are at Mass on Sundays (out of a population of six thousand or more) while, in monthly or two-monthly Masses in the villages, the numbers, though they look impressive, are also fairly modest in relation to the total numbers of inhabitants. It is not that the sects have many adherents in Dulce Nombre – comparatively few in fact; but perhaps Mass attendance is not seen as such a touchstone for the "practising" Catholic as it is with us. At Mass one Sunday, for example, I missed a "pillar of the church" who is a member of the parish council and, when possible, a daily Mass-goer. "Was she ill?" I asked. "Oh, no" I was told, "she runs a small drapery business from her house and is doing the rounds of her clients this morning".

DAILY LIFE

The church is the largest and most prominent building in Dulce Nombre. It is situated in the very centre of the small town, on one side of the *parque* (the main square) which has some trees and benches in it. The principal streets of the town are cobbled, sometimes smoothly and sometimes very roughly and unevenly. Other streets are just made of earth or gravel, often with big stones sticking through.

The houses are one-storey and mostly of *adobe* (earth). As a result, the walls are thick, this being a great advantage when the bullets are flying. I was quite surprised to find how large many of the houses are, some with interior patios. Some houses have rooms with tiled floors and whitewashed plaster walls, but many of the poorer houses have earthen floors and the interior walls are just of bare *adobe*.

Most of the houses have some furniture in them – a table, chairs, a sewing machine, chests of drawers, a statue or two, holy pictures on the walls and, in many, a TV set and even a refrigerator. The distinction between living room and bedroom is not nearly as marked as with us and it is quite common to see several beds in the main room, sometimes curtained off from one another but, in the poorer homes, often not. The beds are simple and basic and often ancient, while bedclothes are minimal – it never gets cold at night. Central heating and fires are unknown and unnecessary.

The houses of Dulce Nombre have running water, available only at limited and unpredictable times of the day – but the water is contaminated. The people drink it because, being used to it, they have probably developed immunity. However, when I was there, it was recommended that, due to the danger of infection and especially of cholera, all water for drinking should first be boiled. As well as sinks, most houses have basic showers, but never hot running water. There is electric light in the homes and even some street lighting, except when the electric supply has been dynamited by the guerrillas.

By our standards, the people are lightly and, I suppose, poorly clad. There is no question of typical costume in El Salvador (as there is in Guatemala) because there is no distinct indigenous population. So, although many of the people are very dark-skinned and/or have obviously a high proportion of indigenous blood in their veins, they all dress in "western" style.

Rice (*arroz*), red kidney beans (*frijoles*) and maize pancakes (*tortillas*) are their staple diet. Chicken is a special treat because many families keep poultry and a hen is often called upon "to fulfil her destiny" when there are guests or a feast day. I was surprised to discover that most people use instant coffee – but then Dulce Nombre is not a coffee-growing area. The places where coffee was a crop have now, in many cases, been abandoned as a result of the violence. Some people eat bread and there are three small bakeries in Dulce Nombre which produce what is known locally as "French bread" or what we would call rolls. For me that alternative was preferable to *tortillas* which I found stodgy and heavy. When I expressed my surprise that people could eat so many *tortillas* at one meal, I was told that it was because they worked hard and so became very hungry. I felt suitably chastened!

Dulce Nombre has quite a number of shops or, rather, stores. They are really just the front rooms of people's homes where food or clothing or "general goods", including Coca-Cola and beer, can be bought.

Although the people are poor and live a very simple life, I did not have the impression that theirs is the grinding poverty that I have seen, for example, in the Mayan highlands of Guatemala. There, even a spoon can be a luxury, there is little furniture, no electricity, no piped water, and cooking is done over a wood fire, and not on a gas stove, with gas canisters, as in many homes in Dulce Nombre.

There is a surprisingly good bus service between Dulce Nombre and San Salvador, a distance of about fifty miles over very bumpy roads. Buses from Dulce Nombre are particularly frequent in the early morning, leaving every thirty minutes or so until 8.00 am. The first bus leaves at 3.50 am and, for the previous half hour, gives frequent blasts on its horn to attract customers. The bus terminus is right outside the priest's house so it was wise to get to bed reasonably early since one's sleep is disturbed from 3.15 onwards. Nonetheless, it is remarkable how one becomes more or less accustomed to the racket and can get back to sleep again after each bus has left. The buses have names: "Gift of God", "Little Queen of the North" (a small and extremely rusty vehicle). All are garishly painted and carry such slogans as "Trust in God and Let's Go!"

Certainly Dulce Nombre is in the Third World. I am sure that everything there, from houses to TV sets and from clothes to machinery, has a longer life than it would have in our own country. I often felt that there was a similarity between Dulce Nombre and small towns and villages of the 1950s and 1960s in Spain.

Apart from the church, Dulce Nombre has only a few public buildings, including a junior school and a high school. There is a "Casa Comunal" where wedding receptions and occasional dances are held and a "Casa de la Cultura" used, among other things, for adult literacy classes. There is only one telephone in the town – in the telephone office – so incoming and outgoing calls are fairly public and difficult. One feature of the telephone office is that its exterior walls are pockmarked with hundreds of bullet holes – and that brings us to the subject that has made El Salvador notorious in recent times.

THE WAR

At the time that this journal was written, El Salvador meant, for many people, the FMLN guerrillas and right-wing death squads. The history of the country is one of centuries of injustice and the maintenance of the unjust *status quo* by repression and terror. The basic problem is the totally lop-sided distribution of wealth and especially of productive land. The comparatively few rich people in El Salvador are extremely rich, and becoming richer, while the great majority live in miserable, insanitary conditions, at or near the poverty line and with no prospect of advancement.

As the poor masses have begun to voice their discontent, often with the help of priests, religious and lay leaders influenced by the Second Vatican Council and the Latin American bishops' meetings at Puebla and Medellín, so those in power have become more ruthless in their repressive measures. Such means have included assassination, torture, disappearances and death threats as well as sheer terror and new legislation passed to make repression easier and "lawful".

Since 1980, the repression has been extremely violent. The army went to war (until the cease-fire in January 1992) against the guerrilla forces, known as the FMLN, who took up arms in an organised way in October 1980. This civil war resulted in many more deaths, of course, and it is estimated that since 1980 seventy thousand people have been killed in El Salvador.

Clashes and skirmishes between the army and the FMLN could and did occur all over El Salvador. In the capital, urban guerrillas sabotaged the electricity supply, attacked military and police installations etc. Outside the city the FMLN operates much more like an army, wearing uniforms, working in detachments and carrying weapons.

Frequently in Dulce Nombre we could hear guns in the distant hills, either the crack of rifles or the muffled explosions from heavier guns. Every few days the army would come into Dulce Nombre and stay, either for a few hours or for a day or two before continuing their patrols elsewhere. A certain tension came over the town when the army arrived – small, very dark young men and not at all pleasant-looking. Many of them would be hanging about the *parque* beside the church and in the streets, all heavily armed and rather sinister and unfriendly. On their behalf, one ought to remember that they were conscripts, recruited simply by being "grabbed" in the street or on a bus and taken away to be trained; in fact, press-ganged. As a result, they were often unwilling and reluctant soldiers, away from their home districts, among a mainly hostile civilian population, and scared of their own officers as well as of "the enemy". Even so, the inhabitants of the town breathed a sigh of relief whenever the army left.

One evening during Mass the altar server came to me at the Greeting of Peace but, instead of the usual words, he whispered "The guerrillas are here". They had come into Dulce Nombre unobtrusively, standing around in the *parque*, moving cautiously about the streets. I must say that I did feel some fear when told, on that first occasion shortly after my arrival, that the FMLN were in Dulce Nombre, but gradually I began to take their occasional visits as fairly normal.

The guerrillas also are in dark green or olive uniforms and carry guns. They were less sinister-looking and more friendly than the army. Indeed, when the server told me of the arrival of the guerrillas in the town, the word he used was not "*guerrilleros*", but "*muchachos*", "the boys". That first evening, their officer in charge had a group of young people from the town round him, chatting and joking. One of the guerrillas painted, in big letters on the outside wall of the priest's house, their current slogan, taunting the army: "*Si quieren nuestras armas, que ganen la guerra. FMLN*", "If you want our weapons, win the war".

A few of the guerrillas were extremely young – perhaps only twelve or thirteen – but even these children were armed to the teeth. It was noticeable also that there were quite a number of girls and young women among the guerrillas, perhaps 10%.

There were frequent skirmishes in the rural areas because the guerrillas live mostly in the thickly wooded hills and their patrols are very mobile and swift. The danger for a town like Dulce Nombre is when one or other side is "in residence" and may be attacked while there.

On Wednesday 17th July the army arrived in some force and they were still there two days later when suddenly, at 1.50 pm, the FMLN burst into the town and attacked them. The guerrillas knew that the army was in Dulce Nombre and had brought up reinforcements to encircle the town. At a prearranged signal the guerrillas emerged from the trees and the maize fields at the edge of the town. They rushed through back gardens and even, in some cases, through the back doors of houses and out through the front doors into the streets of Dulce Nombre. The army was caught unawares – some of the soldiers were having their midday meal, others were resting. The machine gun, rifle and mortar fire was very intense and the battle was waged through the streets until about 4.00 pm. Several of the combatants were killed, but there were no casualties among the civilian population – only terror, especially among the children.

People stay indoors during these "*enfrentamientos*" (clashes) and, if possible, behind *adobe* walls. Many of the houses were struck by bullets and the fighting was particularly severe in the street between the church and the priest's house – not so much hand-to-hand, but firing from houses or from behind walls or peeping round corners. The walls of the church and the house had several new bullet marks on them and one bullet went through a window of the house and shattered a fluorescent light tube.

The army was out-manoeuvred that day – and perhaps outnumbered – so at about 4.00 pm they retreated southwards, towards their barracks about ten miles away. For many of the soldiers, the retreat was something of a rout as they threw away their packs and equipment and even their uniforms and escaped, in twos and threes, to the woods.

While all this was going on, I was not at home but had to wait about a mile outside the town, on my way back from an overnight visit to San Salvador to renew my residence permit. We had been told at the last village before Dulce Nombre of the fighting that was taking place there and so we had no alternative but to stop the car and wait, listening to the rifles and machine guns in Dulce Nombre. Eventually about twenty soldiers came up the hill out of Dulce Nombre and told us that it was now safe to proceed. We had not gone very far, less than a mile, when we came across large groups of guerrillas. They were looking for and/or pursuing the army. It was a frightening moment as we approached them, but they allowed us through, one officer stopping us to ask what army personnel we had seen, where they were and what they were doing.

It was 4.30 when we arrived back at the house. Life was beginning to return to normal, people re-emerging from their houses to discuss the events of the afternoon and to ask about casualties. In the patio of the priest's house, a girl was in a state of shock because the fighting had been very intense near the junior school where the children were in class. A grenade had been thrown and had exploded near her. She soon recovered, the church bells rang for evening Mass, which we began at 5.10, only ten minutes late, and with a large congregation, thankful that casualties had been so few.

THE WAR'S EFFECT ON THE PEOPLE

When Fr Basil left for his vacation two days after my arrival in Dulce Nombre, I felt nervous at being on my own. My feelings must have shown because some of the altar servers informed me that, in addition to their duties at Mass, they had decided to constitute themselves as my personal bodyguards! Most nights two or three of them slept in a spare room in the house and I admit that their presence made me feel more secure – even though they were only ten or twelve years old.

One of them spoke to me one evening of his memories of the war in Dulce Nombre. A few months previously the bodies of two soldiers had been left lying in the street outside the priest's house until taken to the barracks by Fr Basil. The boy described to me in detail where the bullets had entered and left their heads and bodies. Even more graphically, he remembered a street battle in 1989 that had lasted from midnight until 3 am. The FMLN had entered Dulce Nombre in great numbers and my young informant told me how they hunted down the soldiers, finding some hiding in houses and even some cowering on the roof rack of one of the buses. "It was awful", the boy said, "everyone was under the bed and the women were shaking with fear".

Questions naturally arise. What effect has all this violence – and the war being fought out in their streets – done to the ordinary people of El Salvador? How has it affected them and especially the children?

It is very difficult to answer such questions with any confidence or assurance. It is said that the war has brought on a great many psychological and emotional problems. Are there, however, figures to show that such cases are more widespread than in peaceful countries? And even if they are, are they due to the war or to other factors?

Sometimes I was aware of a number of drunken people around the streets, sometimes even lying stretched out on the road. Dulce Nombre has a branch of Alcoholics Anonymous. It does not cost much to get drunk; cheap, locally made liquor is readily available. On my first day alone in the parish, a young man in his late twenties died. He was an alcoholic and, in his depression, he did what several alcoholics had done in the past in the town – he drank pesticide and killed himself.

There is also a lack of community care for "those with special needs" (the mentally and physically disabled). Each village or town seems to have one or two or more of the simple-minded, who roam about the streets. Dulce Nombre's most celebrated is Adilio who, except when he has succumbed to his "weakness" and got drunk, is an amiable soul who comes daily to the priest's house for food, water and 20 *centavos* (less than 2p) for a cigar. Every now and again, when those around cannot fail to be aware of his need, he is induced to have a shower. When a bus arrives from San Salvador, Adilio is always on hand to direct the driver enthusiastically as he reverses and turns his vehicle. Then he often earns one *colón* (about 8p) for cleaning the interior of the bus, though, given his simplicity, "cleaning" must be regarded as a euphemism.

Likewise, for those who have physical disabilities, there is little on offer. A lady told me about her son. He is dumb but he can hear and understand; nonetheless, he has never gone to school because "the other children would laugh at him and throw stones".

Such neglect and lack of social care cause problems in families but can hardly be attributed to the war. What is certain, however, is that many, indeed most, families in Dulce Nombre have had a relative – and often more than one – assassinated by death squads or killed in combat. I was constantly being told of a husband, brother or son who met a violent death (usually in the mid-1980s). I sometimes got the impression that people have a very matter of fact attitude to these deaths and seem to have accepted them and, almost, to have put them behind them. I do not know.

Others with longer experience of living and working in El Salvador have said to me that it is their opinion that, even without the recent countrywide war, El Salvador would be a very violent and lawless place. Many of the people have real or imagined scores to settle: family feuds, long-term grievances and the like. I was told that such people are quite liable to take the law into their own hands to get what they want or to wreak vengeance.

These are imponderables. I feel unable to draw any conclusion or make any judgment about causes and effects. All I know is that death has been and still is very much a part of life in El Salvador. The people seem to have an extraordinary resilience, bouncing back to apparent normality after tragedy as quickly as sunshine can follow a storm.

One aspect of the FMLN that receives little publicity is their fundraising in the towns and villages. From time to time the more wealthy inhabitants get a request for, say, five thousand *colones* to be left at a designated spot in the woods – or else... Sometimes the guerrillas buy food or clothes in a village but, on other occasions, they just "confiscate". For example, a lot of the clothes that had been washed and were hanging out to dry on 19th July in Dulce Nombre were just taken away after the battle.

THE OUTLYING VILLAGES

If the priest resides in a town (*pueblo*) in rural El Salvador, then he will, in all probability, have a number of outlying villages included in the parish. Dulce Nombre is no exception. In addition to weekly Masses each Sunday in the town of Santa Rita and in the large village of Piedras Gordas, the priest celebrates Mass regularly, usually once a month, in ten other villages (*cantones*). They are all within a radius of ten or twelve miles of Dulce Nombre and the parish car can reach all but two of them. The roads to these villages would be considered as no better than rough, narrow tracks in this country and often they are very bumpy indeed, with outcrops of rock protruding, gullies to be negotiated and streams to be crossed. In the rainy season these tracks can become extremely slippery. Driving along them, never easy, is then quite hazardous.

The whole district around Dulce Nombre is hilly and thickly covered with trees, bushes and especially "*la milpa*", i.e. fields of maize, "as high as an elephant's eye". At first sight, the countryside looks like impenetrable jungle because of the fertility of the soil. In fact, however, the land is all divided into small holdings, mostly of maize and of beans (*frijoles*). Even the villages can seem to be concealed because the houses are often separated from one another by quite a distance and almost hidden by the vegetation. These village houses are more primitive than in Dulce Nombre town – *adobe* walls, tiled roofs, earthen floors inside and only very basic furniture. Hammocks are often used rather than beds, being cheaper and needing less space. Each house is surrounded by a kind of yard or garden and nearly always there will be poultry and occasionally a few piglets and a dog – the last only as a pet and sentry, of course!

I was quite surprised at the number of villages which had electric light, though the houses did not normally have running water. Water for washing, drinking and cooking is obtained from the village well while, often, clothes are washed in a nearby stream.

All but three of the villages in Dulce Nombre parish have their own little church and these were normally packed to the doors for the monthly Mass. Many have the Blessed Sacrament reserved in the tabernacle but in only one is there a person who distributes Holy Communion. In the rest, the people make visits of adoration etc. and, of course, they celebrate their Sunday Liturgies of the Word in the presence of the Blessed Sacrament. The monthly Masses were usually quite enthusiastic as well as crowded and there was a fair amount of singing – parts of the Mass and hymns – sometimes with guitar accompaniment. The visits of the priest are much appreciated by the active Catholics in these communities but it is well to keep in mind that the proportion of Catholics who attend these Masses is, in fact, quite small.

Some of the villages have a prominent presence of the sects. This leads to a lessening of a real spirit of unity and community in these places and, when a village has also suffered particularly severely because of the violence, there is a sense of demoralisation prevalent. This is especially noticeable in one or two of the villages – violence, poverty and religious division mean that, somehow or other, the Catholics become disheartened and disorganised. But in most of the villages there is a real atmosphere of vibrant faith and joyful hope, an implicit belief in God's presence and a childlike trust in his providence.

THE "CORPUS" PROCESSION

One of the biggest events of the year in each village is "*El Corpus*", in other words, the Corpus Christi procession of the Blessed Sacrament through the village. Since there are so many villages in the parish, the *Corpus* is held on any suitable day during the year.

After a packed and joyful Mass, the procession sallies forth from the church – men and women, with the ladies of "*La Guardia del Santísimo*" prominent in their white dresses and yellow veils, lots of children, the altar servers with candles and thurible, the priest carrying the monstrance beneath a canopy, more or less held in place by four canopy bearers. The procession goes from "altar" to "altar" located at various spots around the village. These "altars" are shrines built up of tables, benches, boxes and stools to form a large structure on which are white cloths, flowers and candles. The priest places the monstrance on a "throne" near the top of the shrine. This action can be a hazardous and unnerving moment since a false step or a stumble would bring the whole construction crashing to the ground.

The people gather round for a Scripture reading, a reflection and a prayer at each shrine, with hymns between stops. Sometimes, to add to the grandeur of the shrine, two or three solemn-faced girls, in long while dresses, with wings sprouting from their backs and holding in their hands a sheaf of wheat, a loaf or a bunch of plastic grapes, stand statuesquely on the shrine, flanking the monstrance.

Four or five shrines is the normal number but in one village there were eight. I felt really exhausted – and holy – at the end of that procession. But the people's enthusiasm there didn't flag. They asked if the Blessed Sacrament could remain exposed in their church all that night – or at least until midnight.

WEDDINGS

While in Dulce Nombre I officiated at three weddings. There is an incongruous formality, especially in the way that the principals are dressed, looking very uncomfortable in the heat. On one occasion there was some panic. I had a worried request half an hour before we were due to start. Could we delay the Mass for an hour because a relative who lived in San Salvador was going to be late and he was bringing the bridegroom's suit?

Nuptial Masses are not dissimilar to ours, except that the couple can have godparents for the wedding as well as two official witnesses. At one wedding in Dulce Nombre – the bridegroom is chairman of the parish council – the couple elected to do the readings themselves, the groom first and then the bride. When it came to the latter's turn, the lectionary and microphone had to be taken to her since her dress was so full and stiff and jewel-encrusted that she could hardly move.

There are often bridesmaids ("*damas de honor*") as well as pages and flower girls. But they are there for decorative purposes or embellishment, not as the official witnesses. Photographers are much in evidence, with many different permutations of the principals and their families. Even during the ceremony, they can be quite obtrusive at solemn moments in order, for example, to "capture" the bride receiving Holy Communion.

For the reception after one wedding we went down the road to the Casa Comunal (the town hall), situated alongside the bombed-out offices of the local council. Outside, there was a boisterous mob of children and grown-ups, all without invitations but trying, nevertheless, to gatecrash the reception. One man at the door had the almost impossible task of trying to keep them out while allowing invited guests in. There was good-tempered mayhem but, eventually, crushed and squeezed, I got in.

It was a fairly large hall with long tables round three sides, the lights dim, deafening disco music through amplifiers, and one of those many-faceted revolving silver globes hanging from the ceiling so that the effect was of a lighthouse gone mad. I was shown to the top table for the simple meal of chicken, rice, salad, *tortillas* and a sweet fizzy drink from a bottle labelled "TROPICAL". There were no speeches; even ordinary conversation was next to impossible in the din.

As soon as we had finished eating we were asked to move away to allow a second sitting (those would-be gatecrashers, possibly) so I stood around for a little while, vainly trying to hear what people were saying to me. Eventually I decided that I'd hardly be missed in the flashing lights, semi-darkness, deafening music and the dancing that was getting under way. I believe that proceedings ended at 2.30 am.

Other weddings are more modest affairs – fewer maids of honour, fewer cameras and a simple reception in a house. The music is not as loud, conversation is possible and the atmosphere very relaxed and friendly. At one wedding the bride had done the reading at Mass but, when it came time for signing the register, the bridegroom informed me that he was illiterate and could not even write his name.

EATING AND DRINKING

In Dulce Nombre many of the people have cooking stoves which operate on bottled gas. But the poorer people who live in the town, as well as all those in the villages, just cook over wood in a corner of the open verandah that most houses have. The staple diet is *tortillas* (pancakes made of maize flour) along with *frijoles* (red kidney beans) either whole or mashed, boiled rice sometimes flavoured with onion, carrot etc., eggs sometimes, and coffee.

Chickens are a delicacy for special occasions when one of the many hens that wander around each house is killed. Meat, potatoes and wheat bread are unusual items, and never for the very poor. Fruit is quite plentiful – oranges, bananas, pineapples and various squashy tropical fruits – but only in season.

Most families, especially in the country, keep a certain amount of livestock. The relatively rich may have a couple of cows in a field. Others have, typically, a cockerel, hens, chickens, even a pig or two sniffing around the outside of the house; occasionally some ducks and even turkeys.

During my stay in Dulce Nombre I had one meal a day cooked for me and with my First World fastidiousness kept in mind. There was usually a mug of soup with vegetables in it and then, perhaps, a bit of chicken or even meat with flavoured boiled rice, maybe a vegetable such as a beetroot or a *yuca* or a *huisquil* (local vegetables) and, to finish, a jelly or a piece of water melon. Occasionally, and given as a special treat, the mug of soup had, head down in it, a cooked fish; I lacked the courage to demur or dissuade!

At breakfast and in the evening I tended just to have bread, margarine and either cheese, honey or jam with coffee or tea, teabags being obtainable in San Salvador. The heat seemed to ensure that I never had a big appetite but often a great thirst, quenched with tea, coffee, cola, beer or bottled water (from San Salvador). I longed sometimes for the food of home – the variety, as well as the freedom from anxiety about the possible effects on my stomach.

Curiously enough, porridge (Quaker Oats) can be bought in packets in San Salvador. It is called "mosh" or "quacker" and, when I said that in Scotland we used it a lot at breakfast, I was given a present of a packet. So sometimes I treated myself to a plate of porridge and powdered milk to start the day.

HEALTH AND HYGIENE

People drink the ordinary water, either from a tap in their homes if they live in the town or from a communal tap if they live in the country. The water is liable to be contaminated but years of drinking it give the people a degree of immunity from infection.

One day I was invited to attend a meeting, along with the doctor (who comes to Dulce Nombre twice a week), the nurse, the area sanitary inspector and the primary head teacher. We were to discuss with the *alcalde* (provost or mayor) and the four *consejales* (town councillors) the contamination of the water supply in Dulce Nombre. There had been a call for some precautions to be taken in view of the cholera that was widespread in South America and was now appearing in Central America. Some representatives of the four zones of the town were also present. The provost and councillors had been much criticised for their apparent lack of interest in the water problem. We expected a stormy meeting, especially as the five men from the town council kept us waiting for half an hour and, when at last they arrived, were looking rather truculent and nervous.

In fact, the meeting was amicable and constructive. We agreed that there was widespread carelessness about refuse disposal. Most people are unaware of the danger of disease being spread by flies, unwashed hands etc. We were told that the water supply is unchlorinated and that the channels through which it flows are open to cattle. Hopes were expressed that "something would be done" especially by enclosing the water channels and erecting fences to prevent access by cattle. There was talk of a campaign of education and the formation of an action committee. All seemed genuinely concerned and the doctor particularly emphasised the urgency of the matter.

The acquisition of a garbage truck was mooted but, due to the shortage of funds, it was decided instead to hire an oxcart which could go round the streets each week collecting refuse. Each householder would be charged one *colón* (8p) for this service. I hope that, indeed, "something was done".

I might mention here that, during my weeks in the parish, my own health was excellent except for sore ears whose condition I did not help by putting oil in them (at a retired nurse's suggestion). The trouble was that she gave me "3-in-1" oil. Thereafter my earache became worse and I had to go to the health centre where I sat with the other clients, all of them pregnant ladies. When I explained my presence at the clinic, the doctor and the nurse were highly amused at the treatment I had given myself: "that's for door hinges and sewing machines!" They provided me with free antibiotic tablets which had a rapid and much more satisfactory result.

CHILDREN

My first impression was that there seemed to be so many children around! Families are still quite large, especially in rural areas. At a diocesan day in Dulce Nombre for couples in marriage encounter, one husband and wife stood up proudly to acknowledge the applause of all present – they had fifteen children. Double figures are a bit unusual but seven, eight or nine are quite common. Mothers breast-feed their babies quite openly; it is an unfailing remedy for fractious infants at Mass or during their baptism.

Some of the children in the town go to nursery school, but school proper starts at the age of seven. Most places of any size, including villages, have a school but sometimes it will have only three or four grades and, if they are to continue, the children have to walk to a place with a larger school. In primary education there are nine grades but progression is not automatic and you can find, for example, a twelve year old in grade three. Hence many of the children just drop out of school at a fairly basic level, while others can be sixteen or seventeen by the time they reach the ninth grade.

In Dulce Nombre, as in many other places, the primary school has two shifts because of the large numbers: 7.30 am until 11.30 and 1.00 pm until 4.30. Some teachers work only the morning or the afternoon shift, but a few do the double shift – and receive more pay, of course. The classrooms are fairly spartan and, in each class, there can be about forty children. School uniform (blouse and skirt, shirt and trousers) is usual for the towns, but not in the villages, where the people are generally very poor.

In one remote village in Dulce Nombre parish, a new teacher had just arrived. It was three years since the previous teacher had left and the children had been without education all that time. It is difficult, because of the danger and the remoteness, to get teachers to go to such places – and even more difficult to get them to stay. Apart from the loneliness and the very basic conditions, teachers could be threatened because they are government employees.

[On a subsequent visit in 2004 I found that teacher, who had arrived in 1991, still there, but he was now the head teacher with a staff!]

Large towns such as Dulce Nombre have an "*Instituto*" (high school) to which the young people who complete primary school can go. The course there lasts for three years but, in Dulce Nombre at least, standards cannot be high. There are only four or five teachers who, among them, teach all the subjects, including English. I had several visits from one of the pupils who had copied out the story of *Little Red Riding Hood* (in English) and wanted me to hear him read it. Had I not been looking at the text also, I am sure that I could not have deciphered what he was saying.

As in the primary schools, I found the pupils in the *Instituto*, some of them nineteen or twenty years old, to be very open, friendly and talkative. They are ingenuous and unsophisticated and certainly did not give the impression of apathy or cynicism, as can happen in our country.

The children in Dulce Nombre watch television a lot, the *Teenage Mutant Hero Turtles* being the current favourite programme. In another place where there was no television, the children just seemed to chase each other around. Since firearms have had such a baleful effect in El Salvador it was sad to see a four year old brandishing a piece of wood as if it were a gun and pretending to shoot us. I was amused to note that marbles seemed to be a common game played, apparently, according to the same rules as I recall from my own young days at home in Scotland.

THE WEATHER

I was in El Salvador during July, August and some of September, their winter, not because it is cold but because it is the rainy season. Actually it rains only on some days and this occurs nearly always in the afternoon or evening.

I asked why this was so, why did it hardly ever rain in the morning, and was told that, if it rained in the morning, the people would not be able to work in the fields because, when it rains, it really pours down, often with thunder and lightning accompaniment. I pursued my questioning: was it perhaps due to variations in atmospheric pressure in the afternoon or the evening that brought the clouds and the rain? "Perhaps," I was told, "or maybe God in his providence arranges things that way to allow the people to get to work in the morning".

Despite it being the rainy season, there was semi-drought while I was in Dulce Nombre. The water supply was frequently cut off for hours or even days and, more serious, severe damage was done to the crops, especially to the maize.

During the winter the thermometer registers over 30 degrees each day and does not fall below 20 degrees at night, so that even a top sheet was hardly necessary. The coolest period of the year, still very warm by our standards, is around Christmas and the hottest is during Lent – and there is no rain for months on end. This obviously determines the times at which the different crops are sown and harvested; while I was there the maize and beans were harvested but the various kinds of fruit ripen at different times.

Central heating and overcoats are unknown and, if a church or school has windows, they are always wide open.

On the whole I found the weather uncomfortably hot, especially during Mass, when I was often soaked in sweat, yet I think I prefer it to our Scottish climate!

REPOPULATIONS AND OTHER PLACES (i)

Most of my time was spent in Dulce Nombre parish but I also had the opportunity of visiting several other places. Obviously San Salvador itself, the capital city, was among these. Built on undulating land and overlooked by volcanoes, it has endured earthquakes as well as the havoc of death squads, sabotage skirmishes between the army and the FMLN, and the "offensive" by the latter in the first months of 1989. During that offensive, the FMLN were very visible in the working class districts of the city but they caused consternation also by taking over various parts of San Salvador where the wealthy have their beautiful homes and carefully tended gardens, behind high walls and closely guarded gates. It was in San Salvador that Archbishop Oscar Romero was killed as he celebrated evening Mass in the chapel of Divine Providence Hospital on 24th March 1980. Not far away in the city is the University of Central America where six Jesuit priests, along with their housekeeper and her daughter, were assassinated in the early hours of 16th November 1989.

In addition to the ordinary towns and villages where the people have all suffered to a greater or less extent, there are also "*repoblaciones*" (repopulated villages), especially in Chalatenango department and other parts of the north. What happened is that, at the height of the army's savagery in the early 1980s, many thousands of people fled to Honduras. There, they were kept in refugee camps, the biggest of them, Mesa Grande, having ten thousand Salvadoreans living in it. A couple of years ago the refugees began returning to El Salvador under United Nations auspices. Some went to live in existing villages and towns, but the majority set up "*repoblaciones*", either completely new settlements or, in other cases, amid the ruins of abandoned villages. I visited one such "*repoblación*".

In a few cases, the houses there which had been abandoned were able to be made habitable again but often the deterioration had gone too far. The army had set fire to these houses and the elements had done the rest, giving a Pompeii-like effect to the ruins. So most houses were newly built: walls of *adobe* and roofs not of the traditional reddish tiles but of corrugated zinc, donated by First World charities. The people all had terrible tales to tell of members of their family – or even whole villages – being assassinated, after inhuman tortures, and then the decision of the community to try to get over the mountains and the river and into Honduras. Now they are back in their own country, not usually in their home villages, but just as they are allocated. They are subjected to severe harassment by the Salvadorean military and still live in fear of the army. Because the FMLN were all around and sometimes even in the "*repoblaciones*" temporarily, the people there were under suspicion of being subversives or of helping those whom the army called "the terrorists".

Despite their tragic history and their continuing deprivations, I found the "repopulated" people very resilient and determined to make a new life for themselves and their families. They show considerable initiative too, for example in starting up little workshops to embroider tablecloths and napkins or to paint the bright pictures on wood in the primitive style that is characteristic of El Salvador. They are now trying, through the good offices of various contacts, to find profitable outlets for their products, especially in the United States.

What is particularly impressive is the lively and active faith that these people have, in spite of all that they have endured. In the "*repoblaciones*" the church building sometimes survived and could be repaired; if not, a new one was constructed. The people greatly appreciate when the priest is able to come and celebrate Mass. There seemed little or no resentment against God for what had taken place; instead, a deep trust in the protection of divine providence.

Such "*repoblaciones*" are often run as cooperatives, with the people who work on the land, or even in workshops etc., handing over their produce or their income to the elected council of the community. As long as this system can operate, i.e. as long as the people are able to trust one another, it makes for a real spirit of mutual support and care in the village.

Until 1992, of course, the people were living in the shadow of war, with neither the army nor the guerrillas far away. I went one day to a tiny village called El Poy, where the highway crosses into Honduras. There were some souvenir stalls, but very few people crossing the frontier – only the very occasional lorry, one or two people pushing handcarts and the odd, and very intrepid, foreign tourist.

On the way back to Dulce Nombre that evening, we stopped to pick up some very poorly photocopied FMLN propaganda that had been scattered along the road. On another occasion on the same road, the parish car was stopped by the guerrillas and the person driving was told to place the car at right angles across the road, in order to block it. When he successfully protested that it was a church car and on urgent business, the FMLN stopped the next vehicle, a lorry, and used it instead.

Several times during my weeks in Dulce Nombre, the road between us and San Salvador was the scene of clashes between the army and the guerrillas. When that occurred, the traffic was usually halted for reasons of safety; but just to make sure and in order to prevent the army moving up and down the highway, the guerrillas usually stopped some buses, put them at right angles across the road to block it and then, to make certain that they did not try to escape, fired a few bullets into each tyre.

REPOPULATIONS AND OTHER PLACES (ii)

One day, along with a parishioner who often drove for me, I went to a place called Carrizal, to the north-east of Dulce Nombre and very near the Honduran border. The parish is remote and extensive and, at the time of my visit, it had three priests working there – two Irish Franciscans and one priest from Edinburgh. It is a long and tortuous road – or, rather, track, north from Chalatenango town. For the first few miles the going is fairly smooth but then it becomes very rough, slow and tiring. The daily bus takes two and a half hours to reach Chalatenango from Carrizal and, just to make things really difficult, it leaves at three o'clock in the morning!

On the way to Carrizal is the town of La Laguna, pleasantly situated on the crest of a ridge but with a permanent and numerous presence of soldiers. In the past, La Laguna had the reputation of giving assistance to the guerrillas and so, some years ago, the army took over the town and has been there since. Soldiers seemed to outnumber the townspeople. They were everywhere and had made trenches and dug-outs all over the town, between houses, at street corners etc. The army presence had provoked innumerable guerrilla attacks and, because the army is scattered throughout the town, such clashes had inevitably meant loss of life among the inhabitants and wholesale destruction of property. The town had an almost "blitzed" appearance and the people had suffered greatly.

In addition to the frequent violence, the people of La Laguna had also to endure the day-to-day presence of the army – and this brought all sorts of problems. For example, I was taken into a house where an emaciated child was lying in a hammock. A man there told us that the child was thirteen months old and the latest child of his wife, who is an alcoholic and whom we later saw, staggering about in the street outside. The man seemed to accept his wife's promiscuity in a resigned and fatalistic way. I was told that there were many such children in La Laguna, as well as many cases where women and girls have been raped.

About ten miles north of La Laguna and very definitely in guerrilla-controlled territory, lie the villages of Carrizal and, beyond, Ojos de Agua. Living conditions are primitive for the three priests there, as well as for everyone else, and there has been a great deal of violence and suffering. The northern boundary of the parish is the river Sumpul (which divides El Salvador at this point from Honduras) and it was on the banks of this river that one of the worst atrocities of the conflict took place. In 1984 people who had tried to occupy and cultivate disused land were attacked by the army. They attempted to flee across the river into Honduras, but the troops of that country forced them back and up to one thousand peasants were massacred by the Salvadorean military.

Both Carrizal and Ojos de Agua were quiet, even somnolent, on the day I was there. We also visited a small village between the two places and I have three memories from there. The first is the little *adobe* school which, because of the war, had had no teacher for three years. Second, we met a group of six men returning from Chalatenango. They had been at a peasants' demonstration about water supplies and were well satisfied with their day despite the fact that the military had used sirens in an attempt to drown the speakers' voices and had fired over the heads of the crowd to frighten them. Lastly, I recall a woman of about fifty who had only a small part of her right hand remaining, the rest having been severed some months before as she was trying vainly to protect her husband from a man wielding a *machete*. This was one of three murders that the little village had experienced in the previous twelve months, all of them the result of vendettas and family feuds. Violence in El Salvador is not restricted to the army or the guerrillas. As someone said to me, "Many Salvadoreans do not even know the meaning of the word 'forgiveness'".

RECREATION AND SPORT

The older people of Dulce Nombre stand around chatting and the young ones play in the street – and with impunity because the traffic is so light: only the occasional bus, the even more occasional van, a horseman or two. There is not much danger of being knocked down or run over. Even the hens and their offspring love to play "chicken", having an insatiable urge to scamper across the road just in front of the wheels of any oncoming vehicle.

Television is popular in the town. There are about eight channels, all showing very lightweight programmes, often USA productions, dubbed in Spanish, and frequently interrupted by commercials. There is no cinema in Dulce Nombre but videos are obtainable in Chalatenango.

Dulce Nombre has two football teams, both playing in department leagues. The members of the "big" team receive a pittance for playing and a small bonus if they win. They were doing well while I was there and seemed likely to be promoted to a national league until they met one of their great rivals, Citalá. Earlier in the season Dulce Nombre had lost at Citalá in a match marred by violence. One of the Dulce Nombre players was hit by a stone from a spectator's sling, a Dulce Nombre supporter was struck with a *machete*, while a Citalá fan produced a gun and fired it in the air. So the return match in Dulce Nombre was anticipated with a mixture of anxiety and desire for revenge.

The first half was played in torrential rain and, although the rain had gone off by half-time, the pitch was by then sodden and partially flooded. The crowd was lively, vocal and enthusiastic. In order to get the second half started, the referee had a difficult task ushering people off the pitch – strolling spectators, small boys enjoying the chance to score goals, and an ice cream man with his handcart. Sad to relate, Citalá scored the only goal of the game near the end and that more or less ended Dulce Nombre's hopes of promotion.

Dulce Nombre's home games began at 1.00 pm on Sundays (rather than the more normal 11.00 am) because the parish Mass is at 10.00 am. How they manage to play in the torrid heat of the early afternoon is beyond me.

The junior team is even more conscious of religious observance. Each Saturday evening they meet on the verandah of the priest's house for a talk on tactics for the next day's game, followed by an hour of Scripture reflection and faith sharing. The team had a narrow escape while I was in the parish. Travelling to an away game, their bus was passing an army barracks when it was stopped and boarded by the military. The whole team was herded into the barracks and informed that they were being recruited and drafted there and then, as the Central American custom is. After four hours' argument, their manager succeeded in having them released on the grounds that most of them were students and so, for the time being, exempt from military service. But it was a near thing!

The young mothers' club started a softball team and, having heard that the British Embassy had provided sewing machines for the school, wondered whether Her Britannic Majesty the Queen would supply them with bats, balls and gloves. I was asked to make the required approaches and I did so but, I have to admit, in a somewhat half-hearted fashion. The Embassy was very kind but thought it unlikely that they could help. On the other hand, if the young mothers had asked for pads, stumps and bails…

An annual event in Dulce Nombre, as in other towns, is *La Fiesta del Maíz* (The Maize Festival). It is really a money-making affair and, in 1991, profits were being divided between the parish and the football team.

The festival got under way on the Saturday evening with a noisy and crowded dance at which the Maize Queen was chosen. This is done by an unashamedly commercial process. Girls aged from ten to twenty try to sign up as many sponsors as they can, the more generous the better, and the girl who brings in most money is the queen. The runners up are her maids of honour. In 1991 there were eleven candidates, of whom only eight appeared at the dance, the other three presumably having decided that they had no chance.

The following day, after Mass, the candidates are paraded around the town, each standing in a decorated cart drawn by two oxen. On arrival at the front of the church, they dismount and join the platform party for speeches, announcements, votes of thanks etc. Then the victor is crowned by the previous year's queen and given her royal sceptre. The parish priest – or, in 1991, the acting parish priest! – is then invited to invest her with the winner's sash. During the coronation ceremony, Coca-Cola was served to the contestants – only six had turned up on the day – and to the acting parish priest, who, alone, was also given a tumbler. There was a festive air in the town on the day and stalls selling ice cream, fizzy drinks and snacks did good business. Fortunately the occasion was not marred by any military activity, violent or otherwise.

TWO SPECIAL PLACES

Each of the villages served from Dulce Nombre has its attractiveness but, while in the parish, I was particularly anxious to help the two villages furthest away from Dulce Nombre: El Cóbano in the very south of the parish and Ocotal in the far north. Both suffer from their isolation and deserve special attention.

El Cóbano is a low lying and scattered village about ten or twelve kilometres (some eight miles) south of Dulce Nombre and very near the huge lake formed by the river Lempa dam. Somehow or other – because it is not really remote – the people there did not seem to have integrated into the parish community or even to know what was going on in it. When I arrived for the monthly Mass they had not been told about my coming and were quite unprepared. However, the hurried arrangements to have the Mass in somebody's "garden" were a great credit to those involved – and the hens, dogs and pigs moving around us were not a nuisance at all.

There are serious problems among the Catholics of El Cóbano and a demoralised atmosphere, partly due to the considerable encroachments of the sects (right-wing fundamentalist groups, often based in the United States and funded generously from there). One day I asked the people of El Cóbano if they had any representatives on the parish council and the response was "We did not even know that there was a parish council". So, with the president of the parish council and one or two others, I arranged a meeting with the people, to be held a few days later in the village school. About forty turned up and we explained what the parish council was and what it did. We then invited them to elect their three representatives and, to our great joy, five candidates were nominated and the assembly voted three of them to be its representatives.

Apart from the fact that they have no church building – one of the few villages in the parish with none – and are most anxious to have one, there was another very serious problem in El Cóbano. Very few, if any, of the villagers are properly married. A number have been married at a civil ceremony, which is a necessary legal preliminary to the church ceremony, but most are just living together. The result is that not only do the grown-ups not frequent the sacraments but many of the children are not even baptised.

We broached the matter and there was general agreement that it would be a good idea to have their marital status rectified. But then the questions started. How much have you got to pay? Have you got to buy a white dress? And, even when these problems were answered and out of the way, there remained a serious obstacle for these poor people: before a church wedding, they are supposed to go through a civil marriage and that costs 25 *colones* (£2.00) plus the need to get valid certificates of birth (more money) from their place of birth, often quite a distance away, so further expense.

Before I left El Salvador, we were told that there is such a thing as a "collective civil wedding". When many couples wish to regularise their marriages and cost is an obstacle, an official can be asked to go to the place and conduct a mass wedding at a nominal charge. That possibility seemed an attractive one for El Cóbano.

I took a special liking to El Cóbano principally because they seemed to have missed out on so much, spiritually as well as materially. A few days before I left the parish we had another Mass in the village school in El Cóbano. I was accompanied by twenty members of the Dulce Nombre choir. The classroom was jammed with people – more than one hundred must have been inside – and others were standing at the open windows, looking in. There were about twenty-five communicants and two baptisms: a three-year-old girl and an eight-month-old boy, who delayed things a little because he was found to be naked when called and had to be clothed in order to appear decent in front of the congregation. It was a good celebration enjoyed by all and I hope that it encouraged the people of El Cóbano to become more involved in the life of the parish.

[Some years after this, El Cóbano was transferred to another parish.]

Ocotal is definitely in the mountains. The "road" there is rough and rocky as it winds its way tortuously through valleys and along the edge of precipices. The distance is only eleven or twelve kilometres but it takes an hour in the car (which therefore means an average speed of about 7 m.p.h.) Because of the state of the road and because of the guerrilla activity, there is no bus service to Ocotal so the people have to walk to Dulce Nombre. They use trails and paths even more precipitous than the road and do the journey downhill in about ninety minutes, but take considerably longer on the way back.

They are great people in Ocotal despite their isolation and the amount of suffering they have endured in the last decade. I was told that they were living in constant fear of landmines. The people said that animals have been killed and children maimed when they have triggered off a mine. And the people were scared to move about or to go to work in the fields because of the danger. One person told me that, when he complained to the guerrillas, he was told that the solution was simply to stay at home. The feeling was that the mines were there not only to deter the army but also to disrupt daily life and work.

There is a little church in Ocotal and a school which, while I was there, welcomed its first teacher in three years. The people were overjoyed – the parents at least, but I think the children too – that at last the young people were going to get some lessons. Still, with only one teacher for several dozen children who hadn't been in school for three years, it was not clear how much they would learn.

Beyond Ocotal there are a few other villages or hamlets – Los Encuentros, Chorro Blanco – which are accessible only on foot or on horseback. Fr Basil makes the journey to these places but I had to admit defeat, ask their pardon and try to make a special fuss of them when they came down to Ocotal. I felt very humbled when old ladies and young children made the journey of an hour or more, up and down ravines and over the most uneven paths. When I told the people that it was 160 km from the most distant community in our diocese of Galloway to the town where I live, they were astonished; but never again shall I complain of such a long journey in the comfort of a car and on Scottish roads which, even at their worst, are motorways by the standards of El Salvador.

On Friday 30th August we had the sacrament of confirmation in Ocotal – probably for the first time ever in the village. On previous confirmation occasions, the people have had to walk to Dulce Nombre. I thought that, being so remote and so oppressed, they deserved the chance of having confirmation in their own little church.

We arrived at 8.00 am, two hours before Mass time, and agreed with the decision to take all the benches out of the church in order to give more room. As the people began to arrive, I started to hear confessions and was kept at it from before nine o'clock until 10.55, an hour after the Mass was due to begin. Even then, I managed to finish confessions only by dint of shortening the rite to the very minimum and making announcements that just fell short of saying, "only those in mortal sin, please". In place of the expected twenty for the sacrament of confirmation, there were forty-nine. The ceremony was joyful, prayerful and very hot and, as a postscript after Mass, there were two baptisms.

On the way back to Dulce Nombre we gave a lift to a woman and her small daughter. She told me that her husband and three of her sons had been killed since 1980, her husband being one of thirty civil guards trapped and murdered by the FMLN and her sons having been missing now for years, presumably dead, in the war. What the mother said about her youngest son was very poignant. Aged ten, he was "recruited" by the FMLN and, when he came home on leave, she wanted to keep him there because he was crying so much; but the guerrillas told her to send him back unless she wanted "to put earth on her other children".

When authorising me to celebrate confirmation in Dulce Nombre parish, the bishop of the diocese had stipulated that no one under twelve should receive the sacrament. I was very insistent that that instruction be observed but, some days after the Ocotal confirmations, I heard that the community there, anxious that the younger children should have some religious instruction as well as the confirmation candidates, had organised a course for them, with the inducement that the best boy and the best girl on the course would be added to the confirmation candidates without my knowledge. The people of Ocotal deserved a prize for imaginative pastoral initiative.

SECTS

It is well known that in Latin America the "sects" have been very active in recent years. By sects, people mean not the mainline Protestant churches such as Lutherans, Presbyterians, Episcopalians and Mennonites, but smaller and very active organisations, founded often in the United States and funded from there. Their "*bête noire*" is the Catholic Church. As a result, there has been, and still is, a big effort "to win Latin America for Christ", i.e. to get people to join the sects. In general, the campaign has met with considerable success and, sadly, large numbers of Catholics have now joined the sects.

The reasons for this are both sociological and pastoral. The sects do offer a style of religion and worship that is Scripture-based, though in a very fundamentalist and selective way. Their prayer is Pentecostal in style. Their worship is simple, cheerful and attractive, and their preaching offers an assurance of certain salvation after death for those who are "converted".

The sects have little or nothing to say about social justice or building God's Kingdom on earth. Consequently, they represent no threat to regimes where injustice, violence and the violation of human rights constitute a way of life. In fact, such regimes favour the sects because they teach that we must accept whatever God wills for us in this life without protest, so that we may receive our eternal reward in heaven. This attitude can be very attractive to people who live in terror of being killed if there is any suspicion of their being subversives or sympathetic to the FMLN. Moreover, those who join the sects often experience a sense of community that they may never have had as Catholics. In addition, their Scripture teaching seems to speak to them, although in a selective way, of the certainty of their personal salvation and of the joy which that brings.

In Dulce Nombre there are three sects, all with their own temples: Jehovah's Witnesses, the Assembly of God, and the Gnostics. Their numbers are not great, although a few of the villages in the parish have higher percentages of sect members than there are in Dulce Nombre itself. Few or many, they are quite active in door-to-door canvassing. So much so that many Catholics have a printed card on their doors with the words "*Somos Católicos. No insista*" ("We are Catholics. Do not pester us"), alongside a picture of the Sacred Heart or Our Lady.

For a week during my time in Dulce Nombre we had daily visits from an itinerant evangelist who arrived each day at about 3.30 or 4.00 pm, set up his loudspeakers just opposite our church and, for the next two and a half hours, subjected us to a mixture of hymns and preaching (mostly the latter). Each of his sermons lasted over an hour and, to a large extent, were attacks on the Catholic Church, its teaching and its priests. He usually bussed in a few dozen followers from other towns and these provided organised applause and support. Some Dulce Nombre people gathered round to listen – probably a few of the local sect members, but mostly the merely curious.

The disturbance was a great nuisance, especially when there was a five o'clock Mass and we had to compete with the din outside. The parishioners were indignant and complained to the mayor who agreed that, although there was freedom in the law to preach different religions, this was a breach of the peace and a provocation when Mass was on. But nothing happened, except that the preacher asserted that no one could stop him fulfilling his God-given mission of proclaiming the truth.

I heard that sometimes, when sects tried to hold open-air meetings in other towns, the Catholics had been more militant than those of Dulce Nombre. On one occasion, for example, the Catholics brought a statue of Our Lady out of their church and processed around the evangelist, reciting the rosary. Another tactic had been to get a team of parishioners into the belfry to ring the church bells continuously until the preacher packed up in frustration and left.

CONFIRMATION

Not long after I arrived in Dulce Nombre, people began asking if we would celebrate the sacrament of confirmation while I was in the parish. Bishop Eduardo Alas of Chalatenango had been to Dulce Nombre for confirmation within the previous year or two, but clearly there were many young people now who could receive the sacrament. I asked the bishop if I might confirm during my stay in the parish and he very graciously consented, but with the proviso: normally only those aged fifteen or more, and perhaps those from twelve upwards "if they are mature". That phrase "if they are mature" was to cause us difficulties although, in practice, I tended to leave the decision – and its communication to the people concerned – to the local catechists.

Since the numbers were going to be large, we decided that we should have confirmation not only in Dulce Nombre but in Santa Rita as well and, because the people in Ocotal were so far away, there also. For days, indeed weeks, beforehand, candidates were being enrolled, sponsors vetted (if married, they were supposed to be properly so), and "*charlas*" (a course of three or four informal preparatory talks) given in the three places. Besides trying to ensure that enrolment and talks were being seen to and that some preparation for the special liturgies was being made, I had also to provide opportunities for the sacrament of reconciliation for the candidates, their parents and their sponsors. I reckon that, for this purpose, I spent fifteen hours in confessionals, in sessions lasting from one to three hours.

Sunday 25th August was confirmation day in Dulce Nombre, at the ten o'clock Mass. The candidates, their parents and sponsors had been in the church since 8.00 am, their names being checked against the lists we had prepared. Because of the considerable numbers, the 130 candidates and their sponsors were ranged on benches placed along three walls of the large church and grouped according to their home villages or communities. The Mass started promptly at 10.00 am, which was something quite exceptional for special occasions in El Salvador and was the result of careful planning and everyone's cooperation. After a most enjoyable and beautiful celebration, we finished at 11.40.

One postscript to the Dulce Nombre confirmation. I was informed the previous day that several of the football team's best players had been chosen as sponsors, but they had an important away match starting at eleven o'clock. So could I "do" their candidates first so that they could rush off to the game and, even if the match had begun, some at least of them could go on as substitutes? I did not think the plan very appropriate and suggested proxy sponsoring. In the event, the players invited to be sponsors carried out their duties in the church. It would be good to be able to report that divine providence rewarded their sacrifice but, alas, the weakened Dulce Nombre XI went down 6-0, and thus lost its last chance of promotion to the national league.

Santa Rita had its confirmations on Sunday 1st September. Mass there is at 7.30 am but, when I got there just after 6.30, very few people had arrived, despite previous requests, and planning such as making arrangements for seating had not been done. So we had some frantic and fairly intensive preparations, especially checking names against lists and getting people into groups according to their home villages. In spite of my frustration at the lack of planning, all went well, we had a good and cheerful celebration with about one hundred candidates. Before rushing off to the next Mass in Dulce Nombre, I was besieged by people with cameras, wanting me to pose with the candidates and their families.

The confirmation at Ocotal, one of my "special places", on Friday 30th August was the first ever in the little church. I have described it in the section called "Two Special Places".

I was very relieved to have got through all the confirmation celebrations. They were generally regarded as having been very successful. No praise is too high for the various parish council members, catechists etc. whose collaboration, despite their inexperience, was excellent and unstinting. Erasmo, the parish council president, was particularly deserving of recognition especially as, after the confirmations, he took it upon himself to enter all the details of the candidates into the parish confirmation register and onto the forms, one for each candidate, which had to be sent to the diocesan office in Chalatenango.

BIRTHS AND DEATHS

In El Salvador both births and deaths are so commonplace as almost to be taken for granted. During my time in the parish at least two young men took their own lives by drinking pesticide. A week after my arrival in Dulce Nombre I was invited to a combined death commemoration and birthday party. It was Normita's fifth birthday and also the fifth anniversary of the death of her mother (a seventeen-year-old). The event was a strange mixture of rejoicing and grieving. We gathered round a shrine erected in the house for the occasion – banks of flowers, fairy lights, a photograph of the dead girl, a picture of God the Father and God the Son and, above them all, a statue of Our Lady. Led by an indefatigable and indomitable old lady, we prayed non-stop for forty-five minutes with a variety of Our Fathers, Hail Marys, litanies, invocations, prayers for each of Our Lord's five wounds etc., etc. It just went on and on with a kind of relentless inevitability until, at last, the praying more or less collapsed as those present were distracted by the appearance and distribution of pieces of birthday cake and bottles of coke.

There were a number of deaths from natural causes while I was in Dulce Nombre, but considerably more births. Illegitimacy is not uncommon and does not seem to be regarded as a stigma. Several people informed me that they were illegitimate. One very prominent parishioner told me, without any embarrassment, that he had been brought up in great poverty by his maternal grandparents. In hunger and in some desperation he once went, aged fourteen, to see his father and ask for financial assistance. The father did not recognise him and refused him help. He (my informant) had been told that his father was a notorious philanderer who had had about forty children, all over El Salvador.

In my eleven weeks in the parish, I baptised twenty-one children, ten of whom were illegitimate. The baptismal register has a space for noting whether a child has been born in wedlock or not and one day, out of curiosity, I examined the data and noted some statistics. In 1959, there were 316 baptisms, 76 being noted as illegitimate. In 1969 the comparative figures were 372 and 133; in 1979, 364 and 85; in 1985, 210 and 87; in 1989, 120 and 52; and in 1990, 178 and 49. However, I do know that, in recent years, many priests have ceased to note illegitimacy in their baptismal registers, so the second figure that I have given in each pair is probably lower than the reality.

The names children are given by their parents nowadays in El Salvador are not usually the old-fashioned Juan, José, María etc. Among those whom I baptised, there were Melvin, Yobani (= Giovanni), Neftali, Ulises, Osmin, William, Jairo, Yaneth, Evelín, Xiomara, Lucimar, Florinda and, I am pleased to say, Mauricio. Other entries which I spotted in the baptismal register showed a considerable fashion in foreign names, often somewhat disguised; for example, Yasmin, Glendy, Lesley, Hazell, Gisél and Deisi.

FAREWELL

I arrived in Dulce Nombre timorously, but departed very reluctantly! The departure process was long drawn out as I bade farewell to each community on my final visit to it. As the days passed and 9th September drew nearer, the process became harder and harder. There were parties for me and songs and presents from the teachers, the altar servers, the choir, the people who had specially looked after me. There were visits by people from other villages as well as groups of Dulce Nombre townspeople – and a multitude of gifts, touching in their simplicity: a towel, a few coins, five oranges, eggs, a chicken, a bag of beans, some maize, a pair of sunglasses and, from one of the altar servers, his own pack of playing cards, well worn because he loved to play with them. I hesitated before accepting this last gift; it was a big sacrifice for the boy which I could not rebuff.

Sunday 8th September began with the arrival outside my bedroom window of the parish choir – instruments and voices – at 5.30 am. They serenaded me in the chilly air until 6.15. Then I was taken to breakfast in a house where about twenty-five people were assembled. The main item for eating was rice pudding with raisins in it, and there were presents, speeches and photographs.

I had to rush off to Santa Rita for 7.30 am Mass, which became quite an emotional occasion with, afterwards, speeches, photos and gifts, cakes and coke. Then back to Dulce Nombre for Mass in a packed church with many people standing. Again it was very emotional. After lunch with some of the parishioners who had been very close to me and after more visits from sundry well-wishers, including a lady and her two children who had walked from Ocotal to say goodbye, I felt physically exhausted and emotionally drained. I tried to do some packing – which wasn't easy due to the ever-increasing number of gifts being brought to me – before going to Piedras Gordas for four o'clock Mass, my last in the parish.

On my return from there, things became even more hectic as I tried to pack and people continued to call to say goodbye and to give presents. Some I had to leave behind, including a large cushion and a plaster statue of a triumphant figure in a chariot (with horses).

After having supper, with a group of about twelve people, I had to go outside to the main square in front of the church where a large crowd had gathered for my farewell concert. The choir sang and we had solos, sketches, dances and two speeches, one from Erasmo as president of the parish council and the other from me. At the end, there were more photographs and lots of hugs. I finally got to bed at 10.30 pm – very late for me in Dulce Nombre, especially as I had to be up the following morning at three o'clock.

All too soon for me, my time in Dulce Nombre was at an end. In this account of my eleven weeks there I have tried to describe what life was like for the people and what it was like for me. There has been great suffering in Dulce Nombre, as in so many other places in El Salvador, but daily life also has its lighter and brighter side and this I have attempted to portray.

Thank God, a ceasefire was signed and came into effect in January 1992. The open war between the army and the guerrillas in El Salvador has come to an end. Many lives have now been saved that otherwise would have been lost; and many families will not now have to mourn the death of a son, a brother, a husband or a father.

There can, however, be no genuine and lasting peace without justice – and that still seems a long way off in respect, for example, of land reform, equality of opportunity and an end to corruption.

From the people of Dulce Nombre parish I received acceptance, friendship, gratitude and love. My time with them was a wonderful and unforgettable experience for me. I received far more than I could ever give to them. May Jesus the Saviour keep them in his care and bestow on them, and on all the people of El Salvador, his gift of peace.

POSTSCRIPT

I had the pleasure of return visits to Dulce Nombre de María in October 2004 and in January 2008. They were short visits, only two days in 2004 and an overnight in 2008, but very welcome opportunities to see so many friends again and to be in their company.

In the circumstances, only superficial observations and impressions were possible. On the whole, the material conditions of the people have improved and they have more opportunities to enjoy a better standard of living.

There have been changes. The parish priest is Salvadorean, the altar in Dulce Nombre church is now back in the sanctuary at the head of the nave, the church façade has been completely changed and the dome, which suddenly collapsed in a heap of rubble a few years ago, has been less grandly replaced.

Many more of the streets have solid surfaces, the roads to San Salvador and the south have been much improved, some new bridges have replaced the need to cross the beds of streams and even the road north to Ocotal is now good enough to allow an occasional but regular bus service.

Post-war El Salvador suffers from the same kind of widespread violence as Guatemala and, as in most countries, drugs are a baleful influence affecting many people and in various ways. It would be foolish to attempt to predict what the future holds for El Salvador. That depends on so many unknowns both in the country itself and in the wider world.

However, on a personal note let me say this. As long as I live, I shall cherish the memory of my time in Dulce Nombre; it was a profound experience to be with some of the best people I have ever known and loved.

Welcome to Dulce Nombre de María: with flowers, music and an embarrassed newcomer

Welcome to Dulce Nombre de María: each community in the parish has a welcome banner

Welcome to Dulce Nombre de María: en route to the church for the Mass of welcome

Dulce Nombre de María: parish church (with its old façade)

Dulce Nombre de María: the priest's house in the town, with mountains to the north

Dulce Nombre de María: main entrance to the town (from the south)

Dulce Nombre de María: parish church, the Risen Saviour in a rural panorama (oil on wood)

Dulce Nombre de María: with the altar servers (*acólitos*) in the priest's garden

Dulce Nombre de María: tea with the teachers of the primary school

Dulce Nombre de María: telephone office (with bullet holes and FMLN slogans)

Dulce Nombre de María: main square (*El Parque*) with bus ("*Reinita del Norte*" – "Little Queen of the North") preparing to leave for San Salvador

Dulce Nombre de María: church in an outlying village, exposition of the Blessed Sacrament (with *Guardia del Santísimo* and some distracted children)

Ocatal ("a special place"): a remote village of Dulce Nombre parish; church shrine, with statues and adornments

Ocatal: candidates for confirmation

Ocatal: the church, prior to the confirmation Mass

San Salvador Cathedral
(where Archbishop Oscar Romero's body lies)

San Salvador: government propaganda against FMLN, 1984

San Salvador: University of Central America (UCA), place (with rose bushes) where six Jesuits and two women were shot

Dulce Nombre de María: parish church
(with its new façade and bell tower)

Portrait of a Diocese

INTRODUCTION

I wanted in my retirement to do various useful things during the years left to me on earth. This attempt to offer a portrait of the diocese of Galloway will be, I hope, of interest to some people at present and perhaps provide some useful information or material in years to come for those with an interest in the diocese as it was in the last two decades of the twentieth century and the early years of the twenty-first. Even if this ambition or hope is never fulfilled, at least the work of compiling this portrait kept me from mischief and indolence.

This is not my first attempt at a written portrait. In 1991 the opportunity arose for me to spend a few months in a rural parish in El Salvador (Central America) as acting parish priest while the "official" pastor was on leave. The experience that I had in the parish of Dulce Nombre de María in the diocese of Chalatenango made a very deep impression on me, an impression that I wanted to share. So I wrote *Portrait of a Parish* which the Scottish Catholic International Aid Fund published and which now appears as chapter 5 of this book.

During my time in Dulce Nombre de María I received such great kindness and learned so much that the *Portrait*, which I composed on my return to Scotland, seems a very small recognition of my debt of gratitude to the people of the parish in El Salvador. The same is true of this tribute, *Portrait of a Diocese*. To serve the people of Galloway diocese as their bishop has truly been a privilege and I am only too pleased to offer them this *Portrait*, hoping they will find it of interest. At least it is meant as my recognition of what they mean to me. So let me begin to paint the portrait.

THE SUBJECT BEING PORTRAYED

The diocese of Galloway can claim to be the oldest in Scotland, founded as it was by St Ninian, the first known Catholic missionary in the country. The tradition is that he arrived in 396 (though quite probably the correct date is some decades, even a century, later) and established the earliest Christian settlement, which was given the name Candida Casa (White House) and, in the vernacular, Whithorn. The diocese is still officially known in the Vatican as "*Diocesis Gallovidiensis seu Candidae Casae*".

For over a thousand years, Galloway continued as a diocese or, at least, as an ecclesiastical entity. I quote from *The Catholic Directory for Scotland* (2012, p.73): "*The See of Whithorn is associated from the late fourth century with St Ninian, but it is possible that a Christian community existed there before his arrival. There was a continuous succession of bishops in the eighth century. The See was revived c.1128 and recognised the metropolitan authority of York until 1355. It became a suffragan of St Andrews in 1472 and of Glasgow in 1492. The See was, in effect, vacant from the death of Andrew Durie (1541 - 1548) since his successor, Alexander Gordon, conformed at the reformation in 1560, and it remained vacant until the restoration of the hierarchy in 1878.*"

The first four bishops after the restoration were John McLachlan (1878 - 1893), William Turner (1893 - 1914), James McCarthy (1914 - 1943) and William Mellon (1943 - 1952). These bishops had their residences in Dumfries and their cathedral church at St Andrew's, Dumfries. The fifth bishop of the restored hierarchy was Joseph McGee (1952 - 1981); in 1959, to be more central in the diocese which, in 1947, had been given more territory in the north, he changed his residence from Dumfries to Ayr, giving his newly acquired house the name "Candida Casa", an appropriate but slightly incongruous choice since the house is built of red sandstone. In 1961 when St Andrew's cathedral was destroyed by fire, Bishop McGee made Good Shepherd church, Ayr, the cathedral, at least provisionally.

I was the sixth of the post-restoration bishops and, in 2004, was succeeded by John Cunningham. In 2007 Bishop Cunningham changed the cathedral to St Margaret's church in Ayr. Good Shepherd church was in need of extensive and costly repairs, its normal congregation had greatly decreased over the years and the proposal to close it was finally approved by Rome. The building was sold and then partially demolished but with the façade and tower retained as embellishment for the housing built on the site.

It is perhaps worth remarking that none of the seven bishops of modern times have been either natives or originally priests of the diocese of Galloway. Respectively, they were born in Glasgow, Aberdeen, Newcastle-upon-Tyne, Edinburgh, Perthshire, Hamilton and Paisley.

The diocese's name being Galloway can puzzle strangers. There is no town, let alone, city, of Galloway, although there is a village called New Galloway. Galloway is a district, that part of Dumfries & Galloway that extends westward from the river Nith (in the town of Dumfries) to the Mull of Galloway (whose principal town is Stranraer).

In 1947, the territory of Galloway diocese was increased because, when the archdiocese of Glasgow was divided into the archdiocese of Glasgow and the dioceses of Motherwell and Paisley, the parishes in the north of Ayrshire, previously in the archdiocese, were transferred to Galloway. The diocese therefore is located in south-west Scotland and its territory is easily and exactly described as all of Dumfries & Galloway and, except for the island of Arran, all of Ayrshire.

The diocese is divided into a number of deaneries, seven in 1981, but now only four. The number of deaneries has been largely dependent on the number of Catholic secondary schools in the diocese. This is because a secondary school with its "feeder" primary schools gives a certain unity to an area. In recent years, secondary schools in Girvan, Cumnock and Kilwinning have closed and only four remain: in Dumfries, Kilmarnock, Saltcoats and Ayr. In 1981 one new deanery was established (for the Wigtownshire area of Dumfries & Galloway), not because it had a Catholic secondary school but because there was a certain justification for having two deaneries in the extensive sweep of Dumfries & Galloway and, besides, the priests allowed to concelebrate with Pope John Paul II at the Mass in Bellahouson Park on 1st June 1982 were limited to one per deanery!

Each deanery has a certain number of parishes within its boundaries. "Parish" is a legal term: "a parish is a certain community of Christ's faithful stably established within a particular church, whose pastoral care, under the authority of the diocesan bishop, is entrusted to a parish priest as its proper pastor" (canon 515 §1). This definition left me in some confusion, since there were a number of communities with their own church for Mass and usually without their own resident priest. I did not know whether they had been established by one of my predecessors as parishes or whether I ought to establish them; or if they were simply "chapels of ease" of neighbouring parishes. I never was certain if my guess was correct but I did calculate that we had 47 parishes. Over the years, a few of these have been closed or merged (especially those with very few parishioners). In 2012 there were 43.

PERSONAL

My ordination as bishop of Galloway took place in the grounds of Fatima House, Coodham, by Cardinal Gordon Joseph Gray on 9th June 1981. I took up my duties gladly and enthusiastically, without any great fear but, I hope, humbly and with some nervousness. I was aware that I had much to learn and that I would make mistakes. But I wanted to be a good bishop and to do all that I could for the diocese, its priests and all of its people.

I did not have a detailed plan of work but I did want to become known and to get to know the diocese. I wanted to visit the parishes as often as I could and also to visit the religious houses and the Catholic schools. The priests were my closest collaborators and I realised that it was my duty to serve them, care for them, encourage them, consult them and support them in every way that I could.

I was conscious of my inexperience as well as my ignorance of many aspects of the diocese. That meant that I should be greatly dependent on the priests of the diocese and also, I hoped, on my predecessor, Bishop Joseph McGee. I already knew and liked him and admired him as a kindly, intelligent and wise man. However, although I wanted his advice, he never offered it and, out of a wish not to interfere, was reluctant to discuss problems with me. When I sought his counsel, his inclination was to agree with my way of thinking, although I suspect that, sometimes at least, he did so out of courtesy rather than from desire and conviction.

Since Bishop McGee did not become involved in any diocesan activities after his retiral, I cannot say that he exercised much influence on what I did or how I did it. Rather, it seems to me that Bishop Frank Thomson, who had been my bishop when I was a priest of Motherwell diocese, and who had been extremely kind to me since my nomination as bishop in early April 1981, influenced me in the sense that I copied some of his style and manner in carrying out various episcopal duties. Archbishop (later Cardinal) Winning was equally approachable and was quite ready to offer advice. Of course, he and I had been friends since our schooldays. We were in the same year group in Our Lady's High School in Motherwell, and had gone to Blairs College together in 1942, the philosophy course having been located there during wartime, since the Scots Colleges in Rome and Spain were inaccessible. After my three years of army service from 1944 to 1947, we were together again when I was sent to Rome for my theology course. When the dioceses of Motherwell and Paisley were set up as suffragans of Glasgow in 1947, we were both assigned to the former, having been born and brought up there. After our ordination to the priesthood we were priests of Motherwell diocese although each of us spent most of our years working outside the diocese until episcopal ordination took him to Glasgow in 1971 and me to Galloway in 1981.

Church law requires a bishop to have a vicar general. "In each diocese the diocesan bishop is to appoint a vicar general" (canon 475 §1); "he is to be known for his sound doctrine, integrity, prudence and practical experience" (canon 478 §1); "the vicar general has the same executive power throughout the whole diocese" as the bishop, except those matters reserved by law or by the bishop himself (canon 479 §1). Even if there were no law, common sense would dictate the wisdom of having a vicar general. A bishop needs someone in whom he can confide, from whom he can ask advice and guidance, who can point out errors (if possible, before they are made) and who can provide support in difficulties and anxieties.

Mgr Francis Duffy had been Bishop McGee's vicar general. He was extremely well liked in the diocese and had the confidence of my predecessor. I thought that he was also the obvious choice for me and I therefore asked him to continue his important duties. When he retired, I invited Fr (now Mgr) Joseph Boyd to succeed him. He proved to be a man who was liked by the priests and people and who gave me great support as well as acting with complete discretion.

In addition to the general plans which I have already mentioned, there was one initiative which I had very much in mind. This was to make the Second Vatican Council's aim of renewal a feature of diocesan life in Galloway. I shall be more detailed on the subject later but I remember that, when in the very early days I mentioned renewal to people, there tended to be a rather scared and defensive reaction. "Do you mean charismatic renewal?" To have had plans to introduce, or worse try to impose, that practice would have been widely unacceptable and would probably have put paid to any hope of their new bishop being given the kind and sympathetic welcome which I did receive.

EARLY DAYS

It was my wish not only to be known but also to be as pastorally involved in the diocese as possible and to spend only the necessary amount of time in administration. Being pastorally active, of course, meant being willing to drive all over the diocese, getting to know the priests and their parishes, celebrating Masses, preaching, visiting sick and housebound parishioners, spending days in schools and so on. My ordination on 9th June 1981 came towards the end of the annual confirmation season but Bishop McGee had thoughtfully arranged that I should still have some confirmation Masses to carry out. In fact, there was a confirmation on the evening of 10th June, my first full day as a bishop.

Bishop McGee drove me to the parish involved – it was St John Ogilvie's in the Bourtreehill district of Irvine, a "new town" which never achieved its intended size. He left me there, returning alone to his new residence in Prestwick. The parish is in a part of the town that had been recently built and its church is perhaps, of all the churches in the diocese, the most difficult to locate. It is in the middle of a housing estate where no streets are straight and the district seems deliberately constructed to baffle strangers. The church had been opened very recently and that evening it was packed.

I think I managed fairly well, conscious that all eyes were upon me, but I was rather flustered and nervous, not only as the very new bishop but also as a complete beginner at conferring the sacrament of confirmation. The parish is under the direction of religious priests (Fathers of the Sacred Heart, "Dehonians") and I recall that my discomfiture was increased by the parish priest (Fr Jim Feeney SCJ, who died not long afterwards) telling the people that the parish had areas totally unknown to me. "He has never heard of Girdle Toll or Stanecastle or Springside or Dreghorn". It seemed to me that everyone in the congregation was enjoying the joke, so I tried to look as amused as possible also.

At that time, when I became bishop, I began to appreciate the wide variety in the size of parishes and in their distances from Ayr, as well as the times needed to drive to them. Some parishes had 3,000 or so parishioners, others were very small. The diocese is fairly large geographically, the farthest parish (Langholm in east Dumfries-shire) being about one hour and three quarters' drive from Ayr. There were about 500,000 people in the area of the diocese, about 10% of them Catholic and about half of whom were Sunday Mass attenders.

THE PAPAL VISIT OF 1982

The prospects for pastoral and spiritual renewal in the diocese were greatly enhanced, and fortuitously, by the announcement that Pope John Paul II would visit Britain at the end of May 1982. I had begun my episcopal duties in Galloway the previous summer and the news of the papal visit meant that, along with the other Scottish dioceses, we had almost a year to prepare for the unprecedented experience of having a pope present in our own country.

Preparations were started on two fronts, national and diocesan. The bishops' conference appointed Bishop Thomson of Motherwell to lead the national preparations and especially to be in charge of the arrangements for the various events during the pope's stay in Scotland, above all the Meeting with Youth on Monday evening, 31st May, at Murrayfield Stadium, Edinburgh, and the Mass on the following afternoon at Bellahouston Park,

Glasgow. Those two events were extremely well organised and unforgettable successes.

The national preparations were, of course, much wider than simply making arrangements for the events during the pope's two days in Scotland. While Bishop Thomson and his team were engaged in the enormous amount of work involved in negotiations and preparations for the events of the papal programme, various ideas and materials were offered by national sources for pastoral preparations in the dioceses and parishes. These were taken up and used in Galloway – days of prayer, discussions in the parishes, distributing tickets and booking transport to the events and, not least, several collections to meet the considerable and increasing costs of all the events and of the accommodation for the pope and his entourage and their travel to, within, and from Scotland. All of this engendered a great deal of excitement and anticipation which, in themselves, provided elements of pastoral and spiritual renewal in all of our parishes.

It will not be forgotten that, as anticipation of the pope's visit grew, Argentina invaded the Falkland Islands. At first, the ensuing war between Great Britain and Argentina was not reckoned a threat to the papal visit but, as the war continued and became more violent, anxiety increased that the visit might have to be cancelled or postponed. In particular, Argentina declared that a papal visit to Britain would be seen as favouring one of the combatants. This particular complaint was met by Pope John Paul II heroically agreeing to a visit to Argentina shortly after his visit to Britain. That gesture did help, but there was still a real possibility that, given the conflict situation, the Vatican authorities or the British government might decide that the visit was inopportune and would have to be cancelled. Cardinal Gordon Gray and Cardinal Basil Hume went to Rome to discuss matters with officials of the Holy See and with some representative Argentine bishops. Matters were not settled until Archbishop Winning and Archbishop Derek Worlock (Liverpool) followed the cardinals to Rome and bluntly insisted that the visit must go ahead. Their uncompromising view won the day, the situation was saved, Argentina seemed to acquiesce, especially as the pope was to go there after being in Britain.

The pope's days in this country were an unqualified success, with huge crowds, gloriously sunny weather, and a relaxed atmosphere of friendship and admiration throughout the whole population of Scotland. The only exception to this was the presence of a few protesters as the pope stopped for a short meeting in Edinburgh with the Moderator of the General Assembly of the Church of Scotland. In all, the papal visit was a wonderful experience for hundreds of thousands of Catholics and, indeed, for many other people as well.

As an informal postscript to the celebrations, the Scottish bishops were invited, after the Mass in Glasgow, to dinner with the pope in the cardinal's house in Edinburgh, where the pope was staying for his two nights in Scotland. The Mass in Bellahouston had seriously overrun its scheduled time and, although the Pope and a few others were taken from the park to Edinburgh by helicopter, most of the bishops travelled by coach. The result was that it was late when we finally began the meal. The day had been extremely hot, the Holy Father was tired but very content with the Mass and with the enthusiasm with which he had been welcomed in Scotland. Cardinal Gray and his staff had gone to considerable trouble in preparing the meal and it was an enjoyable and exciting experience for those privileged to be there. Two slightly bizarre incidents occurred during the meal. At the main course, when the pope was about to be served, the cardinal attracted his attention. "Your Holiness, the roast beef is prime Scotch beef which I chose myself and bought from a butcher in Hawick, the best in Scotland". The pope smilingly acknowledged the Cardinal's words but without understanding what he said, because he then helped himself, not to the roast beef but to the alternative – a piece of chicken. Then, at the dessert, the cook's speciality was brought in – baked Alaska. However, due to the delay and the lateness of the meal, the confection was a sorry sight of bits of meringue floating on a sea of white liquid.

These were mishaps of no consequence. The entire visit was a complete success, unforgettable for all of us privileged to take part and the best possible foundation with which to set up a pastoral plan of renewal for the local church. Blessed with the graces flowing from the presence of Pope John Paul II in our midst and the response of the people to him – not merely the euphoria attached to the unprecedented event, but a sincere desire to be active disciples of Our Lord – we looked forward expectantly to building up the local church and opening ourselves to the graces of renewal.

PASTORAL RENEWAL

DIOCESAN QUESTIONNAIRE

I thought that the first step ought to be a consultation with the people of the diocese to seek their opinions as well as their hopes for the future. As a result, we spent some time in constructing a questionnaire to be given to every Catholic aged sixteen and over in the diocese or at least to as many of them as we could reach. A considerable amount of preparation, consultation and experience was used to produce the questionnaire. Copies were printed and distributed through the parishes and, although quite detailed, the questionnaire brought an excellent response. I do not know how many copies were distributed – perhaps about 20,000 – and we received 7,772 completed responses. The process lasted longer than we had anticipated, but we did not want to rush things. Compilation, distribution, collection and counting all duly completed, the results were announced in 1984.

The entire questionnaire, with the introductory explanation which I wrote, as well as the statistics in response to each question, is reproduced in the following four pages.

Some of the questions and their responses seem specially relevant and worthy of comment.

Question 1 – Do you think that your parish has become a community?
Although there was a majority for "yes", the alternatives, "no" and "don't know", had sizable minorities. Perhaps the question seemed a strange one in the early 1980s; if so, many would be unsure what was entailed in their parish being a community.

Questions 2 - 6 – Questions on respondents' Mass attendance and parish involvement
Most of the respondents to the questionnaire were at the "active" end of the spectrum of parishioners, although this tended to be limited to regular attendance at Mass with only a minority more active even than that.

DIOCESE OF GALLOWAY

DIOCESAN PASTORAL PLAN
A QUESTIONNAIRE FOR THE PEOPLE OF THE DIOCESE
1983-84

After the success of the pastoral preparations for the Pope's visit in 1982, there was a widespread desire to go on seeking the graces of a spiritual renewal in the diocese. In particular we recognised the value of pastoral planning to meet the needs of the people and the parishes.

Such a plan, and any guidelines for it, cannot be imposed. They must be the result of consultation throughout the diocese.

This questionnaire is an attempt to further such consultation. We ask you, please, to answer the questions frankly so that we can try to build up a picture of our strengths and weaknesses, our needs and concerns, our hopes and aims.

Thank you for your help.

TOTAL RESPONSES RECORDED: 7772

PLEASE TICK EITHER 'YES' OR 'NO'. OR 'DON'T KNOW' FOR EACH QUESTION

	Yes	No	Don't Know		Blanks
1. Do you think that your parish has become a community?	3443	2344	1779	01	15C
2. Do you normally go to Mass on Sundays?	6289	1388	53	02	42
3. Do you sometimes go to Mass on ordinary weekdays?..........	3703	3903	86	03	80
4. Apart from Mass, are you involved in your parish in any other way?...	1819	5777	98	04	78
5. Are you a member of some group in the parish or diocese? ..... If so, which ones?	1335	6010	207	05	220
6. Would you like to be more active in the parish than you are at present?	2481	3557	1592	06	142

	Blanks	Yes	No	Don't Know	
7. a) Do you find prayer important for your life?	63	6596	726	413	07
b) Do you find Mass important for your life?	58	6240	452	522	08
c) Do you find confession important for your life?	70	4498	2336	979	09

8. Should parishioners be involved in the following areas of parish life?

	Blanks	Yes	No	Don't Know	
a) reading at Mass	108	6270	809	585	10
b) giving Holy Communion at Mass when asked by the priest	91	3225	3546	910	11
c) taking Holy Communion to the sick and housebound	96	3174	3523	979	12
d) leading discussion groups	129	5373	1092	1178	13
e) helping to look after parish finances	146	4699	1919	1018	14
f) sharing responsibility for maintenance of parish buildings	115	5750	473	934	15
g) organising youth activities	129	6730	377	536	16
h) visiting the sick and housebound	114	6586	560	532	17
i) helping to prepare engaged couples for marriage	133	3055	3175	1409	18
j) visiting non-attenders to help them keep in touch	121	3030	3025	1596	19
k) working with other Christian churches	144	6238	575	815	20
l) any other activity not mentioned (please specify below)	2919	450	894	3509	21

9. Would you like to know more about any of the following matters?

	Blanks	Yes	No	Don't Know	
a) methods of prayer	291	3936	2565	980	22
b) understanding the bible	240	4818	1898	816	23
c) what Catholics should believe nowadays	211	5629	1328	604	24
d) the Church's attitude to world poverty	212	5869	1049	642	25
e) the Church's attitude to unemployment	195	5644	1216	717	26
f) the Church's teaching on war and nuclear weapons	208	5624	1479	664	27
g) the Church's teaching on marriage and sex	224	4833	1920	795	28
h) moral issues of today	281	5408	1269	824	29
i) any other subject not already mentioned (please specify)	3017	340	1010	3405	30

Please circle here the three you consider most important: 31

a	b	c	d	e	f	g	h	i
1755	1886	3607	2575	1848	2718	1909	2780	148

	Blanks	Yes	No	Don't Know	
10. Do you think that separate Catholic schools should remain?	402	4246	2186	938	32

11. In your parish are you satisfied with the following aspects?

	Blanks	Yes	No	Don't Know	
a) the friendliness of the parishioners	141	5357	1527	747	33
b) the social events that are organised	140	3978	2467	1507	34
c) the atmosphere in the church during Mass	161	5119	1681	811	35
d) the care shown to those in need	165	4175	1284	2168	36
e) good relations with non-Catholics	110	5632	822	1208	37
f) the fact that the parish seems alive	198	3658	2061	1855	38
g) the support offered to married couples	204	2366	1474	3728	39
h) the opportunities given to young parishioners	247	2253	2553	2719	40
i) any other matter not yet mentioned (please specify below)	3058	230	905	3579	41

12. Do you think that enough is done in your parish for the following groups?

	Blanks	Yes	No	Don't Know	
a) pre-school children	317	1533	2914	3008	42
b) children 5 - 10	286	2253	2329	2904	43
c) children 10 - 14	308	2181	2372	2911	44
d) youth 15 - 18	315	1611	3106	2740	45
e) young adults 19 - 30	322	1302	3045	3103	46
f) adults 31 - 45	370	2289	1885	3228	47
g) adults 46 - 60	374	2424	1684	3290	48
h) those over 60	326	2988	1663	2745	49
i) single people	372	1387	2437	3576	50
j) the sick and the housebound	275	3284	1622	2591	51
k) lapsed Catholics	263	1005	2729	3775	52
l) the divorced and separated	304	822	2393	4253	53
m) the handicapped	296	1897	1940	3639	54
n) single-parent families	314	1138	1961	4359	55
o) the unemployed	303	848	2645	3926	56
p) alcoholics and drug addicts	402	754	2362	4254	57
q) another group not already mentioned (please specify below)	3083	124	788	3777	58

Please circle here the **three** groups which you think most in need of support: 59

a	b	c	d	e	f	g	h	i	j	k	l	m	n	o	p	q
541	437	672	1965	979	140	140	776	456	2536	1739	844	1968	1139	1829	2014	69

13. Do any of the following problems cause you worry?

	Blanks	Yes	No	Don't Know	
a) the threat of nuclear war	169	5649	1639	315	60
b) increasing godlessness	235	4953	1579	1007	61
c) abortion	172	5623	1296	681	62
d) Third World poverty	184	6231	730	627	63
e) the present state of the Catholic Church	233	3408	2825	1306	64
f) the shortage of vocations	242	4465	1645	1420	65
g) your children and their attitudes	453	3287	2629	1403	66
h) falling moral standards	238	5311	1212	1011	67
i) your eternal salvation	279	4332	2154	1007	68
j) unemployment in your family	335	3457	3369	614	69
k) ill health in your family	333	3480	2920	539	70
l) another problem not yet mentioned (please specify below)	3258	306	902	3306	71

Please circle here the **three** most important:

a	b	c	d	e	f	g	h	i	j	k	l	
3216	1720	2507	2433	1021	1227	1129	2094	989	1069	1394	127	72

This questionnaire will be given to everyone in the parish over 14.
Please complete it and return it within a week.

YOUR NAME AND ADDRESS ARE NOT REQUIRED —
BUT PLEASE TICK WHAT APPLIES TO YOU BELOW:–

male	3248	73
female	3712	74

age 14 – 18	1479	75
19 – 30	1047	76
31 – 45	1726	77
46 – 60	1524	78
60 +	1460	79

full-time employed	2397	80
part-time employed	630	81
unemployed	536	82
retired	1002	83
housewife	1502	84
student	770	85

IF YOU WISH TO COMMENT ON ANY OF THE QUESTIONS IN THE QUESTIONNAIRE, PLEASE DO SO HERE OR ON A SEPARATE PAPER.

Question 8 – Should parishioners be involved in the following areas of parish life?
Most of the areas suggested received wide approval, although at that time (1983 - 1984) Extraordinary Ministers of Holy Communion and lay involvement with marriage preparation and with non-attenders attracted only minority approval.

Question 9 – Would you like to know more about any of the following matters?
Of the eight topics listed, the responses showed strong majority interest in knowing more about Church teaching, doctrine (including Scripture) and morals, as well as Church teaching on poverty, war and nuclear weapons; but the largest majority was on "What Catholics should believe nowadays".

Question 10 – Do you think that separate Catholic schools should remain?
Although a substantial majority favoured separate Catholic schools, I recall being surprised and disappointed that more than 25% did not. Especially in the south of the diocese, there are a number of parishes without reasonably easy access to Catholic (particularly secondary) schools. Were people in such parishes less supportive of Catholic schools?

Question 11 – In your parish are you satisfied with the following aspects?
In the question, the word "satisfied" was used to gauge people's thoughts. Consequently, the results were fairly favourable, especially the friendliness of parishioners, the atmosphere during Mass, attitude to those in need, relations with non-Catholics and support for married couples. Slightly less favourable opinions were expressed on organised social events and a sense of the parish being alive. The only aspect of parish life that attracted more "no" votes than "yes" (2,553 against 2,251) was on the opportunities offered to young parishioners. This negative vote is not unexpected because, whenever parishioners are asked about needs not being met in their parish, better care of the youth and more facilities for them are nearly always required.

Question 12 – Do you think enough is done in your parish for the following groups?
This question probably covers much the same ground as the previous question, but from the point of view of the various possible ways of providing help (rather than from the different ages of parishioners and also people's personal circumstances). The

resposes indicate that those in need of help were reckoned to be those between fifteen and eighteen, the sick and housebound, alcoholics and drug addicts.

Question 13 – Do any of the following problems cause you worry? This final question was more personal than parochial. The choice of concerns listed seemed to cover most people's worries; the invitation to add further "worries" elicited only 306 responses out of more than 7,000 respondents. The matters that caused greatest concern were the threat of nuclear war, shortage of vocations to the priesthood, falling moral standards, the practice of abortion and Third World poverty. All eleven "worries" listed received more "yes" votes than "no", with "unemployment in your family" emerging as least of the worries. Would the same concerns reappear and in the same order, if the questions were posed today, thirty years later? It is perhaps noteworthy that, even in the early 1980s, concern about a shortage of priests was widespread. That foreseen shortage is now a reality and the concern remains and is even greater because the present scarcity seems certain to become even more serious.

Few respondents gave their names and addresses, but we did ask for gender, age and occupation.

We welcomed the response to the questionnaire which we received, not only because we considered the number of respondents gratifyingly high but also because we had given the parishioners an opportunity to express their opinions and their wishes. All the responses were carefully counted and the results made known to the whole diocese and not only to those responsible for leadership in the parishes.

I considered the results highly informative and interesting, though not really surprising and not at all shocking. They demonstrated the seriousness of so many people in the diocese. The evidence provided by the questionnaire helped to point the way ahead, especially in regard to what could be done by way of pastoral and spiritual renewal.

Perhaps I may make the interjection here that a phrase like "spiritual and pastoral renewal" can be used so frequently that its precise meaning becomes lost in the very familiarity of the phrase which, as a result, becomes a mere cliché. So let me try to be explicit. "Renewal" in the context means an openness to change, based on gifts such as wisdom and discernment being brought to bear on God's will for us, known through Scripture, Church tradition and teaching, and therefore especially through the documents of the Second Vatican Council. The adjectives "pastoral" and "spiritual" are not mutually exclusive; perhaps the former emphasises more the communal dimension and the aspect of good works; while the latter's primary emphasis is internal, on our growth in faith and personal holiness.

The questionnaire told us quite a number of things about the diocese. It assured us that there was a great amount of good will and openness among the people, that those who were practising Catholics (regular Massgoers) were of moderate views, traditional in the best sense of the word, and that there were many people, baptised and brought up as Catholics no longer actively involved in the practice of the faith… These impressions were confirmed by meetings, both formal and informal, with the priests, by my visits to parishes (not only for the sacrament of confirmation but on other occasions such as weekend "pastoral visits" which I made throughout the whole year) and by my custom of an annual visit to each Catholic primary school in the diocese with time spent in every classroom as well as in the staffrooms.

Following the papal visit of 1982, there was a widespread feeling that we should build on that memorable experience. To prepare for the visit we had had national initiatives but there was little in the way of any national follow-up to invest in the experience. It was clear that, if we wanted to have something serious and constructive, we should have to make decisions in and for our diocese.

Although what we ought to do was evident, how to do it was not. Planning spiritual and pastoral renewal for the diocese was presenting a frightening challenge to us but then, providentially and apparently fortuitously, a way forward presented itself.

RENEW

I was in the United States to visit Sister Mary George O'Reilly, a religious of the Society of the Holy Child Jesus. She was a distant relation (second cousin by marriage is possibly the correct description) and, over the years, we had become close friends. At the time, she was employed by the Archdiocese of Newark, New Jersey, in its education services. Talking about the archdiocese one day, she mentioned that they had a pastoral renewal process which they called "Renew". I was immediately interested and so I was taken to Renew's headquarters in Newark and there learned some details of the process.

The need for diocese and parishes to have a planned process for renewal (and not simply urging bishops, priests and parishioners to "do" pastoral renewal) had impelled two priests of the archdiocese, Msgr Tom Ivory and Msgr Tom Kleissler, to plan the details of the process and to provide the necessary materials and specific guidance for its successful delivery in parishes. Msgr Ivory had gone on to other areas of pastoral planning in Newark but Msgr Kleissler had stayed with Renew and had become its executive director. The process had been successful in the parishes of Newark and was already being used in many other dioceses of the United States and Canada.

I was much impressed – and very hopeful that I had found an answer to the problem of how to carry out a programme of renewal in the diocese. The upshot of my discovery of Renew was that I invited Msgr Kleissler and his assistant director, Sister Donna Ciangio OP, to come to Galloway diocese, present an explanation of the process to the priests and parish leaders and then ask them to consider with their parish communities whether they were in favour of taking on Renew for our diocese. The response was overwhelmingly positive and favourable; not unanimous (there were some who said that the process sounded "too American") but a clear majority wanted to go ahead. At the very least, it was a ready made tool, not only saving us a lot of time and trouble but perhaps saving us the embarrassment of attempting something that would have been too much for us and our inexperienced resources. One lady told the gathering that she was "chuffed to bits" at the prospect, an expression that had to be explained to the mystified Americans. In the event, forty-two parishes decided to undertake Renew and five parish priests told me that their parishes had decided against it.

The Renew process was nothing if not thorough. We had to select two people to go to Newark for an international summer school and be trained to lead Renew in our diocese. I chose Fr Archie Brown and Mr Jim McMillan for this task. By sheer coincidence, the latter had been born in Newark and, as an infant, had come to Scotland with his returning parents. The course on which they embarked was of two months' duration in the summer of 1985 and was very intensive. The participants came from various nations and dioceses, especially from Australia, India and England as well as from Galloway and Glasgow. Without any collusion between us, Cardinal Winning had heard about Renew, investigated, and decided to have it in Glasgow. This gave us in Galloway the advantage of having a partner-diocese in Scotland and we worked closely together, especially in producing Scottish versions of the materials (booklets and other resources) used in various activities of the Renew process.

When our two leaders returned to Scotland, we began a full year of preparation for Renew in the diocese and in each parish which had chosen to do the process. Each of the parishes had to choose a lay person to be its Renew coordinator and others to conduct the various aspects of the process in the parish community. There was training provided for the parish coordinators and their assistants, each parish had to be helped to organise the various Renew activities, to encourage as many parishioners as possible to be involved in these activities and to be reassured of what would be asked of them. Extensive materials had to be written, printed, distributed to parishes and participants. The various activities required people to be recruited and trained for their requisite tasks.

The two diocesan coordinators and I were kept very busy, travelling around the diocese to explain the process and encourage participation. We had overnight retreats for those who, in each parish, were to have leading parts in Renew, including the parish priests. It was a hectic time, but also a good time because there was great enthusiasm, many people felt a growing sense of anticipation and of responsible involvement, Thus, for them, the grace of renewal was already very active, whether they recognised it or not. Every now and again during that year of preparation, we had visits from Msgr Kleissler and Sr Donna Ciangio, as well as continuing our collaboration with the archdiocese of Glasgow. I remember that time with great memories of hard work yet increasingly assured prospects for the success of the initiative.

Every diocesan bishop has to send a very comprehensive report about the diocese to the Holy See every five years. My first quinquennial report covered the period from 1982 to the end of 1986. In it, I made these comments on Renew:

"The process is totally parish-based in order to avoid any tendency to elitism or the establishment of separate parallel communities. By means of the Sunday liturgy, small faith-sharing groups, large group activities, and material for use in the home, Renew *leads participants through five seasons (two seasons each year) of spiritual renewal.*

"The first season of Renew *began in the diocese in the autumn of 1986 and, at the time of writing this report, we can thank God for many wonderful graces of conversion, renewal and commitment. The process is based on prayer and organisation and so we can also record the great increase in praying and prayerfulness as well as the large number of laity who, though not previously very active in their parishes, have now assumed various ministries in accordance with their gifts and without any difficulty in accepting the proper authority of the parish priest and the bishop."*

My subsequent quinquennial reports were equally positive. For example, in the report for 1992 to 1996, I wrote:

"The Renew *process was completed at the end of 1988...* Renew *is a pastoral plan that seeks to bring about spiritual renewal in the parish and in the individual...*

"It is my opinion that Renew *transformed the diocese in several ways; viz., thousands of people "discovered" the Scriptures and different forms of prayer; there began a much greater involvement of laity in parish ministries and in small group leadership; the experience of faith-sharing was new but has become accepted in the diocese and treasured by many; in addition (although this is not an easy matter to prove by statistics), I believe that many people were enabled to develop a much deeper and more personal relationship with God."*

In such reports to one's superior authority, the tendency is to speak in glowing terms and to avoid mention of negativities. That tendency is evident in the quotations above. Nevertheless, Renew was a success in the diocese. Nowadays, when I think about Renew or am asked questions such as "What benefits did it bring to the diocese?", I recall that it changed the attitudes of many people, both with regard to their own spiritual life and growth and also in their active involvement in the life of the parish community; it made us more familiar with the Scriptures and with informal and formal prayer; it gave us a familiarity with faith-sharing and discussion; and it provided an impetus for parish and diocesan liturgy to be taken more seriously and more knowledgeably.

There were disappointments too. About half a dozen parishes (or their parish priests) decided not to participate; in the parishes which took part, there were parishioners who avoided any voluntary participation, especially the small groups; and our attempts at "large group activities" such as parish picnics and barbecues as well as gatherings for specifically religious purposes were not as successful as hoped. Perhaps the Scottish climate must share some of the blame... Overall, however, the process was, I believe, highly successful as we advanced through the five seasons from autumn 1986 until autumn 1988. Each of the seasons had its own theme, all of them following a logical sequence of personal and parish renewal: God's Call; Our Response; Empowerment by the Spirit; Discipleship; Evangelisation. It is because of Renew's profound and lasting impact on the diocese that I have dwelt so thoroughly on describing it.

As we neared the end of Renew, there was widespread regret among many parishioners. Liturgy standards remained very high and in some parishes, small faith-sharing groups continued to be organised for autumn and Lent, with booklets providing material for the meetings being written and published in the diocese. I asked the priests if they would like the diocese to continue to provide plans for an "After Renew" process. The clear majority was against continuing diocesan direction and with a preference for each parish to be responsible for planning and organising its own efforts. I accepted this decision as I was anxious not to seem to be ambitious to micro–manage. The principle of subsidiarity is a good one but, in retrospect, I feel that the decision may have been unwise. It is my impression that few parishes achieved much in specific and formal ongoing spiritual and pastoral renewal. Perhaps, however, the process was still going on in ways less visible and organised. Perhaps, too, the time will come when a diocesan plan of renewal will again be judged opportune. I certainly hope so!

ALARMING STATISTICS

The very favourable opinion that I express with regard to the effectiveness of Renew is true of those who remained firmly committed to religious practice, people who probably were already convinced Catholics. The quality of their practice was, I think, notably enhanced. However, it has to be admitted that, despite the papal visit of 1982 and the Renew process, the success of our efforts cannot be measured in terms of numbers.

Here are some sobering statistics.

	1982	1992	2002	2012
Estimated Catholic population	51,400	48,400	47,700	45,000
Sunday Mass attendance	22,267	16,860	12,962	10,214
Baptisms	909	761	568	514
Marriages	413	251	181	128
Parishes	46	47	47	43
Diocesan priests (including retired)	59	60	53	41
Religious priests	22	10	3	4
Religious brothers	23	10	6	2
Religious sisters	73	60	35	22
Retired priests	N/A	7	10	11
Seminarians	11	13	2	1

Although some decrease in numbers is to be expected, some of the statistics are depressing and distressing. Let me make some comments on the various figures.

The "Estimated Catholic population" is partly guesswork. Who or what is a Catholic? How "lapsed" should you be in order to cease being a Catholic? Each parish in *The Catholic Directory for Scotland* gives a figure for the number of Catholics it has, but these figures often remain unchanged for years, while different parishes have different criteria of "Catholicity". The customary belief was that Catholics comprised about 10% of the population of the area of the diocese, higher in Ayrshire (especially in North Ayrshire) and lower in Dumfries & Galloway.

The "Sunday Mass attendance" is based on an annual count in every parish on a weekend in early November. As a result, the totals are fairly accurate. The drop in numbers over the period is very great indeed. There are many reasons for this – growing secularism, loss of faith or of the sense of sin, other attractions on Sundays, boredom at Mass. (So is Mass boring?) Whatever the reason in each case, the fact is tragic since participation in the celebration of the Eucharist is not only an obligation but should be the necessary centre of our lives as baptised Catholics who want to love God.

The decrease in the number of baptisms indicates that less importance is given to the sacrament by some Catholic parents but the figures for marriage in church are even more startling. Nowadays the great majority of couples are either of mixed religion (Catholic and Protestant) or of what is rather quaintly called "disparity of worship" (Catholic and unbaptised). In addition, the figures show fewer Catholics marrying in their parishes, choosing instead either a Protestant church or, more often, a registry office or, by far most often, not formally marrying. This last option used to be called "living in sin" but nowadays is more politely included in the expression "partners" (rather than "husband and wife").

The steep fall in Mass attendance, baptisms and marriages is alarming. The first statistic is now less than half of what it was thirty years ago; the second is a little more than half; and the last is only between a third and a quarter. Is the precipitous trend stoppable?

Perhaps it is worth noting that, in the diocesan questionnaire of 1984 (which, of course, was open only to over-sixteens), of the 7,772 responses, 6,289 said they were regularly at Sunday Mass and 1,388 said they were not. Since the attenders figuring in the annual count in the early 1980s were three times the number of questionnaire respondents but less than half the estimated Catholics in the diocese, it may be that the only valid conclusion to be drawn is that more attenders than non-attenders responded to the questionnaire.

The decreases in the number of diocesan priests and of seminarians are directly related, of course. Like all other mortals, priests retire from active work and die. The drastic dearth of seminarians is very troubling. Why is the priesthood attracting hardly anyone? At the present time, most applicants/candidates are older than was the custom some years ago; an applicant straight from secondary school is the exception. Perhaps the trend to older men is wise but few of them are available, especially because of the celibacy rule. Young men in their late teens are fewer than years ago. In addition, so many of them these days seem to have abandoned the practice of faith and religion some years before they finish school, that it is not surprising that so few are attracted to the priesthood. Further reflection on the decreasing number of priests is to be found below, in the section "The Priests".

The recent introduction in the diocese of permanent deacons gives some help but, since they neither celebrate Mass nor celebrate the sacraments of reconciliation and anointing of the sick, their help is limited and in crucial areas non-existent.

The figures for members of religious congregations (priests, brothers and sisters) are perhaps most drastically fallen of all. Much of the decrease is due to the closure of a number of convents and religious houses that were previously in the diocese. Religious also grow older and recruitment, especially of those wishing to be religious brothers or sisters, is minimal. We miss the presence, work and witness of the numbers we used to have in the diocese and of the religious centres which were much used by the people of the diocese. Nowadays, many of the religious who remain reside fairly quietly in ones and twos and in much smaller accommodation. In 1982 two parishes were staffed by religious (Norbertines and Dehonian Sacred Heart Fathers). Now, only the latter are still in the diocese. Since the turn of the century, two priests, a Passionist and a Mill Hill Missionary have come to the diocese; one is parish priest in Newton Stewart and the other was parish priest in Annan until 2013 when he retired (though still resident there). These arrangements are personal ones for them.

So in terms of numbers, the picture in the diocese of Galloway is a gloomy one. Years ago I remember the prognosis of the great German theologian, Karl Rahner SJ. He foresaw that the Church would be much reduced in numbers, at least in Europe, but that the people who remained would be more committed, with a deeper faith and more fervent practice, than before. Certainly the first part of that prophecy has been fulfilled.

THE PRIESTS

In a Catholic diocese, priests are very special people and their work is vital and essential. The priests are the closest collaborators of the bishop. Their relationship with him is that of both sons and brothers; and, with the bishop, they serve the people as their pastors, their shepherds, proclaiming the gospel to them, providing them with Mass and the sacraments, leading them in lives of faith, hope and charity by their presence, their teaching, their constant care and the example of their lives.

That may not be a definition of the ordained priest nor may it give a complete picture of his vocation and role, but I hope that it is some use in describing the life and work of a diocesan priest in our day.

When I came to the diocese of Galloway in June 1981, I wanted, during my years as bishop, not only to exercise good leadership and gentle authority for the priests but to serve them as wisely and well as I could and to be as close to them in friendship as was possible. I am not sure how well I have fulfilled that last desire or intention of my ministry towards the priests; others will judge but, to the extent that I fell short, I ask their pardon.

Prior to becoming bishop, I already knew many of the priests – Scotland is a relatively small place and, although our work is confined to one diocese, we do know and meet priests of other dioceses from time to time. Moreover, since I had spent many years in seminaries, quite a number of the Galloway priests had been with me while I was a seminarian in Rome, a lecturer in St Peter's College, Cardross, or the rector of the Scots College in Spain. And since the total number of priests in the diocese when I became bishop was around sixty, it was easy, within a few weeks of my arrival, to get to know those previously unknown to me.

In a few cases, establishing friendship was not as easy as I had hoped. Some priests perhaps found it a little strange to meet me as friend and to be relaxed socially with me. I think also that one or two suspected that I wanted to use the "friendly" approach as cover for a desire to check or snoop on them. That attitude was very exceptional and, generally speaking, I hope that the priests did not resent my efforts or misunderstand my motives. However, sometimes I did wonder whether I was trying to be too close for comfort to some of them. I am sorry also for the opportunities I probably missed of showing care, compassion, respect and understanding for such good men, the priests of the diocese.

On the whole, I found the priests supportive, helpful, cooperative, friendly and kind. It is from that standpoint that I now speak of their place in the diocese of which I am attempting to draw a portrait.

During the years since I became bishop (that is, from 1981), the number of priests in the diocese has decreased noticeably and, given the lack of applicants in recent years, the decrease is alarming. There has been a dearth of vocations to the priesthood or, perhaps more accurately, a reluctance to respond to God's call. Even so, when I think of my experiences in Central America and in some countries of South America where many people have Mass only occasionally, the situation here may be considered still reasonable. Nevertheless, it worries me that, while some countries in Europe and some areas of Britain now seem to be enjoying an increase in applicants, they are still few and far between in Galloway.

The statistics are worth noting. In 1981 there were 56 priests active in the parishes of the diocese; they included six who belonged to religious congregations and eighteen who, though priests of Galloway diocese, had come from Ireland to work in Scotland. There were a further seven priests of this diocese, some of whom were retired and others working in seminaries or as chaplains in the forces. Now, in 2012, there are 27 priests active, a number which includes only one Irishman and four religious. There are also eleven priests retired, as well as two who are forces' chaplains and one who works outside the diocese.

A significant figure in those statistics is the drop in Irish priests working in Galloway, from eighteen in 1981 to one in 2012; likewise, from six religious priests thirty years ago we have now only four. The decrease in Irish and religious priests from twenty-four in 1981 to five in 2012 provides a partial but important explanation of the overall fall in numbers over the period.

The Scottish priests of the diocese were educated at various seminaries – the Pontifical Scots College and the Beda College in Rome, the Royal Scots College in Spain (at Valladolid until 1988 and now at Salamanca), St Sulpice in France, St Andrew's College at Drygrange near Melrose and at Scotus College in Bearsden. Over recent years the seminaries in Scotland have closed and, at present, no students from Scotland are sent to Salamanca or Paris. They all go to Rome and the Scots College there. It is worth remarking, however, that a considerable number of the Galloway priests are products of the Scots College in Spain. That predilection for Spain is probably and at least partly due to the association that two recent bishops of the diocese had with the college there, Bishop Joseph McGee having been a student for seven years (1922 - 1929) and I the rector for nine years (1965 - 1974).

The Irish priests in the diocese were educated in various seminaries in their home country – All Hallows in Dublin and the colleges in Kilkenny, Carlow, Thurles, Waterford and Wexford, none of which is still functioning as a seminary.

At the beginning of the period under review, most students had gone to the seminary directly after completing their secondary education, either at Blairs College or at a local school, and "late vocations" were the exception. Nowadays, however, candidates (very reduced in numbers) have usually completed their tertiary education and/or have been working for some years before going to a seminary, while someone "straight from school" is a rarity.

In the 1980s Galloway seminarians, when ordained, spent some years as assistant priests under the guidance and authority of a parish priest, thus benefitting from the experience of an older man. However, as numbers have gone down, a newly ordained priest will spend only a few months or, at most, a year as an assistant priest and then will find himself installed as a parish priest. Since the newly ordained are now usually older, they are probably more capable of taking early responsibility as parish priests than someone who has had no experience of having lived independently and having worked for a living.

One sometimes hears the complaint that, these days, priests no longer visit the parishioners unless they are housebound through illness or disability. I have heard people say that, in their young days, "Father So-and-so was never out of our house", which must be something of an exaggeration since, in that case, every other family in the parish would feel rather neglected. But the point is a valid one and deserves a response.

Apart from the fact of there being fewer priests, there are now evening Masses, meetings in the parish and elsewhere, and a considerable number of other duties since nearly all priests are parish priests and, as such, have administrative tasks that assistant priests (curates) do not have. It may be that priests today could manage some "old fashioned parish visitation", but there are also difficulties from the point of view of the families to be visited. People are much more mobile these days, less likely to be at home and, if they are at home, many do not particularly want to be interrupted from the television or the computer. Even in the 1970s, when I was a parish priest and tried to visit, I was conscious of interrupting people's TV enjoyment. Some people switched off the TV when I visited but others simply lowered the sound and couldn't resist glancing at the screen, which made me feel awkward and not particularly welcome. Some priests would ask the family to switch off the television, but I never had the courage to do that. So there, if you like, is another reason why many priests no longer visit families in a systematic way as they used to do.

Nowadays, "ongoing formation" is on the agenda for all priests. It is something that wisdom urges, especially as we live in times that are so subject to change. Moreover, we owe it to those whom we serve. Ongoing formation is prescribed by the Second Vatican Council and also by Blessed Pope John Paul II and his successors. It comprises spiritual, intellectual, social and physical efforts to keep ourselves active, up to date and "fit for purpose". Clearly, it requires a certain determination and asceticism to be faithful and persevering in our efforts.

The diocese provides some help and encouragement for our ongoing formation with retreats and days of recollection. There have been attempts to update us on contemporary scholarship in regard to Scripture and Church teaching on faith and morals and so on. However, I must confess that, perhaps through lack of opportunities and perhaps, even more, due to lack of enthusiasm and dedication, our organised efforts have probably been no more than half-hearted and not always well supported. We have occasional social events, such as Mass followed by lunch, for various celebrations, especially, for example, priests' jubilees. And one deanery holds a very enjoyable monthly Sunday night supper for its priests. The former custom of groups of priests gathering on Sunday night to play cards no longer takes place and even the annual golf tournament for the priests of the diocese to contest the Bishop's Cup is a thing of the past.

However, one very important and interesting initiative was undertaken when, after consulting the priests, I invited Fr Vincent Dwyer OCSO, an American Cistercian, to introduce his "Ministry to Priests" scheme to the diocese. Although a member of a contemplative religious order, Fr Dwyer was aware of the loneliness of many diocesan priests and the scarcity of opportunities for growth in spirituality in their lives in parishes. He therefore designed and constructed his "Ministry to Priests" initiative. It consists in two main areas of activity: (a) one-to-one meetings and (b) small groups. The first invites a priest to choose a brother-priest whom he trusts, not to be his confessor or spiritual director but rather to be a friend or confidant with whom he can discuss any topics of personal concern to him, whether about his spiritual life or his work or relationships. The other priest's role is not to solve his friend's problems but to provide a sympathetic ear and, if asked, to offer some thoughts that may be helpful for his friend's personal growth or reassurance. The second activity of the Ministry to Priests scheme is for a number of priests, say between five and ten, to meet together regularly, perhaps monthly, for an overnight and at a place away from their own homes. At these meetings they will pray together, eat together, have some social time and probably celebrate Mass together; specifically, each group will also choose some type of activity that will be a feature of every meeting – for example, a paper by one of the group followed by general discussion of some topic of Scripture or liturgy or theology; another group might choose a topic of current affairs or history or literature; other groups' specific activities might be sport or music or a visit to a place of interest.

Before embarking on the Ministry to Priests activities, those of us who wished to participate in the scheme had a few preliminary meetings at which one or two people from the Ministry to Priests headquarters in the United States explained the programme to us, told us how to be involved and asked us to elect, from among those participating, a priest who would be diocesan director and a few others to help him with the work. The overwhelming choice for co-ordinator was Canon Nicholas Murphy, parish priest of St Mary's, Saltcoats.

In addition, we were invited to complete written psychological tests; our papers were sent to the United States for assessment and then, some time later, returned to us individually with a confidential report on our psychological strengths and weaknesses, our needs, attitudes and personal traits. I think that some of the priests found this part of the preparatory sessions "too American" and somewhat threatening. I remember, with some embarrassment, that my answers showed that I lived too much in the future and should be more concentrated on the present; in my own defence, I did a lot of thinking, during those early years of my time as bishop, about the needs of the priests and lay people of the diocese and so gave the impression of being too concerned with what might be, rather than what was the then present reality in my life. Well, you can't just sit around, waiting for things to happen!

With the preliminaries completed, the priests embarked on the programme proper. The first activity, the "one-to-one", was taken up by a number of the priests, but a minority. On the other hand, nearly all joined a small group of one kind or another. The groups continued for a number of years and were very enjoyable, not only for relaxation but for beneficial reasons too. However, numbers gradually dwindled as the numbers of priests decreased, small groups got smaller and eventually the Ministry to Priests activities in the diocese have more or less ceased. I do not know the story of the programme in the other three or four Scottish dioceses which adopted the scheme, but such things do not last for ever and I am satisfied with what the programme achieved in Galloway. Nonetheless, ongoing formation is still required and should be taken seriously by each priest and by the presbyterate as a whole.

At what may be termed the business level, the priests have a variety of meetings. The number of deaneries has been reduced from seven in 1982 to four in 2012. The four are St Margaret's deanery (South Ayrshire), St Joseph's deanery (East Ayrshire), St Mary's deanery (North Ayrshire) and St Andrew's deanery (Dumfries & Galloway). There are statutory meetings of all the priests in a deanery and additional meetings if and when necessary. Each deanery elects representatives to be members of the diocesan Council of Priests which the bishop attends and to which he nominates several additional members, usually those holding certain diocesan offices. The bishop can also call meetings of every active priest in the diocese, as needs require.

There are also meetings of the members of the chapter of canons. There are seven canons, the most senior (that is, longest ordained) of the priests of the diocese, provided they accept the bishop's invitation and nomination. The canons used to be a bishop's close advisers and he can still consult them as he wishes; but since the new Code of Canon Law was promulgated in 1983, a new office of Consultor was introduced. The College of Consultors, a group of up to twelve priests of the diocese, chosen by the bishop, are now his statutory advisers; moreover, when a diocese becomes vacant, it is the Consultors who meet to choose an Administrator who has (limited) authority in the diocese until a new bishop takes charge.

On the whole, I have a very high opinion of the priests of Galloway diocese. They are good men and with a genuine desire to serve the people of the parishes. They work conscientiously to "build the Kingdom" in this local Church. Each priest, of course, has his own unique character and personality, as well as his own strengths and weaknesses. There is genuine friendship among them and great kindness towards the bishop, whom, because the diocese is small and the clergy not numerous, they get to know very well.

Things were not always perfect, of course, because priests (and bishops) are human. Perhaps the area that was most difficult to manage well was that of asking priests to accept changes and to move from parish to parish. I tried to do what was best, not only for the parishes concerned but also for the priests. However, such occasions naturally caused upset to those priests who were involved and, in addition to the inconvenience, I know that they sometimes caused dismay, disappointment and even anger. Canon Law decrees that priests have a certain stability and should be asked to move only for serious pastoral reasons. Applying this law is not easy. What are "serious pastoral reasons"? Is it better for a priest to remain more or less permanently in the same parish or should he transfer after a reasonable time in a parish? And, if so, how long is "reasonable"? Leaving one parish and starting afresh with a different parish community is very hard, especially if the priest is no longer young.

During my first year in the diocese, I asked some priests to change their parishes. They agreed, but some did so reluctantly and some of the moves were criticised. So from that time I had the advice of an appointments committee of the vicar general and three priests chosen by the Council of Priests. This proved very helpful to me and I believe that the priests appreciated it as well. Despite this, a situation arose that caused great distress in the diocese and much unwelcome publicity, especially through press reports.

This very serious situation arose following an assembly of priests of Galloway which we held in 1990. One of its recommendations (not unanimously approved) was that priests should not remain "for ever", especially in those parishes which were considered among the "best" in the diocese. When I put this recommendation into effect and asked some priests to transfer to other parishes, they declined. Without going into details, suffice to say that the dispute was finally decided by the Church's highest court, the *Signatura Apostolica* in Rome. That court found in the priests' favour, advising me that I had made errors in procedure and that, if I wished to proceed, I should correct such procedural errors. However, since the whole business had already caused bitterness and had been widely reported, I had no stomach for prolonging the dispute.

It was a sad experience for all of us who were concerned and there will always be disagreement about the wisdom, or lack of it, of my actions... But since 1990 or thereabouts, I confess that I have asked priests to change only when it was necessary and not in cases where I thought such changes would be merely beneficial. As I said, priests' changes are never easy. For me, they were a source of real distress.

Still on the subject of priests being asked to transfer from one parish to another, should not the lay members of the parishes affected be consulted? Ideally, of course, they should. Not only with questions such as "Are you happy that the priest at present in your parish should remain with you?" but also "What qualities should your new parish priest possess?" But the ideal is not feasible, particularly in a relatively small diocese suffering from a chronic dearth of priests.

An attempt to respond to parishioners' satisfaction or dissatisfaction with their parish priest by transferring in the latter case and excluding transfer in the former is impractical. How to measure satisfaction or dissatisfaction? Even if the latter is clear, is another parish to be compelled to have him? The bishop's better response if there are serious or widespread complaints from parishioners about their priest is to take the matter up with him and proceed from there, not simply to transfer him to another parish.

Regarding the proposal that parishioners should be consulted about the kind of priest they would like to have, their response would be very predictable: "someone who is friendly, hard-working, dependable...". Yet the choice facing the bishop is very limited, in fact usually restricted to one priest. I think that most parishioners realised the impracticality of prior consultation and that was the reason why I received very few requests for it.

Besides, to have held consultation in the prevailing circumstances would have suggested that such consultation was no more than a meaningless pretence.

A rather more general subject, but nevertheless related, is that of bishops' and priests' accountability. All such men are, of course, accountable to God and we shall have to give an account of our stewardships when we die. In theory, also, bishops are accountable to the pope and diocesan priests to their bishop. But in practice, a situation has to be very serious before that accountability is effective. Moreover, the relationship between bishop and priest is not that of employer and employee and so does not encourage such a confrontational attitude, apart from the dire shortage of priests being exacerbated if the bishop decides on drastic action.

So can an unsatisfactory bishop or priest rest unperturbed and undisturbed? Are there no ways to assess, judge and correct such cases? Probably not, unless in extreme cases. The superior can urge, encourage, even threaten but, in contrast to inadequate performance in other professions, bishops and priests do enjoy a freedom from rigorous assessment of their work. Sanctions are possible up to ordination but, thereafter, the bishop or priest knows that his only effective judge in this life is his own conscience. It is a serious responsibility. "When a man has had a great deal given him on trust, even more will be expected of him" (Luke 12:48). Although the situation is not ideal, the maintenance of the good relationship that ought to exist between pope and bishop as well as between bishop and priest is so important that the effect of introducing anything that would destroy or weaken that bond is probably the principal reason for maintaining the prevailing state of affairs. How significant, therefore, are those words of Jesus just quoted: "When a man has had a great deal given him *on trust*...". Of course, a wise bishop or priest might well seek an informal and unbiased appraisal from someone whom he trusts, provided that the person asked is someone who has a proper awareness of a priest's or bishop's work and the ability to make true judgments and give a useful appraisal and helpful advice.

There are now a considerable number of retired priests in our diocese. When a priest is seventy-five years old, he offers his resignation to the bishop who may accept or defer it (canon 538 §3). Some of the retired priests live outside the diocese. Those who remain in the diocese and are fit are usually willing to give some help in a parish, normally by offering Mass when requested. Retired priests no longer have the burdens and responsibilities of a parish priest but they should have the pleasure and satisfaction, if they wish, of continuing to have some pastoral involvement when needed and convenient. I think that there is a similarity between, on the one hand, the relationship of a grandparent to the younger generation and, on the other, of a retired priest to a parish. Neither the grandparent nor the retired priest should be regarded as unwanted or unavailable.

When the issue of the sexual abuse of children arose and, in particular, the fact that the guilty persons sometimes were priests, we had to take the whole matter very seriously indeed. In Galloway, we had training days which all our priests had to attend. At these, we were instructed, by professionals in the field, about how to behave correctly with children and how we should act if cases occurred, or were suspected, of child abuse by fellow priests or by others who were engaged on any business connected with the parish. Since the issue first became a prominent scandal, there have been developments in the way in which the evil should be prevented, reported, treated and so on; in these respects, we have had to invest a great deal of time, effort and money in order to do everything possible to prevent abuse, to protect the vulnerable, including some adults also, and to deal with offenders or suspected offenders. In this diocese, and until the present, we have not gone unscathed but, compared with other places, the dioceses of Scotland have emerged less afflicted.

It is not difficult to realise how much this issue of the abuse of vulnerable people has affected the priests. We have felt compassion for the victims and anxiety to help them in any way that we could, we have been ashamed of those priests who have been guilty of abuse, we have endured the widespread suspicion and opprobrium engendered by the publicity, we have been more vigilant than before about our own behaviour and that of others involved with our parishes. It has been a time of suffering for priests and yet they have continued to do their work and live their lives in as conscientious and exemplary a manner as possible.

With regard to permanent deacons, there were none ordained for the diocese and none in training during my years as bishop. I consulted the clergy, especially the Council of Priests, on two or perhaps three occasions, and the general opinion was not in favour of their introduction. The prevailing view was that, since they can neither celebrate Mass nor confer absolution nor anoint the sick, their usefulness was unfortunately limited; moreover, lay people, both men and women, can carry out many of the duties that deacons perform. It seemed a pity to "clericalise" ecclesial ministry even more than before and thereby, especially, reduce women's involvement. However, my successor, Bishop John Cunningham, has introduced permanent deacons in the diocese, a decision that I am happy to accept, especially because the permanent diaconate now exists in the Roman rite and it is therefore good to use it; and already all the other seven Scottish dioceses have introduced the practice of having permanent deacons.

RELIGIOUS

The numbers shown in "alarming statistics" are stark. They show a great decrease in the number of religious, both male and female, in Galloway diocese between 1982 and 2012. The fall in men religious (both priests and unordained brothers) was from 45 to 6 and, in religious sisters, from 73 to 22.

The reasons for the decreases differ in the two cases, men and women. In 1982 there were five male religious congregations in the diocese: Passionists, Norbertines (Premonstratensians), Verona Fathers, Sacred Heart Fathers ("Dehonians") and Marist Brothers. All had sizable numbers in the diocese, the first four being almost entirely composed of priests and two of them were in charge of parishes: Norbertines and Sacred Heart Fathers. The Marist Brothers had three houses: St Joseph's College in Dumfries, Kinharvie Centre near New Abbey, and St Columba's College in Largs. Today, all have gone with the exception of the Sacred Heart Fathers, who take care of St John Ogilvie's parish in Irvine and Smithstone House of Prayer and Spirituality in Kilwinning.

Soon after the end of the Second World War, the Passionist Fathers opened several houses in the diocese. When I came to Galloway in 1981, there was only one left, Fatima House at Coodham, near Kilmarnock. Within a few years, extensive dry rot was found and very costly repairs were undertaken. Unfortunately, further damage to the building was discovered some years later and the Passionists understandably decided to cut their losses and put the estate on sale. The departure of the Passionists from Coodham, around 1990, was a particularly heavy blow as the large house and modern extension offered a magnificent pastoral and spiritual resource for the diocese and indeed for the whole country. Coodham provided residential courses and retreats, days and weekends led by members of the Passionist community and/or renowned speakers from Britain and abroad. In addition, the accommodation was always available for our diocesan use, especially during the years of the Renew process and the introduction of the Ministry to Priests programme as well as many other occasions. On a personal note, I also mention the fact that I received episcopal ordination in the Coodham grounds in front of Fatima House on 9th June 1981, a rather cold and windy, but ultimately sunny, afternoon.

The Marist Brothers came to the diocese in 1872 to establish St Joseph's College, Dumfries. Consequently, when they left after such a long association, their going, and especially the loss of their rightly famed educational gifts, was deeply regretted. At present, the only male religious community in the diocese are the Sacred Heart Fathers who have been in St John Ogilvie's parish since it opened in the late 1970s and in Smithstone since purchasing the house and grounds in 1970. The latter, due to the shortage of priests to staff it, does not at the moment provide any pastoral or spiritual resources for the diocese or the wider public, again a very regrettable situation. Partially offsetting the bad news, two religious priests came to the diocese some years ago as individuals; one is parish priest in Newton Stewart and the other was parish priest in Annan and continues to live there in retirement.

At the start of the period under review, there were in the diocese nine convents of women religious. Today there are seven. The Benedictine Adorers of the Sacred Heart of Jesus (of Montmartre) are different from the others, being the only enclosed contemplative community in Galloway diocese. The original establishment was a community of Benedictines of the Blessed Sacrament (whose mother house is in France). They were in charge of a secondary school for girls, attached to their convent in Dumfries. When the community became very reduced in numbers, the nuns closed the school and the girls were transferred to St Joseph's College, which then became coeducational. This had, in fact, several advantages, perhaps the most important being that Catholic secondary education for girls was no longer limited in numbers, a situation that had deprived an indeterminate number of girls of a proper secondary education. The few nuns still in Dumfries voted to be received into the Benedictines of the Sacred Heart, whose mother house is Tyburn Convent, London. A few years later, a decision was made to move from the convent in Dumfries to a large building purchased in Largs, where the community of some eight or nine members now lives, prays, works and accepts guests for private retreats, visits and hospitality.

The six other houses of female religious have much smaller communities, ranging from one to three persons In most cases, however, the sisters are still very active, either in the parishes in which they reside or in duties ranging further afield. Nor should it be forgotten that many of these women, in earlier life, carried out a valuable service either in teaching or in nursing and that some of them served in missionary countries in arduous and even dangerous and hazardous conditions.

Both the contemplative religious and those who belong to "active" congregations are important elements of the diocese, through their exemplary presence, their prayers and their work. The decrease in numbers and the lack of applicants for both male and female orders and congregations is a cause of concern. It is true that some were established to educate the young and to nurse the sick in the nineteenth century when there was a shortage of lay people to undertake such work, a shortage that is not nearly as severe now. But the absence of religious from our dioceses would be a sad loss, especially for the exemplary witness of faith and dedication that they provide for us all.

However, the global picture is not as bleak. In the so called developing world, in Africa and parts of South Asia, the number of recruits to religious congregations is gratifyingly on the increase. This is very fitting in those areas where religious, especially women, do necessary work in the traditional fields of education and health care. What I find very heartening is not only the increase in numbers but also the fact that many of the congregations are now appointing people from these new areas of the world to positions of high responsibility in their ranks. Religious life in our world is not moribund but its "centre of gravity" is moving.

EDUCATION AND SCHOOLS

The Church in Scotland is proud of the network of Catholic schools that there are in the country. Originally they were set up and paid for (including teachers' salaries) by "the pennies of the poor" until the early years of the twentieth century. In 1918 negotiations resulted in the Church handing over their school buildings to the local authorities, namely the various county councils of Scotland. These assumed the responsibility of maintaining the properties, building new schools as necessary, appointing and paying teachers and other staff, and supplying all necessary equipment, including books, stationery and furnishings. The legislation allows the Church to retain certain rights, especially that teachers' appointments must be approved by the local bishop, that a certain time each week is devoted to the teaching of Catholic faith and practice, and that the Church may appoint priests to have access as chaplains.

The arrangement on the whole works very well and, in particular, it relieves the Catholic community of the burden of funding the schools. From time to time, difficulties have arisen in operating the system but usually these have been settled, more or less to the satisfaction of the local diocese and the local authority.

Of course, in areas of Scotland that are sparsely populated, and especially where Catholics are not a large percentage of the local inhabitants, separate Catholic schools are not provided. This is a reasonable restriction but it does call for efforts by the local priest or parish community to provide alternative arrangements for the religious education of the Catholic children of the district, a responsibility that is fulfilled in a variety of ways.

In the diocese of Galloway, the number of Catholic primary schools in 1982 was in the mid-thirties. Since then, a number of the smaller schools, perhaps around ten of them, have been closed. I was in the habit of making an annual visit to each school and spending some time in each classroom, as well as having a meeting with the head teacher and going to the staffroom with all the teachers at the morning interval and, if I were still in the school, at lunch time. Since I am not a trained and professional schools inspector, I did not attempt any assessment of the quality of religious education on offer. My reasons for visiting the schools were pastoral – to encourage staff and pupils, to demonstrate my interest and friendship, to say something helpful that might strengthen their faith in Jesus Christ and their fidelity to Catholic practice. Of course, not all the children in the schools are Catholics and, even among those who are, many are strangers to Sunday Mass. The visits were tiring, especially in the bigger schools. The largest primary school in the diocese was St Peter's in Ardrossan and the smallest was All Souls' in Wigtown; closely rivalled by St Margaret's in New Cumnock and St Thomas' in Muirkirk, all three now no more. I was invariably received with kindness and courtesy and, for me, the visits were personally very rewarding.

Visiting the secondary schools was much more difficult for me. It was not only their size and their complexity but, even more, the classes were constantly on the move from subject to subject, from room to room and from teacher to teacher. Those factors, plus the feeling that a visit by me would not always be convenient for the school, deterred me with the result that my visits to secondary schools were rare and nearly always on the occasion of some specific event.

In 1982 there were eight Catholic secondary schools in the diocese. Over the years, the two smallest have closed – Sacred Heart Academy in Girvan and St Conval's High School in Cumnock; in Dumfries the Benedictine Convent School was also closed and the pupils, all girls, went to St Joseph's College; and in North Ayrshire, St Michael's Academy in Kilwinning and St Andrew's Academy in Saltcoats were amalgamated as St Matthew's Academy, located on the Saltcoats campus. Queen Margaret Academy, Ayr, and St Joseph's Academy, Kilmarnock, remain as they were. Consequently, there are now four Catholic secondary schools in the diocese.

Apart from the widespread reluctance of Catholic teenagers to persevere with practice of their faith, especially as regards attendance at Mass, the rolls of the secondary schools contain a percentage of teachers and pupils of other faiths (and none). As a result, although in primary schools it is relatively easy to "deliver" the religious education curriculum, the same does not hold in the secondary schools. In each of them there is a specific RE department with properly qualified teachers, but for them to achieve a satisfactory outcome of their efforts must sometimes be a problem. I have great sympathy for those teachers and pupils who are conscientious and dedicated Catholics, as also for the priests, appointed to part-time chaplaincies in each school.

The celebration of Mass in school, whether primary or secondary, causes concern and on more than one ground. For example, on holy days of obligation, should there be a Mass in the local school, if possible? Is such a Mass much more than a too easy way to fulfil an obligation? On days of obligation and on other occasions, did a school Mass or a class Mass not mean that those who never went to Mass in the church just received Holy Communion merely because everyone present did so? And those who were not Catholics? Furthermore, I found that the standard of liturgy at school Masses generally left a lot to be desired, even making allowance for the conditions and circumstances. Of course, the counter argument is that, by having Mass in school, an opportunity is given to those who otherwise would never be at Mass.

As I have already noted, the people's commitment to separate Catholic schools, as shown by the questionnaire, is far from overwhelming. That is a negative factor. Sometimes, while I was bishop of the diocese, I confess that I had doubts about the value of separate Catholic schools. Was the religious instruction as good as it ought to be? Why did it not appear more effective, at least as far as Sunday Mass attendance showed? Sometimes I got the impression that children who attended non-denominational schools, either by their parents' choice or through lack of any alternative, were more likely to be at Sunday Mass than those at Catholic schools. Such thoughts are depressing and worrying. I hope they are also mistaken.

However, on the positive side, the establishment some years ago of the Scottish Catholic Education Service, under its excellent director, Mr Michael McGrath, has been a success and SCES is doing outstanding work. Its recently published RE programme *This is Our Faith* has been widely praised and is now being implemented in all of our schools. May it help to bring a rediscovery of faith and of God's loving call to our adolescents and young adults.

There are local authority schools (non-denominational) for children with special needs, although the tendency is to have as few children as possible at such schools and as many as possible in mainstream education. In my early years in the diocese, there were "St Francis Clubs" in Ayr and Kilmarnock where Catholic children with special needs were welcome. In the 1990s these groups ceased because we adopted, for Catholics with learning difficulties (and not only children), the system known as SPRED, Special Religious Development. Begun in Chicago in the 1960s, SPRED is "designed to assist those with developmental disabilities and/or learning problems to become integrated into parish life through a process of education in faith". Since its introduction in Galloway, SPRED has been directed by Sister Kathleen Hogg DC and has now several centres in the diocese. The system has enabled many "friends", as they are called, to develop an awareness of the presence and love of God and to receive sacraments which, otherwise, might not have been offered.

Some mention ought also to be made of adult education in faith, even although it is a voluntary matter and not something organised and obligatory, as is the case with children's religious education. Our most important and effective instrument in adult education in faith was undoubtedly the Renew process, which is described in its own section.

For some years the diocese also sponsored a scheme known as the Certificate in Pastoral Ministry. This was begun by the diocese of Dunkeld in collaboration with Abertay University, into which Galloway also entered. It was a three-year part-time course of classes, essays and required reading on a variety of theological and pastoral subjects. The classes or lectures were given by qualified priests and lay persons, the participants were lay people recommended by their parish priests as involved or able to be involved pastorally in their parishes. On completion of the course, the students were awarded a certificate to show their competence in pastoral matters. The scheme lasted for a number of years and, in the diocese, something over a hundred people did the course.

In some parishes, schemes such as Alpha and CaFE were introduced and, at deanery and diocesan levels, many series of talks have been held, all with the aim of fostering a greater interest in theological, scriptural and pastoral areas of knowledge.

By its very nature, adult education in faith has to be "bitty" and we have to be content with what is achieved; hence, there always remains the desire to do more. Active Catholics hear a weekly homily, of course, and many copies of the *Catechism of the Catholic Church* were bought when it was published in 1994. Not many people would read it from cover to cover but, one hopes, it is a frequently consulted reference book. Finally, if the Year of Faith (October 2012 to November 2013) was to be effective, it had to encourage not only that we invite the Holy Spirit to revitalise and deepen our belief but also that we sincerely try to widen our knowledge of God's revealed truth.

THE CELEBRATION OF MASS

The Mass should, and does, hold a special place in our lives as Catholics. Perhaps in the days before Vatican II, when the Mass seemed so unchangeable, we did not pay great attention to how we celebrated it. The priest knew the rubrics, the missal provided him with all the words, the people were little involved except as devout spectators – that was that and Mass was Mass. But, thanks to the Council's Constitution on the Sacred Liturgy (*Sacrosanctum Concilium*) and to subsequent official documents, things are very different nowadays. Every Mass requires careful preparation and diligent, devout celebration by all those present, each of us fulfilling his or her own role and with an awareness of what we are doing as sharers in Christ's priesthood and as the community of his Church. That is the ideal. To what extent do we achieve it, or approach it, in this diocese of Galloway?

Personally, I had a great desire, as bishop, to help the parishes to celebrate Mass well. I had taught liturgy to the students in the Scots College in Spain and have welcomed the reform and the renewal of liturgical practice decreed and inaugurated by the Second Vatican Council. I had to implement the directives and the guidance of the *General Instruction of the Roman Missal* when I was a parish priest in East Kilbride in the diocese of Motherwell. That aim was confirmed and intensified when I was made a bishop and especially when I was appointed to be the Scottish member of the Episcopal Board of the International Commission on English in the Liturgy and, even more, when elected chairman of that body in 1997.

From the beginning of my time in Galloway, I encouraged the full use of lay ministries at Mass – Scripture readings by lay people, singing of those parts of Mass which are meant to be sung, the availability of Holy Communion under both kinds at all Masses.

Nearly all the priests were of similar mind as I was in these matters, although there were a few priests and parishes that perhaps were less enthusiastic in having as much lay participation in certain parts of the Mass or in making Holy Communion under the form of wine available to all.

A matter in which we could have done better in some parishes was in the effort to have Holy Communion for the lay people provided from hosts consecrated at the Mass being celebrated. For obvious reasons, complete success in that direction is not possible, but to have a full ciborium of hosts in the tabernacle and already consecrated to be distributed at a later Mass is wrong. And the practice has been discouraged and deplored by popes from Benedict XIV in the eighteenth century to those of the present century.

On a few occasions of the year there are diocesan Masses in the cathedral church. Such Masses are the highest and best expression of the Church's worship because they involve bishop, priests, deacons, religious and laity from all the parishes, that is, all the elements that comprise the local Church. Such a celebration of the Eucharist, led by the bishop, the principal liturgical figure of the diocese, and with the entire diocese represented, is a wonderful act of faith and merits every effort to make it an impressive and memorable occasion.

There is one particular diocesan Mass that, year by year, shows the diocese at its best. I refer to the Mass of Chrism, celebrated in Galloway on the Tuesday evening of Holy Week. The cathedral is packed, people have come from the farthest parts of the diocese, from Largs and elsewhere in the north to Dumfries and neighbouring parishes in the south. The music is well chosen and the singing full-throated and wholehearted. The great majority of the priests are present and publicly renew their promise of commitment to priestly life and service; the sacred oils are solemnly blessed and then distributed to the parishes for use. The Mass of Chrism is a splendid occasion that affords us a spiritual experience of liturgy at its best, its most participatory and sacred.

To introduce a bleak realistic note, the relatively low percentage of baptised Catholics who regularly take part in Mass on Sundays, and the fact that that low rate continues its fall, is very worrying and perplexing. It should challenge us to try to encourage those who are "inactive" Catholics to be open to God's invitation and desire for them to worship him in the perfect way left to us by our Saviour. However, since we are told so often by those who do not go to Mass, and by some who do, that "Mass is boring", I do think that, although Mass is not celebrated as an entertainment to be enjoyed by spectators, parishes should frequently be aware that their Sunday Masses should try to be as attractive and interesting as possible and avoid the tendency to a routine and dullness that can legitimately be criticised as boring. As the people leave the church, is their good humour the result of what and how they have celebrated or merely a sense of relief and gratitude that "it's over for another week"?

THE SACRAMENTS

It is useful to make some comments on certain pastoral aspects of the sacraments, aspects that are relevant to life and religious practice in the diocese.

BAPTISM

The number of infants and young children being baptised has reduced greatly in the thirty years from 1981 to 2012. This is partly due to the decrease in the size of families but more to the fact that many people who, in a previous generation, would at least have observed this most basic practice of a Christian family, no longer do so.

Most Catholics would agree that parents, asking to have their children baptised, should receive some instruction about the Church's teaching on baptism and its effects, as well as on their responsibilities as parents, After all, the liturgy describes them as "the first and most important teachers of their children". It is clearly to be hoped that they themselves will be practising Catholics or, in the case of a mixed marriage, that the Catholic partner should be. When there is little sign or founded hope of Catholic practice in the parents, should baptism of the children be refused? Most would probably say no, but that the sacrament might be delayed for a short time, in the hope that there would be a change for the better.

For those of a later age who seek to be Catholics, the process leading to baptism is normally the Rite of Christian Initiation of Adults (RCIA) or, in the appropriate case, the Rite of Christian Initiation of Children "who have reached catechetical age". In our diocese, the RCIA process usually lasts from September to the following Easter Vigil. In fact, however, we find that a majority of those seeking to become Catholics have already been baptised, with the result that their status during the time of preparation is different from that of the unbaptised, the catechumens, although, in practice, they accompany the catechumens in the various courses of instruction.

Care is taken that the RCIA process should be followed very seriously, not only in the various liturgical rites during it but also in the teaching offered to the candidates for full initiation into the Catholic Church. On the First Sunday of Lent, the bishop invites the catechumens to the cathedral for the Rite of Election, as they begin the final and intense period of preparation; those already baptised are also invited, recognised and enrolled. After their reception into full communion at the Easter Vigil in their parishes, the new members of the Church should carry out, along with the parish community, a period of mystagogia, "a time for the community and the neophytes together to grow in deepening their grasp of the paschal mystery and making it part of their lives through meditation on the Gospel, sharing in the Eucharist and doing the works of charity" (RCIA §234).

I sometimes wondered whether we were fulfilling these instructions about the period of mystagogia as well as we should. It would not be correct to generalise, either in criticism or in complacency, but there were reports and there was evidence that, in some cases, those who had been through the RCIA process and had received the sacraments of initiation did not persevere in the practices of Catholic life.

Despite the recommendations of some liturgical scholars, we do not yet have baptism by immersion, either of infants or of adults; but, rather, our method is simply by water poured on the heads of the recipients of the sacrament. Perhaps the Scottish climate and the time-honoured norms of seemly decorum provide powerful deterrents.

CONFIRMATION

During my time as bishop, we introduced the practice of conferring confirmation on children before first Holy Communion. Thus we restored the correct order of the sacraments of initiation into full membership of the Church, as recommended by the official documents of the Church. This order had been upset over a century ago when St Pius X decreed that, once they reach the use of reason, children should be admitted to Holy Communion. Previously, that sacrament had been delayed until early teenage and normally after the sacrament of confirmation.

Some other Scottish bishops also restored the official order, although others did not. The bishops did attempt to achieve unanimity on the matter, but unfortunately failed to do so. When the change was made in this diocese, I think I did not succeed in convincing most people of its rightness or wisdom. This was due to a number of practical difficulties that the change brought in its wake. Let me outline three such difficulties.

First, since, having received baptism and confirmation, children have a right to receive Holy Communion, we decided that confirmation and first Holy Communion should be received at the same Mass. This meant that, since the appropriate season for the sacraments of initiation is Easter time, the bishop cannot manage to go to most parishes for the administration of confirmation. Some of the solemnity and specialness of confirmation is thereby lost and, moreover, it is overshadowed by first Holy Communion.

Second, teachers felt that children in primary 4 class and therefore eight or nine years old were too young to appreciate the Church's teaching on confirmation; besides, since the class teachers had to prepare the children for two sacraments, the work became a rushed and unsatisfactory task. To this, of course, it can rightly be responded that full knowledge of the meaning of a sacrament is not necessary prior to its reception – think of baptism! – but could and should continue to develop afterwards. In fact, the Church's teaching on confirmation is rather vague and tentative. And (a personal observation), the emphasis placed on the "Seven Gifts of the Holy Spirit" is confusing and detracts from the New Testament teaching, especially St Paul's rich theology of the gifts of the Spirit.

Third, it is argued that teenage confirmation provides an opportunity for the recipients to make a mature commitment to be faithful disciples of Christ and members of his Church. However, in reply, the facts do not seem to bear out these claims and reception of the sacrament of confirmation is not a very effective guarantee of faithful commitment. In fact, it is not the purpose of the sacrament that it should be used as the occasion of making such a faithful commitment. The time for that is the Easter Vigil when all of us, not just teenagers, are called to make a solemn renewal of our baptismal commitment. If this were taught and advertised properly, it would provide an excellent and annual opportunity for all of us to pledge ourselves publicly to Christ and his Church.

A fully satisfactory solution to the dilemma about the order of Christian initiation of children seems unlikely, mainly because the Church's theology on confirmation is so meagre and tentative, and particularly on the relation between baptism and confirmation. What does confirmation add to baptism? Should the two be separated when baptism is administered to infants? Whatever we do in practice, it seems bound to be open to criticism.

There is another issue connected with children's initiation that, theoretically, should be easier to solve but that, in practice, seems very resistant. It is the emphasis, probably also increasing, that many parents put on the material aspects of the event. Costly and unsuitable outfits for the children, expensive gifts, special cars, unnecessary hotel or restaurant catering – all these detract from the true importance of the day and can be a gross waste of money that some people can ill afford. But the peer pressure is very strong and it seems to emanate from those with an inadequate awareness of where the true importance of the celebration really lies.

EUCHARIST

The Mass is, of course, the principal celebration of the sacrament of the Eucharist; thorough consideration of it is the subject of the first chapter of the present book and so is not repeated here. Of course, there are other expressions of this sacrament that derive from the Mass. One of these is Holy Communion for the sick at home or in care, as well as for the housebound. This ministry is carried out by the priest and also by properly commissioned lay people. A few of the recipients prefer to be visited only by a priest, but most enjoy Holy Communion brought by a lay person, often also providing the opportunity of a short chat.

With the increasing shortage of priests and therefore the difficulty of daily Mass in every parish of the diocese, the rite known as Liturgy of the Word with Holy Communion, carried out by lay people with one of them, male or female, presiding, is becoming more common. Since, by the nature of things, the priest is not present, I have sometimes wondered if the rite is being carried out in a fully correct manner. This is a matter that should be courteously checked by the priest. There is no doubt, however, that the rite is celebrated with care and devotion and is appreciated by those who used to be, and would still like to be, daily Mass-goers.

Benediction of the Blessed Sacrament and processions are now, in most parishes, rare occurrences. But many parishes have weekly periods during which the Blessed Sacrament is exposed in a monstrance to allow people to come to the church and spend some time in prayer, whether by contemplation, adoration, thanksgiving, petition, or propitiation. This is a form of devotion that is much encouraged by recent popes.

When I came to the diocese in 1981, there was still a programme for each parish to have the Forty Hours Devotion, namely exposition of the Blessed Sacrament for the daylight hours of three days. The days, Sunday to Tuesday, were assigned so as to have Forty Hours in a different parish in as many different weeks as possible in the year. Sadly, the practice was very difficult to sustain for a variety of reasons, some very understandable, and soon was discontinued.

RECONCILIATION

The Second Vatican Council and subsequent official instructions brought about a renewal of the sacrament of reconciliation. The main change is that there are now three forms of celebrating this sacrament: individual and private (where the celebration directly involves only the priest and the penitent); communal, but with individual confession and absolution (in which the community celebrates a liturgy of the word to prepare, to express repentance and to give thanks together); and general (with no individual confession, but only a communal expression of repentance followed by a general absolution by the priest). This last form is permitted only in exceptional circumstances and with, if possible, prior permission of the bishop and later confession of all serious sins absolved.

The third form is rarely, if ever, encountered in this diocese. The other two forms are in use, the first much less than before Vatican II. The second form is popular with many people and, in each parish, it is celebrated with quite large numbers and several priests assisting, every Advent and Lent.

Concern is sometimes expressed about the relatively few people who use the first rite of the sacrament of reconciliation. Naturally and as a result, the times set for the first rite to be available are much shorter than in the days before the Second Vatican Council, although, if a person wished to use this form of the sacrament, a priest would always be ready to oblige when requested. We should keep in mind also that, over the centuries, this sacrament has experienced a great range of ways in which it has been used. There were times when it was celebrated only once in one's lifetime and therefore tended to be delayed until as near death as seemed likely. At other times, it came to be used with great frequency by some people, not only weekly but even daily. It is said that one king of Spain in the eighteenth century was likely to need his confessor several times a day. So, given such great variations in the use of the sacrament, I can accept, without great concern, that many people, who used to have frequent (weekly or monthly) confession, now receive the sacrament less often. My concern is for those who, it seems, never receive the sacrament in any of its three forms.

At celebrations of the second form of the sacrament of reconciliation, we remind the people that they should confess any serious sins not previously absolved and, if they have none to confess, as is usually the case, they should at least briefly mention some area of their conduct or some incident for which they feel truly repentant. The individual confessions are usually very brief and, if a person seeks a longer time with the priest, it is better to arrange private and individual celebration of the sacrament.

To revert for a moment to the subject of the frequency with which this sacrament ought to be received, we should remember that most practising Catholics who confess occasionally but not frequently are not aware or guilty of regularly committing serious sins. Less serious sins can receive God's forgiveness in many other ways, for example by celebrating Mass and/or receiving Holy Communion, incidentally a practice much more frequent than it used to be. There are other areas that perhaps should be of greater concern to us than the infrequency of reception of the sacrament. For example, have many of us lost a sense of sin or of sinfulness in our lives? Do we realise that some behaviour is still seriously wrong? And how much should psychological factors be seen as affecting, and perhaps lessening, the culpability of our actions?

ANOINTING OF THE SICK

In addition to the administration of the sacrament of anointing of the sick in people's homes and in hospitals etc., most parishes have occasional Masses with the sacrament offered to the sick and the elderly who wish to receive it. Such an occasion is pastorally very valuable, not only for those being anointed but also for families, friends and parishioners in general present at the Mass. It is a source of satisfaction, an opportunity to pray for sick and old parishioners and a chance for the parish community to celebrate its faith when some of its members are present who normally are not able to be there. Besides, the provision of transport to and from the church and the opportunity to entertain the recipients socially after Mass are excellent ways of showing our love and care for those in need.

There are still, in people's minds, the vestiges of the time when the sacrament was called "extreme unction" or when the sick were given "the last rites". As a result, the impression, even subconsciously, is prevalent that this anointing is the sacrament of the dying, rather than of the sick. The consequence, especially in hospitals and nursing homes, can be that a priest is not called until the person is near death or already dead. Furthermore, when a person who is ill is offered this sacrament, he or she has to be reassured that this does not imply that death is near and that the truth has not been divulged.

Another misapprehension that I think may be widespread is that, if a person has died without receiving anointing or viaticum, the former, or even both, sacraments can still be given. To attempt to give a sacrament thus may provide some consolation to the bereaved family members but I hope I may suggest, without offence, that the anxiety to confer a sacrament after someone has died may betray a very limited sense of God's infinite mercy, as if that mercy was not operative if a person had not been anointed; besides, the omission was one for which the person who died was in no way responsible.

MATRIMONY

The drastic decrease in the number of marriages celebrated in our parish churches in recent decades, as shown already in the statistics given earlier, is a matter of serious concern. The implication that many Catholics either seek to solemnise their marriages elsewhere or, more often, prefer to live together unmarried, is extremely depressing. Perhaps social and/or economic factors play their part, especially in the latter situation, but there is also evidence that many Catholics simply are not aware of the Church's regulations on marriage and of the conditions for it to be valid.

Another sad fact is that, nowadays, the great majority of Catholics who do marry in accordance with the Church's rules do not have Catholic spouses. In the case of such mixed marriages, does the Catholic partner ever do or say anything that would suggest to the other the idea of becoming a Catholic? An incident that occurred in the early 1950s, shortly after I was ordained, remains in my memory. I asked an excellent Catholic lady and "a pillar of the Church", whose husband was not a Catholic, if the situation caused any friction between them. "None at all", she replied, "we never discuss the subject of religion". By the way, I now recognise that my question was an unwarranted intrusion, and I am sorry for my impertinence.

Another related matter. There are no statistics, but I wonder in regard to mixed marriages, (a) what proportion of Catholic partners remain active in practising their faith, and what proportion do not; (b) what percentage of the non-Catholics become Catholics; and (c) what percentage of the children of mixed marriages are given a Catholic upbringing at home and in school?

On the subject of weddings themselves, I have great sympathy for those who have to meet the very large costs incurred. Clothes, flowers, photographs, car, organist, other musicians and singers, various extras as well as the cost of the reception including food, drinks and accommodation; all those, and probably other expenses of which I am unaware. Is there not some way of reining in the huge expenditure? How much influence do such considerations as "Nothing is too good for our daughter" or "We have to do it because everyone else does it" play in the planning and decisions? People are very susceptible and vulnerable when they approach hoteliers, caterers and the like. Moreover, all the emphasis on the material aspect of the wedding detracts from an occasion that is primarily religious, sacred and serious.

The lavishness of the entertainment and other expensive aspects that increasingly accompany sacramental occasions is a matter of concern. Undoubtedly, the expenses that have to be met, so as to "keep up with the Joneses" and not be called a skinflint, can be a crippling financial burden for some and an unwelcome expenditure for most. In addition, removing the emphasis from the religious event to the subsequent hotel reception means that the local parish community cannot play its proper part in the sacramental celebrations of its members. Does that merit any consideration?

ORDINATION

Since there is a whole section of this "Portrait of a Diocese" on the priests of the diocese and since ordinations to the priesthood have became so scarce, the following is the only point which I make here.

During my twenty-three years as bishop of Galloway, I ordained many priests, both for this diocese and for various religious orders and congregations. Those occasions were, for me, invariably times of tension, great privilege and sacred wonder. To be empowered to confer the share in the priesthood of Christ that ordination gives was always a spiritual experience that I found as awesome as it was fulfilling.

FUNERALS

Although not a sacrament, a funeral is, to some extent, a similar ceremony and is one of the group of rites and quasi-rites called "sacramentals".

I believe it is true to say that, when a death occurs in a parish, the community and the priest show truly Christian compassion for those who are bereaved. Perhaps, however, in some cases, we forget to ensure that, if the bereaved need continued compassionate help of a specific kind, even an occasional visit, that that work of mercy is not overlooked.

Most deaths see the dead person's body brought to the local church, usually the evening before the funeral although, recently, that ceremony is sometimes being delayed until immediately before the funeral Mass. Funeral Masses generally take place at the normal morning Mass time; on some occasions the time may have to be changed to suit the cemetery or crematorium schedule. There are three crematoria in the diocese and the number of Catholic funerals using them is, I think, slowly increasing. Most funerals, however, go to one of the local cemeteries. The crematoria are more welcoming for the mourners in bad weather, but no doubt the decision between the alternatives is made, by the deceased or the bereaved family, on grounds of preference for one or other manner of treatment of the body after death.

Fifty years ago, black vestments were worn for funeral Masses. Later, the usual colour was purple but, in the last twenty years or so, when white became a possible choice, most funeral Masses seem now to use that colour, based on the fact that death is not the end of our existence but the entry into eternal life, sharing in the Lord's resurrection. Nevertheless, the funeral Mass is offered for "the repose of the soul" of the one who has died and this intention of praying for the deceased should be the principal reason for the funeral Mass. I fear that, perhaps due to theology of the Reformation or the outlook of people with no religion, the impression is sometimes and unfortunately given that the Mass is mainly a celebration of the life of the deceased, even though the official prayers of the Mass constantly ask God to give a merciful judgment to the one we mourn.

ECUMENICAL RELATIONS

The bishops of the Catholic Church in Scotland have occasional but regularly scheduled meetings with the bishops of the Scottish Episcopal Church, at which various topics are chosen for discussion and any matters of mutual concern are also on the agenda. No similar statutory meetings with the leadership of the Church of Scotland take place but, as occasion demands, there are meetings between relevant commissions of the Catholic Church and the Church of Scotland. A Catholic observer is invited to attend the annual General Assembly of the Church of Scotland, a duty normally fulfilled by a bishop.

At the diocesan level, there are no regular meetings between our bishop and leaders of the reformed churches or non-Christian faiths. However, informal relations at parish level are usually good, often very friendly and warm. Various occasions during the year, for example, the Week of Prayer for Christian Unity, Remembrance Sunday, Advent carol services, are opportunities for joint meetings or services of prayers and hymns. Many Catholics in the diocese assist in the work of Christian Aid (in addition to their commitment to SCIAF). There are various local ecumenical contacts in different towns in Ayrshire and in Dumfries & Galloway and there is at least one ecumenical prayer group which has been meeting weekly for many years and continues to do so very successfully.

However, it has to be admitted that, generally speaking, although relations are friendly, formal ecumenical activity does not seem to have a very high profile in our diocese, either at diocesan or at parish level. Perhaps we should be more zealous and proactive, but neither does one detect great enthusiasm from the reformed churches or communities. Perhaps a contributory factor to this state of affairs is the differences that exist in boundaries, structures and methods of operation between the neighbouring parishes of the Church of Scotland and the Catholic Church.

FINANCE

I recall Bishop McGee, in my very early days, telling me that the diocese had no debts, with one exception – the costs incurred in building the church, house and hall of St John Ogilvie's parish in Irvine. During his time as bishop, many new churches had been built, others had had repairs and alterations. To have cleared all the debts was a record of which he could be proud, but he was very apologetic about the one exception, especially as the amount of debt was considerable. The explanation seems to have been that, during the months of construction, several changes had been made in the plans and additions had also been requested. Eventually, we managed to pay all the bills, as I shall explain later.

Despite Bishop McGee's success in paying all but one of the debts, the diocese is not wealthy. There were, and are, no investments and very little income apart from that generated from the levies collected from each parish, as a percentage of its ordinary income. When I came, the levy was, I think, at 12%. I raised it to 15% but with the promise that, in future, the diocese, rather than the parishes, would pay the annual contribution to what was known as the Retired Housekeepers and Domestics Fund, a national fund to pay the beneficiaries a modest pension.

At the start I felt very anxious about the small amount of income coming to the diocese. Early in 1982, Bishop Thomson was kind enough to give us an interest-free loan from the funds of the diocese of Motherwell. It was of £6000, a greater sum then than it would be nowadays, and we managed to repay it by the beginning of 1985. We also inaugurated, copying Motherwell, a Parochial Investment Fund, whereby parishes with money to spare would lend their surplus to the diocese at a fairly low rate of interest and with the guarantee that the loan would be repaid immediately on request. This brought in a considerable amount of money and, with the income from the levy on the parishes, I began to feel that we were more financially secure.

Occasionally the diocese was left bequests and then, some time in the1990s, I was informed that the lawyers of the archdiocese of St Andrews and Edinburgh had rediscovered a fund known as the Taggart Bursary. It was a bequest for the education of students for the priesthood in that archdiocese and in our diocese, the former to have two-thirds of the income and Galloway one third. That provided a few thousands each year. A small number of other bequests were also in our "portfolio", but the income from them came to very little indeed.

In the 1980s, Lady Carmont established the Carmont Settlement for the financial relief of "necessitous priests" in Scotland. It was administered by a firm of Edinburgh lawyers and the trustees were lay people, with the exception of the bishop of Galloway, an *ex officio* trustee. Although the beneficiaries were individual priests, there was a clause in the Settlement stipulating that, if the income were insufficient, Galloway priests were to have priority. This clause was the result of the association that Lord and Lady Carmont had with Dumfries. Since the income never was insufficient to support all the applicants, the trustees agreed to my suggestions that, because it seemed as if the priority for Galloway priests would never have its effect, the Settlement might invest some of its funds in purchasing three houses for retired Galloway priests, the diocese to pay a small annual rent to the Settlement. This was agreed and so, in an indirect way, the Carmont Settlement also benefits the diocese.

The ordinary collection at Sunday Mass remains in the parish and the levy is paid from it. Parishes should, of course, encourage parishioners to Gift Aid their contributions to their parish, thus enabling the parish to augment its income. In the early days of the Covenant scheme, before Gift Aid, a few parish priests, not properly understanding the scheme, claimed more money from the Inland Revenue authorities than their entitlement; the authorities discovered this when a full inspection of parish accounts and records took place, and the offending parishes had to repay the excess of their claims. The consequences of the mistake might have been worse!

Around the year 2000 we made a diocesan-wide effort to ask parishioners to review the amount which they each paid weekly to their parish. If they then realised that the amount was lower than they thought reasonable and/or it had not been increased for years, they were asked to consider raising their weekly offering. Volunteer lay people went to each parish and, with permission, made their appeal in a short address at the end of Masses on one Sunday. The results were good – not spectacular but certainly worth the effort and, since the address was gently phrased, no offence was given and no complaints reached me.

When there are special collections, they are usually for national or international purposes but a few, for example for retired priests and for students, go to the diocese.

These are the sources of income for the diocese. So what is the expenditure which the diocese incurs and the expenses it has to meet?

One of the largest is the annual payment to the Bishops' Conference of Scotland. The amount is calculated on a *pro rata* basis, each diocese paying according to its size. If I remember correctly, Galloway pays around 8% of the total required each year. Pensions and other expenses for retired priests are also a considerable cost, only partially met by the annual collection. Nowadays, with so few seminary expenses, that particular collection and the Taggart Bursary will cover the cost. The upkeep of the bishop and his house, the salaries of diocesan employees, subsidies to small parishes, the Retired Housekeepers and Domestics Fund are all considerable, and varying, expenses.

When parishes embark on expensive projects, such as construction, alteration or repair of property, the diocese will repay any money which the parish has in the Parochial Investment Fund and, if it is requested and can, it will lend money at low interest to the parish. In cases where the parish has to seek a loan from a bank, it was my custom to suggest the Bank of Ireland because the interest charged to the parish tended to be slightly lower than from Scottish banks. In such cases, the diocese usually had to give "a letter of comfort" to the bank to guarantee repayment.

The diocese with its parishes is a charity, its accounts have to be audited professionally and are published and open to inspection.

Priests receive board and lodging from the parish where they work. From the same source they receive a modest remuneration (less than £3000 per annum) and a mileage allowance when they use their cars for their work. They can keep fees received for marriages, baptisms and funerals as well as Mass offerings, but not any quarterly or Christmas or Easter collections in the parish. Some retired priests reside, rent free, in diocesan or Carmont Settlement property; others may live in houses owned by themselves or relatives. In addition, they receive a monthly pension from the diocese, an award of; at present £350 per annum from a charity called the Mitchell Bequest and, if in need, an allowance from the Carmont Settlement; all this in addition to the state retirement pension.

DEANERY BY DEANERY

ST ANDREW'S DEANERY
(Dumfries & Galloway)

In St Andrew's deanery lies the parish of **Whithorn**, the place of St Ninian's arrival in Scotland. At Whithorn he established the first Christian community in the country and the base for his missionary work. Very little is known for certain of the saint revered as the person who first brought Christianity to Scotland. In the village of Whithorn today there is, following recent and extensive excavations, important archaeological evidence of the saint's early followers, as well as a small museum containing contemporary ecclesiastical objects found there and in the vicinity. Alongside is the Priory, belonging to the Church of Scotland and built on the exact site of the medieval church.

On the other side of the broad main street is the Catholic church of St Martin and St Ninian. The decision to name two saints is due to the tradition that, on his way from Rome, where he is said to have become a Christian, a priest and a bishop, St Ninian spent some time with the bishop of Tours, St Martin. Since the latter died in 397, it is suggested that that is also the year of Ninian's arrival in Whithorn. On the other hand and following recent "digs", some scholars believe that the Whithorn foundation is more likely to have occurred in the fifth century The present Catholic church is modern, opened in 1960, and designed by the celebrated London architect, H. S. Goodhart-Rendel. It replaces an inadequate building known as "the iron church", a gift from the Marquis of Bute and which had been in use since 1882.

Whithorn was a famous place of pilgrimage in the Middle Ages but, after 1560 and the Protestant Reformation in Scotland, pilgrimages ceased. It is probable that they did not resume until 1924 but, since then, they have been held annually on the last Sunday of August. The pilgrimage Mass normally is celebrated at St

Ninian's Cave on the seashore, three miles from the village. In some years and for various reasons, the Mass has been in Whithorn itself, in the grounds of the church. In recent years, there have been two simultaneous pilgrimage Masses, the principal one, with the bishop as chief celebrant, at the Cave and the other in the parish church, for those unable to undertake the difficult and tiring walk down a muddy and wet track through the glen and then along a stony beach to St Ninian's Cave.

The annual Mass at the Cave attracts several hundred pilgrims, who arrive from all over the diocese as well as from further afield, by bus or by car or on foot. The duties of readers, homilist, cantor and choir are fulfilled by each deanery in turn; generator, microphones and portable toilets are hired; and, despite the terrain, Holy Communion under both kinds is carefully and safely provided. Even a piper is at hand, to play the bishop and other pilgrims across the beach before and after Mass. The only uncertain item is, of course, the weather. Most years it has ranged from beautifully sunny to tolerable but three occasions when the weather added its penitential element to the pilgrimage remain in my memory. On one of these, a high tide and a very stormy day almost succeeded, during Mass, in bringing the waves to the altar. In 2010, the rain was so heavy that Mass was celebrated with as much speed as decorum allowed, the homily being simply omitted. And in 1997, the sixteen hundredth anniversary of the saint's arrival, there was heavy driving rain and very slippery conditions down the muddy track and along the stony beach for all the pilgrims, who included, for that special anniversary, the bishops of Scotland.

For years the feast day of the saint was observed on 26th August but, although the date of the pilgrimage is unchanged, we have now reverted to the previous custom and restored the feast to 16th September. By a happy coincidence, this was the date which Pope Benedict XVI spent in Scotland during his visit to Britain in 2010 and the papal Mass in Bellahouston Park that sunny afternoon was that of St Ninian.

It is interesting that, in official documents of the Holy See, written in Latin, this diocese is called *Diocesis Gallovidiensis seu Candidae Casae*, thus conferring on us the alternative names of Diocese of Galloway or Diocese of Whithorn. Geographically, one name is that of the western, rural part of St Andrew's deanery and the other that of a small, but historic, parish in the same deanery.

Whithorn no longer has a resident priest, since its parish priest is also parish priest of, and lives in, **Newton Stewart**, beside the beautiful church of Our Lady and St Ninian (1876), built at the expense of the Marquis of Bute and Sir David Hunter-Blair of Dunskey. The same priest also serves the parishioners of **Wigtown** and its church of the Sacred Heart (1879), also a gift of Sir David Hunter-Blair. When I came to the diocese in 1981 there was also a church in Creetown – St Joseph's, served from Newton Stewart. The church was built in the early 1840s as the property of the Free Church of Scotland and was acquired by the Catholic Church in 1876. In those days there was a priest also resident in Whithorn, who served Wigtown. The congregation in Creetown had dwindled to a very few, augmented by some who travelled from Newton Stewart for an early Sunday Mass. St Joseph's was closed in the early 1990s and then sold to the Creetown Town Band as a place to store their instruments and hold their rehearsals.

The other Catholic church in Wigtownshire is St Joseph's, **Stranraer**. Built in 1853, it was enlarged in 1886. The parish has its own parish priest. Next to the church, there was a convent of the Sisters of St Joseph of Cluny. They were invited to the town towards the end of the nineteenth century to staff the new Catholic school, but the community withdrew at the start of the present century because of their falling numbers.

Wigtownshire has two Catholic primary schools, one in Newton Stewart and the other in Stranraer. There used to be a very small Catholic primary school, with all the pupils in the one classroom – All Souls', in Wigtown. This school is remarkable on two counts. First, Mrs Bridget Mills was appointed as the only teacher, and therefore also head teacher, immediately after qualifying as a teacher and she spent her entire career there, the only teacher, until her retirement. Second, despite several efforts by the local education authority to close the school, these attempts were foiled by vigorous campaigns of the parents, their appeals upheld by the full local Council, until finally the parents were defeated and the school was closed, early in the present century.

Most Catholic children of primary school age in Whithorn and other villages attend the local non-denominational schools. There is no Catholic secondary school in Wigtownshire and the Catholic children attend either Douglas Ewart High School in Newton Stewart or Stranraer Academy.

In the Stewartry of Kirkcudbright, east of Wigtownshire, there is now only one priest serving the area. Residing in **Kirkcudbright** (in the house which adjoins the church of St Andrew & St Cuthbert), he also serves Castle Douglas, **Dalbeatie** (St Peter's) and **Gatehouse of Fleet** (Church of the Resurrection) and celebrates Mass in the last two of these places. The Kirkcudbright property was once the county prison but was bought in 1884 and converted to its present uses. There was a priest resident at St John the Evangelist's church (1867) in Castle Douglas until a few years ago but now, sadly, even the church is closed. It is in an unsafe condition and, even if repairs had been feasible, they would have been very costly. Catholic schooling in the area is also sparse; in fact, only St Peter's primary school in Dalbeattie continues in existence.

Special mention should be made of Dalbeattie because, until recently, there has been a priest there since the middle of the eighteenth century, originally residing with the Catholic owners of the mansion house of Munches, a mile from the town, and then in the house attached to St Peter's church, built in 1814 and therefore the oldest Catholic church continuously in use in the diocese.

St Peter's possesses a further distinction. It was there that, for the first time in the diocese, I saw altar girls. It was something of a surprise for me when I met them one Sunday morning before Mass. But there was another novelty. One of the girls said to me, pointing to her colleague, "She's not going to receive Holy Communion". I was puzzled at this announcement but discretion prevented me from asking the reason. However, my confusion soon was removed. My informant added "She's a Protestant".

East of Dumfries, there are a number of Catholic parishes, all of which are now under the pastoral care of the priests who live in Dumfries. They serve St Columba's parish in **Annan** and also Holy Trinity parish in **Lockerbie** and St Luke's in **Moffat**. St Columba's was, until 1838, known as the Meeting House and had been a Congregational church. St Luke's, a timber construction, was built in 1865 for the Episcopal Church but became a Catholic church in 1886.

The church in Lockerbie, situated in the centre of the town, was built in 1874 and was acquired by the diocese from the Church of Scotland in 1973, the Catholics having previously had Mass in a structure, elegantly known as "The Tin Hut". Lockerbie used to have its own priest. In fact, the then parish priest was in his house on 21st December 1988, the night of the disaster when PanAm 103, en route from London to New York, crashed in the town and 270 people were killed. The largest piece of the plane fell only a few yards from the parish house where the priest and his mother had a very narrow escape. Nearly all the casualties (259) were in the plane but eleven Lockerbie people were killed, seven of them Catholics.

St Ninian's church, Gretna, was built by the British government during the First World War to meet the needs of the many Catholics who had come to the town to work in nearby munitions factories. Until recently, there was a resident parish priest in Gretna; in fact, the last in the series was, appropriately for Gretna, part-time assistant to the local blacksmith. As well as regular Masses in Gretna, the priest also went on Sundays to celebrate Mass in Eastriggs, using the Scottish Episcopal church there, by courtesy of their local and diocesan authorities. When St Ninian's closed, Mass attendance had dwindled to a handful of people. The building was sold and its new owners use the former church as a location for the celebration of marriages since Gretna is very popular with people from various countries as a venue for their weddings. My memories of St Ninian's are of a brick building but with some notable Byzantine-Romanesque features. The church always seemed damp and was bitterly cold. Until he retired, the organist (playing a small harmonium) had a very limited repertoire of hymns and was alleged sometimes to play wedding music at funerals and vice versa. It must be said in his defence that he was almost totally blind.

In Langholm there was, until around the turn of the present century, a residential care home for the elderly. The home, called Erkinholme, was owned and run by the Franciscan Missionaries of Our Lady. One of our priests was resident chaplain and there was daily Mass in the convent chapel (which Catholics from the town could attend). When the home closed and the sisters left, the diocese bought a former Protestant church in the town. The building was repaired, refurbished and refurnished and opened as St Francis of Assisi church. The interior arrangements were excellent. The altar was at one end, the lectern at the other and, completing an oval, two arcs of chairs between the two focal points and facing one another, with the presidential chair in front of the altar; the Blessed Sacrament chapel was in the church crypt.There was a small but regular and active congregation, served from Annan, but unfortunately the arrangement was discontinued a few years ago, mainly because the shortage of priests necessitated retrenchment in services provided.

The only Catholic school in the area east of Dumfries is St Columba's primary in Annan. For secondary education, some go to St Joseph's College in Dumfries. The dearth of Catholic education in this area (and in others in the diocese, particularly in this southern deanery) prompts the question: do Catholic children who attend non-denominational schools, primary or secondary, suffer deprivation in their religious education? Clearly, the curricula of the schools they attend do not include Catholic RE; but (a) is that loss compensated by their parents and/or parish? And (b) (a very radical question) how much value does RE in Catholic schools have in the lives of those who have access to them? The Bishops' Conference of Scotland and its agency, the Scottish Catholic Education Service, are aware that that latter question must be asked, and strenuous efforts are being made to improve the current situation. Furthermore, when, as bishop of the diocese, I used to make regular weekend visits to each parish, I had the impression that there seemed sometimes to be a higher proportion of teenagers present at Mass in parishes without Catholic schools than there were in parishes with such schools. If that is true, what is the explanation? Adverse peer pressure in Catholic secondary schools, a deterrent that is not so prevalent in non-denominational schools?

North of Dumfries there is, in the deanery, an extensive but sparsely populated area with a few towns and some villages. This part of the deanery had one parish, that of St Conal in the small town of Kirkconnel. The church (1921) and parish were closed in the summer of 2013. The parish had a resident priest until the mid-1980s, and was then served from St Teresa's in Dumfries. Although the weekend (Saturday Vigil) Mass had a congregation of less than twenty, the liturgy was good, well prepared and participatory.

Until the beginning of the present century there was Sunday morning Mass in Thornhill, north of Dumfries. The Mass took place in the Drumlanrig Café, where the space was very restricted both for the twenty or more who attended, as well as for the priest. Consequently, the liturgy was not particularly vibrant or imaginative. However, as I remember from occasional experience, it was enjoyable, when the congregation had dispersed, the tables and chairs rearranged and the crucifix on the wall replaced by secular decorations, to be invited to sit down and eat a cooked breakfast before the shop reopened for normal business.

In **Dumfries** itself there are two parishes. The older, in the centre of the town, is **St Andrew's**. When the Scottish hierarchy was restored (having disintegrated in 1560), St Andrew's church, which had been built in 1813, became the cathedral of the diocese of Galloway. A disastrous fire in 1961 totally destroyed the old building and the present church was built and opened in 1964. The only remnants of the old church are the two towers, which had been added in 1843 but are now some twenty metres away from the new building. Bishop Joseph McGee had already changed his residence from Dumfries to Ayr to be nearer the centre of the diocese, several parishes in the north of Ayrshire having been added to the diocese in 1947. After the cathedral in Dumfries was burned down, the bishop also transferred the diocesan cathedral, on a provisional basis which was to last almost fifty years, to the new church of the Good Shepherd in Ayr.

In St Andrew's parish, the Daughters of Charity of St Vincent de Paul had a convent from 1892 until a few years ago, when the community had to leave because of decreasing numbers. Their departure caused much disappointment among the parishioners, especially those whom the sisters visited and cared for, and among the itinerants for each of whom the sisters always had a packet of food.

St Andrew's parish was also the location of a large community of Marist Brothers, who arrived in Dumfries in 1872. Their principal work in Dumfries was St Joseph's College, a secondary school for boys, both boarders and day pupils. The College had an excellent reputation and was highly prized in the town and in the diocese but sadly dwindling numbers forced the brothers to withdraw from the College. Some of them continued to live in retirement nearby, but even they are now gone. St Joseph's College, with its buildings, continues to exist, now as a local authority Catholic secondary school, coeducational but not boarding, and with a fully lay staff. Although it is a Catholic school, a large majority of the pupils belong to other denominations and faiths, or to none, which makes the maintenance of a Catholic ethos a difficult task. In the school grounds stands St Joseph's College chapel, a substantial and free-standing building erected in 1925 as a war memorial.

Currently, there is one priest resident in the large house beside St Andrew's parish church, a house that was the original residence of the Marist Brothers and then, until a separate house across the river was bought, of the bishop of the diocese. The parish priest, in addition to new responsibilities in Annan and district, also serves the village and little parish of St Mary's, **New Abbey**, where the church, built in 1824, stands just a stone's throw from the ruins of Sweetheart Abbey, a Cistercian foundation of 1273 and where Lady Devorgilla, the foundress, buried the heart of her husband, John Balliol.

The second **Dumfries** parish**, St Teresa's**, was established in the 1950s and the church was opened in 1958. The parish is on the north side of the River Nith and serves the people who live in the housing estates developed after World War II. The priest at St Teresa's also serves the large territory north of Dumfries to the Ayrshire border at New Cumnock, an area that includes Kirkconnel. Since Kirkconnel is twenty-seven miles from St Teresa's, and the road is winding, difficult and lonely, the Saturday Vigil Mass was at 2pm on the reasonable grounds of allowing the priest to drive as many as possible of the fifty-plus miles before nightfall. That duty is now ended, as a result of new duties at Lockerbie and Moffat (as already noted).

Within St Teresa's parish territory, on a prominence known as Corbelly Hill, are the priory, church and school, formerly of the Benedictines of the Blessed Sacrament. The community of contemplative nuns came to the town in 1884 and had a secondary school for girls. The school closed in the late 1980s and the nuns left, two for France, but most to their new priory in Largs (see later). The closure of the school also ended an anomalous situation regarding Catholic secondary education for girls in Dumfries. The convent school was selective, St Joseph's College was for boys only; and, as a result, some girls were denied a Catholic secondary education. This situation was rectified when St Joseph's College, already non-selective, became coeducational.

Both Dumfries parishes have Catholic primary schools. St Andrew's school was very recently built to replace old and inadequate accommodation; its pupils are, in the main, Catholic. On the other hand, St Teresa's school, inaugurated in 1963, has a large majority of non-Catholic pupils, the result of the school's good reputation but creating a situation less than ideal.

ST JOSEPH'S DEANERY
(East Ayrshire)

The long road from Dumfries to Kirkconnel, winding and narrow for the heavy vehicles it has to carry and therefore not easy driving, continues in a north-westerly direction into Ayrshire and to the town of **Cumnock** and its parish of St John the Evangelist. The resident priest here also serves the parish of Our Lady of Lourdes and St Patrick in the town of **Auchinleck** and the parish of St Thomas in the town of **Muirkirk**. In 2011, the parish of St Joseph in Catrine, and which also embraced Mauchline, was closed. There used to be a parish also in New Cumnock with a small stone church of St Margaret, now demolished. Many years ago there was a parish in Birnie Knowe, but both church and village have disappeared. Some older people still remember the tragic death of one of the religious sisters who taught in the school there and who was killed by a train as she crossed the railway tracks.

St John's church in Cumnock is not a large church but was built and opened in 1884, with help from the 3rd Marquis of Bute, who owned property in the area and especially the mansion known as Dumfries House. Influenced by his hopes that it would be a place of liturgical excellence, the church design has certain pretensions, especially a chancel where a choir would sing the Divine Office. That grandiose hope was not realised but the chancel, which before Vatican II separated altar from nave, since the liturgical reform separates tabernacle from altar.

St Margaret's in New Cumnock had no architectural or liturgical pretensions but older people still tell of the occasions when the bishop came to confirm children of the parish. The recollection is not of any ceremonial nature, but rather gastronomic. Since there was not a priest's house nearby and the episcopal visitor had to be fed after Mass, the little church was filled, towards the end of the ceremony, with the aroma of bacon and eggs being fried in the sacristy, to be set before His Lordship on a specially set makeshift table.

Still on the theme of cooked breakfasts but bringing the subject up to date, the parish hall of St Thomas' in Muirkirk lies about one hundred yards from the church and directly across the road from the local kirk. On Sunday morning once a month, a group of St Thomas' parishioners prepare a full cooked breakfast in the hall at ten o'clock for those coming from the nine o'clock Mass and also for the Church of Scotland parishioners prior to their service at eleven o'clock. It is a very popular event and is a novel and imaginative way of encouraging a pleasant form of ecumenism.

The whole area of Cumnock and neighbourhood used to be a thriving district of coal mines but all of these are now closed and employment opportunities are scarce. Some parishes have closed, as has been noted. At one time there were five parish priests and two assistant priests resident in the district. Now one priest serves the entire area.

Four Catholic primary schools, at Cumnock, Auchinleck, Muirkirk and New Cumnock, are now reduced to St Patrick's in Auchinleck. St Conval's High School in Cumnock, which for many years provided the first four years of secondary education for Catholics and then, for some years, increased to all six years, has gone. Families, wishing to have a Catholic secondary education for their children, have to send them to Kilmarnock. Nevertheless, and despite the reduced state of the district, the people retain a sense of community and mutual support that is characteristic of mining towns. The Catholics of the area are noticeably friendly and caring people and with a readiness, in fact a desire, to share with others and to offer a generous helping hand to those who require it.

The more populous part of St Joseph's deanery and of East Ayrshire is **Kilmarnock**. The town has, in comparison with other parts of the diocese, a relatively high proportion of Catholics and there are still four parishes there: **St Joseph's** (dating from 1847) in the town centre and the other three built after the Second World War: **St Matthew's** (in New Farm Loch), **St Michael's** (in Bellfield and Shortlees) and **Our Lady of Mount Carmel** (in Onthank). There are priests resident in the first three of these parishes, while the priest in St Michael's serves Our Lady of Mount Carmel parish and, indeed, also Our Lady and St John's in

Stewarton, some five miles beyond Onthank and north of Kilmarnock.

Until recent years, Our Lady of Mount Carmel and Stewarton were in the charge of a community of Norbertine Canons (Premonstratensians), whose abbey is at Kilnacrott, Co. Cavan, but who, due to declining numbers, had to withdraw from the diocese at the start of the present century. Their former residence at Mount Carmel is now used by a small community of Sisters of Marie Reparatrice. Nazareth House, adjoining St Joseph's church, was a large building and a very well used home for the elderly. It closed early this century due to decreasing numbers of Poor Sisters of Nazareth, in whose charge it was.

St Joseph's Academy, recently housed in new buildings in New Farm Loch, is the Catholic secondary school for the deanery. Nearby is St Andrew's primary, also in a new building, which replaces two primary schools, St Columba's and St Matthew's, now closed. One other Catholic school is situated in the town – Mount Carmel primary school, near the church in the Onthank area of Kilmarnock.

Along the River Irvine eastwards from Kilmarnock, in an area known locally as "The Valley", there lie the two parishes of St Paul's in **Hurlford** and St Sophia's in **Galston**; in the latter parish but in the town of Darvel was the church of Our Lady of the Valley, a converted hall bought from the Church of Scotland around 1990 and recently closed. Formerly, both parishes, Galston and Hurlford, had their parish priests but now one priest is responsible for both. There is a Catholic primary school in Galston, but the school that used to be in Hurlford closed in the 1990s.

St Sophia's, opened in 1886, was also the recipient of the generous benefactions of the 3rd Marquis of Bute, as can be deduced from its appearance and design. It is a remarkable church, built in Byzantine style, of red brick, and modelled on Hagia Sophia in Istanbul (formerly Constantinople). Its capacity is less than might be imagined from its exterior since one of the arms of its Greek cross construction is an empty chancel, originally intended for a choir and a choral liturgy. The church's outstanding feature is its central dome, a very prominent landmark in the area. When St Sophia's needed very extensive repairs around the year 2000, a local hall belonging to the Church of Scotland was placed at the disposal of the parishioners for temporary, but long term, use and without cost. Non-Catholics also contributed to the funds which helped to meet the costs of the repairs at St Sophia's and there was a generous donation from the local Freemasons and publicly presented to parish representatives.

I remember an incident in the parish hall in Hurlford when, during a meeting, the loudspeakers failed. The person at the microphone, a parishioner, told us not to worry because "we've all got loud voices here". However, he was speaking in a local accent and "loud voices" came over as "lewd vices". Few seemed to notice the *double entendre*...

A couple of miles to the south of Kilmarnock lies Coodham or, to give it the full name it had when it belonged to the Passionists, **Fatima House, Coodham**. For more than forty years, from 1949 until it was sold, Coodham served as an excellent pastoral centre for the diocese and far beyond. Its closure was a serious loss.

ST MARY'S DEANERY
(North Ayrshire)

This deanery, the largest in terms of numbers of Catholics, can be considered as having two groups of parishes. One is the series along the coast of the Firth of Clyde; the other comprises the parishes inland from the coast.

Beginning with the coastal series and in the north, the first is **Largs**, a very popular town for excursions and days "at the seaside" because of its situation and the many attractions for visitors. The views across the Firth of Clyde are, in good weather, magnificent, my favourite being from above the town, on the Haylie Brae. The Catholic church, Our Lady, Star of the Sea, but commonly known simply as St Mary's, dates from 1962. It has a striking location on the sea front and is one of the finest churches in the diocese.

Another religious feature of the parish is the monastery of Benedictines of the Sacred Heart (Tyburn nuns). Their monastery is a former hotel and, in addition to the community of nuns, it offers residential accommodation for private retreats as well as a welcome for those simply wishing to visit the chapel and small historical museum. These Benedictines came to the rescue of the Benedictines of the Blessed Sacrament who, in their Dumfries convent, had reached crisis point and seemed destined to close. The Tyburn nuns sent a few of their number from London to assume control of the situation and, a few years later, the remaining Dumfries nuns, at the invitation of Tyburn and with permission of the Holy See, opted to become Tyburn nuns and the merged community left Dumfries for Largs.

In the very north of the parish, in the village of Skelmorlie six miles from Largs, there is a large house, known as Lincluden, on the sea front. It belonged to Archbishop Charles Eyre, archbishop of Glasgow (1878 - 1902), who bequeathed it as a holiday home to the Sisters of Notre Dame de Namur, who had come to Glasgow to teach in a number of newly opened Catholic schools. More recently, the sisters have made the house a place suitable for people coming for retreats and conferences and other meetings. Sadly the property, which is known as the Notre Dame Apostolic Centre, has been sold because the sisters can no longer continue the work.

Largs has a Catholic primary school. The Catholic secondary school is in Saltcoats but many children simply transfer from St Mary's primary school to the adjoining non-denominational Largs Academy.

There is one "overseas" parish in the diocese, on the island of Cumbrae, just under two miles across the Firth of Clyde from Largs. There is a frequent ferry service between Largs and the island; the road round the island is about twelve miles long. At the south end of the island is the only town, **Millport**, and it is there that the church, Our Lady of Perpetual Succour, built in 1958, is located.

Previously, the Catholic church had been a small stone building, originally part of the stables in the grounds of The Garrison House. This latter, a large, handsome structure in the centre of Millport, had been built in 1745 for the accommodation of the captain and crew of the Revenue cutter *The Royal George*, used to combat smuggling in the Firth of Clyde. The 3rd Marquis of Bute bought The Garrison in the nineteenth century and it was then that the little building in the grounds, having served for a time as a Sunday school for children of the Episcopal Church, was given over for Catholic use. That old church had a very distinctive and curious arrangement of seating since the chairs and benches and pews seemed to have been garnered from a wide variety of sources. In those long-gone pre-World War II days, a priest was brought over on Sunday mornings in summer from Largs in a small motor boat, weather permitting.

The present church had a resident priest until a few years ago. Latterly I made strenuous efforts and indulged in extensive advertising in attempts to find a priest to take over the attractive work as parish priest on the island. These efforts were only partially successful, some priests soon leaving, others being unsuited to the task. Now, Millport depends on the parish priest of Largs and, sometimes, on the kindness of one or other retired Scottish priest.

Millport possesses one ecclesiastical building of which it is justly proud. On the same road as the Catholic church, but a little higher up the hill, stands the Cathedral of the Isles and the Collegiate Church of the Holy Spirit, which belongs to the diocese of Argyll and the Isles of the Scottish Episcopal Church. The cathedral, a result of the munificence of the Earl of Glasgow in the mid-nineteenth century, is a small and very beautiful gothic building standing in its own grounds and providing a very fine adornment for the island.

Catholic children in Millport attend the only primary school on the island and, for secondary education, cross daily in the ferry to attend Largs Academy.

Following the coast southwards from Largs, the next parish is St Bride's, **West Kilbride**, which also serves the adjoining town of Seamill. The parish has a resident parish priest but no Catholic school. Most Catholic children attend the local non-denominational school while some go to the Catholic primary in Ardrossan.

A little further south are the "Three Towns", Ardrossan, Saltcoats and Stevenston, all situated contiguously along the shores of the Firth of Clyde.

Ardrossan is the largest parish, numerically, in the diocese of Galloway, the Catholic population, according to *The Catholic Directory for Scotland*, being 4000. The church is St Peter in Chains', an early work of Jack Coia who later became well known as the principal partner of Gillespie, Kidd & Coia, Architects, who were responsible for several Catholic churches in Scotland, mainly in Glasgow, as well as for St Peter's College, the inter-diocesan major seminary in Cardross, near Dumbarton. The seminary is a large concrete structure which, although praised by architectural and other authorities, unfortunately proved unsuitable for its proposed purpose and lay derelict and abandoned for many years. All Coia churches are distinctive in style, the early examples, as in Ardrossan, being of brick and the later of concrete. Although impressive architecturally, some of the buildings are of debatable success pastorally and liturgically.

In 2004 fire broke out in the presbytery in Ardrossan and the parish priest, Fr Michael Lynch, died in the blaze. The tragedy occurred very soon after my successor's arrival as bishop and was compounded by the house being so badly damaged that it had to be demolished. The house, being listed (along with the church), had to be replaced by a new building exteriorly almost identical to it.

Saltcoats, until recently, had two parishes, Our Lady, Star of the Sea, usually called St Mary's, (1856) and St Brendan's (1961). The latter developed serious defects and became unsafe. It was demolished and was not replaced. Instead, the two parishes were united. Like St Peter's in Ardrossan, St Mary's is situated very near the sea front and, although these are very favourable locations, the churches are not central for the parishioners. St Mary's is by far the oldest Catholic church in the three towns and its exterior retains the dignity of mid-nineteenth century gothic. However, with the liturgical changes of the 1960s, the interior underwent a transformation with the high altar and sanctuary now occupying the centre of what originally was a side wall. The main entrance is opposite the sanctuary and the original entrance and sanctuary have become lateral spaces or shrines. The resulting 90 degrees change allows the congregation to be nearer the altar, but the sanctuary, although adequate length-wise, is somewhat cramped in front of the altar.

Among the parishioners of St Mary's is Peter Reilly, well into his nineties, who has been a daily Mass server for over eighty years and still exercises that ministry each morning.

St John's church in **Stevenston**, built in 1963 and centrally situated, replaced an earlier church constructed over school classrooms and increasingly inadequate as the town extended inland in the years after World War II. The present church is remarkable for the extensive and beautiful stained glass which provides much of the side and rear walls of the buiding and was designed and produced by the celebrated French master, Gabriel Loire of Chartres.

Each of the three towns has its own Catholic primary school. Catholic secondary education for the three towns and, in fact, for the whole deanery, is provided by the recently opened St Matthew's Academy, a school which results from the amalgamation of two schools, now closed, St Michael's Academy in Kilwinning, and St Andrew's Academy in Saltcoats, on whose site the new school is located.

Like the coastal parishes of the deanery, the inland parishes also follow a line approximately from north to south.

In the north is **Kilbirnie**, an industrial town that is, these days, a place of relatively high unemployment but it also has its religious inheritance in a fine pre-Reformation church, still in use but as the "Auld Kirk" and belonging to the Church of Scotland. The local Catholic church of St Brigid dates from around 1860 and, in the last century, was enlarged by moving the sanctuary further back and filling the resultant space with an extension of the nave. The parish priest died in 2013 and so St Brigid's is now served from Dalry. The primary school has the same patron as the church but, curiously, with a different spelling – Bridget.

The church in **Beith** was built in 1816 and had been a Protestant church until bought by the diocese in 1947 and placed under the patronage of Our Lady of Perpetual Succour. It is a small building, square in shape and with two side aisles. In that respect and in having a tiny, cramped sacristy, it is similar to Holy Trinity church in Lockerbie, which also started life as a Reformed church. Beith had a resident parish priest until a few years ago but is at present served from Dalry.

The church of St Palladius in **Dalry** is the second oldest Catholic church in Ayrshire, built in 1851. The nave is similar in size and shape to that in Beith, but the sanctuary is spacious. There have been considerable renovations in St Palladius' during recent years, both in the church and in the house. The parish has a resident parish priest and a Catholic primary school. The international pharmaceutics firm, Roche, provides much of the local employment.

The church of St Winin in the relatively large town of **Kilwinning** is located away from the main thoroughfares and can, in consequence, be difficult to find. In the years following the

Second Vatican Council, the interior had a 90 degree reorientation similar to that in St Mary's in Saltcoats, although it was built much later, in 1937.

The parish has two Catholic primary schools, St Winning's (note the different spelling) and St Luke's, an indication of the sizable Catholic population in the town, in spite of Kilwinning's reputation as a stronghold of Freemasonry and the Orange Order. Perhaps at one time in the past there was overt hostility and bigotry. If such attitudes exist today, they no longer constitute a serious hazard or nuisance for Catholics.

Kilwinning's most important and famous building is the abbey, founded by Benedictine monks from Kelso between 1162 and 1188, but pillaged at and after the Reformation and now with only the walls still extant. I was invited to an ecumenical event to mark the eighth centenary of the abbey's foundation and, as we entered the precincts, the local minister remarked to me that there was a certain appropriate significance in our both being there. "The abbey belonged to you for its first four hundred years and to us for the next four hundred". ("*Quam dispar exitus!*", the thought occurred to me). Passing into the open lawn of the nave, we disturbed two little boys playing football and both dressed in miniature outfits of Celtic F.C.!

Just outside the town, on the Dalry road, the Sacred Heart Fathers (Dehonians) own **Smithstone House** and its grounds (bought 1970). This "House of Prayer and Spirituality" has been a place of great pastoral and spiritual benefit for the diocese and beyond, offering retreats, courses, talks, spiritual direction and opportunities for adult growth in faith and prayer. Unfortunately, it is not active at present, due to declining numbers of Sacred Heart Fathers as well as ill health and increasing age among them.

It is probably unfair to include the historic town of **Irvine** among the inland places of the deanery since it lies at the mouth of the River Irvine. However, it is not normally considered "a seaside town" or a place for holidays but, rather, commercial, industrial and residential.

The original Catholic church, still thriving (and with a new parish hall) is **St Mary's** (1875). It is somewhat hidden in what may be described as a central backwater, as a result of post-war rearrangement of streets. Irvine was designated "a new town" in the 1950s and several new parishes and churches were planned for the much enlarged town. In the event, the extension was less than first proposed and so only two new Catholic churches were built, one of which was closed at the end of 2012.

The church of St Margaret of Scotland (1982) was a building which also served as a hall. Located in the Castlepark housing estate in the town, it had an enthusiastic community with a lively liturgy. Latterly, the parish no longer had its own priest, but shared with St Mary's, the parish into which St Margaret's has now been absorbed. The hall-church, house and connecting passages of the former St Margaret's complex are all of simple construction, designed locally and at comparatively low cost.

The other Catholic church in Irvine serves those parts of the "new town" to the east of the older section of Irvine. Bishop McGee, my predecessor, entrusted this parish, whose patron is **St John Ogilvie**, to the Sacred Heart Fathers, who also are at Smithstone House. They have served the parish well since the church was inaugurated in 1979. The parishioners are "Glasgow overspill" and live in a number of districts, each with its own name. There is a good sense of community among those who attend church, but there also seems to be a considerable number of families who are not regular attenders, as well as other family homes where the husband/father is no longer there and another man has moved in. Sadly, many of the children who present themselves for the sacraments of confirmation and Holy Communion are seldom, if ever, seen again at Mass. And, of course, there are numerous homes, nominally Catholic, but with no Catholic involvement, either at church or at the local Catholic primary school. Undoubtedly, similar situations to these exist in most, probably all, parishes in the diocese, but St John Ogilvie's seems to be among those where the problem is particularly acute.

St John Ogilvie's church is in the district called Bourtreehill and it has another problem in addition to those just mentioned. The church/house/hall complex of buildings is an elaborate, ambitious and costly structure which, in many ways, has proved impractical in use, subject to leaks and other defects and with a financial burden that is far beyond the ability of the parishioners to meet; after all, they were not responsible for incurring the expense. Eventually, once the parish had valiantly raised a reasonable amount of money, all the remaining debts were paid off by the diocese, but only after many meetings, complaints and threats, much unpleasantness and disclaiming of responsibility among architects, contractors and tradesmen. The building has won several awards from artistic, cultural and professional groups, none of whom has to live in the house, worship in the church or pay for the construction or for the regular repairs.

Irvine is at the southern extremity of North Ayrshire, bordering South Ayrshire and St Margaret's deanery, the final stage of this tour of the diocese of Galloway.

ST MARGARET'S DEANERY
(South Ayrshire)

Like St Mary's deanery, St Margaret's deanery also has some parishes on the coast (five of them) and some inland (four).

Troon is the most northerly of the coastal parishes. Its handsome and impressive listed church, built in 1911, has, as its patrons, Our Lady of the Assumption and St Meddan. The latter is a local saint and there is also, in the town, a Church of Scotland place of worship called St Meddan's. Details of the saint's life are obscure, in fact unknown. The Catholic primary school, called St Patrick's, is a new building which replaces older, cramped and now demolished premises, one section of which was the original church of the nineteenth century. The parish priest also has responsibility for the villages of Symington and Dundonald, but the latter no longer has a Sunday Mass in the public hall.

There are golf courses throughout the diocese, but perhaps especially in South Ayrshire. Three of the most celebrated are Troon Old Course, Prestwick Old Course and Turnberry (near Girvan). The first and third of these are regular venues for the Open Championship, while the second, though no longer hosting that event, was in fact the venue, in 1860, of the very first Open Championship.

Prestwick is also a coastal parish, a few miles south of Troon. The patron of its church is St Quivox, another local but obscure holy person, commemorated not only in Prestwick but also in a nearby hamlet, itself called St Quivox and with a pre-Reformation church of the same name and still in use, but as the local kirk of the Church of Scotland.

The Catholic church in Prestwick was quite small when built in the 1930s but was skilfully enlarged after the Second World War and recently has had a new hall/parish centre attached. The Catholic primary school is St Ninian's, possibly thus named to avoid the error of thinking it to be in the hamlet of St Quivox.

The name of the town denotes its clerical origins ("place or district of the priest") but perhaps Prestwick is best known for its international airport, which dates back to the very early days of aviation. It narrowly escaped the ignominy of being officially named Elvis Presley International Airport on the extremely flimsy grounds that, during or after the Second World War, a US military plane, on which the singer was a passenger, had landed there to refuel.

The parish priest of Prestwick is also parish priest, non-resident, of St Ann's, **Mossblown**, a couple of miles inland. This parish comprises not only Mossblown but also the villages of Tarbolton and Annbank, the place from which the parish derives its name.

Also inland, but to the south of Mossblown, is St Clare's, **Drongan.** This parish, which also includes the village of Coylton, is in the anomalous position of being partly in East Ayrshire (Drongan itself) and partly in South Ayrshire (Coylton) but wholly in St Margaret's deanery. In fact, the entire territory of the parish (Drongan and Coylton) is much nearer to Ayr than to Kilmarnock, or even to Cumnock.

Both parishes (St Ann's and St Clare's) are in former coal mining areas but, with the pits now closed, there is a high rate of unemployment and of the elderly retired. But the traditions of neighbourliness and hospitality, characteristic of mining communities, are still very much alive. Neither parish has a Catholic school within its boundaries any longer and, like St Ann's, St Clare's is also served by a non-resident priest, in this case, from Ayr.

The church of St Francis Xavier in **Waterside** (or Dunaskin) is on the main road from Ayr to Castle Douglas. The place used to have large iron works with rows of cottages and some shops owned by the company and for the use of the employees. But the industrial site is gone and Waterside is now reduced to a single row of cottages. St Francis Xavier's church has the dubious distinction of being the only one in the diocese which is situated on a road with no speed restriction for vehicles except the general 60 mph limit. The church once had a presbytery and a convent next door;

there is still a hall adjoining, but the other two buildings have gone, victims of dry rot as well as of the shortage of priests and religious sisters. The church, served by the priest from St Paul's in Ayr, still survives, although looking very lonely and isolated. Parishioners come from Patna and Dalmellington, both four to five miles distant, Patna to the north-west in the direction of Ayr, Dalmellington to the south-east, towards Castle Douglas. Surprisingly, since it is not large, the parish which, defying logic, is in East Ayrshire, has a Catholic primary school, St Xavier's, formerly near the old iron works but now re-established in new premises in Patna.

The fourth inland parish in the deanery is **Maybole**, situated between Ayr and Girvan. The church, Our Lady and St Cuthbert's, is a beautiful neo-gothic stone building (1878). It has a spectacular and lofty location which enhances its appearance but tests the parishioners' lungs, especially of the elderly. The inclusion of St Cuthbert in the church's name reminds us that the village of Kirkoswald is not far distant; thus two Northumbrian saints of the seventh century, a king and a bishop, are commemorated in neighbouring Ayrshire towns.

Two miles south of Maybole are the ruins of Crossraguel Abbey, built in the early thirteenth century for a community of Cluniac Benedictines. Just after the collapse of most Catholic life and practice in Scotland when the Catholic Church was proscribed in 1560, the abbot of Crossraguel, Quintin Kennedy, a zealous Catholic and thus something of a rarity at the time, challenged John Knox to a public debate. The confrontation took place in the open air in Maybole and lasted for three days. In fact, at the end of the third day, the two were still disputing on the first argument adduced by the abbot in his chosen task of vindicating the sacrificial nature of the Mass. With such little progress made and no agreement in sight, the debate was not resumed on the fourth day. Perhaps spectator – or sectarian – interest was exhausted by then and the two men no longer had an audience.

The southernmost parish of the deanery and one of the largest in area in the diocese is centred on the seaside town of **Girvan**. The church was opened in 1860. The parish has the unusual title of Sacred Hearts of Jesus and Mary and has the distinction of having there a community of the Sisters of St Joseph of Cluny since 1879. They were invited to Girvan to be in charge of the Catholic school which, for years, had both primary and secondary sections. The school also accepted boarders as well as day pupils. Over the years, the boarding facility closed and the primary section became a separate school. The secondary section continued as Sacred Heart Academy, but with fewer and fewer religious sisters teaching there. Eventually, with the number of pupils only around the sixty mark for the whole secondary course of six years, Sacred Heart Academy closed, its pupils having the option of either Queen Margaret Academy in Ayr or the non-denominational Girvan Academy. The large building, comprising both convent and school, property of the sisters, was sold and transformed into flats, the small remaining community of Sisters of St Joseph of Cluny occupying the flat that adjoins the church, allowing them direct private access to it.

Some two miles north of Girvan is the large country mansion known as Trochrague. This property was gifted to the Sisters of St Joseph of Cluny after World War II and they ran it as a guest house, particularly for those who sought a quiet holiday in rural tranquillity and a religious setting. In the 1990s the Congregation donated Trochrague to the Jericho Society, who use it to provide holidays for families and others who would normally find such facilities beyond their means.

By the roadside at the north entry to Girvan there is a memorial stone marking the spot at which a policeman, Alexander Ross, was killed trying to prevent an Orange procession from entering the town on 12th July 1831.

The resident parish priest of Girvan has now also assumed the duties of parish priest of Maybole, where he resides for a couple of days each week. The small inland town of Dailly is within the parish boundaries of Girvan, as is the village of Ballantrae, some thirteen miles south of Girvan and only a few miles from the boundary with Dumfries & Galloway.

Ayr has two churches and two parishes, **St Margaret's**, the cathedral parish, and **St Paul's**, in the south part of the town and opened in 1967. Both have resident priests and, attached to the church buildings, their parish halls. The priest in St Margaret's acts as chaplain to the Ayr Hospital as well as the Ayrshire Hospice. His opposite number in St Paul's, in addition to serving St Francis Xavier's parish of Waterside, is chaplain to Ailsa (psychiatric) Hospital.

The Catholic secondary school for the whole deanery is Queen Margaret Academy, situated in St Paul's parish. There is only one Catholic primary school in the town and it is in St Margaret's parish but called St John's, an appropriate recognition of the patron of the town, St John the Baptist.

St Margaret's church was erected and opened in 1827 and is the oldest Catholic church in Ayrshire. Because of its age and since it is close to the busy centre of Ayr, it has always been seen as the mother church of the area and it was fitting that it was chosen and designated as the cathedral of the diocese in 2007. It underwent a very thorough makeover and rededication in the 1990s and early years of this century, with completely renovated sanctuary and new furnishings, a central aisle, stained glass windows, new organ, new large sacristy and toilet and many other improvements, including a brighter colour scheme for the ceiling and walls, new lighting and new central heating. All the improvements were costly, but substantial grants from Heritage Scotland and the National Lottery plus some very successful and imaginative fundraising saw the bills paid off in a remarkably short time.

The parish already had a new presbytery (1970s) and a new hall (1980s) so the complex serves very well as a liturgical and social centre for the diocese. Admittedly, the church is not large but there is only one annual occasion when the lack of space is a serious problem. That occasion is the Mass of Chrism on the Tuesday evening of Holy Week, which is always a most impressive liturgy with the bishop presiding and priests and laity gathered from all over the diocese, a truly moving and beautiful event.

The church of the Good Shepherd, built in 1957 and situated in a large post-war housing development in the north-east of the town, was a good choice to serve as the cathedral for about fifty years. Larger than St Margaret's and in a poorer district of the town, it had those points in its favour. However, by the year 2000 there were three large problems. The building needed extensive and costly repair work; normal Sunday attendance, two Masses, had dropped to about eighty people; and, with no proper parking places, cars left in the surrounding streets had become subject to frequent vandalism. Bishop John Cunningham, my successor, received the authorisation of the Holy See to make St Margaret's the cathedral church and to have Good Shepherd church demolished. On the site where the church stood, there is now an attractive cluster of flats which preserve some of the architectural features of the church, especially the whole façade with its tower and statue of the Good Shepherd. This outcome is some compensation for the unavoidable loss of a well loved church.

A COMMUNITY OF COMMUNITIES?

In the Apostles Creed we proclaim our faith in the "Communion of Saints" (although, strangely and sadly, that item is not found in the Nicene Creed). The Communion of Saints applies not only to those "who have gone before us in faith" but to us still on earth. The Church, both universal and local, is the People of God, the Mystical Body of Christ, and therefore the Communion of Saints and, *a fortiori*, a community. The local Church is strictly speaking the diocese but the reality of community is more effectively felt in the parish. The persons who form a community have a sense of belonging, of being accepted by the others in the group, of being important to them, cared for by them, missed by them if absent; and this awareness is reciprocal and shared. "Communion" adds to community the element of the presence of Jesus Christ, the Good Shepherd and all that that title means to us.

The sense of community which a parish should have is best exemplified in the congregation at Sunday Mass. In practice, it is best felt in parishes where there is only one Sunday Mass. Where there is more than one and people attend "their" Mass, those at one Mass do not, in general, know those who are at the other Mass(es).

The parishioners who are frequently at weekday Masses have their own sense of a small community; likewise the members of small faith-sharing groups, where such exist. The same is, or was, the case with members of societies, guilds, confraternities and the like which used to play an important part in parish life, but much less so nowadays.

An area where community is very evident is that of pilgrimages. Galloway diocese has its pilgrimage annually to Whithorn and St Ninian's Cave. A greater awareness of community is apparent in the diocesan pilgrimages to Lourdes every second year and, perhaps most of all, in diocesan pilgrimages to the Holy Land.

These latter take place every second year, alternating with Lourdes, although unfortunately, due to unrest in the Middle East and increasing prices, they have been less regular in the last few years. Parishes also have organised pilgrimages, especially to Rome and to Salamanca, and there is no doubt that, apart from other benefits, these greatly foster community.

The very first question in the diocesan questionnaire of 1982 intrigues me. "*Do you think that your parish has become a community?*" That question probably intrigued many of the respondents and puzzled them too. A majority answered in the affirmative, a sizable minority in the negative and something approaching a quarter of the respondents did not know. In fact, the "no" and "don't know" votes combined exceeded the "yes" votes 4,173 to 3,443. Of course, it all depends on what you mean by "community". My own answer to the question would, I think, be "yes", but understood in the sense that most parishes are on the road there. The awareness of being a community (or not) will vary greatly from person to person but, slowly, the recognition of the call to be a community and to achieve that aim is gradually developing in the parishes. Perfection will never be fully achieved, but we must keep trying.

The Renew process was very effective in bringing people together, especially through small groups. The reformed liturgy with its emphasis on participation, today's ecclesiology expressed in homilies – these are also some of the factors operative in forming community. Here are some others that I think play their part:

Socialising before and after Sunday Mass
Taking part in weekday Masses
Masses for particular occasions, especially for sick, with anointing
Attending parish social events and occasions
Visits/Holy Communion to sick, housebound, lonely, bereaved
Reporting from pastoral councils, both diocesan and parish
Various societies and groups
- St Vincent de Paul
- Union of Catholic Mothers
- Justice & Peace
- Catholic Men's Society
- Charismatic Renewal etc.

Weekly parish bulletins, preferably interesting and attractive

The Galloway News (and its more modest predecessor, *The Galloway Newsletter*)
Adult growth in faith groups, viz.,
- Rite of Christian Initiation of Adults
- Certificate in Pastoral Ministry
- Small faith-sharing groups (in the manner of the Renew process)

Responding to appeals for new ministers or tasks.

For a parish to be a community, relationships among and between its members should be correct, respectful and friendly. There is one relationship whose correctness is a vital one – the relationship that the priest has with the parishioners. Although the priest is the pastor and leader of the faithful laity, he should always remember that, generally speaking, they lived there before he arrived and will continue to be there when he goes; this fact plays its part in the laity's feelings and attitudes, and rightly so. The priest should be constantly aware of it, and especially when he thinks it necessary to use his authority. "*Suaviter in modo, fortiter in re*" is good advice.

The Catholic Church lays down a number of laws and norms to regulate activities and govern relationships in parishes (*Code of Canon Law*, canons 515-552). Specifically, each parish must have a finance committee and, if the bishop "considers it opportune" (which I did), a pastoral council (canons 537 & 536) but these bodies have only a consultative vote. This last point should never be seen as practically allowing the priest to ignore their opinions or to neglect to consult them. If fact, if he is wise, the priest will listen carefully to their opinions and take them fully into consideration. On the other hand, lay people should remember that in "churchy" subjects (liturgy, doctrine, canon law), the priest is a trained and experienced professional so that his lack of enthusiasm for a proposal should not be presumed to be due to obscurantism or clerical quirkiness.

Why should the parish be a community? Because the teaching of Jesus is that his disciples should not be individuals but should be united in faith, hope and love, working together to form the Kingdom of God and to consider themselves brothers and sisters in the family of God. Above all, the great event of the Mass calls us to be united with Christ, taking part together with him in the renewal of his Paschal Mystery. In fact, we are called to be not merely a COMMUNITY of people who are friends with one another and act in collaboration, but through baptism and our union with Jesus Christ, we become that deeper unity that we call COMMUNION, the "COMMUNION OF SAINTS".

To conclude on a positive note, the diocese is a community of communities, a communion of communions, because it is truly a church, a local church, one of thousands of local churches that, united, form the communion of the worldwide Catholic Church.

The Holy Land: Pilgrim memories

INTRODUCTION

If matters had gone according to plan, my first visit to the Holy Land would have been in 1947. I was in the British army, stationed in India. That great country was preparing for independence and therefore thousands of British soldiers were being withdrawn. Like many of them, I was transferred to the Suez Canal Zone of Egypt.

At that time, Palestine was under the Mandate of Great Britain and one of the principal duties was the maintenance of law and order. This was becoming increasingly difficult due to the Jewish desire for a national homeland in Palestine, as had been promised by the Balfour Declaration of 1917. After the end of the Second World War, various Israeli groups in Palestine, impatient for political change, were responsible for a campaign of violence, much of which was directed against the British army units in the country.

So I found myself one of many British soldiers being held in Egypt, awaiting transfer to Palestine to strengthen forces there. The prospect of being stationed in the Holy Land would normally have been a very pleasant one; but in the circumstances of violent and lethal attacks by such Israeli elements as Irgun, Hagannah and the Stern Gang, the Holy Land had lost much of its attraction.

In the event, while on hold in the Canal Zone, I was given a short home leave; and, during that time in Scotland, I received notification that, as a student, I was to be allowed early release from military service. Since then, I have often wondered what happened to those colleagues who were not so fortunate and who awaited, with trepidation, the dreaded order ro proceed to Palestine.

It was not until sixteen years later, in 1963, that I made my first visit to the Holy Land. I was a member of the teaching staff at St Peter's College, the major seminary of the archdiocese of Glasgow and the dioceses of Motherwell and Paisley. Our summer holidays lasted for two months and I made use of the annual opportunities to travel. Mostly, my destination was westwards, to the United States and Canada where I visited many places, defraying my expenses by supplying in different parishes. However, in 1963, a colleague and I decided to go eastwards for a change and to make a pilgrimage to the Holy Land.

With two months at our disposal, we planned to see as many places as possible. From Munich we travelled on the Orient Express, via Yugoslavia and Bulgaria (very daring in those days of the Cold War and of Soviet domination in Eastern Europe) and across the north of Greece to Turkey and Istanbul. Actually, the Orient Express broke down about fifty miles short of its destination and, along with all our fellow passengers, we had to scamper across the railway tracks and clamber aboard a slow local train which took us to Istanbul.

After some days there, we went to Izmir (for Ephesus) and then took the long bus journey to Konya (Iconium, in the New Testament) and a train through the mountains of Cilicia to the south coast of Turkey at Mersin. (I have described our travels through Turkey in chapter 3, *Being a Bishop in Scotland*, in the section entitled *The delights of Turkish travel.*)

Our original plan had been to continue from Turkey into Syria in order to visit Damascus and some other places before going to Jordan and the Holy Land. However, the Syrian authorities denied us the necessary visas. Plan B had to be put into operation: a plane from Adana (Turkey) to Beirut (Lebanon), a night in that city and then a short flight to an airport near Ramallah, a few miles north of Jerusalem.

Here I must explain the political situation in the Holy Land in 1963. In those days the state of Israel consisted of Galilee (in the north of Palestine/Holy Land) and the western parts of Samaria and Judea; the city of Jerusalem was divided, Israel having the western, newer section of the city, the Arabs retaining the eastern section (the Old City). The eastern parts of Samaria and Judea, as well as the Old City of Jerusalem, were incorporated into Jordan.

Our first few days in Jerusalem were spent in the Old City where many of the sacred sites are located, above all the Holy Sepulchre basilica which contains Mount Calvary and Christ's Tomb. Bethlehem, a few miles to the south, was also accessible, but by a circuitous route since the direct road went through Israeli territory and was therefore closed.

After our stay in the Old City we crossed into Jewish Jerusalem, a crossing which, in those days, was possible only by passing through the so-called Mandelbaum Gate (which was very near the Anglican Cathedral of St George, in the north of the city). An Arab taxi took us to a spot from where we had to walk, with our cases, a couple of hundred metres along an open road to where the Israeli taxis waited. One of these completed our transfer from Arab to Israeli Jerusalem. I recall that we made the crossing on a Saturday and, as we passed through the strict Jewish district of Mea Shearim, some passers-by showed their anger at a car being driven through the area on the Sabbath.

On our second or third night in west Jerusalem we were awakened by gunfire. It was rather frightening, mainly because we were unaware of its seriousness. Might it be the outbreak of another war between Israelis and Arabs? In the morning we were informed that such gunfire (with light weapons) occurred from time to time between army units of the two sides. Our lodgings were near the "frontier", just alongside the church of the Dormition of Our Lady. This church has a high tower which Israeli soldiers occupied; from it they fired at the Arab units who directed their return fire at the same tower. Our fears were quietened to an extent, but we were advised that perhaps we should not delay our departure, just in case…

We went north that day to Galilee and found there beauty and peace, staying on the Mount of Beatitudes in a hostel run by Italian nuns and with a view down to the Sea of Galilee and beyond, in the distance, the Golan Heights. We were very fortunate to meet a friendly trio from Genoa (two priests and their sister) who invited us to accompany them in their car to visit the sites associated with Jesus in Galilee.

When our time in the Holy Land came to an end, the two of us took a ship from Haifa to Piraeus (with time ashore *en route* in Cyprus and in Rhodes) and then, a few days later, a ferry from Patras to Brindisi. On that latter crossing, our ship, on leaving Patras harbour, collided side to side with a smaller ferry, dragging off part of its bridge and a lifeboat or two as its passengers threw themselves to the deck in astonishment and horror; our ferry sustained little damage – the hull slightly dented – as we continued on our way without stopping. Perhaps such collisions are fairly routine in the busy harbour at Patras. When last seen, the other ferry was still afloat.

Since I became a bishop, my pilgrimages to the Holy Land have become quite frequent. The first was just a few weeks after my ordination and, in fact, had been arranged prior to my nomination. That pilgrimage, in July 1981, was with two friends from East Kilbride, where I had been parish priest for the previous seven years.

Conditions in the Holy Land were much changed since my previous visit eighteen years earlier. As a consequence of the 1967 war, Israel now occupied all of the west bank of the Jordan river so that the whole of Palestine was under Israeli rule and the Mandelbaum Gate was history.

In Jerusalem we stayed at the Casa Nova, run by Franciscans and very near the Holy Sepulchre basilica; in Galilee, we found accommodation in the Church of Scotland hospice in Tiberias, right on the waterfront of the Sea of Galilee.

All my subsequent Holy Land visits, perhaps ten or twelve in number, have been on pilgrimages organised by our diocese of Galloway. These began in the mid-1980s and normally have taken place every second year, alternating with our diocesan pilgrimages to Lourdes. On one or two occaions, however, our Holy Land pilgrimages have had to be foregone, for safety reasons. Flights have been by various airlines, including El Al. In recent years we have sometimes managed to charter a plane so that we can fly nonstop from and to our local airport in Prestwick. Security is always very strict before boarding the plane, both in Britain and in Israel. Luggage is thoroughly checked and searched and passengers are taken aside by Israeli security people and questioned individually, both about themselves and about their luggage. The process is slow and irritating, but accepted as a necessary inconvenience.

Our custom has been to divide our time between Judea and Galilee and to use hotels in Jerusalem (or Bethlehem) and Tiberias (or Nazareth). The coaches at our disposal are modern and comfortable and skilfully driven; hotels are satisfactory, whether in Judea (Arab hotels) or in Galilee (Jewish).

Before I say something about the holy places to be visited, it should be noted that, at present, the Holy Land, though wholly under Israeli control, is divided into Israel proper (i.e. Israel as it was until the 1967 war) and what is called either the West Bank (of the Jordan river) or the Occupied Territories; the latter has a certain amount of Arab autonomy but not as an independent state. In addition, the West Bank has many Israeli Settlements which, along with their access roads, are for Israeli residents only and have been built in defiance of UN resolutions. The fact of the settlements, as well as the desire of many Arab Palestinian refugees to regain their property in Israel occupied by Jewish people for decades, and the problem of the future status of Jerusalem (to be capital of Israel? or capital of Arab Palestine? or a divided city?) constitute the three major obstacles to real progress towards a peaceful and lasting solution for the political future of the Holy Land.

Let me now give some fuller descriptions of the holy places of the Holy Land, following the general chronology of our Lord's life, which is different from a usual pilgrimage itinerary. (These sections were written in 2011.)

ANNUNCIATION AND INCARNATION (NAZARETH IN GALILEE)

In Our Lord's time, Nazareth was a rather insignificant village, off the beaten tracks of travellers and commerce. Its citizens, if not despised by other Galileans, had no great claim to religious, political or historic importance.

Nowadays it is a large and busy town, situated (as the whole of Galilee is) in Israel proper. The population of the old part of the town is Arab, both Christian and Muslim; there is a growing new part, Upper Nazareth, which is mainly Jewish.

The outstanding building in Nazareth is the Basilica of the Annunciation, a huge construction of the 1960s and completed in 1969. It has two levels and an open crypt containing the remains of what are believed to be the house in which the Virgin Mary lived when the angel Gabriel appeared to her to announce God's choice of her as the human mother of his incarnate Son.

I have to admit that I find the basilica rather unattractive, too grand or even grandiose, and somewhat overpowering and triumphalistic. In the spacious courtyard which surrounds the basilica, the boundary walls have a series of mosaics representing many nations. Scotland's mosaic has a number of motifs (but the choice of these is not necessarily the most obvious and the spelling of the identifying words is not perfect).

The basilica is on the main street which runs through the Old Town. Next to it is a public square or garden on which the Muslim authorities had begun to construct a mosque that was to rival or exceed the basilica in size, until construction was stopped by the civil authorities.

In addition to the basilica, there are some lesser Christian churches in Nazareth, claimed to be built, for example, on the sites of the Holy Family's house and St Joseph's workshop. There is also a public fountain to which, even in the time of Jesus, people went to draw water.

Nazareth should be an attractive place, but somehow I do not find it so. Perhaps it is because the basilica is so dominating, perhaps because on one of our visits there was a sudden cloudburst which caused immediate flooding, perhaps because the main street is so crowded with shops, people and, above all, impatient and noisy traffic. I admit, of course, that this negative judgment about Nazareth is very subjective and possibly unfair.

THE VISITATION (EIN KAREM IN JUDEA)

Ein Karem was, until recently, a quiet and pleasant Arab village, just south-west of Jerusalem. It is still a pleasant place to visit but now it is a suburb of the city and populated mainly by Jewish people.

There are two Catholic churches in Ein Karem. The church of the Visitation (of the Virgin Mary to her cousin Elizabeth) is on a hillside and is reached by a fairly steep and narrow road, about a kilometre from the centre. The church and its surroundings are quiet and peaceful and, from the front of the church, there are fine views of tree-clad hills to the west and north.

The other church, commemorating the birth and circumcision of John the Baptist, is in the village, just a short walk from the main street. It is larger than the church of the Visitation, and an older and more sombre construction. The interior walls are adorned with some beautiful tiles from Talavera in Spain since the church has been served for many years by Spanish Franciscans. In the paved area in front of the church, the enclosing wall has a number of large panels of Spanish ceramic tiles, each panel with the text of the *Benedictus* canticle in a different language. (St Luke's gospel tells us that Zechariah proclaimed the canticle when he recovered his speech at the circumcision of his son.)

BIRTH AND INFANCY OF JESUS (BETHLEHEM)

Bethlehem is a town I love to visit. Not only because it is there that Jesus was born, not only because it has a proud Old Testament history as well, but every time I have been there I am aware that it has a very special character of its own, a character that evokes sympathy as well as admiration. The prophet Micah (5:1), speaking in God's name and addressing those who lived in the town (and, by extension, the town itself), proclaims: "But you, (Bethlehem) Ephrathah, the least of the clans of Judah, out of you will be born for me the one who is to rule over Israel". The immediate subject of the prophecy is King David. Much later, the prophecy is recalled in St Matthew's gospel where we read that, when Herod inquired of his advisers where "the Christ was to be born", they told him that he would be born in Bethlehem because: "This is what the prophet wrote: And you, Bethlehem, in the land of Judah, you are by no means least of the leaders of Judah, for out of you will come a leader who will shepherd my people Israel" (2:4-6). Thus, in the gospel, the subject of the prophecy is extended to include David's descendant, Jesus, and Bethlehem itself has been upgraded from "the least" to "by no means least".

Bethlehem is only a few miles south of Jerusalem. In any normal country, it would be a dormitory town in danger of becoming a suburb; but Jerusalem has been declared by the government of Israel (and unilaterally) to be the capital of that country while Bethlehem is an Arab and West Bank town. Moreover, these days it is separated from Jerusalem by the high barrier wall which Israel has built, ostensibly to protect itself from the danger of terrorists. Where the wall crosses the road between Jerusalem and Bethlehem, there is an opening and a checkpoint guarded by armed Israeli soldiers and reminiscent of the checkpoints of recent years in Northern Ireland. Coaches carrying pilgrims or tourists are usually allowed to pass through after inspection (though sometimes the passengers have to leave the coach and submit to individual checks and questioning). On the other hand, inhabitants of Bethlehem have little chance of being allowed to pass through, a prohibition that has caused great hardship since many citizens of Bethlehem used to go daily to work in Jerusalem.

Bethlehem is suffering grievously from the present situation. The people feel, and practically are, imprisoned, impoverished and fearful of the future. Violence might occur at any time, either across the divide or by an incursion of the Israeli army. Although the plight of the people of Bethlehem is obvious to Christian pilgrims, the barrier wall is meant to separate Israel proper from the whole length of the West Bank.That, in itself, causes great hardship to inhabitants throughout the latter as most are barred from Jerusalem and other towns in Israel proper. But that is not all. Although the wall is supposed to follow the line of the border, it frequently encroaches into West Bank territory and, in many cases, encloses land belonging to Palestinians (olive groves in particular), denying the owners of the land access to the sources of their livelihood.

Bethlehem is completely Arab and, in a limited sense, may even be described as a Christian town. There are the Basilica of the Nativity and some other Christian churches; Bethlehem University is a Catholic foundation although both staff and students are mixed, both Christian and Muslim; and there are two Catholic parishes in addition to the Franciscan community based at the basilica. There are, moreover, a number of houses of religious sisters engaged in educational and caring work. In addition, there is a custom that the mayor of Bethlehem is always a Christian.

Sadly however, the population, once at least 50 per cent Christian, is now largely Muslim. As has happened all over Palestine in the years since World War II, there has been much Arab emigration and the majority of those who have departed have been the Christians. A serious, even tragic, situation exists now that the exodus of Christians from the country has reduced the Christian population to a small and dwindling minority.

The Basilica of the Nativity is a remarkable church. It is a large, stone building, oblong in shape, with a central nave and two aisles on each side, separated by columns. The church was completed in 565 in the reign of the Emperor Justinian I. It is still largely unaltered from the original Byzantine construction. Centuries ago, the original main door was reduced in size to a low narrow entrance, allowing people to go in only one at a time and stooping, almost crouching. Why the bizarre alteration? Because the basilica was seen as a potential fortress and the severely reduced size of the door was regarded as an essential element of the building; a defence from attack and any attempted intrusion. (Even in very recent times, the basilica has been no stranger to violence. In 2002 a group of Palestinian militants occupied the church, taking refuge there from the besieging Israeli army. The confrontation, and the mayhem and casualties that ensued, provided a tragic and lamentable microcosm of the situation in the Holy Land today.)

Once inside, the majesty of the building is revealed. The original mosaic floor is covered by wood nowadays, but there are areas left uncovered to allow the ancient mosaic to be admired. The church is mainly Greek Orthodox, and the furnishings, especially in and around the sanctuary, show this clearly – icons, lamps, hangings and a great many bits and pieces of dull and dusty metalwork. To the left of the high altar there is a small separate area, set aside for Armenian liturgy.

Beneath the high altar and sanctuary, there are a number of small rock caves and recesses clustered together. These are reached by a short flight of stone steps at the side of the sanctuary. The main cave (Orthodox), at the foot of the steps, has a large brass star set in the floor to mark the exact spot of Our Lord's birth; an adjoining cave ("Latin", i.e. Catholic) is reputed to be where the manger was placed.

The Catholics have no locus in the basilica itself, but there is a sizable 19th century church, dedicated to St Catherine of Alexandria, which is located alongside and parallel to the basilica. It is in St Catherine's that any large and formal Catholic liturgies are celebrated, notably, of course, the crowded Midnight Mass of Christmas. As is the case in most of the Catholic holy places in the Holy Land, including St Catherine's, Franciscan friars are in charge;

but at midnight on 24th/25th December the principal celebrant of the Mass is the Latin Patriarch of Jerusalem (i.e. the local bishop). Pilgrims from many countries are there and the head of the Palestinian Authority (a Muslim) is also present.

To visit and venerate the site of Our Lord's birth may need patience. The wait to get down the steps to the cave can be a long one if, as usually seems to be the case, there is a big crowd of people in an unruly queue at the top of the steps, all of them intent on preventing others from jumping the queue (and perhaps, at the same time, not averse to doing that very thing themselves). The delay is due to the narrowness of the stairs, the confined space below and the fact that most of the pilgrims want to kneel and kiss the star marking the place of the Saviour's birth.

Sometimes our pilgrims were few enough to allow us to have Mass in the "Catholic" cave, a memorable experience but not always without untoward incident. On one occasion the start of our Mass was delayed because a Franciscan had gone ahead to tidy the cave and brush the floor. He got into an angry altercation with an Orthodox cleric who accused him of brushing in such a way that the dust was being swept into Orthodox territory. Another time, the priest who was reading the gospel at our Mass moved a yard or two to be nearer a better light; almost immediately an Orthodox official noisily interrupted him to inform him that he had strayed into their area, meanwhile pushing him back "over the line". Just two small incidents that illustrate the constant tension that exists between the different churches as they jealously guard their rights and claims in the basilica (and equally, or even more so, in the Church of the Holy Sepulchre in Jerusalem).

One of the great doctors of the Church had a close association with Bethlehem. St Jerome (c.340 to 420), born on the Dalmatian coast (now part of Croatia), in later life went to live and work in Bethlehem. It was he who first translated the Bible into Latin (a translation known as the Vulgate). One of the caves near the Nativity cave is thought to have been used by St Jerome and, in the little garden in front of St Catherine's church, his statue has a place of honour. St Jerome lived an austere, ascetic life and he is reputed to have been frank and forthright, someone who called a spade a spade and who once described bishops as "a necessary evil" in the Church.

In contemporary times, the Catholic Church continues to foster study, learning and research in Bethlehem, and especially in the university there. The university is owned by the Church and funded by the Holy See, with students of both sexes and without discrimination of faith. In these days of Israeli restrictions the university has had to endure difficult times. It continues to be a beacon of hope for Bethlehem and for Palestine.

When going to the Holy Land on pilgrimage, we are frequently urged not to limit ourselves to visiting the holy places and the sacred shrines, but also to make contact with the diminishing Christian and Catholic communities there. This is not as easy as it may sound. The agencies responsible for arranging pilgrimages seem unfamiliar with such an initiative; nor can groups of Arab Christians be summoned or produced on request. We have had several attempts at contacts or meetings, but only on two occasions can we claim any real success.

One time, the (Catholic) mayor of Bethlehem and some Catholic families came to our hotel one evening. We had some shy and hesitant fraternisation before being more relaxed when the evening took on a musical character with songs and dances from both Arabs and Scots.

On the other occasion our pilgrims went to Sunday Mass in the Catholic parish in Beit Jala in the western outskirts of Bethlehem. It was an enjoyable encounter, though somewhat contrived. After Mass we went into the parish hall where we were joined by some of the parishioners. The atmosphere there was pleasant and convivial and some home addresses were exchanged.

Beit Jala is at one edge of Bethlehem. At the other is the district of Beit Sahur. It is here that the Shepherds' Field is located, reputedly the place where the shepherds, watching over their flocks one night, saw and heard the angels proclaim the birth of the Saviour. The Shepherds' Field area is now a beautiful park, quiet and peaceful, with trees, flowers, lawns and avenues. In the centre is a chapel, one of the many Catholic shrines built last century by the Italian architect Antonio Barluzzi under the direction of the Franciscans. As always with Barluzzi, the chapel is tasteful and attractive, filled with appropriate symbolism. In this case, the building is partly sunken to remind us that the shepherds would be sheltering in a cave or hollow; the night sky and the stars as well as the shepherds themselves and their sheep are prominent in the decoration of the ceiling and walls. The Shepherds' Field is a place of calm and tranquillity, a refuge from the indefatigable importunities of sellers of postcards and rosaries.

THE PUBLIC MINISTRY OF JESUS

After the hidden years that Jesus spent in Nazareth, he began his public work, aged about thirty. Two events inaugurate his ministry: his baptism and his forty days in the wilderness.

John the Baptist was baptising at the river Jordan, at its southern end. The Jordan leaves the Sea of Galilee (also called the Lake of Gennesaret or the Sea of Tiberias) and flows south to end its course in the Dead Sea. The place where tradition locates John the Baptist's activity and therefore the baptism of Jesus is just a short distance north of the Dead Sea. Nowadays this area is, politically and militarily, very sensitive since it forms the border between Israel (West Bank/Palestine territory but under Israeli control) and the Kingdom of Jordan. Tourists and pilgrims generally are not allowed at present to visit the area.

The town of Jericho is not very far off but we shall describe it later. Between Jericho and Jerusalem there is the Judean wilderness, a grim district, barren and mountainous, where Jesus spent forty days and nights in seclusion, prayer and fasting and withstood the temptations of Satan. Near Jericho, the eastern end of the wilderness ends with a high, forbidding cliff. A ledge high on the face of the cliff can be reached by cable car, at the upper terminus of which is a rather incongruous café. Further along the ledge, a small Orthodox monastery seems to cling to the cliff face, but visitors are not admitted.

PUBLIC MINISTRY OF JESUS IN GALILEE

CAPERNAUM, NAZARETH AND THE SEA OF GALILEE

After these two preliminaries (baptism and wilderness), Jesus went back north to Galilee, which he regarded as his homeland. His ministry was one of constant travel, by foot or by boat, to various places in Galilee (and beyond), but he made his headquarters or base at Capernaum. In those days this was an important town on the north shore of the Sea of Galilee and on the busy trade route between Syria and Egypt. Today Capernaum is merely a partially excavated archaeological site, to which there is an entrance fee. Within the compound there are the considerable and restored remains of a third or fourth century synagogue, probably very similar to the earlier one which Jesus attended and in which he preached. Nearby are the ruins of a house, traditionally said to be that of Simon Peter and his relatives. Jesus was no doubt a frequent visitor to the house, perhaps slept there and, on one occasion, cured Peter's wife's mother of an ailment. A few decades ago, a new and very modern church was constructed over the ruins of the house; it is a fine place for liturgical celebrations, being in the form of an amphitheatre; but as for the appropriateness of a large concrete building, balanced immediately above the ruins, there are many who doubt and perhaps regret the decision.

Two thousand years ago Capernaum was much bigger and more important than Nazareth. The reverse is the case today, of course, and the New Testamnt recounts only one notable visit of Jesus to his home town. It was the Sabbath day on which Jesus attended the synagogue in Nazareth, read to the congregation the passage from Isaiah about the future Messiah (61:1-2) and then, to his astonished and admiring listeners, proclaimed himself to be that person. However, when Jesus (perhaps on a different occasion) complained that the people of Nazareth were lacking in faith, their mood changed, the atmosphere became very hostile and Jesus had to make a rapid escape from the synagogue, pursued by those who wanted to throw him over a cliff.

It is also worth mentioning that, with Capernaum now only an archaeological site, pilgrims in Galilee these days usually find accommodation in Nazareth or in Tiberias. The latter is a very pleasant town on the south-west corner of the lake. It is some hundreds of feet below sea level, of course, and has a very mild climate. The citizens are almost all Jewish and, as well as Christian pilgrims, many Israelis go to Tiberias for a vacation. It is a town of hotels, restaurants and a lively lakeside promenade. Hidden among the modern buildings is the beautiful little church of St Peter, staffed by a small community of Franciscans. The church is a gem, still largely in its original form as built in the time of the Crusaders.

A few miles south of Tiberias, where the river Jordan flows out of the lake, there is now a specially built area with some enclosed pools of the Jordan where people can renew their baptismal promises, either sprinkling, washing or even immersing themselves in the waters of the river. This is the contemporary substitute for the spot further south where Jesus was baptised, access to which is not allowed by the Israeli authorities. If and when this latter area does become accessible again, it is very uncertain whether the present facilities near Tiberias will still be used. If they were to close, it would also mean the end of the huge souvenir emporium there, which obviously does a very profitable trade.

It was on the shores of the Sea of Galilee that Jesus recruited several of the apostles. Many of them were fishermen, no doubt like hundreds of men of that district. A fishing boat, dating from that era, was recovered from the floor of the lake some years ago and can now be seen at a special exhibition site on the shores of the lake. Quite often Jesus was taken across the waters of the lake by the apostles and the gospels give several accounts of sudden storms which Jesus calmed.

One of the highlights of a pilgrimage is a sail on the lake. Some of the boats to be hired are designed as replicas of the fishing boats of Jesus' time, but with engines and propellers. Even on the calmest days, there is always a slight swell on the waters and it is easy to imagine that, with the surrounding hills making a huge bowl or amphitheatre, unexpected squalls can rapidly occur. We have to remember also that so much water has been taken for irrigation that the water level of the lake is now much reduced from what it was in former times. This is truly a problem, even a crisis, affecting Jordan as well as Israel and having repercussions not only at the Sea of Galilee but also on the river Jordan itself and on the Dead Sea which now is of considerably less extent than formerly.

During the sail on the lake, it is easy to imagine Jesus and the apostles on these same waters, seeing exactly the same surrounding hills. Pilgrims are provided with a memorable religious experience. One can also enjoy the beauty of the scene as well as its history, such as (to the west) the Horns of Hittim, two prominent hills and the valley between them where the Crusaders suffered a devastating defeat at the hands of Saladin and his Arab army in 1187 and (to the east) the hills known as the Golan Heights which the Israelis captured from Syria in 1967 and still retain.

CANA (WEDDING FEAST)

Cana is a busy little town just a few miles from Nazareth. Pilgrims usually make a brief stop here to visit the Catholic church, built, it is claimed, at the spot where the wedding took place which Jesus, his mother and the apostles attended. Water jars similar to those in use at the time are on display. During the visit to the church, married couples are invited to renew their vows. It is a moving event, very significant and emotional for the couples themselves and they can obtain a certificate as a memento of the experience.

An Orthodox church nearby disputes the Catholics' claim about the location of the wedding feast but pilgrims are more interested in visiting the souvenir shop across the road from the Catholic church. All the usual devotional objects are on sale, plus bottles of a liquid labelled as "Cana Wine". I have tasted it and found it a disappointing drink, undoubtedly far below the standard of the wine for which Jesus was responsible.

MOUNT OF BEATITUDES (THE SERMON ON THE MOUNT)

One of the most pleasant pilgrim visits in Galilee is to the Mount of Beatitudes. The traditional site of Our Lord's Sermon on the Mount is on the hillside, rising up from the north-west corner of the Sea of Galilee. An area of a few hectares has been fenced off and now contains some well tended gardens, a convent of Italian nuns, a hospice for pilgrims (being rebuilt and extended) and the little church whose exterior is famous because photographs of it frequently feature on brochures and postcards. The exterior of the church, one of Barluzzi's finest, is octagonal and therefore symbolically explicit. It is grey and white in colour and the arcades are surrounded by a walkway and surmounted by a dome. I find the interior a little disappointing, smaller and more cramped than one expects. But the exterior, in its setting of flowers and trees, with the lake below and the Golan Heights in the distance, is stunning. (It was in the hospice here that I lodged on my first Holy Land pilgrimage in 1963.)

A small but important complaint. Many pilgrims find, to their disappointment, that the gates into the whole area are firmly closed each day for an early and extended "lunch hour".

MOUNT TABOR (TRANSFIGURATION)

Perhaps my favourite place in Galilee is Mount Tabor, in all probability the scene of Our Lord's Transfiguration, as he was leaving Galilee to go south to Judea, Jerusalem and Calvary. Mount Tabor is a few miles south-east of Nazareth, its height and prominence accentuated by its isolation in the Plain of Jezreel. Coaches reach only to the beginning of the ascent so, except for those fit enough and anxious to make the climb up a very steep track to the summit, the pilgrims transfer to minibuses. Until a year or two ago it was a fleet of Mercedes cars that awaited the pilgrims at the base of the hill. The Arab drivers took a perverse delight in scaring their passengers as they rounded the twenty or so hairpin bends – they would remove both hands from the steering wheel as they shouted "Alleluia". The road has now been widened, fit for minibuses and not now so enjoyably scary.

The church on the summit of Mount Tabor is another Barluzzi construction and, as always with him, impressive, beautiful and full of symbolism. The sanctuary is on two levels to symbolise Jesus transfigured and, on each side of the entrance to the church, there are two side-chapels (for Moses and Elijah). The atmosphere inside the church is, for most people, very prayerful indeed. This experience of sacredness is heightened as one reflects on the significance of the Transfiguration which, I think, can be expressed in one word: reassurance. Reassurance for Our Lord to continue his journey to Calvary and his sacrificial death; reassurance for the apostles to remain faithful followers; reassurance to each one of us that God is with us on life's journey and despite our fears of what may lie in the future.

Outside the church, there is evidence of some earlier churches and, in clear weather, magnificent views north, south, east and west. There are pines with their fresh smell to enjoy before reluctantly leaving this special place, to be taken down once more to the plain and to the resumption of normal life.

OTHER GALILEAN PLACES

Caesarea Philippi, where Jesus asked the apostles whom they thought him to be and where he proclaimed Simon as Peter, the rock on which the Church would be built, is now only a deserted place amid trees and scrub and rocks in northern Galilee. I have been there only once, on the occasion when I also had the chance to reach the Israeli frontier with Lebanon (soldiers, guns, barbed wire) and to drive up to the plain above the Golan Heights, territory still occupied by Israel after its capture from Syria in 1967; from there the present border could be seen and, just beyond, a Syrian village. These two fortified borders are a reminder of a grim and sombre reality, an intimation of a very troubled part of the world and of the many unsolved and festering problems that still exist.

THE WAY SOUTH

There are three main roads connecting the north and the south of the Holy Land. A modern motorway runs along the coast of the Mediterranean from Haifa in the north to Tel Aviv. The highway passes close to the impressive ruins of Caesarea, a town built by Herod the Great in the style of a Roman city with stadium, amphitheatre and several other buildings, now archaeological sites. It was in Caesarea that Peter baptised the Roman centurion, Cornelius, and his family – the first non-Jews to receive Christian baptism. The ancient port of Joppa, where St Peter restored Tabitha (or Dorcas) to life, is now known as Jaffa; it is these days a southern suburb of Tel Aviv, but still has its Catholic church of St Peter.

The central route from north to south passes through Samaria and the town of Nablus. In recent decades, Nablus has acquired a reputation for outbreaks of violence and so the central route is not normally used by pilgrim groups. However, I recall travelling that route on one or two of my earlier times in the Holy Land. Samaria is the land of the Samaritans, people whom religious Jews shunned and despised as heretics who had separated themselves from orthodox Judaism and were therefore beneath contempt. Hence the impact of Christ's choice of a Samaritan as the "hero" in the parable of good neighbourliness. On those early visits it was interesting to see Mount Gerizim (sacred to the Samaritans and on which they built a temple) and the Greek Orthodox church at Jacob's Well where Jesus met and conversed with the Samaritan woman (to the dismay of the apostles). I recall an ancient cleric displaying an ancient scroll, with the claim, if I remember, that it was a Samaritan scroll from Old Testament times and the oldest document in the world.

These days, the journey between north and south in the Holy Land is usually by the route along the west bank of the river Jordan. At several points the road is only a few hundred metres from the river and it is quite easy to see buildings and other features across the river in Jordan.

JERICHO AND THE DEAD SEA

Shortly before turning west towards Jerusalem, the road near the Jordan comes to the West Bank town of Jericho. The town is a large and very fertile oasis in otherwise arid terrain. Jericho claims to be the oldest continuously inhabited town in the world and there are extensive archaeological excavations there. It is famous, of course, for its wall which "came tumbling down" when it was besieged by Joshua and the Israelites as they ended their forty years' journey from exile in Egypt and crossed the river Jordan into the Promised Land.

The town is also the place where Zacchaeus, the senior tax collector, climbed a sycamore tree to gain a better view of Jesus as he passed. A sycamore tree in the town, fenced off to protect it from would-be imitators of Zacchaeus, is a stopping place for pilgrim coaches and photographs, although the guides explain that this is not *the* tree which the little man climbed. On a personal note, since my eyesight is poor and failing, I like to remember that it was on the outskirts of Jericho that blind Bartimaeus was begging when he was told that Jesus was passing. To his pleading, Jesus responded by granting him sight and faith.

The town is totally Arab. In fact, on its southern outskirts, there is a large refugee camp of Palestinians who were expelled from their homes by the Israelis after 1948 and 1967 Arab-Israeli wars. Jewish families now occupy the Palestinians' former properties, particularly in the Jerusalem area.

There are several shops in Jericho which sell many kinds of fruit, especially locally grown dates, grapefruit and oranges. They do a brisk trade with pilgrims and the quality of their wares is truly first class. There is also a very large restaurant, situated at the foot of the barren mountains where Jesus spent forty days and nights, fasting and praying. This popular eating house is appropriately and cheekily named "Temptation Restaurant".

Continuing south from Jericho, one comes, after a few miles, to a crossroads. The road to the east goes towards the river and the place where Jesus was baptised by John the Baptist. South from the crossroads is the Dead Sea as well as Masada, the ruins of the Qumran settlement and the caves where the Dead Sea Scrolls were found in 1947 (and until 1956).

The Dead Sea is "the lowest spot on the surface of the earth" at 1290 feet below sea level. It is nowadays considerably smaller in area because so much water has been taken from the river Jordan. There are a few "beaches" for bathing – a unique experience in thick, warm "water" full of unpleasant chemicals; the water is so dense that it is impossible to sink in it and the chemicals are painful, even dangerous, if they get in one's eyes or are swallowed. A bathe in the Dead Sea is an experience worth doing once, but only for future storytelling and boasting.

Masada is a high flat-topped hill, towards the southern end of the Dead Sea. Hundreds of Jews took refuge there, besieged by a Roman army. The latter painstakingly built a huge ramp to enable the soldiers to capture the hill. When, in 73 AD, the situation became hopeless for the Jewish families on Masada, they committed mass suicide rather than be captured. The mountain is now accessible by cable car, although there are still some intrepid climbers who use a narrow path to the summit, in the blazing sun and fierce heat.

Qumran is at the north end of the Dead Sea and, for the archaeologist, there are interesting ruins of the monastic community of (or similar to) Essenes who dwelt there from about 150 BC to 68 AD and therefore contemporaneously with John the Baptist and Jesus. The most important of the community's documents, the Dead Sea Scrolls, unknown for almost two thousand years, are now in the Museum of the Shrine of the Book in West Jerusalem.

THE ROAD TO JERUSALEM

Back to the crossroads near Jericho and then turning westwards, the road ascends into the barren mountains of the Judean desert. Pilgrims usually make a photo stop at the roadside sign indicating sea level. The road to Jerusalem continues its ascent, past a cluster of buildings known as the Inn of the Good Samaritan. Of course, it is not really that, but it tries to combine the style of an ancient hostel for travellers with attractions for today's passing pilgrims and tourists.

The road is good. Occasionally, there is a Bedouin encampment just off the road – black square tents, camels and, incongruously, a couple of modern cars as well as washing hanging on a line to dry. Then, still some miles from Jerusalem, the Israeli settlements come into view – modern flats and houses grouped into small towns on hilltops. These settlements are one of the most acute reasons for tension between Israel and Palestinians. They are, of course, on the West Bank, the "Occupied Territories", conquered by Israel in the war of 1967. Several UN resolutions have declared the settlements illegal. Nevertheless, they continue to be built, encroaching more and more on Palestinian land and now, with a network of roads connecting the settlements, rendering all the less realistic the possibility of a viable and independent Palestinian state. The Israeli settlements are a blatant injustice but, with the United States unwilling to react in any meaningful way, their continuing growth appears unstoppable.

Jerusalem is overlooked, from the east, by the Mount of Olives, which now has a number of prominent buildings on its crest including a hospital, hotels and churches. On the eastern slopes of the Mount of Olives lies the village of Bethany, where Lazarus, Martha and Mary lived. Jesus developed a close friendship with them and, on the occasions when he came to Jerusalem, he would be likely not only to visit them but also to stay in their house. Two events concerning them, both well known, are recounted in the gospels. First, the occasion on which Jesus was visiting and Martha became flustered and angry because her sister remained speaking with Jesus while she was left to do the work of preparing the meal. Second, when Lazarus fell ill, died and was buried; the sisters told Jesus that, if he had arrived sooner, he might have healed their brother, to which Jesus responded by going to the tomb where Lazarus was and restoring him to life. Bethany and nearby villages have Arab populations and modern Catholic and Orthodox churches marking the sites of the family house and of the tomb of Lazarus. As at every other shrine and church in the Holy Land, vendors of postcards, rosaries and other pious objects are on hand to besiege the pilgrims.

THE MOUNT OF OLIVES

When we reach the crest of the Mount of Olives, a magnificent panoramic view of the city lies before us, across the Kidron Valley. Morning is the best time to enjoy the sight, with the sun behind us in the east and shining on the resplendent walls of the Old City and on the Dome of the Rock. The present city walls were built in the sixteenth century in the time of the Ottoman sultan and emperor, Suleiman the Magnificent, while the Dome of the Rock dates back much earlier, to 691 AD. In Our Lord's time, the walls of the city, which were newly constructed under Herod the Great, did not follow the same line as those we see today; hence, in the first century AD, Calvary was outside the city walls whereas now it is inside the walls. The "pinnacle of the Temple", mentioned in the gospel account of the temptations of Jesus, is usually pointed out at the south-east corner of the walls.

Before leaving the crest of the Mount of Olives, we should mention two shrines. One is a convent of Carmelite nuns, built in the nineteenth century. There is a small church attached and, in the grounds, remains of Byzantine and Crusader churches as well as the foundations of a 1920 church which was never completed. Most interesting, however, is the fact that this is reputedly the place where Our Lord taught the apostles to pray the "Our Father"; on various walls in corridors and alcoves, ceramic panels have been placed, bearing the text of the prayer in more than seventy languages (among recent additions being a version in Lallans, i.e. Lowland Scots).

The other shrine, nearby, is a walled enclosure with a small minaret; within the enclosure is an octagonal stone kiosk inside of which is a stone slab with, it is claimed, the footprints left by Jesus as he ascended into heaven from this spot. Despite the minaret and the Muslim custodian, the place is no longer used as a mosque. In Byzantine and Crusader times there was a church here, but nowadays there is no Christian involvement, apart from the pilgrim visitors.

The walk down the western slope of the Mount of Olives towards the Kidron Valley is interesting. First, there is a Jewish cemetery where the dead await the call for the General Judgment which, many hold, will take place in the valley. About halfway down the hill there is a small Christian park in which is the chapel called Dominus Flevit to commemorate Our Lord's weeping over Jerusalem as he foretold that it would be totally destroyed (an event that indeed occurred in 70 AD). From the park there are further views of the city but particularly famous is the view from inside the chapel, through a window behind the altar. That view is often reproduced in books, brochures and postcards. The architect of the chapel is, once again, Antonio Barluzzi and the exterior is said to have the shape (greatly magnified, of course) of a tear. The road continues down, past the convent of Saint Mary Magdalen with its community of Orthodox nuns and its chapel (very conspicuous onion domes but seldom open to visitors), to the valley floor. It is estimated that, in Old Testament times, the valley may have been much more of a ravine with its floor between fifty and a hundred feet lower than at present. At all events, the western slope of the Mount of Olives now ends with the Garden of Gethsemani and an abundance of traffic and vendors.

JERUSALEM

THE TEMPLE

On Palm Sunday, Jesus descended from the Mount of Olives, crossed the Kidron Valley and, through a gate in the city walls, entered the area of the Temple (the "Temple Mount"). The eastern line of the walls is still where it was in the time of Jesus so we can easily picture him, mounted on a donkey, crossing the valley, going up the slope and entering the walled city and the Temple Mount. There is, however, only one part of the Temple area still remaining from Christ's day – a section of the Western Wall, some massive stones that formed part of the foundations of the enclosure, dating from the era of Solomon in the tenth century BC. Jewish people can now approach the Western Wall (from the outside) to pray; this is because, following the 1967 war and the Israeli capture of the Old City, the Arab houses which crowded right up to the Wall have been demolished, leaving a large space in which people can walk about and which allows them to pray at the Wall itself (separate stretches for men and women) and to place written prayers in between the stones.

Pope John Paul II and Pope Benedict XVI also did this on their pilgrimages to the Holy Land. Non-Jews may freely approach the Wall to pray, to insert a written prayer or merely to look, though a man must cover his head – a cardboard skull cap (*gamulka* or *kippah*) is available free at the entrance.

The interior of the Temple area is completely under Muslim control. Once admittance is gained after passing in a long queue through some strict security, it is a very pleasant and tranquil area with trees and open spaces. It contains two buildings that are sacred Islamic shrines: the Al-Aqsa mosque and the Dome of the Rock. With regard to the latter, the building of which was completed in 691 AD, the two words of the name disclose its principal features: first, the magnificent dome, recently restored and with new gold leaf covering its exterior; and second, the rock, inside the shrine and surrounded by a screen. The rock is supposed to be Mount Moriah, the spot on which Abraham was about to sacrifice his son Isaac until a ram providentially was caught in bushes and was killed in the boy's place; it is sacred to Muslims as the spot from which Mohammed ascended to heaven.

The mosque called Al-Aqsa ("the farthest") is the third holiest in Islam. A mosque has stood on this spot since the late seventh century. The present building dates from the eleventh century. Muslims believe that Allah brought Mohammed here during his lifetime. In 1099 the Crusaders captured Jerusalem and Al-Aqsa became for a time a palace and a church. The mosque has been restored and additions have been made in subsequent centuries.

Both the Al-Aqsa mosque and the Dome of the Rock can be visited, although non-Muslims must be careful to behave with respect and care, especially in the former. Even in the open grounds of the Temple Mount, one has to be alert and prudent. On one occasion, a small group of us, pilgrims, were together under the shade of a tree and we very quietly began to say the Lord's Prayer. Almost immediately, a gentleman whom we had not noticed angrily interrupted us and, though speaking in Arabic, made it clear that he knew we had been praying and that, for non-Muslims, this was strictly forbidden.

To this sacred Temple area, now totally Muslim, Jesus was brought as an infant (Presentation, with Simeon and Anna) and as a child (Jewish feasts and Finding in the Temple). He also came on several occasions during his public ministry, notably when he berated those engaged in inappropriate buying and selling and money changing and when he confronted Jewish religious officials and authorities.

THE SACRED TRIDUUM – LAST SUPPER, AGONY, TRIAL, PASSION, DEATH, RESURRECTION

In the southern part of the Old City, there is an "Upper Room" which is venerated both as the place of the Last Supper (for which reason, the room is often called the Cenacle: *coenaculum,* supper room) and also the site of the Descent of the Holy Spirit on the apostles at Pentecost. The present upper room is a medieval construction that, for some time, was used as a small mosque. It is not used formally as a religious building nowadays but, since it is thought to be where the original Upper Room was located, it is visited by Christian pilgrims. On the most recent occasion on which I was there, the room was packed almost to suffocation by several different groups. There must have been over one hundred people in the room. One of the groups comprised Pentecostal Christians whose praise and worship were so loud that the other groups had little chance either to hear their guides' explanations or to have any Scripture reading or prayer themselves.

Close to the Cenacle, there is a Jewish shrine, claimed to be the tomb of King David. It is much venerated by religious Jews and, if Christian pilgrims visit it on their way to the Upper Room, males must cover their heads.

After the Last Supper on Maundy Thursday evening, Jesus and his apostles went down the slope out of the city, across the Kidron Valley, to the Garden of Gethsemani at the foot of the Mount of Olives. The Garden still exists, although the road from the Mount of Olives now cuts through it and divides it into two quite small sections. The olive trees are gnarled and ancient; some of them, it is thought, may date even from the time of Our Lord. The Basilica of the Agony, which is in the Garden, is in the care of Franciscans. The interior of the church, dark and gloomy, is symbolic of the fact that the Lord's agony took place at night and, of course, that it was a very sombre occasion. In front of the high altar there is an expanse of rock, marking (or depicting) the spot on which Jesus prayed that night. Many pilgrimages make a nocturnal Holy Hour in the church to commemorate Our Lord's plaintive appeal to the apostles: "Could you not watch one hour with me?" The basilica, one of Barluzzi's most famous works, is also called the Church of All Nations since many different countries contributed to the cost of construction in the 1920s. There is an appropriate dramatic and well known mosaic on the façade of the basilica.

From the Garden of Gethsemani, Jesus was taken to the house of Caiaphas, the high priest at that time. The site is now occupied by the church of St Peter in Gallicantu ("at the crowing of the cock"). It is quite near the Cenacle but outside the present walls of the Old City. It overlooks the area where King David established his city around 1000 BC, but which is now the village of Silwan and closely packed with Arab Palestinian houses. The church of St Peter in Gallicantu is a beautiful, tranquil place and it has several crypts or spaces beneath it. The lowest of these is a cave which seems to have been a prison or dungeon since, although there is now a modern stair down into it, there was, in former times, only a hole in the roof as access. It is possible that this is the very place in which Our Lord was held captive during the night hours between Holy Thursday and Good Friday morning.

There is a very old path with some stone steps that descends past the side of the church and down to the floor of the valley. I find the steps and the path evocative because they are clearly so old and without any later attempt to adorn or beautify them. Might Jesus himself have used this ancient route between the city and the Mount of Olives?

In the Arab village of Silwan, below St Peter in Gallicantu church, there is the area where the City of David was located, just south of the present Old City. It is here that Hezekiah's Tunnel is still to be found. It is a narrow passage which runs underground, through the rock, from the Gihon Spring to the Pool of Siloam. This remarkable construction dates from the eighth century BC in the reign of King Hezekiah. Its purpose was to bring water from the Gihon Spring into the City of David, while the latter was under siege by Sennacherib and the Assyrians. The tunnel is about a metre wide and, in height, varies from something over a metre to several metres. It is 533 metres in length (just under 600 yards) but, because of the tools and means of calculating in use at the time, there are twists and turns in its trajectory. Hezekiah's Tunnel can be traversed on foot although the floor is uneven and the water level variable (from ankle to waist height). A torch is a necessity and the adventure should not be attempted by those who suffer from claustrophobia. To achieve the feat is not really too difficult for the able-bodied and it provides a topic of conversation with which to interest, impress or bore. On one occasion, I saw a group of Israeli children about to walk through the tunnel, accompanied by an adult armed with a Kalashnikov rifle. Not, I presume, because Israeli children are as unruly as that!

The official trial of Jesus took place before Pontius Pilate, the Roman procurator of Judea. He had come from Caesarea on the coast, his normal residence, to be in Jerusalem during the Jewish festival of Passover. The location of Pilate's seat of authority in Jerusalem is not certain but the traditional view is that it was in the north-eastern corner of the Old City, a few hundred metres west of St Stephen's Gate (Gate of the Lions) and just outside the precincts of the Temple.

Near this location nowadays is the large college of the Missionaries of Africa ("White Fathers"). In the same enclosed grounds are two impressive and historic places: the beautiful and dignified church of St Anne built in Crusader times on the spot thought to have been where St Anne and St Joachim lived and where the Virgin Mary was born; and the "Sheep Pool", where Jesus cured the cripple who had waited in vain for many years in the hope of being healed in the waters there (John 5:1-9).

Immediately west of St Anne's church and the Missionaries of Africa building is the convent of the Sisters of Our Lady of Sion. In its crypt, there is a paved area dating, it is said, from the time of Our Lord. On some of the flagstones on the floor there are geometric designs scratched or chiselled into the stones and which are pointed out as used by Roman soldiers for games of chance (and therefore, possibly, how lots were drawn for the garments of Jesus). This crypt was a street-level courtyard two thousand years ago but is now several metres below ground level. At the latter level, there is a chapel of the Flagellation (Scourging of Jesus) and it is in the little garden outside that wooden crosses are kept, available for pilgrim groups as they begin to follow the Way of the Cross, starting in the street outside. Early on Friday afternoons, a large group directed by Franciscan friars embarks on the Via Dolorosa. Other groups (and individuals) are, of course, free to make the Stations of the Cross at any time.

The different Stations are marked by plaques on the walls of houses and shops and the pilgrim processions make their way through the bazaar, where buying and selling and ordinary life continue noisily as normal. The Arab citizens pay little attention to the praying groups; but there is always a photographer on hand to take pictures of the pilgrims as each gets a turn of carrying the cross. It has been said that, if there had been cameras two thousand years ago, even Jesus would have been pestered by photographers (or perhaps postcard and rosary sellers) as he made his way to Calvary.

After the eighth Station, the Way of the Cross proceeds to the roof of the Church of the Holy Sepulchre for the ninth Station and then, through the small dark chapel of the Ethiopian Orthodox monks on the church roof, before descending again, to enter the church for the final five Stations.

The Church of the Holy Sepulchre is an astonishing and confusing place. The first building was constructed around the year 330 by the Emperor Constantine and his mother Helena. After the destruction of this church, new building took place in Byzantine times; in fact, two churches were built, one at Calvary and the other, nearby, at the Holy Sepulchre. The Crusaders carried out repairs and additions and made changes, the main one being to unite the previous two churches into one large church. It is this church that we have today, still with some Byzantine and many Crusader parts. The church is dark and sombre, complicated and seemingly shapeless. Greek Orthodox clergy are principally in charge, but Catholics (called "Latins" here) have various parts and Orthodox Armenians have a small section.

There are two main focal points in the Church of the Holy Sepulchre: Calvary and the Tomb.

Mount Calvary is reached by a short, steep, narrow staircase, at the top of which is the crowded, dark, square (perhaps ten by ten metres) area of Calvary. Three of the Stations of the Cross are located here (tenth, eleventh, twelfth). A Greek Orthodox altar is in central position at the rear of the square, at the actual place of Our Lord's Crucifixion. A small Catholic altar is immediately to the right. Mount Calvary was never a hill of any great size or height but, in order to build the present construction, the top of the hill was cut away; and, of course, ground level today is some metres higher than it was two thousand years ago. Nonetheless, I find the Calvary chapel so dark, so crowded and so full of various furnishings and adornments that any sense of prayer or attempt at reflection or contemplation, let alone of "composition of place" – in other words, being fully aware of where I am – is very difficult. But should I complain? Perhaps on the very day of the Crucifixion things were equally distracting.

Downstairs from Calvary, there is an early nineteenth century, oblong-shaped stone table ("The Stone of Anointing") suggesting a place where bodies might have been laid so that they could be prepared for burial. The thirteenth Station can be prayed here, before going to the Tomb.

The Tomb or Sepulchre is mainly in the custody of the Greek Orthodox but it is possible for pilgrims to visit it. Sometimes this requires a long queue and a patient wait. The "Tomb" (technically known as "the Aedicule" i.e. "little house") is like a shrine or a small chapel. The interior dates from 1555 and the exterior from 1810. Its style has been described, rather disparagingly, as Ottoman Baroque. Marking the spot of such a sacred event as Christ's resurrection, the Aedicule is badly in need of repair or, better, replacement. The entrance is very narrow and surrounded by lamps and candles. Only a few people at a time can get inside, where there is a narrow floor space alongside a replica tomb or stone shelf. Nothing of the original tomb is visible there now. So, once again, pilgrims are often dismayed or disappointed. The tawdry ugliness of the shrine, the wait of an hour or more in a queue, the rude and peremptory treatment by the Orthodox clergy in charge – all these are a severe trial for what is the climax of the pilgrimage. (Outside and at the rear of the shrine, the Coptic Orthodox have a small altar behind which, they claim, it is possible to see part of the original sepulchre. I do not know if the claim is valid.)

The first time that I was in Jerusalem, in 1963, pilgrims were much fewer and I had the double privilege of celebrating Mass, one day at the Catholic altar at Calvary and, on another day, on the "tomb" itself, during the hour or so that the Greek Orthodox authorities allow the Catholic authorities (Franciscans) to be in control.

The main exclusively Catholic section of the church is a side chapel, called the chapel of St Mary Magdalen, where most Catholic groups can celebrate Mass. However, on a recent Holy Land pilgrimage even that proved impossible for us. Our pilgrims had queued for well over an hour to visit the Tomb and, after that, we were told that the St Mary Magdalen chapel had been double booked and that the Franciscans (who have charge there) had nowhere else to offer us, not even in the nearby Franciscan parish church of the Saviour. There was no alternative but to return to our Bethlehem hotel where we were provided with rather basic equipment that finally enabled us to celebrate Sunday Mass in an atmosphere of calm that soothed nerves sorely troubled by our experiences at the Church of the Holy Sepulchre.

Some reflections on the Holy Sepulchre Church. It is built on the spot which, for Christians, is the most sacred in the world. To be there is, indeed, truly a great privilege. Moreover, the church witnesses to Christian faith and devotion down through the ages, from Helena through the Byzantine period, the Crusades, the Ottoman centuries, right to the present day. But, while historically rich, the building is such a confused and confusing place that it leaves the pilgrim with a jumble of impressions. Above all, Calvary seems so incongruous as a cluttered chapel at the top of a stairway of twenty steps. Devoted but misplaced zeal has left both the place of Our Lord's death and that of his resurrection with a surfeit of ugly and unworthy decoration. The uncooperating and even bitter rivalry between the various Christian churches as they grimly fight (sometimes literally) to uphold their "rights" is very disedifying in these supposedly ecumenical times. All of this, together with the crushing and the queueing and the rudeness of the official and officious clergy, means that the impression that many people carry away with them is one of disappointment – but also, in retrospect, of gratitude to God for having been given the chance to be in the place where our redemption was wrought by Jesus Christ in the paschal mystery of his death and resurrection.

The Old City of Jerusalem has many sites of great historic and devotional interest, but it is also a most frustrating place. I suppose that that is because it is a largely Muslim city nowadays and there is the tension arising out of the hostility between the Palestinians and the Israeli police and army; one is aware of Israeli control and Arab resentment. Moreover, the Old City is a Middle East city, very foreign for us and, while the inhabitants try to live their lives independently of the pilgrims/tourists, the latter are seen as a source of income for myriads of very persistent vendors.

One place of calm that should be noted is the church of the Dormition of Our Lady, staffed by German Benedictine monks. The architecture of the church is imposing and impressive. (Earlier, I mentioned the tower of this church, used by snipers in the years before 1967 when the city was divided between Israel and Jordan.) The upper church of the Dormition is dignified and quiet, the crypt has a beautiful statue of the Blessed Virgin, lying just after her death and awaiting her bodily assumption to heaven. This church implies the claim that Our Lady died in Jerusalem, despite the very public devotion, far away, at the place venerated for her death and assumption near Ephesus, in Turkey.

FROM THE RESURRECTION TO THE ASCENSION

After Christ's resurrection, the gospels recount several appearances of the risen Lord. Jesus appeared to Mary Magdalen and some other women in the vicinity of the tomb as well as to his apostles and disciples in the room in Jerusalem where they had assembled behind closed doors "for fear of the Jews" (John 20:19). It was there, John narrates, that Jesus gave the Holy Spirit to the apostles and conferred on them the power of forgiving sins in his name. Popular tradition assigns this event to the Cenacle, the place of the Last Supper.

There are three appearances of Our Lord outside of Jerusalem that are recorded in the gospels. Luke (24:23-35) tells the moving story of Jesus, at first unrecognised, joining two of his disciples as they walked, disconsolate, to Emmaus; the climax of the story, when they recognised Jesus "in the breaking of bread", is dramatic and heart-warming. But where is Emmaus? There are two, or even three, claimants because all we know of the location is that it was probably about seven miles from Jerusalem. The two principal claimants are Latrun (west of Jerusalem, on the road to Tel Aviv) and El Qubeibeh (nearer Jerusalem, to the north-east of the city, and in an open, rural district).

The other two recorded appearances of Our Lord away from Jerusalem took place in Galilee. One of these was on the shore of the Sea of Tiberias (Lake Gennesaret). The account is in John's gospel (21:1-23): seven disciples (Simon Peter, James and John, Thomas, Nathanael and two unnamed) had spent a night on the lake without making a catch; Jesus, unrecognised, calls from the shore and urges them to try once more; they make a huge catch and thus recognise Jesus; ashore, Jesus prepares breakfast of bread and fish for them and then, three times, asks Simon Peter if he really loves him; after Peter's three embarrassed replies, asserting that of course he does, Jesus orders him to "feed my lambs, feed my sheep".

This whole incident is commemorated by two neighbouring churches, each in its own grounds on the north-west shore of the Sea of Galilee. At Tabgha, German Benedictines have the church of the Loaves and Fishes. The floor of this little church is covered by ancient mosaics with images of flora and fauna but in the centre, at the altar, is the famous mosaic (reproduced in patens, chalices, plates etc.), of a basket of loaves, flanked on each side by a fish, reminders of the breakfast which Jesus prepared for the seven.

Alongside the Tabgha enclosure is another, which Franciscans look after. In the grounds is the church of the Primacy, built of basalt rocks and stones and commemorating Our Lord's commission to Peter which confirmed Peter as being charged with the responsibility of primacy in Christ's Church. The waters of the lake are now about a hundred metres away from the church but I remember how, on my first visit there in 1963, they lapped the wall of the church. The lake, like the Dead Sea, is now much smaller because so much water has been drained for irrigation and reservoirs.

Each of these places, Tabgha and the Primacy, is outstanding, both for natural beauty and for peaceful tranquillity. They provide memorable opportunities for the celebration of the Eucharist in the churches or outside in the grounds.

St Matthew's gospel (28:16-20) ends with Jesus commissioning the apostles to proclaim the Good News and to baptise; "go, make disciples of all the nations". The location is the mountain in Galilee "where Jesus had arranged to meet them". Which mountain this is, or whether it is an actual location or merely symbolic, is unknown; there is no earlier mention of an arrangement to meet.

The traditional sites of Our Lord's Ascension and of the Descent of the Holy Spirit at Pentecost are, respectively, the Mount of Olives and the Cenacle. Since I have already described them and neither is, nowadays, a developed shrine for Christian worship, nothing further need be said about them.

It is sufficient now to conclude the pilgrimage journey, a journey that provides abiding memories of Nazareth, Bethlehem, Jerusalem and Galilee – grateful memories that furnish lifelong material for reflection and prayer.

Our thoughts and prayers must, in a special way, be about those whose home is in the Holy Land. With the problems and painful issues that are so evident there and with so little prospect of solutions, humanly speaking, we ask a merciful God to give reconciliation, justice and lasting peace to that Land made Holy by the presence and work of his Son.

Bethlehem: Church of the Nativity; note the very low and narrow main entrance, 1963

Bethlehem: Nativity Square (facing away from the Church of the Nativity), 1963

River Jordan near its outlet to the Dead Sea: thought to be the place of the baptism of Jesus by John the Baptist), 1963

Jericho: a sycamore tree (recalling Zacchaeus), 1963

Jerusalem: Gethsemani, Basilica of all Nations; in the background, convent of Russian Orthodox nuns, 1963

Jerusalem: Garden of Gethsemani, ancient olive trees, 2006

Jerusalem: Basilica of the Holy Sepulchre, 1963

Jerusalem: Basilica of the Holy Sepulchre, façade and principal entrance, with scaffolding lest the structure should collapse, but now repaired, 1963

Jerusalem: Western Wall; Jews pray here, barred from entry to the temple area, 2006

Part of the barrier wall, erected by Israel, between Jerusalem and Bethlehem, with graffiti; the wall extends the length of the border between Israel and the West Bank, 2006

27298854R00233

Made in the USA
Charleston, SC
08 March 2014